CONSTITUTIONAL LIMITS AND THE PUBLIC SPHERE

Constitutional Limits and the Public Sphere

A Critical Study of Bentham's Constitutionalism

OREN BEN-DOR

• HART •
PUBLISHING
OXFORD – PORTLAND OREGON
2000

Hart Publishing
Oxford and Portland, Oregon

Published in North America (US and Canada) by
Hart Publishing c/o
International Specialized Book Services
5804 NE Hassalo Street
Portland, Oregon
97213-3644
USA

Distributed in the Netherlands, Belgium and Luxembourg by
Intersentia, Churchillaan 108
B2900 Schoten
Antwerpen
Belgium

Hart Publishing Ltd is a specialist legal publisher based in Oxford, England.
To order further copies of this book or to request a list of other
publications please write to:

Hart Publishing Ltd, Salter's Boatyard, Oxford OX1 4LB
Telephone: +44 (0)1865 245533 or Fax: +44 (0)1865 794882
e-mail: mail@hartpub.co.uk
WEBSITE: http//www.hartpub.co.uk

British Library Cataloguing in Publication Data
Data Available
ISBN 1 84113–111–3

Typeset by Hope Services (Abingdon) Ltd.
Printed and bound in Great Britain by
Biddles Ltd, www.biddles.co.uk

To my parents

MIRIAM and MEIR BEN-DOR

Table of Contents

Acknowledgements

THIS BOOK has developed out of a doctoral thesis at UCL. I would like to thank Dr. Philip Schofield, the Joint General-Editor of Bentham's Collected works, who acted as my thesis supervisor. I am grateful for his continuous faith, patience and encouragement at times when the argument assumed an impenetrable form. I also thank him for countless detailed and thoughtful remarks on the substance and style of the text.

Without the critical and painstaking readings of this manuscript by Dr. Michael Quinn, whose heart is as big as his mind, this work would not have taken off, let alone have been completed. I have learned a lot and have benefited greatly from his comments, which helped me to avoid many confusions and obscurities.

My final single debt is to Dr. Andrew Halpin of the Faculty of Law at Southampton for reading various parts of the manuscript. I had the benefit of his truly incredible empathic ability to extract immediately and accurately the central problems and resonances a text contains but not yet elucidates. His remarks assisted me tremendously both to clarify and to put in perspective many issues in Chapter 1 and Part 2.

I wish to thank my thesis examiners Professor James Burns and Professor Neil MacCormick for their critical comments. I was fortunate to be a pupil of Professor William Twining whose teaching drew me closer and closer to Bentham and whose painting of wonderful jurisprudential pictures continues to awe-inspire. I have learnt a lot of Jurisprudence, both formally and informally from Professor Stephen Guest. Dr. Ariella Atzmon provided fruitful exchanges and linguistic turns which sparked me off to broaden the perspective and scope of what Bentham's thought might be about. I was inspired by many discussions with Eccy de Jonge and Dr. Michael Drolet. Many helpful strategic comments were made by the anonymous reader of my thesis for which I am deeply grateful. At Southampton, I am grateful to Dr. David Owen for his insightful and constructive comments on Part 2. I thank Professor Nick Wikeley who read and offered valuable general comments on the whole manuscript, Kit Barker who read and commented on Part 2 and Emma Laurie who proof-read the whole text.

The hospitality offered at the Bentham Project, especially by Dr. Jonathan Harris, Catherine Fuller, Dr. Tony Draper and Dr. Colin Tyler, proved invaluable during the years at UCL. The Anglo-Jewish Association and the Ian Karten Charitable Trust furnished me with generous grants. I thank Robert Mangold for his permission to reproduce "Five Color Frame". Last but not least, I have been fortunate to work with Richard Hart, Hannah Young and Lyn Truesdale

Aitchison who have made the publishing process a friendly, efficient and informal delight.

Keren's loving partnership and sensitive containment at moments of exhilaration and dispair transcends any description. My sisters Sidi and Ruth have always been there for me. It is to my parents Miriam and Meir, the well of my Being, that I dedicate this book.

O.B.
Faculty of Law
Southampton.
2000

Abbreviations

Bowring	*The Works of Jeremy Bentham,* published under the super-intendance of his Executor, John Bowring, 11 volumes, Edinburgh, 1838–43.
PT	*Political Tactics* (CW)
Colonies	*Colonies, Commerce, and Constitutional Law: Rid Yourselves of Ultramaria and other writings on Spain and Spanish America* (CW)
Comment	*A Comment on the Commentaries* (CW)
Constitutional Code	*Constitutional Code,* vol. 1 (CW)
Correspondence	*Correspondence of Jeremy Bentham* (CW)
CW	*The Collected Works of Jeremy Bentham* (1968–)
Deontology	*Deontology together with A Table of The Springs of Action and Article on Utilitarianism* (CW)
First Principles	*First Principles preparatory to Constitutional Code* (CW)
Fragment	*A Fragment on Government* (CW)
IPML	*An Introduction to the Principles of Morals and Legislation* (CW)
OLG	*Of Laws in General* (CW)
PJP	*Principles of Judicial Procedure,* Bowring, ii. 1–188.
SAM	*Securities against Misrule and other Constitutional Writings for Tripoli and Greece* (CW)
UC	*Bentham Papers at University College London (followed by box number in Roman Numerals and folio number in Arabic).*

Notes

In quotations, bold characters are used by the present author for purposes of emphasis. Words emphasised by the original author appear in italics.

Throughout the book, any reference to individuals made in the male gender indicates both male and female.

It is so difficult to find the *beginning*. Or, better: it is difficult to begin at the beginning. And not try to go further back.

L. Wittgenstein, *On Certainty*, 471.

1

Introduction

> I define a "classic", in literature, in music, in the arts, in philosophic argument, as a signifying form which "reads" us. It reads us more than we read (listen to, perceive) it. There is nothing paradoxical, let alone mystical, in this definition. Each time we engage with it, the classic will question us. It will challenge our resources of consciousness and intellect, of mind and body . . . The classic will ask of us: "have you understood?"; "have you re-imagined responsibly?"; "are you prepared to act upon the questions, upon the potentialities of transformed; enriched being which I have posed?"
>
> G. Steiner, *Errata: An Examined Life,* London, 1997, p. 18.

I

Bentham's legal and political thought was wide-ranging and voluminous. Based on the principle of utility, Bentham's thought offered insights on subjects as diverse as epistemology, psychology, morality, legislation, analytical jurisprudence and constitutional theory, where he offered a utilitarian defence of democracy. In parallel with his theoretical endeavours, Bentham devised institutional schemes with a view to the implementation of his ideas. These included prison reforms, poor law proposals, and many practical suggestions for the reform of political and legal institutions.

Bentham is well known for the volume and the diversity of his writings. This diversity has created a particular feature which characterises Bentham scholarship: it has not yet arrived at a stage of maturity where all scholars agree on definitive sources for argument. Study of the Bentham manuscripts in University College London, and of the new critical edition of the *Collected Works*, has provided fresh sources for exploring the complexity and subtlety of Bentham's arguments. Bentham scholarship has therefore developed not only on the basis of argumentation about existing texts, but also from the continuous emergence of new texts. Further, the emergence of these texts has enabled new readings of some of Bentham's already well-known writings.

One example of how a discovery of a new text has totally changed the nature of Bentham scholarship is *The Limits of Jurisprudence Defined*,[1] now known as *Of Laws in General*.[2] Before the publication of this work in 1945, Bentham's

[1] C.W. Everett (ed.), *The Limits of Jurisprudence Defined* (New York, 1945).
[2] H.L.A. Hart (ed.), *Of Laws in General* (CW) (London, 1970).

theory of law was seen very much in the shadow of John Austin's command theory of law. The new materials showed a fresher and much more subtle exposition of the command theory. The result of this discovery was that old debates about the nature of legal positivism were reopened among legal theorists.[3] *Of Laws in General* led H.L.A. Hart to develop in a more sophisticated fashion, in *Essays on Bentham,* the criticisms he had developed against Austin's command theory of law in *The Concept of Law*.[4]

The appearance of previously unpublished writings by Bentham has also led to a number of revisionist interpretations of Bentham's principle of utility and of his theory of law, which have presented Bentham's arguments in a new and provocative light.[5] A utilitarian theory of distributive justice, based on Bentham's writings on the civil law, has been defended.[6] There have been new studies in Bentham's constitutional theory, following the publication of the first volume of *Constitutional Code*.[7] All these revisionist interpretations have aimed to challenge Bentham's previous image as a master of scientific method who was concerned with the attainment of security *rather than* having any inherent commitment to liberty and liberal values.[8] As will be discussed in detail in the next section, the present book develops a new approach to reading Bentham—that of constructive/creative interpretation. Arguably, it departs both from the received and the revisionist interpretations, which arguably are still too restricted and conventional in their approach to Bentham's writings.

On a general level this book undertakes a reconstruction of Bentham's conception of constitutional limits. As such, it connects the answers to two questions which lie at the heart of legal and political theory. First, why do people establish a political authority over themselves? Second, how far should centralised coercion encroach upon an individual's life-plan? In this book, the utilitarian characteristics which answer the first question are shown to be dependent on a dynamic social process in answering the second. It is argued that the answers to both these questions develop a perspective from which

[3] See, for instance, J. Raz, *The Concept of a Legal System* (Oxford, 1980).

[4] H.L.A. Hart, *Essays on Bentham: Studies on Jurisprudence and Political Theory* (Oxford, 1982), and *The Concept of Law* (Oxford, 1961).

[5] G.J. Postema, *Bentham and The Common Law Tradition* (Oxford, 1986).

[6] P.J. Kelly, *Utilitarianism and Distributive Justice: Jeremy Bentham and the Civil Law* (Oxford, 1990).

[7] See F. Rosen, *Jeremy Bentham and Representative Democracy: A Study of the Constitutional Code* (Oxford, 1983), and *Bentham, Byron and Greece: Constitutionalism, Nationalism, and Early Liberal Political Thought* (Oxford, 1992); see also L.J. Hume, *Bentham and Bureaucracy* (Cambridge, 1981) and R. Harrison, *Bentham* (London, 1983).

[8] Examples of scholars who interpreted Bentham as "illiberal" are E. Halévy, *The Growth of Philosophic Radicalism* (London, 1928), pp. 487, 490–1, 506; J. Steintrager, *Bentham* (London, 1977); D. Long, *Bentham on Liberty: Jeremy Bentham's Idea of Liberty in relation to his Utilitarianism* (Toronto, 1977), pp. 87–95, 125–7, 159, 168–75; C.F. Bahmuller, *The National Charity Company: Jeremy Bentham's Silent Revolution* (Berkeley, 1981), pp. 201–6; J.E. Crimmins, *Secular Utilitarianism: Social Science and the Critique of Religion in the Thought of Jeremy Bentham* (Oxford, 1990), pp. 73–92, 156–8, 273–302; S.R. Letwin, *The Pursuit of Certainty: David Hume, Jeremy Bentham, John Stuart Mill* (Cambridge, 1965 (reprint 1993)), pp. 140–6, 150–4, 187–8.

Bentham's legal and political enterprise as a whole can be better understood and defended.

These two general questions about constitutional limits lead to more particular issues. A socially dynamic conception of constitutional limits links issues such as sovereignty, the duty to obey the law, forms of government and the possibility of a role for some collectivity, which Bentham referred to as the Public Opinion Tribunal, and which will be discussed, borrowing Jürgen Habermas's term, under the name of the "public sphere".[9] All these issues, which feature in the reconstruction of Bentham, constitute different aspects of the same field of enquiry, namely the nature of constitutional limits.

Both the understanding of Bentham's particular preoccupations, and the connection between them, can facilitate a response to a hitherto unresolved series of questions which have been asked with regard to Bentham's legal and political theory. How could Bentham offer a command theory of law on the one hand, and provide for a constitutionally limited government on the other? How could the powers of a *supreme* commander in a state be limited? Could the command theory of law account for the idea of "validity", rather than "legality" or "legal permissibility"? How could Bentham reconcile his claim, on the one hand, that sovereignty could be constitutionally limited in given areas, with, on the other hand, the provision in his later constitutional writings for a government to whose power no limits were prescribed? An attempt to answer these questions will be made, and it will be argued that these puzzles are not insoluble once the central role played by the public sphere in Bentham's legal and constitutional theory is appreciated.

The reading of Bentham in this book involves two dimensions. The first is a reconstruction of the most general argument about Bentham's legal and political enterprise, given his most abstract theoretical assumptions—a task that Bentham did not himself undertake. This I shall call the *reconstructive* dimension. The reconstruction establishes a link between Bentham's early legal and political writings and his mature constitutional ones. This link consists of the argument that Bentham's legal and political enterprise provided for a socially dynamic conception of constitutional limits which were to be determined and effectuated by a popular collective judgement. As has been mentioned above, the reconstruction involves an analysis of many particular aspects of his theory

[9] The "public sphere" is regarded by Habermas as the public grouping of *private* individuals who debate issues bearing on state authority: see C. Calhoun, *Habermas and the Public Sphere* (Cambridge, Mass., 1992), p. 7. In *The Structural Transformation of the Public Sphere: An Inquiry into a Category of Bourgeois Society* (Cambridge, 1989), p. 27, Habermas refers to the public sphere as

> "the sphere of private people come together as a public; they soon claimed the public sphere regulated from above against the public authorities themselves, to engage them in a debate over the general rules governing relations in the basically privatized but publicly relevant sphere of commodity exchange and social labor. The medium of this political confrontation was peculiar and without historical precedent: people's public use of their reason."

See also ibid., pp. 54, 79, and his *Between Facts and Norms* (Cambridge, 1996), p. 360.

in the light of this link. As a reconstruction of Bentham's legal and political thought, the argument does not question Bentham's basic assumptions, which were essentially those of the Enlightenment, namely the desire to establish a systematic understanding of morals and society. More specifically, it attempts neither to question Bentham's assumption that two sovereign masters—pain and pleasure—formed the foundation of psychology and morality, nor his assumption that communication problems might be solved by the development of language. The second dimension involves a critical discussion of Bentham's thought within the context of contemporary debates in legal and political philosophy. Here Bentham's utilitarianism and his command theory of law is defended against various contemporary criticisms. This dimension I shall call the *critical* dimension. The two dimensions, despite being clearly separated in the text, have mutually reinforced one another in the course of formulating and refining the main argument. In general terms, it was a puzzle of a critical nature with regard to contemporary Bentham scholarship, an admittedly opaque puzzle, which ignited my intuitions in the direction of undertaking an imaginative reconstruction of Bentham's writings. This intuition was coupled with a close reading of the texts in the course of formulating the reconstruction. In turn, this reconstruction substantiated and refined my early opaque criticisms of contemporary scholarship.

It may be helpful to explain the way in which the two dimensions interacted in the course of building my argument. In the first place, long before engaging in a close reading of Bentham's legal and constitutional texts, I was puzzled on a very general level. Being generally familiar with the vast range of Bentham's preoccupations, it seemed that contemporary criticisms of him, both in legal and political theory, were deeply misguided. All these criticisms, I felt, were confined within the limited perspective of the agenda the critic aimed to defend. This limited perspective gave rise to oversimplifications, as well as to a lack of imagination, and failed to do justice to Bentham's arguments. There have been no attempts to challenge the very doctrines under which Bentham's enterprise was understood as functioning, such as "legal positivism". Given the breadth of Bentham's endeavours, it seemed to me that those who criticised him subjected him to their own purposes and paradigms. This led to a doubt as to whether Bentham's texts had been properly interpreted. Further, my intuition contributed to a certain sympathy with Bentham's objectives. This sympathy persuaded me to attempt to relate Bentham's texts to one another in a way which would go beyond any received interpretation, rather than merely to respond to such an interpretation.

Let me give an example of one such insight which relates to a dominant contemporary account of legal positivism, namely Hart's theory in *The Concept of Law* and *Essays on Bentham*. In spite of Hart's lucid criticisms of certain distinctions overlooked in Bentham's thought—distinctions which would make sense to lawyers—it is puzzling that *The Concept of Law* has been so generally recognised as paving the way, in Hart's own words, towards a "fresh start" in thinking about the main paradigms of analytical jurisprudence. How could Hart, a scholar who utilised a far narrower philosophical basis, and had far narrower objectives than Bentham, successfully produce a conceptual theory which undertook to refine Bentham's wider, more fundamental and philosophically richer, as well as more meticulous, social and political enterprise? Bentham attempted to show *detailed* connections between many different philosophical, social and political preoccupations, and based these connections on such elementary concepts that any attack on a *single* aspect of this enterprise *in isolation*, such as his theory of law, seems misconceived. That this *is* a misconception remains the case even when one admits that the terms Bentham used to discuss legal phenomena are rather dated for the present-day lawyer who lives in a modern liberal democracy, and who uses terms such as "validity" without a second thought.[10] An example of this misconception goes to the heart of Hart's own methodology. Hart's methodology, which he called "descriptive sociology",[11] produced a number of perceptive distinctions, such as those between legality and validity, validity and effectiveness, a command and a rule, "being obliged" and "having an obligation", the external and internal points of view, and legal and moral rules. However, it is not clear that these distinctions give rise to a better description of social states of affairs associated with law, than notions which are far wider and more elementary, such as pain and pleasure, desire, expectation, relationship of superiority and subordination, the unification of duty and interest, the expression of a wish by a superior in relation to a given act, and various types of sanctions. In contrast to Hart, this book uses Bentham's elementary concepts in order to help analyse the novel, and in some cases arguably cruder, distinctions drawn by Hart. As such, the argument in the book aims to transcend the constraints of Hartian paradigms in interpreting Bentham and may, therefore, be characterised as presenting a jurisprudential account of "Bentham after Hart".

The second factor which contributed to my own reading of Bentham's works was a familiarity with certain accounts of modern legal, social and political theory. One major influence in constructing the argument was that of theories of interpretation. Ronald Dworkin's interpretative methodology in legal and political theory, in contrast to positivistic studies of these disciplines, made me

10 See pp. 13–19 below.

11 In the preface to *The Concept of Law*, Hart announced his intention to provide a *conceptual* analysis of law, not according to reductionist methods of definition, but in terms of the social context in which legal terms were used. He criticised any attempt to define law as a "command" which failed to investigate whether the social use of terms associated with, and thus the understanding of, law corresponded to such a definition. Under the command theory of law, terms which were associated with law such as "rights", "obligations", "rules", "a legal system", were defined in such a way that a conceptually consistent theory was the result. Yet this command theory was a socially detached account of legal phenomena. It ignored many social connotations which formed the necessary context for any assertion of legal terms; see also H.L.A. Hart, *Essays in Jurisprudence and Philosophy* (Oxford, 1983), pp. 26–35. For an explanation of Hart's methodology, see P.M.S. Hacker, "Hart's Philosophy of Law", in J. Raz and P.M.S. Hacker (eds), *Law, Morality and Society—Essays in Honour of H.L.A. Hart* (Oxford, 1977), pp. 1–25, at 8–10.

receptive to the idea of reading Bentham's texts in a less conventional, more imaginative way. Further, and more substantively, Bentham's legal positivism seemed to be questionable and his utilitarian enterprise seemed to function rather as an interpretative theory. A second major influence has been that of Habermas, whose "Theory of Communicative Action" conceives the existence of an emancipatory potential in the public sphere. Free communication in the public sphere can emancipate authentic rationality from the encroachment of various epistemic systems. A third major influence was the works of legal sociologists such as Ehrlich, Gurvitch and Pound. Ehrlich's arguments about the "living law" contributed to my socially dynamic interpretation of Bentham's enterprise.

In the third place, while closely reading Bentham's various texts it became clearer how limited were the perspectives which criticised his work. Both received and revisionist interpretations of Bentham, whether in jurisprudence or political theory, were still too unimaginative and all-too-often formalistic. Although the leading revisionist Bentham scholars, namely Postema, Kelly and Rosen, relied on unpublished texts, their arguments were predetermined by too limited an ambit of what those texts actually said. Nowhere in their writings was there an argument which had the potential of addressing both unpublished and familiar Bentham texts within a novel context. Consequently, their interpretation could not transcend the limited context within which the texts were read.

Further, all major interpretations of Bentham, including the revisionist ones, were limited by historical or thematic prejudices. Let me give some examples. In respect of his legal and political preoccupations, Bentham's thought has usually been divided into two distinct periods. During the early period, he was mainly preoccupied with the reformation of the moral and the legal world. In the later period of his life, Bentham turned to radicalism and discussed detailed issues in constitutional theory.[12]

The fact that Bentham concentrated on different theoretical fields at different stages of his life has led to two different limitations of perspective amongst Bentham scholars. First, there have been scholars who have discussed Bentham with reference to only one temporal period, that is in relation to *the time at which particular texts were written*. Examples of this approach are Hart and Long, who simply do not consider Bentham's mature constitutional writings.[13] A second limitation in interpreting Bentham's work has been thematic. There have been scholars who have discussed in depth certain themes in Bentham's

[12] For the reasons which may have led to "another Bentham", see J.R. Dinwiddy, "Bentham's Transition to Political Radicalism 1809–10", *Journal of the History of Ideas* 36 (1975) 683–700; J.H. Burns, "Bentham and the French Revolution", *Transactions of the Royal Historical Society* 16 (1966) 95–115, and "Jeremy Bentham: from Radical Enlightenment to Philosophic Radicalism", *Bentham Newsletter* 8 (1984) 4–14, at 6–7.

[13] See, for instance, Hart, *Essays on Bentham*, especially chapter 9, and "Bentham on Sovereignty", in B. Parekh (ed.), *Jeremy Bentham—Ten Critical Essays* (London, 1974), pp. 145–53, at 149–52; and Long, *Bentham on Liberty*, pp. 87–8, 95.

thought, almost to the point of neglecting others. Examples are Rosen, who has considered both Bentham's early and mature constitutional theory, but hardly refers to Bentham's legal theory, and Postema, who has mainly discussed Bentham's legal theory, and therefore approached Bentham's constitutional writings almost only from that perspective.

Rosen does not seek any common rationale underlying Bentham's legal and political thought. As far as Postema is concerned, although his account is thorough and thought-provoking, and despite his analysis of some texts from later in Bentham's career, he does have a rather limited perspective, namely a discussion of Bentham's legal theory. Nowhere does Postema try to establish a connection between Bentham's legal thought, concerning how political society should deal with the issue of constitutional limits, and the treatment of related issues in Bentham's mature constitutional theory. Although his insight into the interactional element between the people and the government in Bentham's theory of sovereignty was a breakthrough in the understanding of Bentham's conception of sovereignty, an insight which has been much relied on and developed in this book, Postema did not develop fully the nature of this interaction, and did not assess the *implications* such an interaction might have for the understanding of Bentham's constitutional writings. Further, he failed to investigate the extent to which Bentham's legal and political thought might have a unified rationale.

As a result of this lack of unity of treatment,[14] Bentham's thought has been exposed to criticisms, for instance that it did not provide strong enough protection for individual rights, through, for instance, their entrenchment as constitutional limits. An example of what I regard as a grossly distorted overall picture of Bentham's endeavours is provided by Steintrager:

> "Constitutional questions were abstract and remote from the normal interests of the common man whose primary concerns, after all, must be with his family and his fortune. If, as seems the case, Bentham held to the view that truth would win out in the market place, it was not because he had great confidence in the people, but because he counted on a few men who would be responsive to popular needs as articulated by thinkers like himself. Even though he was insistent that the feelings of the people must be taken into consideration, his very concept of the legislative function suggest[s] that change would come from above and not from below."[15]

In an attempt to emancipate Bentham from limited interpretative perspectives, by adopting a new interpretative approach, I shall seek to challenge every single sentence of this quote. In fact, the argument of this book is that the role of the people underpinned Bentham's utilitarian enterprise. In the course of the argument, various criticisms of Bentham scholars will be advanced. The common theme in all these criticisms is that scholars have not gone, or could not

[14] An exception to this lack of uniformity is D. Baumgardt, *Bentham and the Ethics of Today* (Princeton, 1952), in which a detailed discussion of Bentham's psychology and morality is undertaken in relation to the competing Kantian moral theory.

[15] Steintrager, *Bentham*, p. 53.

go—because of inaccessibility to many of Bentham's texts—far enough in developing and defending an argument which would present Bentham's legal and political enterprise as a coherent and unified whole.

Finally, the reconstruction of Bentham's texts unveils their contemporary potential. By interpreting Bentham's texts creatively, it is apparent that they have the potential to furnish original approaches—and moreover, arguably, superior ones—to foundational problems discussed in contemporary legal and political philosophy.

II

As a result of the examination of the newly-published and as yet unpublished constitutional texts, it is now possible to reconstruct Bentham's legal and political enterprise as a whole. It might, of course, be that Bentham did not in fact intend his enterprise to be unified in the way suggested here. However, in view of Bentham's "enlightenment" project of producing a complete code of law, a *pannomion*, which was to combine a utilitarian theory of legislation with a consistent epistemology, it is plausible to argue that he aspired towards the establishment of a unified whole. He did not allow sufficient time for reflecting generally upon his all-embracing legal and political enterprise. He devoted his life to detailed expositions of various theoretical and practical subject-matters, and, as a result, provided no general discussion about how all these parts might be welded into a coherent whole. Thus, while it is possible that Bentham had a clear conception of an underlying rationale, he did not in fact reflect generally on the continuity and consistency of the various branches or fields of thought which he considered.

In reconstructing a unified argument from Bentham's texts, the methodology of the book involves by and large what William Twining calls a "discussional" approach, rather then a historical or literal one.[16] A literal approach would involve an original exposition of published texts by Bentham and an introduction of new texts. A historical approach, by contrast, would provide an interpretation of Bentham which would attune to the perspective of what Bentham might or might not have meant with reference to the period in which he lived, and the ideas by which he might have been influenced.[17]

[16] W.L. Twining, "Reading Bentham", Maccabean Lecture in Jurisprudence, in *Proceedings of The British Academy* 75 (1989) 97–141, at 107–28.

[17] The objective of this book is not a Skinnerian one of writing a history of ideas: see Q. Skinner, "Meaning and Understanding in the History of Ideas", in Q. Skinner and J. Tully (eds), *Meaning and Context: Quentin Skinner and his Critics* (Cambridge, 1988), pp. 50, 64–7. I am not looking to see by whom Bentham was influenced or understand the particular historical context in which he lived. However, being an account of Bentham's constitutionalism within utilitarian theory, the argument is historical in that Bentham's understanding of certain terms, such as an "individual", would confine the context in which utilitarian terms such as pleasure and pain are understood. Any description or explanation would therefore imply some historicity, but such historicity does not contain the whole truth of the terms used, such truth being by and large ahistorical.

By contrast, the discussional methodology, though it implies *some* historicity, both on the part of the person who discusses and the object discussed, rejects the commonly made compartmentalisation of Bentham in respect of a certain period in his career, such as a "legal reformer" or a "political radical". Put generally, the method is to construct the most coherent interpretation on the basis of a close reading of Bentham's texts given his most basic theoretical assumptions, namely that it is ultimately for pain and pleasure to "point out what we ought to do, as well as to determine what we shall do".[18]

The discussion with Bentham's texts is interpretative. The aim of the book is to defend a coherent argument about Bentham's utilitarian enterprise in a way which consistently unites many of his texts. The argument defends a constructed coherence between Bentham's texts against other interpretations of them. The interpreter undertakes a detailed "discussion" with Bentham's particular texts, and tries to fit them into a generally constructed argument which encompasses the enterprise as a whole.

An obvious methodological difficulty exists regarding the authenticity of interpreting *Bentham*. Where does Bentham end and the interpreter's argument begin? To what extent is the reader offered a "real" Bentham, and to what extent a "hypothetical" or a "constructed" one? Essentially, these questions pertain to theories of interpretation and literary criticism. This is not the occasion to address fully the complex problem concerning the plausibility of separating text and interpreter-imposed context in interpretation. Nevertheless, it is in order to mention the general position taken in this work. The position adopted here is that, for the purposes of textual meaning, it is impossible completely to separate a text from the context imposed on it by an interpretative argument. Though the interpreter closely engages with the actual texts written by Bentham as a source of interpretation, the *meaning* of those texts must always depend on the interpretation which is conferred upon it by future interpreters. Once one rejects a formalistic reading of Bentham's texts and moves to an interpretative attitude, any truth-claim in the form of "Bentham said such and such" meshes text and interpreter.[19] Any methodology which both presents itself as interpretative and also professes to separate clearly texts and interpreter, is formalistic in fact. The actual words of the text, being an object of interpretation, are significant in themselves only to the extent that they serve as a common, agreed, source of argumentation. To be sure, one cannot say whatever one likes about Bentham. There are constraints about what one can say about Bentham's texts if one is said to interpret *Bentham*. Indeed, the texts themselves, which require a close reading, Bentham's basic assumptions, the fit between the general argument and the texts' own complexity—all constitute constraints on the interpreter's potential creativity. Another important constraint is the influence of the interpreter's values which opens the possibility of imagining new general arguments about the texts.

[18] *IPML*, p. 1.

[19] See R. Dworkin, *Law's Empire* (London, 1986), pp. 47–8.

Despite these constraints, my aim is to read Bentham with an open mind. In order to achieve the required open-mindedness, the interpreter should "clean" the reconstruction in two respects. In the first place, previous interpretations of Bentham should play as little a role as possible. Whichever way Bentham's texts are closely read, their interpretation has to be conducted imaginatively. Initially at least, the interpreter must not try to respond to any received criticisms or interpretations. For example, it is not the aim of the work to show that Bentham's enterprise can accommodate ideas such as fundamental rights, or that it accounts for notions like "validity" and "normativity" which are at the forefront of Hart's concept of law. To engage with those arguments would, from the very beginning, reduce the potential encapsulated in the texts. Any response to received criticisms would reveal that the interpreter is already trapped in certain paradigms. Indeed, a major criticism that this book levels against modern interpretations of Bentham is that they reduce Bentham to their own co-ordinates of argumentation. The aim, in short, is to let the text, through the interpreter, say something new. The discussion of other interpretations only takes place *alongside* the reconstruction, and where possible, *after* it has been formulated.

Second, somewhat paradoxically, the interpretation has to distance itself from many aspects of the historical Bentham, namely from the real person. Historians will probably object to such a methodological move, but it is essential in order to assume a perspective from which novel arguments about Bentham can be developed. This distancing is required precisely because deducing what the real Bentham could or could not have said, in terms of the events or ideas by which he was influenced, may limit the potential that his own work might carry. The horizon of possibilities that the real Bentham envisaged for his texts must necessarily have been limited by him being who he was, located in his historical situation. Instead of confining oneself to a conventionally held "real Bentham" in closely reading Bentham's texts, one has to ask what parts of the conventional argument about "what the 'real Bentham' might have been" are compatible with an argument about a "constructed" Bentham. As was argued above, it is only the main theoretical assumptions of the real Bentham that are left intact. Put differently, the interpretative process tries, within acceptable constraints, to generate a hypothetical reflection that would be made by a "putative" Bentham upon the whole of his legal and political enterprise.

Let me explain this methodology in more detail in order to prepare the reader for the arguments to come. The reconstruction of Bentham's text—the "discussion" with them—is argumentative. The approach to the reconstruction is influenced by Ronald Dworkin's account of interpretation in general, and of "law as interpretation" in particular.[20] Dworkin distinguishes between a conversational interpretation and a constructive/creative one. The former takes place in any dialogue with a real person, or for our purposes the real person's (Bentham's)

[20] Dworkin, *Law's Empire*, chapters 1, 2.

"text". Conversational interpretation presumes that utterances/texts contain the conscious mental state of a speaker/an author. It emphasises the speaker's conscious intention rather than the interpreter's convictions. It presumes a real person with whom one converses. A conversational approach to interpretation assumes that Bentham—the real person—could only interpret the text within certain, historically-given co-ordinates. In other words, such an approach assumes a finite, factual personality whose conscious intention can be used as a limit to the context within which arguments can be made about the words of the text.

By contrast, constructive/creative interpretation involves arguments about an author's enterprise as a whole. A constructive/creative approach to interpretation shifts the emphasis from the actual creator of the object of interpretation (speaker/text), to the interpreter who uses his own convictions and historically-oriented background to argue for the overall coherence of the text in question. Thus, the interpreter "imposes" coherence on the text. By comparison to the constructive/creative method of interpretation, conversational interpretation is arguably too modest, and therefore has too limited a scope in extracting the potential of a text. The limited scope of conversational interpretation holds unless the term "conversation" becomes a metaphor to be dissolved by a constructed argument by the interpreter. If this happens, though, the term "conversation" would mean the imposition of coherence in the manner described above.

Thus, in undertaking a constructive/creative approach, the interpreter's own views, though in accordance with the author's general assumptions, can construct a different, less historically-orientated interpretation of the text. The interpreter can be faithful to the author despite transcending the latter's evident, historically-oriented intentions for the text. An ever-renewed, multi-perspective preoccupation with the same texts, texts which contain some force and to which people come back to rethink, though never to exhaust, is arguably the feature which makes ideas of great thinkers timeless. Furthermore, as Dworkin, drawing on Cavell, argues, even their own intentions are not fully transparent to authors of texts and are being constructed by them continuously during their lifetime.[21]

This book adopts a constructive/creative interpretative methodology. Bentham becomes a "constructed author" for the purpose of this book. A discussion takes place with his text not in the ordinary conversational sense, but in the metaphorical sense. A discussion takes place in order to achieve coherence between the general argument constructed by the interpreter and the complexity that a close reading of Bentham's text generates. Given Bentham's presumptions about the predominance of the principle of utility in morality and psychology, what arguments can be constructed which will consistently weld his various texts into a coherent whole? This book examines the way in which the particular texts under discussion might fit into a larger whole, even if Bentham

[21] Dworkin, *Law's Empire*, pp. 55–62.

may never have explicated that whole consciously. Further, the main argument is used to resolve apparent incoherences and gaps in Bentham's more specific arguments. In other words, certain conflicting views with regard to a particular text are discussed in order to determine which one of them makes the best sense of Bentham's legal and political enterprise as a whole.

In adopting this methodology, it is assumed that in reading Bentham one encounters tensions, or puzzles, or gaps in his argument, both in each specific text that he wrote, and in any attempt to construct unifying themes in relation to his thought. Disagreements among scholars in relation to such tensions do not relate to questions about what Bentham actually wrote, but are of a more theoretical nature. The question at the core of such disagreements is something like this: "What possible justification can be provided to support an argument to the effect that Bentham's claim was such and such?"

Any such justification, at the most general level, integrates Bentham's legal and political theory. In reading Bentham in an integrated way a general argument is formed according to which the basic tenets of his theory can be viewed as a consistent whole. This approach serves two purposes. First, it constructs a consistent general justification for Bentham's theory. A large proportion of particular inconsistencies within and between individual texts can be resolved in the light of this general justification. With a view to integrating Bentham's enterprise, both what Bentham said and what he did not say in any specific text may be equally interesting. It is only after certain general arguments about his legal and political enterprise are advanced that apparent theoretical incoherences in his thought can be accounted for. Second, the construction will itself be justified and defended against rival general interpretations, and against criticisms, which, it will be argued, follow from less consistent and less comprehensive adherence to the main tenets of his argument.

It is possible to be sceptical, and to claim that Bentham's work is too inconsistent, that he contradicted himself too frequently and that he repeatedly changed his ideas over the years. As a result of this inconsistency, so the sceptical argument goes, any global claim about his theory is doomed to failure. This kind of argument is what Dworkin calls the "internal sceptic's" argument.[22] Such a sceptic, in our case a sceptical scholar, would advance *the interpretative argument* that Bentham's enterprise is too indeterminate. However, the aim of this book is to construct the best possible argument which presents Bentham's enterprise as a whole, *despite* these inconsistencies. Thus, if the argument is successful, it will refute such internal scepticism. The only way for the reader to pass judgement on whether to prefer the interpretation suggested by this book, or another interpretation, would be to ask which of them makes better sense of Bentham's enterprise, all things considered. In the course of the book, a justification for many particular arguments in relation to Bentham's texts is furnished by reference to the most general and unifying argument which I advance for his

[22] Dworkin, *Law's Empire*, pp. 76–85.

utilitarian enterprise, namely that constitutional limits were determined and effectuated by the public sphere.

III

The term "ought" has potential to mislead. It can signify many things. The present book features four possible senses of the term. In the first place, it signifies a normative attitude which features in any exercise of authority. In the second, it signifies the status of an alleged universal description according to which a discourse ought to be understood. In the third, it signifies an ideal, that is a critical standard to which whatever exists should aspire. Finally, in the fourth, in the specific context of the present book, it signifies a justificatory claim in an interpretative discourse. The way in which this book relates to the last-mentioned sense of "ought" has been discussed in the previous section. However, the argument also involves a discussion of the other three senses of "ought", though the most problematic distinction is that between the second and third senses of the word.

Bentham claimed to be engaged in a project of a "universal" theory (or more specifically, universal jurisprudence) about individuality, morality, law and society. This project differed from an "expository" account which described the central features of a particular culture, at a certain stage of development.[23] Bentham claimed that he was developing a universal theory which would form the basis for an understanding of morality, legislation, political society, law, private ethics and constitutional theory.[24]

On no occasion did Bentham discuss the meaning of "universality". He simply assumed the meaning of the concept in relation to some parts of his thought. Hence his claim was that his descriptions of legislation and of law, for example, would function "beyond time and place". Some reflections on what universality might mean may alter the perspective from which his works are approached. The term "universal theory" implies that the given account would necessarily form the basis for any particular application of it. Universal jurisprudence would necessarily form the basis for *all* descriptions of legal discourse, for all places, for all cultures and for all time. A universal theory would describe features inherent in any aspect of legal activity. The identification of a universal "theory of law" implies that all descriptions of law contained in a more particular "theory of law" would presuppose the universal theory of law, and be consistent with it in all the distinctions the more particular theory made at its own level, distinctions which, of course, would be subject to ideology, culture and

[23] *Fragment*, pp. 397–8; see also "The Influence of Time and Place in Matters of Legislation", Bowring, i. 170.

[24] See Twining, "Reading Bentham", pp. 133–8, and "General and Particular Jurisprudence—Three Chapters in a Story" in S. Guest (ed.), *Positivism Today* (Aldershot, 1996), pp. 119–46, at 120–25.

time. For example, the notion of what law is might be very different in socialist, liberal, anarchic, and tribal or family-based groups. However, a universal theory of law would apply equally to all of them.

There is a strong case for treating Bentham's theory as aspiring to universality. Bentham devised a method which relied upon the elementary terms of pain and pleasure, as well as a linguistic epistemology. Elementary terms such as "pain" and "pleasure" constituted a level of theorisation which, for Bentham, would constitute the foundation of *any* meaningful discussion about morality and law. In other words, Bentham would insist that if a theory were to constitute a foundational and complete philosophical system, there would have to *be* an elementary level of discussion attempting to answer a question like "what is the human condition which enables "moral talk" or "legal talk" to make sense?"[25] Such an insistence need not be taken to say that the way in which basic terms were understood could not be refined. However, it does imply that such basic terms have some force which *cannot* be fully replaced by other terms. Although both his understanding of pain and pleasure and his epistemology have been contested by modern philosophers and social theorists, Bentham's theorising at this basic level does mean that his legal and political theory interacts intensively with general philosophy and aspires to defend a complete philosophical system. This interaction with, and aspiration towards, a general and complete philosophy, means that his theory aspires to universality much more convincingly than any theory of law which merely purports to describe this or that aspect of legal practice, as commonly understood by people in general, and

[25] Utility, for Bentham, did not aim at (providing an ideal for the substantive resolution of) moral questions, for example, to justify universally one substantive principle for the distribution of resources or rights. The enlightening thing about Utility was that it invoked, and constantly reverted back to, a basic human condition to explain moral possibilities, rather than being about justifying one particular substantive moral judgement. It did not attempt to justify *the* true morality. For Bentham, a *description* of the nature of moral approval or disapproval, and hence the *horizon of possibilities* of having genuine moral feelings, would constitute a broader and more basic enquiry than any a priori justification for an actual moral conviction. What is involved in asserting and assessing the "truthfulness" of any moral judgement was more important in his view than finding the *best* substantive moral judgement with which the intuition of every agent could be universally identified. This was so because a utilitarian description could accommodate different perspectives from which actual moral convictions could be made and interpreted as making full sense. If one described and understood the evaluative (and psychological) process which went on in other people's minds, one would be able to understand other people without need to attempt to articulate a common bridge between one's own substantive moral view and theirs. One could differ from other people in the perspective for making moral justifications. This is empathy. In this respect, utilitarian talk about *possibility*, though prone to the charge of nihilism and relativism, is enlightening precisely because it provides a critical principle which transcends any moral perspective. As far as one's own moral intuition is concerned, such a description of *possibilities* connects a weak, never fully resolved moral intuition to the human condition in a way which makes enough justificatory sense in one's consciousness but never a complete intuitive sense with which one's considered actual judgements are identified. One route out of the nihilistic and relative implications of the inability to form a universal intuition—the inability to articulate fully a universal ethical intuition—is to develop an ethical theory in the language of *possibility*. Another would be to attempt to articulate an ultimate and *pure* substantive moral principle. This will be discussed further in part 2 of the book.

by lawyers in particular, be it the phenomenon of a "rule", or "a theory of adjudication". To put the point differently, having a complete philosophy arguably means that the field of enquiry opened up by the employment of basic terms must be presumed in more complex situations, the discussion of which commonly employs different terms and involves more particular fields of enquiry.[26] The field of enquiry undertaken by a complete philosophical system would have, by the supposition, to serve as the context of more particular enquiries. There is a connection which cuts across jurisprudence, political theory, moral and ethical theory and the theory of practical reason. Arguably, only a field of enquiry which employs basic terms can connect all those respective fields. There is a point beyond which the terms which feature in a common description of a social phenomenon are unable to go unless paraphrased into more elementary terms. The common user of terms might regard such paraphrasis as reductionism and so would object: "Although it is possible, does it *really* make sense to talk about this situation in this paraphrased form?"[27]

This is why, at times, an analysis of social phenomena in basic terms seems an odd way to talk about common, more complex situations. However, a theorist who employs these basic terms could claim that it would, on the contrary, be arbitrary to call a certain situation "novel", or "new", if the situation could be accounted for in more basic terms, however reductionist it may seem. This arbitrariness could result in too hasty, and therefore inadequate, theoretical conclusions. For example, it is one of the conclusions of this book that an unduly hasty defence of legal positivism results from regarding as "reductionism" the translation of the notion of "validity" into the simpler language of expression of will and relationship of subordination and superiority. To emphasise the point again, a universal theory presumes that there must be some basic way of understanding a state of affairs, otherwise there is no *point* in devising a complete philosophical system. I shall dwell upon this last point shortly. Hart's method of "descriptive sociology" would be regarded as aiming at a universal description of law. For Bentham, however, such a method, if it is to be convincing as a universal theory, must assume the notion of an act and an expression of will with regard to this act, with some kind of sanction attached, in order to explain the normativity of law. In other words, a description of a rule could never be a better universal social description of legal phenomena than some expression of will (a command being one of them), because an expression of will forms part of the generically-basic conception of law as a discourse, namely exercised in a context of superiority and subordination, a conception which any account of "law as a system of rules" would have to accommodate. Bentham would claim that a theory of law based on the idea of "a rule" is not sufficiently engaged with elementary conceptions of basic terms to present a claim for universality.

[26] See in this context, A. Halpin, "Concepts, Terms, and Fields of Enquiry", *Legal Theory* 4 (1998) 187–205.

[27] See Hart, *The Concept of Law*, pp. 38–41.

It will be argued that Bentham's most famous works in legal and moral theory (*Fragment*, *IPML*, *OLG*, *Deontology*), and some aspects of his main works in constitutional theory (*First Principles*, and the parts of *SAM* which *do not* discuss actual forms of government), can be interpreted together as constituting a universal description of particular applications. The description of law might accommodate different regimes of property distribution, or degrees of state intervention. However, as was argued above, it should be emphasised that my argument does *not* contest Bentham's basic and most general psychological and ethical assumptions. It merely tries to make the best sense of his theory *within those assumptions*.

Having said this much about universality, new distinctions, which would refine the universal description, might arise. For example, the understanding of "desire" might change from a conscious atomistic "want" into an unconscious symbolic "lack". Should the idea of "desire" change, the content of the universal account which employs the term "desire" within it would also change. The content which had been "universal" in terms of the previous understanding of "desire" would then become particular. In the context of an enterprise like Bentham's discussion of an imperative theory of law, it is possible that the understanding of "a will" as the drive of an atomistic, self-contained, rational individual would come to be disputed. A different understanding of the foundation of "a will" might mean that far more complex ideas of manifestations of will, and the relationship of subordination and superiority, would be developed. This process is usually referred to as a "linguistic turn". This "turn" constitutes a *necessary* move in the process of growth in the conceptual understanding of a theory. "Time" at this level of universal theory would relate to the moment of "advance" at which a transformation in the basic understanding of the terms occurs. A universal account would be historically sensitive only in regard to the development of its own internal distinctions. The "old" basic terms which had made up the "old" universal account, though still featuring in the new one, would be dressed with an almost completely new meaning. It would be appropriate to say that the universal account had undergone a process of self-reflection, though it had retained the use and essential meaning of the same terms. Again, if the term "desire" underwent a fundamental change, then terms which are related to it, like "pain" and "pleasure", and accordingly "utility", would also undergo a fundamental change.

However, such a transformation in the understanding of terms does not remove the universal force from Bentham's intuitions about the human condition, and from many of his legal and political accounts which are firmly based on them. Although such a transformation means that Bentham's account of utilitarianism cannot be complete, there would be some insights immanent in, and foundational to, his account—insights which are all connected to the central role the maximisation of pleasure has for psychology and morality—which could survive self-reflection on Bentham's own understanding of the basic terms he used. There is something deeply authentic, and *in this sense* deeply true, in

Bentham's arguments, although, quite expectedly, being manifestations in the history of the understanding of this authentic truth, his argument could not possibly articulate it fully. Borrowing a Levinasian metaphor here, the truth Bentham wanted to reveal continuously caresses us through his arguments but is never fully revealed. Bentham's constant, and largely consistent, engagement with-basic terms, although it does not exhaust the understanding of those terms, does nevertheless force us to return constantly and invites us to remain open to, the social complexity generated by the basic human condition. Bentham's vision was necessarily limited, because there is always a gap between intuitions one could have about the universality of a condition, and the interpretative restriction upon the more particular, historically contingent, self-description of those intuitions by that very author. It is left for future interpreters to assess the limitations upon the author's own description of his insights (i.e. substituting them with others) without totally discrediting implications of his description to the, never to be completed, unveiling of the universal.

In this context of discussing universality, it is no doubt problematic to claim that Bentham's account fully expounds the complexity of legal and political phenomena. It might be argued that the terms used by Bentham are not capable, on the face of it, of accounting for such complexity (for example to account for the phenomenon of "validity"). Now, in the face of increasing complexity, there are two divergent methods of analysis. One method presumes that an ever-growing situational complexity can be explained by the refinement of the context in which very simple terms, such as pain and pleasure, are used. Such a refinement can take place, for example, by describing a more complex interdependence between different agents, individual or collective, who are able to feel pain and pleasure, or through the revision of the understanding of the very terms "pain" and "pleasure". Although other terms will no doubt be needed for that refinement, the purpose of their employment would be to describe better the way more simple terms might relate to one another. Such a method of analysis would result in the articulation of some "sameness" at the heart of many complex situations which are commonly characterised by different terms. This method of analysis, namely the refinement of basic terms, would need to identify the essence which basic terms like pain and pleasure convey (including in this identification some justification of a conception of "essence"). *Some* truth regarding this essence will hold sway irrespective of any temporal elucidation and falsification of the context in which the basic terms are used. Something will always continue to provoke people to think about this essence.

By contrast, a second analytical method of dealing with a new situation would be to assign a different term, as well as a given context in which this term is used, to signify the new situation. Such a method would attempt to justify the completeness, or the wholeness, of a certain phenomenon to the extent that no refinement of an old usage of terms could really make sense in accounting for that phenomenon. Indeed, such a presumption of "newness" of the phenomenon, itself unexplained, would be the justification for developing a term which seems better to account for it. This method of analysis assumes a common agreement, itself again unexplained, that a phenomenon is indeed new, and it further implies that it would be reductionist, in a distorting manner, to sanctify a certain basic term to account for this new phenomenon.

However, the choice between these two methods of analysis is in truth between two forms of reductionism: the first method sanctifies certain terms; while the second reduces the potential for identifying similitude in what appear to be different social situations. This book chooses the first method of analysis. It assumes that Bentham's account needs refinement, but it also assumes that his account, being so basic, can carry the mantle of such refinements convincingly. For example, allegedly different accounts of "liberty" can be shown to function interdependently under a utilitarian theory, and thus the "difference" between them can be shown to be less marked. My approach assumes that the fact that at some point it *seems* that certain terms cannot bear the descriptions of some social phenomena is insufficient in itself to discredit those terms. There is a good case to defend such an approach of adhering to basic terms with Bentham because his language was simpler than many other accounts in legal and political philosophy, in that it assumed less conventional contexts and less "baggage of terms" in describing certain social phenomena. In that sense he was indeed a reductionist and so arguably *less* susceptible to the charge of too quickly describing a certain situation as "new". Discussing allegedly "new" social phenomena such as "validity", using the language of expression of will and sanctions, can expose fundamental truths which are considered as being a non-question once the term "validity" marks the limitation of the analysis, limitation which rules out the need for further magnification.

What would the term "ought" mean in the context of a universal theory? When Bentham gave an account of universal jurisprudence, there was no difference between what IS and what OUGHT TO BE. Indeed, there could not be. By the supposition of universality *any* description ("this is") must be what it ought to be. The idea represented in the statement "this is" would have been put in the way it ought to be described. Any refutation of this would deny the supposition of universality. Any theory which claims universality would have to insist on this unification of the IS and the OUGHT. The very unification between the IS and the OUGHT is what makes plausible a claim for the universality of a theoretical discourse. If any distinction between IS and OUGHT were permitted at a universal level, it would contradict the universal feature of the enterprise described. To give an example from Bentham's corpus: in *OLG* Bentham claimed to have given a universal *definition* of a law for all places, all cultures, and all times. A law, as *described* there, *ought* to be understood only in that way in all places, in all cultures, and at all times. The same claim might be made, for instance, in relation to Bentham's description of human psychology and morality, based on pain and pleasure, as expounded in *IPML* and *Deontology*. Thus, from this perspective, the distinction between a universal expository account, which would be confined to the definition of terms, and a universal censorial account, which would be some ideal theoretical model of law, cannot exist. Entities like "pain", "pleasure", "desire", "relationship of subordination and superiority", as well as the relationships between these entities, would be defined in terms that would survive changes in place, culture and time.

The second aspect of "ought" which can be identified in Bentham's writings, relates to a temporal unification of IS and OUGHT *within the context* of a universal theory. Theories would be formed in a given socio-historical context by the people of a given social group who communicate and reflect upon the quality of the group's own internal arrangements. This would mean that in the history of a social group, in an existing state of affairs, at a given point in time, an aspiration to a better state of affairs could arise, for example for a change from a pure monarchy to a representative democracy. The OUGHT in this case would simply involve a better normative application of the universal theory. Once an opportunity for such a superior normative application arose, a new arena of "is" and "ought" would be settled according to a succeeding newly-desirable state of affairs. In other words, what *used* to be considered an ideal normative application according to which all existing arrangements were evaluated would, after a certain time, become unsatisfactory, and hence particular, by virtue of a new normative application of the universal theory. The crux of this historical understanding of the "ought" is that the IS and the OUGHT would still remain unified under the auspices of a universal theory. As far as the relationship between these two senses of the "ought" is concerned, within the basic set of distinctions which make up universal *theory*, many ideologies might be successively accommodated. A temporal change in the universal theory, which would be, by the supposition, made at a slower rate than changes in ideology, would give rise to new ideological possibilities. The distinction between these two senses of the "ought" might be exemplified in the difference between works like *OLG*, which were universal in their nature, and *Constitutional Code*, Bentham's normative application of his universal ideas in the institutions of a representative democracy.

The second sense of "ought" assumes the possibility of the practical application of the universal description to which all existing systems ought to aspire. The difference between the two senses of the "ought" would be that the first, universal sense, would constitute a speculative observation. It would therefore usually start from very basic notions, and would generalise an all-embracing explanation of a discourse from these basic notions. The historical discourse (the second sense of the "ought") would involve simply participation in a discourse. It would involve the making of normative claims while taking part in the history of facts or events. As such, it would always be undertaken from the point of view of a participant in social practice under the influence of a given culture and ideology. In short, the second sense of the "ought" would be much more culturally oriented and historically contingent than the first. The quality of striving for the greatest happiness of the greatest number belonged to Bentham's universal account. However, for Bentham, a censoring (critical) historical sense of "ought" might produce an aspiration towards a particular system which would achieve the greatest happiness for a given community. This would amount to no more than saying "my project is to make what I consider the best normative application of the universal description". This would be the paradigm, for instance, of censorial jurisprudence, namely that existing systems should aspire to the conceived "ideal" normative application. For example, when Bentham divided offences in Chapter 16 of *IPML*, or when he devised a chapter at the end of *OLG* which he called "the uses of this book", or when he provided for a representative democracy in *First Principles* and *Constitutional Code*, he argued for the best utilitarian application, or the most just application, of the first sense of "ought"—the universal description. Censorial jurisprudence should here be understood as the ideal normative application for a particular society, rather than a universal description.

However, these applications by Bentham of his own universal description were limited by the extent of his own practical vision. His best normative application (representative democracy) might later be replaced by another arrangement which would fit another society at a different stage of its development. An improvement on the institution of representative democracy might arguably be achieved *while still accepting his general propositions about legislation and law*. For example, the basic assumptions Bentham made for the justification of authority, and the factors which would determine the quality of that authority and its limits, would still hold, whether the necessity of a republican state is conceded (which was provided for by Bentham's *Constitutional Code*), or whether another kind of community, much more localised and self-sufficient, was envisaged, a community in which centralised, institutionally based authority would be much less necessary. In this sense, even Bentham did not exhaust the potential of his own universal account, namely the provision for a society which would maximise the happiness of the greatest number of its people.

The parts of this book which analyse the ideas of sovereignty, political society, constitutional law and limits, consensus formation, the dichotomy of public and private ethics and the different types of community, are parts of the universal account and as such relate to the first, universal sense of "ought". They constitute the bulk of the argument. However, the idea of free government, including Bentham's institutional proposals in *Constitutional Code*, his understanding of obstacles to communication, are all derived from writings dealing with the second, historical sense of "ought". Sections II and IV of Chapter 4, certain parts of sections II and III in Chapter 5, and section IV of Chapter 6, attempt to relate these two senses of "ought" to Bentham's legal and political enterprise.

A final point should be made with regard to the relationship between the IS and the OUGHT, which involves fundamental questions concerning the nature of moral theory. The point is that Bentham's theory has been criticised for committing the naturalistic fallacy, by deriving the OUGHT from the IS.[28] This

[28] For a discussion of the naturalistic fallacy in relation to Bentham, see Kelly, *Utilitarianism and Distributive Justice*, pp. 45–8.

charge is unjustified. Bentham would insist that a proper understanding of the OUGHT should be immanent in a proper understanding of the IS, whether the IS is related either to some communal good implied in any ethical judgement, or to a more authentic existence of the agent. More will be said about this in Part 2 of the book. However, for introductory purposes, it suffices to say that Bentham believed that there was no OUGHT which was totally divorced from the IS. For example, the idea of moral justification could be understood only in terms of the actual function and formation of desire (and will), as well as that of understanding. For Bentham, an abstract moral statement which was allegedly detached from desire would be vacuous.

One of the main contentions in this book is that Bentham was a social theorist for whom the transparency of communication between people, a communication which was at the heart of utilitarian interpretation and evaluation, was the proper, socially dynamic, basis for a moral theory. The formation of obligations in general, and of moral obligation in particular, depended on the quality and complexity of social interactions, rather than on a type of metaphysics which adopted a priori principles. Indeed, Bentham would argue that it was nonsensical to conceive "morality" as an entity whose content, even ideal content, could be arrived at independently of actual communication and communal interpretation.[29] Moral deficiencies would therefore be treated by Bentham as immanent in actual social function, as disturbances in the mutual understandings of people. An "ought" for him (an emancipatory ideal) could emerge and be crystallised as a result of antagonisms in free communication. A re-evaluation and transcendence of the norms of conventional morality would be achieved through communication and utilitarian interpretation and evaluation. I am not saying that there is not a potential metaphysics in utilitarianism, only that if there is a metaphysics, it will not consist of abstract first principles in the form of the Kantian conceptions of the Categorical Imperative. Bentham was attempting to provide a socially dynamic account of normativity, the substance of which could change as the extent and quality of communication changed in a social group. Any posited norm functions in a communal interpretative context which might change in the course of the history of the particular group in question. Formation and crystallisation of ideals and communal obligations were understood by Bentham as related to an understanding of how actual motivations operate in communication. An ideal would evolve and be refined and transcended owing to the random exercise of influences between people. Mutual influences could nourish a desire for emancipation and enlightenment which could in turn lead to the formation of alternative ideals. The improvement in the quality *of function* in the IS would produce a new OUGHT, and accordingly the IS itself could progress and regress. In the course of communication, alternative conceptions of pain and pleasure could be crystallised into moral obligations. Further, as will be argued in Chapter 6, moral obligations might have an

[29] See, for instance, *Deontology*, pp. 136–7.

obligatory status in the mind of each individual, by virtue of the feeling of sympathy that they create in him. The communication which cultivated sympathy would be, *inter alia*, responsible for the development of morally sensitive beings. Any ideal would relate to a generalisation which would stem from the actual being of actual people. For example, an ideal that "minorities should be accounted for", could not be divorced from social interaction which gave rise to a proposition backed up by some moral (or communal) sanction. A discussion of an ideal could not be totally divorced from the explanation of social operations (which would involve motives, sanctions, desires). The obligation by which the ideal was communicated would be immanent in these social operations. The outcome of a communicative process might lead to a generally accepted communal proposition which could advocate, for example, sympathy to minorities.

Morality therefore, for Bentham, was not subjected to the perspective of a metaphysical ideal, but related to a description of the dynamic formation and dissolution of conceptions of harm, themselves stemming from the mutual influences of actual desires in communication. Despite Bentham's general opposition to metaphysics, I shall argue in Part 2 that utility had to have some metaphysical basis were it to achieve disinterestedness. In short, how could utility achieve universality, namely an Archimedean point from which any socially-embodied point of reference could be transcended? Arguably, this question needs to be answered by *some* metaphysical underpinning. However, the metaphysics that utility might rely upon is very different from Kantian metaphysics of morals. An Archimedean point based on some version of a categorical imperative might be a source of abstraction and obscurity, by which a great deal of misery would be caused by the improper use of prejudicial justifications such as "legitimacy", "gratitude", "honour", "fair play", "balance", "integrity" and last, but not least, "liberty". Indeed, one of the assumptions which enabled Bentham to speak about universality was precisely his lack of commitment to *any* a priori moral rules. Theoretically valid observations would be based solely on a method of understanding the principles according to which moral evaluation was made *possible*, not upon any investigation of what was a priori *desirable*.

IV

As was mentioned in the first section, this book involves two dimensions, namely the reconstructive and the critical. These dimensions reflect the need to interpret Bentham's work in a constructive and creative fashion. In the first place, a reading which endorses both dimensions is important for a proper understanding of the scope of Bentham's arguments. It is vital to emancipate Bentham scholarship from the paradigms to which contemporary liberals such as Rawls and Dworkin, and legal positivists such as Hart, have confined it. Contemporary Bentham scholarship, including the most recent revisionist interpretations, are preoccupied by those paradigms. Having this emancipatory aim at heart, the reconstruction is carried out by treating Bentham's writing no less imaginatively than meticulously. An interpretation of Bentham's vast legal and political enterprise should not be confined to conventional questions such as "does the command theory of law account for the normativity of law?" or "can utility respect individuals as ends in themselves?" or "can utilitarianism account for the primacy of the right over the good?" Although the book engages closely with all these important issues, the objective is not to turn Bentham into either Dworkin or Hart. It was these leading thinkers' perspectives which highlighted the need for a new and imaginative interpretation of Bentham. This book attempts to avoid being merely an apologetic response to their arguments. The engagement with their arguments, alongside a constructive and creative interpretation, shows a way in which Bentham can differ from, rather than be assimilated into, their preoccupations.

In the second place, the reconstruction of Bentham in this book opens up new possibilities for Bentham's thought, and more generally, for utilitarianism, to engage critically with many aspects of contemporary debates in legal, political and critical social theory. The arguments in the reconstruction are developed, and their implication explored and used, in order to interact with a contemporary agenda. The arguments of this critical dimension, which build on the reconstruction of Bentham's arguments, reflect the layers of argument with which this reconstruction engages, namely, legal theory (e.g. the implications of the nature of sovereignty and the duty to obey the law) and political, ethical and critical social theory (e.g. the implications of the analysis of consensus formation and the evolution of communities and Bentham's mature constitutionalism). Let me outline the main areas of contribution to contemporary debates:

Legal Theory

First the present interpretation of Bentham's work has the potential to form a bridge between some seemingly opposing conceptions of what legal theory should be about. The book offers a possible link between the analysis of legal concepts and the sociology of law. It is difficult for Hart's "descriptive sociology" to answer criticisms made by sociologists of law. The central tenet of those criticisms has been that whatever allegedly universal social features one attributes to legal concepts, an analysis of a legal system as a *union* of primary and secondary rules cannot fully account for legal pluralism, or for the "living law", or the law of the people.[30] Any allegedly universal account of *the* concept of law runs the risk of not being able to account for the complex operations, influences and dynamism which characterise particular societies. For an account of law which provides a bridge between analytical jurisprudence and the sociology of law, it must explain the conceptual connection between the complexity of

[30] See D. Nelken, "Law in Action or Living Law? Back to the Beginning in Sociology of Law", *Legal Studies* 2 (1984) 157–74, at 173–4.

normative relationships in a particular society, and an informed *understanding* of legal concepts. The relationship between the idea of constitutional limits, which is a part of the *conceptual understanding of law*, on the one hand, and the particular collective judgement of an entrusting body, on the other, can arguably serve as such a bridge. A socially dynamic conception of constitutional limits must be understood as an anthropologically sensitive generalisation of particular societies. A socially dynamic account of constitutional limits is committed to "descriptive sociology" in a way which also has micro-sociological significance. Such a dynamic account does not detach the understanding of legal concepts from the fabric of the social group in which legal discourse operates and from the dynamic change in such a group which affects the ambit of constitutional interpretation within it. It is only in a theory with as wide a philosophical basis as Bentham's that the possibility of such a bridge between the conceptual and the empirical can be seriously envisioned.[31]

Secondly, Bentham's conception of constitutional limits as determined in a socially dynamic process is interpretative. This means that constitutional limits are the justificatory conclusions of an interpretative communal process. They are not static entities that one just knows or finds in a code of law. Bearing this interpretative conception of constitutional limits in mind, the reconstruction of Bentham's utilitarian enterprise combines elements of both legal positivism and an interpretative theory of law. Contemporary analytical jurisprudence is very much divided along these lines. A positivistic theory of law is a model which adheres to, and advances, the values associated with clearly presented, publicly accessible criteria, namely that of certainty, and finality, or as Bentham called it, security. An interpretative theory exposes the unhelpful nature of a positivistic theory in tackling the problem of sense in law, namely the sense according to which a legal proposition can be *justified* as being true or false. Knowing and formally accepting the validity of legal rules, for example, cannot account for the justificatory process which establishes the truth value of legal propositions made by lawyers and judges. In short, the main claim of the interpretative school of thought is that the "reality of law" is argumentative, namely that the clear sources for argumentation serve at most to provide materials for pre-interpretation or, in other words, as "raw material" for interpretation.[32] The argument in this book combines the positivistic and interpretative approaches in the following way. Utility requires security and clarity in order to facilitate communication and, in turn, interpretation of, reflection upon and transgression of commonly accepted conceptions of harm and thus, of constitutional arguments. The articulation of prescriptive propositions associated with the law is conceived not as an end in itself but as an important element in utilitarian, communal interpretation.

More generally, in the context of discussing the connection between utilitarianism and positivism (not only *legal* positivism), it will become apparent in the

[31] See R. Cotterrell, *The Sociology of Law* (London, 1992), pp. 38–41.

[32] See Dworkin, *Law's Empire*, pp. 65–8.

course of the book that I point towards the possibility of justifying the connection between utilitarianism and interpretative theories, and by the same token attempt to destabilise the long-established connection between utilitarianism and positivism. Such a destabilisation is a big task and requires a separate work. Nevertheless, whenever appropriate, I shall point out possible implications my interpretation of Bentham bears for the reassessment of the connection between his utilitarianism and positivism. On the basis of his epistemology and his sanction theory of duties, Bentham scholars have hitherto combined his utilitarianism with legal positivism and positivism in ethics. As far as legal positivism is concerned, a central tenet of Bentham scholarship has been that *knowing* what the law is and the minimisation of judicial discretion—itself a desirable state of affairs from the utilitarian end of maximising security—was complemented by utilitarianism as a critical evaluative theory.[33] This combination of utilitarianism and positivism is arguably a central limitation which has inhibited Bentham scholars from capturing what Bentham was about. It follows from my socially dynamic interpretation of constitutional limits under Bentham's utilitarianism that neither positivistic elements which characterise the *form* of the ideological, and therefore ethical, foundations of politics—a form which constrains, and thus enables, any interpretative coherence in politics (Chapter 7), nor legal positivism (Chapters 2 and 4) follow from adopting Bentham's epistemology and sanction theory of duties. Moreover, legal positivism does not follow from Bentham's theoretical basis for, and actual implementation of, the complete codification of law. In short, I hope that this book succeeds in raising the possibility of claims that Bentham's utilitarianism, and by implication utilitarianism generally, was interpretative and not positivistic.

As far as *legal* positivism is concerned, Bentham's conception of sovereignty, involving as it did a socially dynamic, critical self-reflection, allows criticism of the unacceptable reductionism involved in describing formal criteria of authenticity as the basis for legal validity, and in turn of criticism of legal positivism. The interpretation of sovereignty brings Bentham's account into line with modern accounts of Natural Law, which advocate a universal model according to which legal validity and moral worth are conceptually unified in relation to the *purpose* of law. In these accounts, and in Bentham's, the whole distinction of just/unjust legal systems becomes secondary to, and can be plausibly talked about only in the context of, a purposive realm in which the description of law identifies legal validity and moral worth. Bentham's doctrine of sovereignty can be interpreted as pointing to yet another purposive dimension which involves some conceptual unification of law and morality. Despite a degree of compatibility between Bentham's conception of sovereignty and the general claim of legal positivism, Bentham's theory can be seen to assert that the existence of the "morally just" law would be an *enhancement*, or *augmentation*, of certain formal features of law which involve moral postulates. In the context of the

[33] See Postema, *Bentham and the Common Law Tradition*, chapter 9.

argument of this book what is "morally just" has to be understood in a socially dynamic transient way. Understood as such, the greater the number of the people who participated, and the more transparent the communication between them, the more extended would be the conceptual overlap between what was "legally valid" and what was "morally just".

Thirdly, the argument about the limits of social justifications for the employment of centralised coercion highlights the connection between jurisprudence, constitutionalism and public law. As far as constitutionalism is concerned, the argument shows that, essentially, constitutionalism is about a community whose continuous utilitarian-based evaluation and self-reflection justify and restrains a common political authority. This interpretative social process of justification and restraint of a common political authority involves a general conception of harm. This harm must be averted, either by enabling or by restraining a political authority. The conception of harm changes as the community changes and the particular meaning of constitutional limits changes with it. In this abstract sense of constitutional limits, politics cannot survive in the face of incompatible conceptions of harm. For politics to make sense and to have a social "bite", there has to be an agreed common conception of harm which justifies and restrains political authorities. At a general level, this conception of harm, with the form of political authority which is justified and restrained under it, would be intolerant to other conceptions of harm. There will be no point of reference in relation to which one conception can be justified as better than the other. This universal connection that utilitarianism establishes between, on the one hand, constitutionally limited government, and, on the other, social communication, interpretation and reflection, is shown to be a central theme that preoccupied Bentham throughout his career, and in fact serves as a criterion by which his whole enterprise can be united and indeed, be taken further.

Further, the argument casts some light on the meaning of the rule of law and its relationship to constitutionalism. The idea of the rule of law as a constitutional principle which legally limits governments has always been in conflict with the idea of the sovereignty of Parliament, in that the rule of law cannot accommodate constitutional limits on the *validity* of *primary* legislation. These two ideas can loosely coexist only if, as Dicey held, the limits on sovereignty as a power to legislate, or legal sovereignty, coincide *in the long run* with the dictates of popular sovereignty in a democracy. In the absence of entrenched constitutional limits which take precedence over government activities, there is, under Dicey's scheme, no immediate protection for the rights of minorities.[34]

[34] See P.P. Craig, *Public Law and Democracy in the UK and the United States of America* (Oxford, 1990), pp. 15–17, 30–41; see also J. Jowell, "The Rule of Law Today", in D. Oliver and J. Jowell (eds), *The Changing Constitution* (Oxford, 1994), pp. 57–78, at 72–3. Jowell conceives the rule of law firstly as a rule of institutional morality under which the certainty of the rules and procedural fairness guide official action; and secondly as a limitation to official action, namely as a rule which *disables* government from abusing its power. When Jowell comes to view this in relation to the sovereignty of Parliament, he admits that all the rule of law can amount to, in the absence of a Bill of Rights and constitutional adjudication, is the democratic prospect of popular criticism of

However, the Dicean notions of legal and political sovereignty are given a new interpretation within Bentham's utilitarian enterprise. A proper understanding of the concept of sovereignty would have prevented Dicey from making the distinction between internal legal sovereignty (law-making powers) and external popular sovereignty (popular judgement). In putting the emphasis on the participatory public, Bentham designed a government which did not give officials the ultimate authority.

This book argues that constitutional limits are a mirror of communal evolution and dissolution. As such, constitutional limits can be entrenched as parts of the law, in a way which would prima facie limit legislatures, whose powers would always be subject to communal critical moral judgement. It will be shown that Bentham, in effect, made legal and popular sovereignty coincide conceptually, and took this coincidence as far as he could in his democratic design of a constitutionally limited government. Bentham provided for constitutional adjudication in which judges would interact with the public, and would give execution and effect to constitutional self-limitations imposed by the government. The rule of law as a constitutional principle cannot only account for constitutional limits, but also has participatory citizenship and public judgement at its core.

Political Theory

First, the arguments in the book interact with contemporary debates about the fundamental nature of individual rights. Although Bentham has gained the reputation of being hostile to natural rights, I show that utilitarianism in Bentham's thought could and did accommodate entrenched fundamental rights, which *limited the competence* of a sovereign legislature. However, the perspective from which utility is shown to approach rights does not involve their a priori justification. Utility only makes sense of the notion of fundamental rights from within the context of a vibrant debating and hermeneutic community. The argument acknowledges that communities can develop differently and adopt ultimately incompatible conceptions of harm and moral thresholds. All utilitarian policy-making on the part of the legislature would be *limited* by a communal consensus which had both interpretative (as far as utility derived from expectations was concerned), and consequential features. Thus, modern claims that rights trump utility do not take into account the different levels at which utilitarian calculation was involved in, and interacted with, policy-making activity. The argument in this book is that not only does utilitarian theory recognise the existence of fundamental rights, but that it also sees the ultimate power, a power which makes constitutional law, as *judicial* in nature—a power which can judge

primary legislation. In making this admission, Jowell puts forward a very narrow view of the connection between the rule of law, popular judgement and limits to legal validity. Such a view will be challenged in the course of the book as stemming from an all-too-positivist, as well as socially static, theory of law.

the justification, and hence the permissibility, of measures originating from the policy-making body. A utilitarian political theory can accommodate the claim that certain moral parameters can *limit* the scope of policy-making considerations. Such a theory can account for the communicative possibility that people would arrive at prescriptive propositions which were not vulnerable to the dictates of immediate expediency.[35] On the other hand, utilitarian political theory resists the ultimate justness and social entrenchment of any single conception of harm to which a prescriptive proposition gives effect.

Thus, the claim that a non-prescriptible, rights-based political theory, which relies on the intuitive moral justness of rights, trumps a utilitarian-based theory, is contested. To be plausible, such a claim would have to provide a more coherent epistemological and social basis for the explanation both of such intuitions and of rights than one grounded on utility. In other words, the issue at stake is which of the two theories, namely one which relies on what is already regarded as intuitively just as a necessary perspective for communication, or one which relies on communication as a tool to influence and modify intuitions about justice, can provide a better social and epistemological account of fundamental rights. Both recognise the social possibility of *asking the question* but have very different ways of defending *the answer* to it. The position adopted in this book is that an argument about the fundamental nature of rights can always be made by the people who are subjected to them. However, for such an argument to take root in the consciousness of a people, both transparency in communication, a crystallisation of a conception of harm, and in turn a degree of empathy and sympathy, have to be achieved. It is the tutelary force of sympathy which causes an agent facing a *moral* dilemma to recognise a moral threshold which signifies some pattern which is expressed in a distribution of rights which is regarded as fundamental, rather than to act on considerations of immediate expediency.[36]

Secondly, and more generally, the argument about fundamental rights takes Bentham's socially dynamic account of constitutional limits into the ethical foundations of political theory. It casts light upon the communitarian/liberal debate. Utilitarianism denies the plausibility of an intermediate layer of moral reflection between, on the one hand, a historically-particular evaluating self, constituted in part by a particular cultural-historical paradigm, and, on the other hand, an ultimate Archimedean point for moral evaluation. Utility denies the plausibility of any allegedly universal moral perspective with which an agent can identify, situated intermediately between those layers of moral evaluation, one conventional, the other ultimate, which claims to be constitutive of an all-embracing conception of what is "right".

[35] See above pp. 157–8.

[36] See A. Gewirth, "Can Utilitarianism Justify any Moral Rights?", in J.R. Pennock and J.W. Chapman (eds), *Ethics, Economics and The Law NOMOS* XXIV (New York, 1982), pp. 158–93, at 164–73, and K. Greenawalt, "Utilitarian Justification for Observance of Legal Rights", ibid., pp. 139–47; see also H.L.A. Hart, "Between Utility and Rights", in A. Ryan (ed.), *The Idea of Freedom* (Oxford, 1979), pp. 77–98, at 93–9.

Let me explain. My argument is that utility, as an evaluative theory, operates on an indeterminate basis. This indeterminacy is manifested in so far as it is not possible for an evaluating agent to have a universal vantage point from which to evaluate his moral perspective. This is not to say that utility collapses into total relativism, being sceptical about evaluation and normativity, but only that it fiercely resists a universal moral perspective for evaluation and interpretation. Utility is silent regarding a priori justifications of a moral perspective. Utility supplies an evaluative principle which is based on the human condition, rather than an overarching substantive distributive principle, such as can attune itself to many social matrixes. This gives it flexibility, an asset which means that the theory does not collapse into a particular cultural/historical interpretation of its evaluative master principle. This book criticises from a utilitarian perspective the connection that modern liberals try to establish between a universal conception of the "right" and liberalism. The objection of deontological ethical theories, namely that utility does not have an *inherent* respect for individuality, and more generally, that it does not give priority to the right over the good,[37] is thus recast in this book as utility's main asset.

By being flexible between moral perspectives, utility achieves a similar result to a true, pure, metaphysical deontological theory. Pure deontological theories are in need of interpretation. For example, one needs to interpret Kant's Categorical Imperative in order to arrive at a justification of a scheme according to which actual political institutions can be evaluated.[38] Such an interpretation was undertaken by Rawls in A *Theory of Justice*. Rawls argues, in accordance with the basic deontological premise, that what is right has an ethical priority over what is "good". The right cannot be derived from any maximisation of the good. However, Rawls attempts to articulate a basic conception of liberal harm which both justifies and constrains coercive political action. In doing so he attempts to universalise a moral perspective from which a conception of what is right can be intuitively appreciated.

However, as communitarians argue, the priority that Rawls gives to the right over the good is a sham. In fact, he presumes a given communal "good" which supplies the perspective from which his principles of justice can be assessed as intuitively right. Sandel argues that if one finds oneself in intuitive agreement with Rawls's conception of liberal harm and, in turn, with Rawls's conception of the right, it means precisely that one already "belongs" to a certain community and subscribes to a given social and anthropological matrix. However, the whole point of pure deontological theories is to avoid such a conclusion. To avoid this was Kant's purpose. A true moral theory has to transcend any belonging, otherwise the person who is governed by this theory is not sufficiently free to reason about and to judge moral actions to be right in themselves, as opposed

[37] J. Rawls, *A Theory of Justice* (Cambridge, Mass., 1971), pp. 22–7.

[38] See in this context I. Kant, *Foundations of the Metaphysics of Morals* (New York, 1990). See also H.J. Paton, *The Moral Law: Kant's Groundwork of the Metaphysics of Morals* (London, 1948).

to their rightness being anthropologically contingent.[39] In order to achieve authentic freedom one has to transcend any culturally-oriented moral perspective. Kant achieved such transcendence through a metaphysics which adopts a priori moral principles. Only in this way could he articulate a unified moral theory amidst incommensurable perspectives of theorising. Communitarian criticisms of liberal theory assert that it creates a kind of a partially-metaphysical alternative to Kant's metaphysics.[40]

The common thrust of communitarian criticisms is not reducible to the claim that the self must be understood as constituted by social matrixes. In their different ways, all communitarians insist on reflection upon actual constitutions of selves, which is achieved through interpreting a communal good as a point of reference. This point involves, however abstractly, a communal conception of harm. Communitarian thought, having revealed the already existing cultural perspective upon which liberal theory is based, is therefore sceptical about any intermediate universal, partially-metaphysical perspective by reference to which a political scheme can be universally evaluated. It is not hard, therefore, to find a direct continuum between their arguments about the incommensurabilities of fundamental conceptions of communal harm as between communities, and genuine pure deontological theories. Ultimately, communitarians elect to be silent between moral perspectives, an attitude that Kant, *but not liberals,* would be willing to entertain. Communitarians, in short, challenge a multicultural idea at the level of abstract conceptions of harm. Communitarians criticise a multi-perspective conception of politics that some liberals try to enshrine.

Utility is *in part* sympathetic to communitarian arguments. The argument in this book is about the principle of utility as an interpretative principle according to which many perspectives, and hence possibilities, for the organisation of government can be communicated and justified. I will adopt an approach which centres on communicative possibilities giving rise to the formation of fundamental conceptions of harm upon the basis of which political authorities can be justified and limited. I said "in part" because utility goes beyond communitarianism. My approach is not about a dogmatic justification of a given conception of harm. Utility, in the way it is constructed here, offers an alternative theory of transcendence to that offered by a priori metaphysical substantive moral principles. The principle of utility is offered here as a decision principle according to which social norms can be interpreted differently and, if need be, replaced, as

[39] Kant wrote: "[Everyone] must concede that the ground of obligation here must be sought in the nature of man or in the circumstances in which he is placed but a priori solely in the concepts of pure reason, and that every precept which rests on principles of mere experience, even a precept which is in certain respects universal, so far as it leans in the least on empirical grounds (perhaps only in regard to the motive involved) may be called a practical rule but never a moral law": *Foundations of the Metaphysics of Morals*, p. 5.

[40] See in this context A. Gutmann, "Communitarian Critics of Liberalism", in S. Avineri and A. de-Shalit (eds), *Communitarianism and Individualism* (Oxford, 1992), pp. 120–36, and W. Kymlicka, "Liberalism and Communitarianism", *Canadian Journal of Philosophy* 18 (1988) 181–204.

communication within communities changes. Thus interpreted, utility does not succumb to the moral dogmatics that characterise modern liberalism, but rather claims to involve calculations and the formation of moral obligations in a socially dynamic way. Thus, *if* utility is involved with any metaphysics, this metaphysics would be very different from the one of a priori substantive moral principles.

According to utility (and also to metaphysical deontological doctrines) there is no scheme of social organisation the foundational justifications of which are not ultimately subjected to a more radical re-evaluation. Again, thus interpreted, utility competes as a philosophy of practical reason with a priori metaphysics. However, it shares with this type of metaphysics a scepticism about the moral dogmatics that modern liberalism brings with it. As such, utility, and Bentham's universal enterprise within it, represent rationality not as a blueprint for moral solutions but as a critical theory.

Thirdly, the argument here relates to the limits of justified coercion and hence concerns liberty. Bentham's engagement with the concept of liberty has been the subject of considerable debate. Traditionally it has been argued that, for Bentham, liberty had the consistent negative meaning of "absence of coercion". However in his legal and political writings Bentham replaced the term "liberty" with "security", be it security of expectations, or of property, or security against misrule. Bentham thought that liberty, understood essentially as absence of coercion, should not be confused with the coercive intervention needed in order to attain security of person and property, and security of the public interest in the face of a bad government.[41] To discuss the requirement for law in terms of liberty would be to confuse liberty and security. However, despite the evident importance of security for Bentham, this book attempts to reintroduce liberty into Bentham's arguments. It shows that a proper reconstruction of Bentham's universal enterprise carries with it a continuous engagement with liberty.

As this book is about constitutional limits, it may seem that the argument is concerned solely with the political implementation of a negative conception of freedom.[42] However, Bentham's universal utilitarian enterprise, according to which constitutional limits were to be determined and effectuated by the public sphere, entailed a special sense of freedom, one which was about free communication and entailed a free, communicating and self-determined self. This freedom of communication would functionally connect positive and negative elements of freedom in a socially dynamic way which could transcend any particular political system. A freely communicating and self-determined self would be free, in that it would not succumb to a single, dogmatic formula which entailed an ultimate communal conception of harm and with it a politically given sphere of negative liberty. In turn, community and self would be emancipated from a moral perspective that enabled choice and individual inviolability

[41] See chapter 4, pp. 130–1, and chapter 5, pp. 146–9 below.

[42] For discussion of negative and positive liberty, see I. Berlin, "Two Concepts of Liberty", in *Four Essays on Liberty* (London, 1969), pp. 188–72 and Introduction, pp. xlv–xlix.

only from a single point of view. Freedom was to be found in communication and possibilities of evaluation. This view of freedom has implications for politics with regard to toleration of conceptions of good within a political community as well as between political communities.

Critical Social Theory

In its main thrust, this book aims to direct attention to the possibility of how Bentham's notions can contribute to modern accounts of social theory. It has to be conceded that there are many aspects of Bentham's thought which do not fit modern society. Nevertheless, his thought can be seen as contributing to many of the ailments of modern individualistic, over-regulated society. The normative application which he made of his universal arguments did not take into consideration the systemic division of society today, the loss of sense of community, the rise of multinational corporations as major players in political affairs, and the rise of the mass media. Bentham's model of centralisation and governmental control is a prototype of a "political system", as featured in Habermas's discussion.[43] Habermas criticises the transformation of the public sphere from a sphere in which focused public debate is conducted into a sphere which gathers its rhetoric of communication from various systems, such as "politics" and from the mass media. As a result of this colonisation by systemic, technocratic thought, public debate loses its focus and critical edge, in turn, its emancipatory potential. Bentham's idea of democratic participation would, on the face of it, succumb to the strains resulting from the subjection of public opinion to the political system, rather than succeed in identifying and protecting means of communication, free from domination by "system", which would in turn protect genuine individuality.

Having said that, some of Bentham's theoretical presumptions about consensus formation could be adapted for today's world and still serve as useful tools in understanding modern society, although this would involve applying them "beyond Bentham". First, Bentham's idea of "constitutional limits" in its general sense, namely as a concept which is arrived at and reflected upon in a "learning process", during which a community changes, brings his thought in line with the primary concern of critical social theorists such as Habermas. In other words, a new formulation of the notion of the "protection" of individuality from the encroachment of "system" would have to be made in order to render Bentham's idea of constitutional limits relevant to modern, late-capitalist society.

Secondly, the operation, as a critical standard, of "utility" or "usefulness", of pains and pleasures, as well as entities related to them like sympathy, empathy, influence and sanctions, could serve to establish a formal universal account of

[43] See J. Habermas, *The Philosophical Discourse of Modernity* (Cambridge, 1987), chapter 12. See also W.T. Murphy, "The Habermas Effect: Critical Theory and Academic Law", *Current Legal Problems* 42 (1989) 135–65.

inter-subjective communication. These entities could feature at the heart of a critical theory which combines a philosophy of consciousness (idealism) with the alternative which Habermas calls "communicative rationality" or inter-subjective communication. There is a plausible case to argue that some notion of usefulness, entailing ideas of types of influence, and sanctions of sympathy, would have to be at the heart of any formal idea of universal pragmatics and consensus formation, of the type Habermas advocates.

Utilitarian notions, in short, could have a large part to play, not only in terms of the instrumental applications of the kind for which Bentham wanted to use them (in the context of legislation and law, for example), but also within a theory of inter-subjectivity wherein they would relate to a more symbolic function of communication. This communication would pave the way towards a different form of social organisation, towards the crystallisation of some new "useful" conception of the relationship between self and collectivity. From the perspective of such a society, liberal utopias, as envisaged by Bentham and Mill, would appear oversimplified and relatively primitive.

V

The interpretation offered in the main part of this work involves a close reading of Bentham's texts both published and unpublished. It is based on largely unexplored constitutional texts which have recently been published in the *Collected Works* edition. Passages from these texts have been included in some recent scholarship but there has not yet been a thorough and systematic discussion of them. A study of the relationship of these newly published texts to Bentham's other writings has hitherto not been undertaken. These newly published texts include *Securities against Misrule and other Constitutional Writings for Tripoli and Greece*; *First Principles preparatory to Constitutional Code*; *Official Aptitude Maximized*; *Expense Minimized*; *Colonies, Commerce, and Constitutional Law: Rid Yourselves of Ultramaria and other writings on Spain and Spanish America*; and *Political Tactics*.[44] In addition, unpublished material is used. This material consists of *Preparatory Principles* (UC lxix.), and some of Bentham's writings from the period of the French Revolution not included in *Political Tactics*. In the case of the latter, direct reference is made to the relevant essay in the manuscript. These essays are *On the Efficient Cause and Measure of Constitutional Liberty* (UC cxxvi. 8–18; cxxvii. 4, 5. clxx. 168), *Necessity of an Omnipotent Legislature* (UC cxlvi. 15, 18–25, 27–50), and *On the Influence of the Administrative Power over the Legislative* (UC cxxvi. 1–5). Passages from the Bowring edition of *Constitutional Code*, and *Principles of Judicial Procedure*, which have largely been ignored by other scholars, have also been relied upon. Finally, better known works by Bentham, such as *A Fragment on*

[44] See the bibliography for full references.

Government and *Deontology*, are given a new interpretation, which, in turn, suggests new argumentative connections with the newly published volumes in the *Collected Works*.

Generally, as far as terminology is concerned, I reject the rigid manner in which terms coined by Bentham have been interpreted, which in turn has been responsible for many misconceptions about his work. Here, the formula "constitutional limits as determined and effectuated by a collective communal judgement" replaces the much-criticised formula of "sovereignty as determined by the habit (or disposition) of obedience". Again, "the command theory of law" is replaced by "the command theory of *a* law", in order to emphasise the different preoccupations Bentham had with regard to, on the one hand, the institution of "law" (a social undertaking in which coercive mechanisms would unify duty and interest according to some conception of harm), and, on the other hand, his theory of the individuation of a law, which would be the product of an exercise in analytical jurisprudence. These were different preoccupations despite the fact that the second, jurisprudential sense, was undertaken in the context of, and could not be divorced from, the idea of "law" in the first, broader, sense.

Chapter 2 interprets the idea of sovereignty in Bentham's earlier writings. It relies mainly on *OLG* and presents sovereignty as a "split", and therefore an interpretative, idea. Sovereignty relates to the social justification of political authority and is taken to be an outcome of critical interaction between two bodies in a socially dynamic way. This conception of sovereignty is central to the argument in the book. The interpretation of sovereignty in Bentham's early writings is followed by a critical discussion of contemporary interpretations of Bentham's account of the relationship between sovereignty and legally limited government.

Chapter 3 discusses two other socially orientated and dynamic features of sovereignty in Bentham's earlier writings. It discusses the hierarchical relativity and horizontal plurality of sovereignty in a social group. The argument, relying primarily on *Fragment* and *OLG*, shows the connection between legal pluralism and a unified social manifestation of centralised political authority. It then locates the purpose of Constitutional Law as the arbiter of the boundaries between unity and plurality in a social group.

Chapter 4 is a clear instance of constructive/creative interpretation. It interprets one of Bentham's best-known works—*A Fragment on Government*. I argue that already, in this young man's work, Bentham showed a clear inclination to see the body of the people as determining and effectuating limitations on coercive authorities. It was the work in which the conception of constitutional limits was conceived as socially dynamic. This reading of *Fragment* goes on to defend an interpretation of the most general operation of the principle of utility in the light of this social dynamism. This chapter continues the interpretation of sovereignty offered in Chapter 2 and anticipates the discussion of Bentham's mature constitutional writings in Chapter 5. Reading *Fragment* with a socially dynamic conception of constitutional limits in mind can broaden its scope, allowing for its interaction with issues never before conceived by either received or revisionist interpretations. This chapter discusses the duty to obey the law or, more precisely, the lack of such a duty found in this work, and its relation to constitutional limits. It defends a utilitarian conception of anarchism from the perspective of Bentham's universal theory. The constructive/creative interpretation of *Fragment is* then defended against the contemporary revisionist interpretation offered by Postema and Kelly.

Chapter 5 reads Bentham's mature constitutional writings in the light of the socially dynamic interpretation of his early legal and political works. It develops several points of continuity with Bentham's earlier writings. These points of continuity, which all involve themes found in *Fragment* and *OLG*, are as follows: the enabling rationale for government; the conceptual fusion between the quality and the quantity of the exercise of powers; the relationship between constitutional limits and securities against misrule; the determination of constitutional limits by popular judgement, and if necessary, by an act of collective disobedience; and the recognition of collective judgement, and if necessary, disobedience, as a prime value in a free government. In general terms, Bentham's texts show that, both in his unpublished writings during the time of the French Revolution, and later in his mature constitutional writings, including *Constitutional Code*, he continued to advocate a socially dynamic conception of constitutional limits. As the reconstruction of Bentham's legal and political thought is almost complete at this stage of the argument, issue is taken with a number of contemporary Bentham scholars, namely Hart, Postema, Rosen and Kelly. The level at which the argument engages with their writings is very general. It shows that all of them, in a different way, have a rather limited perspective from which they generalise and assess Bentham's endeavours. As a result of this limited perspective they do not extract the fullest potential from Bentham's texts.

Chapter 6 constitutes the functional supplement to the reconstruction. It undertakes a mutually enforcing analysis of Bentham's *Deontology* and manuscript materials from the time of the French Revolution. The argument is that Bentham offered a detailed functional analysis of social communication based on influence, motives and sanctions. The chapter analyses the motivational basis for normative communication and consensus formation. In his mature constitutional writings, Bentham discussed at length a body which could deliberate and determine the limits of sovereignty, or constitutional limits. This body was the Public Opinion Tribunal (POT), the outcome of the communication with which was to be reflected not only in the institutional make-up but in the constitutional limits that a centralised coercive authority imposed upon itself. The chapter offers a detailed analysis of the operation of the POT.

On a broader level, *Deontology* is shown to be the work in which Bentham reflected upon the development of communities, from communities of law into communities of sympathy. This development was mirrored in the socially dynamic demarcation between law and public arguments within private ethics.

The argument which unites the first five chapters forms the interpretative context in which the text of *Deontology* receives its meaning in this chapter.

Part 2 summarises the reconstruction of Bentham's work but also expands on the implications which could be drawn from it. Chapter 7 discusses the nature of the connection between ethics and politics. Arguing the connection to be socially dynamic in nature, the analysis exposes an indeterminacy at the basis of every harm politics tries to avert. It shows that this indeterminacy has its roots in a general aporia which characterises the philosophy of practical reason, namely the problem of arriving at a universal conception of harm which claims to mirror a universal conception of "right". In the light of this indeterminacy, the argument criticises the limitations of liberal political theory and politics, in particular with reference to their claim to produce unifying, institutional solutions with the purpose of averting harm. Secondly, the argument connects this indeterminacy of harm, and hence of the connection between ethics and politics, to the communitarian/liberal debate, as well as to the distinction between negative liberty and positive freedom.

Chapter 8 discusses critically five contemporary accounts in political theory which attempt to face the dynamic relationship between ethics and politics. My argument is that although most of these contemporary authors are motivated by intuitions which probe and perturb them to engage with this dynamism, most of them fail to do so convincingly. A final end note argues that utility can be seen as a theory of practical reason which is related to authenticity and as such avoids the moral dogmatics of which contemporary conceptions of liberal political theory fail to rid themselves.

Part 1

A Reconstruction of Bentham's Constitutionalism

2

Sovereignty and the Nature of the Normativity of Law

I

This chapter interprets the concepts of sovereignty and the normativity of law, relying on a close reading of Bentham's early works. The jurisprudential claims that are advanced here form a central theme which runs along the remainder of the argument in the book. The rest of the chapters do not only corroborate the interpretation of Bentham's account of sovereignty but they also show how a theory of sovereignty can be a part of a much larger social and political utilitarian scheme. The analysis of sovereignty will join subsequent chapters' examinations of the duty to obey the law, constitutional limits, and the idea of the public sphere. The argument of this chapter sets the framework for the rest of the reconstruction of Bentham's constitutionalism. However, the full magnitude of the argument will be properly noted after reading the reconstruction as a whole. My aim is to set the basic socially dynamic interpretative approach to the justification of authority which is the central argument of the book. The more immediate aim is to free Bentham's account of sovereignty from legal-positivist shackles that have been put on it even by some of the most revisionist interpretations.

The interpretation suggested here of Bentham's theory of sovereignty contributes to a discussion which has occupied analytical jurisprudence for the last four decades, since the appearance of Hart's *The Concept of Law*, concerning the precise nature of the normative elements in the exercise of political authority. "Normative" in this sense refers to a feeling of being under an obligation experienced by people who participate in a social discourse. This feeling of being under an obligation and therefore "normativity" in this context, connotes the idea of justification for that feeling. In the debate over the "justificatory" element, the question has been whether an appeal is to be made to *moral* reasons in ascertaining the validity and acceptance of the actions of a centralised coercive authority. This jurisprudential debate about authority sprang from criticisms levelled by Hart in *The Concept of Law* against Austin. These criticisms were developed by Hart in a more subtle form against Bentham in *Essays on Bentham*.[1]

[1] The debate about the kind of reasons involved in the exercise of authority has been developed by J. Raz. See, *The Authority of Law* (Oxford, 1979), chapter 1; *Practical Reasons and Norms*

The main argument of this chapter is that Bentham's theory of sovereignty was based upon a socially dynamic interpretative process, the account of which informed a universal concept of law. Bentham conceived "sovereignty" as an historically-oriented, ongoing social activity of an interpretative critical nature, which could not be generalised and reduced to a static "test" according to which the formal legal validity (a criterion of authenticity) of coercive measures could be assessed. Further, sovereignty could not be reduced to value-neutral conceptual terms which explained the "acceptance" of law by a group of people who were governed by it. In short, sovereignty was understood by Bentham as encapsulating an ongoing, socially dynamic moral stance between governors and governed. His account of sovereignty linked the authenticity and acceptance of law to the critical social justification of the exercise of centralised coercion. Sovereignty was about the critical justification of a "political authority".[2]

My argument is that a theory of sovereignty which provides merely for the recognition of a coercive measure as "law" cannot properly account for any contextual critical justificatory dimension which forms a conceptual part of such recognition. Reasons for the recognition of law *qua* law were an important part of Bentham's conception of the origin and persistence of a political society. Any conceptual discussion of the foundation of authority and law which ignores these justificatory reasons will not be persuasive in social terms.[3] The argument has implications for Bentham's common status as a legal positivist. Following strong intuitions of social dynamism, Bentham rooted the validity of legislative commands in moral interpretation, which, as I shall show in the next chapters, developed into a communal, historical interpretation. It is a key point to his universal theory that validation statements were conceptually connected to an interpretative moral judgement. This connection meant that *any* conceptual account of sovereign power *had to* entail some minimal necessary limitations on the exercise of sovereign power. The concept of sovereignty, understood as a communally interpretative concept, meant that it did not make sense, socially speaking, to talk about an unlimited political authority. In other words, Bentham's conception of validity was connected to a socially dynamic moral justification of authority. This moral judgement was made by the population and concerned the justification of the centralised institutional authority in the community. The reinterpreted view of the moral nature of obligation in Bentham's theory of sovereignty shows that he did not fully subscribe to the positivist view which divorces legal validity from moral worth, *at the level of description of an individual law*.

(Princeton, 1990), chapters 1, 4, 5, and *The Morality of Freedom* (Oxford, 1986), chapters 2–4. Much of what Hart says in *Essays on Bentham* has to be read in the context of Raz's arguments. For the purposes of the following discussion Hart's analysis will be used as it interacts directly with Bentham's account. Raz's arguments will be referred to whenever necessary.

[2] A "political authority" is to be understood as one which promulgates coercive measures. As such it should be distinguished from theoretical authority (such as an expert's advice) although some overlap can be said to exist.

[3] See chapter 1, p. 5, note 11 above.

II

In this section, I shall summarise two critical accounts of Bentham's theory of sovereignty and its relationship to his theory of law, namely those of H.L.A. Hart and G.J. Postema. Hart's criticisms of Bentham's command theory of law were put forward in *Essays on Bentham*. His first criticism related to Bentham's confusion of legal validity and obedience; that is, of legal validity and the effectiveness of the law. Hart embarked on this criticism because Bentham described sovereignty in terms of the "habit" or "disposition" of the people to obey a person or a body of persons. A constitutional limitation was valid, and therefore a law transgressing it could be held invalid by the courts, irrespective of whether the population obeyed this law. Alternatively, it could be held valid even if the population disobeyed it.[4]

Hart's second main criticism of Bentham was that he failed to distinguish between the aspects of legality and validity of a legislative measure. Hart's understanding of the difference between these notions was that the term "legality" conveyed the notion of acting in a way permitted by the law. The term entailed what was legally permissible or impermissible. "Validity", on the other hand, marked the extent of competence. It signified the extent of authority, and so would constitute a boundary to power. Holding a measure invalid would mean that a body was not conferred powers to act in the first place, so its act should be considered not in the realm of legal permissibility (because it might in certain circumstances be legal), but as *ultra vires* and hence void *ab initio*. This power, in short, ought not to be recognised *as* a power which could produce any legal consequences in this particular area.

Because, Hart claimed, Bentham saw all powers as legally based (conceived or adopted by a sovereign), his ability to distinguish between these two notions was limited. Bentham could not distinguish between legal validity and invalidity on the one hand, and between a legally permitted and prohibited act on the other. He thought of all law as an expression of will, and hence a legal limitation for him would come *only* under the dichotomy of legally permitted and prohibited.[5] This failure by Bentham to distinguish between validity and legality seriously undermined his account of the concept of law. For example, Bentham failed to describe coherently legal powers whose function in many everyday situations, like contracting and conveyancing, gave rise to the above distinction.[6] Another example was constitutional limits. Bentham could not account for the fact that a government might be both legally limited (by a legal measure), and also limited in terms of competence (constitutionally limited) by law. This was so because for Bentham, Hart claimed, sovereignty could not be a *legal* power,

[4] Hart, *Essays on Bentham*, p. 234.
[5] Ibid., p. 225.
[6] Ibid., p. 214.

and therefore he could not conceive any legal limitation on it: "Bentham's difficulties in accommodating the possibility of legal limitations on supreme legislative power sprang from the conception that the legislative powers of the sovereign are not conferred by law."[7]

Hart's final, yet most fundamental, criticism of Bentham related to Bentham's partial understanding of the notion of obligation. This criticism was more fundamental than the others because it was not restricted to jurisprudential enquiry but extended across the whole field of normative discourse. It was more fundamental than criticisms of Bentham's account of sovereignty, because the manner in which sovereignty was viewed would ultimately depend upon how a discourse about political authority dealt with the normativity of such an authority. In the final chapter of *Essays on Bentham*, Hart sought to demonstrate that Bentham's idea of a command failed to explain the normative basis of law. What did Hart mean by "normativity"? Normativity related to the likelihood of social criticisms of individuals in the case of their deviation from a given course of action, or from social norms. A normative attitude would encompass an "internal point of view":

> "What is necessary (for the existence of feelings of compulsion with regard to a social rule) is that there should be a critical reflective attitude to certain patterns of behaviour as a common standard, and that this should display itself in criticism (including self-criticism), demands for conformity, and in acknowledgements that such criticism and demands are justified, all of which find their characteristic expression in the normative terminology of 'ought', 'must', and 'should', 'right' and 'wrong'."[8]

Normativity constituted for Hart the main characteristic which distinguished a social rule from mere habitual behaviour, or from behaviour determined by the imposition of sanctions (or threat of sanctions). In order to account for such distinctions, Hart differentiated the idea of "being obliged" (a command which induced compliance by the threat of sanction), from that of "having an obligation" (normative acceptance of social rules). It is with this idea of the normative aspect of a rule in mind that one ought to read Hart's final chapter in *Essays on Bentham*. The crux of his argument was that the notion of command failed to explain the normativity of the command itself. In other words, the *fact* that a command was uttered could not explain the normativity which the command possessed *qua* an authoritative measure. Hart sought to give a further explanation of his own notion of the "normativity of rules" in order to show that the mere fact of a command being uttered could not account for the normativity of such a command.

Hart, following Raz, claimed that inherent to a command was the intention for it to operate as a peremptory reason on the subject's mind. The command would operate to cut off independent reasoning by the subject as to its justifica-

[7] Hart, *Essays on Bentham*, p. 224.
[8] Ibid., p. 56.

tion. Its utterance would operate as an exclusionary reason.[9] Hart also maintained that the command operated as "content independent" in the sense that a commander might issue many commands which would be different in content, would be addressed to different people and would all operate as peremptory reasons.[10] These two characteristics, Hart claimed, were the main ingredients of the normativity of an authoritative utterance. Hart dubbed these two characteristics in the phrase "content independent peremptory reason" for action (hereafter CIPR). The fact that a punishment would often be attached to a command, in order to reinforce the motive of compliance on the part of the commandee, would be secondary in importance and would not go to explain the normative status the command had *as such*.[11] The prediction of punishment in the case of disobedience should not be confused with the wider idea of normativity of law which it presupposes rather than explains.

This point requires an explanation. A command *in itself*, Hart argued, could not explain its own status as CIPR. To explain the normative attitude which people had with regard to the command, that is their conception of it as authoritative, one had to go beyond the "fact of commanding". CIPR would operate as a description of the ingredients of the phenomenon of "a command", but it could not explain why the commander's utterances were perceived *as* CIPR.

Reasons for normative acceptance, Hart claimed, could be diverse. They could include custom or simple conformism, and so would not have to emanate from the threat of sanctions.[12] However, all such reasons were *exterior* to the "fact of commanding". Hart, in effect, backed up the notion introduced in *The Concept of Law* of an ultimate social rule, the reasons for the normative acceptance of which could be diverse. On a cognitive level, this master rule operated as the ultimate source for the recognition as valid law of authoritative utterances manifested in social rules. This recognition would confirm a certain status certain social rules have, as opposed to the status of other social rules. The "fact of commanding" could explain neither the notion of legal validity, nor the normative acceptance of authoritative utterances, both of which were essential to an account of the existence of legal *limitations* on the exercise of government powers: "The legal limitation of a commander's power to legislate would simply be

[9] See in this context J. Raz, *The Authority of Law*, pp. 14–20, *Practical Reasons and Norms*, pp. 36–41, 63, 82, 100, and *The Morality of Freedom*, chapter 3; see also chapter 4, pp. 99–100, note 11 below. Essentially for Raz, an exercise of a legitimate political authority involves second-order reasons which exclude either an action, or refraining from action, for first-order reasons. These exclusionary reasons are authoritative when they first become "protected" reasons, namely themselves being accepted as first-order reasons, *and* secondly, when they become "pre-emptive", namely excluding any dependence-in-reasoning on, that is utilisation-in-reasoning of, antecedent first-order reasons. An authority is manifested through exclusionary reasons which are protected and depended-in-reasoning upon its own reasons. Thus understood, authority would be conceived as legitimate because, although not necessarily exercised either in a morally best way, or even in the best interest of the subject, it would be accepted as existing for reasons which apply to its subjects.

[10] Hart, *Essays on Bentham*, pp. 252–5.

[11] Ibid., p. 254.

[12] Ibid., p. 257.

a reflection of the fact that the sphere of conduct in relation to which his words are recognised as constituting peremptory reasons for action is limited."[13]

On the basis of reading *together* Hart's accounts in *The Concept of Law,* and *Essays on Bentham,* concerning the nature of the normativity of law, his arguments about the validity and acceptance of law might be summarised thus: the reasons which made a commander such, resulted from practices that led to his utterances being perceived and accepted as CIPR. As far as validity is concerned, an ultimate validating social rule in a given society would enable *all* the people in that society to recognise the legislator as an authentic source of valid rules of law. In analysing the ideas of the normativity and "recognition" of law, Hart endeavoured to show that the notion of "validity" would be distinct from saying that a given measure was legally permissible or impermissible by the "fact of commanding". Further, as far as the nature of acceptance of legal rules was concerned, acts of "recognition" of commands as valid "laws", which operated as CIPR, needed not consist in a fully-fledged *critical reflective* attitude. The CIPR status of utterances could stem from qualitatively different reasons for the people in a community on the one hand, and for the officials on the other. It was sufficient for a legal system to exist if the notion of "validity" entered both as a "recognition" test for the people with some minimal normative reflection in it, and as the critical reflective internal attitude for officials. In other words, there could be a considerable difference between the normativity of the law as the people might see it, and as officials had to see it. However, *both* officials and people would perceive the rule of recognition as "normative", or as an "ought", or as CIPR. In this respect it seems that Hart's claim in *The Concept of Law* that as a minimum requirement for the existence of a legal system the people need only to obey, may be seen as a too-restrictive, and potentially misleading description.[14]

Postema's account of Bentham's theory of law and sovereignty attempts to answer Hart's objections as to the relations between validity and effectiveness, validity and legality, and the normativity of law. He attempts to show that there are many similarities between Bentham's account of sovereignty and Hart's account of legal validity and acceptance. He does so by arguing that Bentham, in his earlier writings, developed a theory of customary-based sovereignty. Bentham provided for a network of customary rules recognised by both governor and governed. The normativity of these customary rules related to a complex web of mutual expectations on the part of governor and governed.

First, Postema shows that Bentham furnished an account of custom. In his *Comment on the Commentaries* and some other unpublished writings, Bentham classified different types of customs. The common denominator between them was that custom was a practice which could become obligatory. A group practice could become obligatory and normative because of the fact that it created

[13] Hart, *Essays on Bentham*, pp. 258–9.
[14] Hart, *The Concept of Law*, p. 113.

expectations between members of the group. These expectations would be interpersonal and would cause each member of the group to conform to some recognised regular pattern of behaviour. These expectations would give this pattern a prescriptive force.[15]

Secondly, Postema draws on *Fragment* to assert that Bentham drew a distinction between an "immediate" disposition to obey a coercive measure, and an "ultimate" disposition on which obedience to *any* particular law rests.[16] According to Postema, Bentham, when arguing that the authority of the governor was constituted *by* the habit of obedience of the populace, had meant that one should not look only as to whether a *particular* law is obeyed, but also whether there was a general recognition of the person as governor.[17] This important, yet arguably undeveloped, insight by Postema[18] changes the nature of the argument about Bentham's account, that is, from an argument about how sovereignty is created by obedience to a particular measure, into an argument about general validity as signified by the collective judgement which could affect the collective obedience of the people.

Thirdly, in order to account for how a customary rule is formed, Postema relies on Bentham's Cartesian ontology, according to which rules are a product of personal belief, or inference from observation. Postema argues that for Bentham a customary rule was a result of an expression of opinion on a matter of fact, the facts here being reasons for such an opinion. In other words, Bentham conceived customary rules as the opinions of the observer of the practice, to the effect that such practices constituted reasons for actions.[19]

Fourthly, Postema attributes to Bentham a notion of sovereignty which, like Hart's, involves an ultimate criterion of the validity of laws. For, Postema argues, Bentham saw sovereignty as a publicly identifiable and accessible criterion for recognising a coercive measure as "law", as opposed to any other kind of coercive measure:

> "Such criteria have an 'ontological' function: they define conditions which entities—rules, principles, norms, commands, acts—must meet for them to *be* authentic legal entities in a given legal system. . . In addition, such criteria may also be assigned the 'epistemic' function of defining tests by which authentic rules, principles, or act-in-law can be identified and distinguished from inauthentic or spurious rules and the like."[20]

In order to fulfil this epistemic task, the criterion of validity would have to specify the *persons* who purported to be recognised as law-makers, and the *procedure* they had to follow in order to produce coercive measures which would

[15] Postema, *Bentham and The Common Law Tradition*, pp. 222, 226–230. In this way, Postema (and therefore Bentham) would dispute Raz's claim that a conceptual analysis of rules rooted purely on their being "in practice" cannot account for their normative character: see Raz, *Practical Reasons and Norms*, pp. 56–8.

[16] Postema, *Bentham and The Common Law Tradition*, p. 240.

[17] Ibid.

[18] See chapter 4, pp. 126–31 below.

[19] Postema, *Bentham and The Common Law Tradition*, pp. 224–5.

[20] Ibid., p. 231.

be identified as "law". In a way analogous to Hart's rule of recognition, Postema argues, the criteria of validity of law for Bentham were not related to the moral worth of the content of the law, but only to the conditions necessary to satisfy the authenticity of law.[21] Thus, Postema claims that Bentham identified the validity of law in a similar fashion to Hart.[22]

Fifthly, Postema attributes to Bentham an account of custom the nature of which was interactional rather than mechanical. By using the term "interaction", Postema means that a customary rule could be inferred by the people as a part of the complex network of expectations in the group. This interactional model of custom could provide the explanation of the basic social practice from which customary rules of sovereignty could be inferred.[23] The interaction occurred when there was some collective public inference regarding the identification of the rules of sovereignty which created and limited law-making authority. However, the authority which was created by these rules could also change the customary practice, and hence the inference of customary rules by the collective body of the people. Therefore, although sovereignty was created by the practices of the people, it could also be shaped by the authority in question. Interaction both shaped sovereign legislative power and could be shaped by the exercise of the sovereign legislative power. In part, power issued from the legislature, though ultimately it rested on the practice of the people.[24]

Postema contrasts the interactional model of customary practice and rule-inferring with a "mechanical" model of custom. Under this "mechanical" model, there would simply be an inference of rules from existing practice by the population. This inference would then give rise to the habit of obedience. There would be no account of the two-way relationship between governors and governed. As has been argued above, Hart's general criticism of Bentham's theory was that the conceptual connection between the ideas of "sovereignty" and "a command which is habitually obeyed" could not furnish an explanation for the

[21] Ibid., pp. 238–9.

[22] Postema restricts his use of the term "authenticity" by not mentioning the substance of law as a possible criterion of authenticity. This is arguably a reductionist, but understandable, move by him. The inclusion of the beliefs in the community, which led to the formation of rules which signified substantive limitations for the authenticity of law, might not fit easily into the rest of Postema's argument. The inclusion of substantive limitations would obviate a doubt as to whether "authenticity" could be *convincingly* accounted for purely in terms of an epistemic *test* (this doubt being applicable, but perhaps somewhat better concealed, in the more "bureaucratic" realm of personnel and law-making procedures). More particularly, such an inclusion would perhaps undermine the appropriateness of the conceptual separation between the social use of the terms "acceptance" and "validity". Further, as will be argued below, it may undermine the whole idea of *formal* acceptance which conceptually runs in parallel to *formal* legal validity, this dual formal aspect being essential to the success of positivistic talk about law. In short, to enter substance into the equation of authenticity may end up risking the requirement of "content independent" from the normativity of law so essential to legal positivism. See also in this context, N. MacCormick in his comment on Postema's essay "The Normativity of Law", in R. Gavison (ed.), *Issues in Contemporary Legal Philosophy: The Influence of H.L.A. Hart* (Oxford, 1987), p. 106, criticising the view that the normativity of law is content independent.

[23] Postema, *Bentham and The Common Law Tradition*, pp. 229, 232–7.

[24] Ibid., p. 237.

ultimate normativity, *outside this fact of habitual obedience*, which provided for reasons for obedience in the first place. Hence, Bentham's argument which connected sovereignty to obedience was circular.

The interactional model operated at the ultimate level of obedience as opposed to the immediate level. However, even on this ultimate level, a mechanical mode would be prone to the charge of circularity, for if the population obeyed a sovereign, an explanation would be needed as to what established this sovereignty in the first place. Only an interactional model of customary obedience could provide an explanation of an ultimate criterion of validity. This is because the disposition of the people to obey would also modify the limits of sovereignty, as opposed to such a disposition being determined solely *by* the action of the sovereign. Sovereignty, under the interactional model, would be a dynamic state of affairs, involving the body of the people *and* the body which produced coercive measures. An interactional model, by allowing mutual modifications of the limits of sovereignty, would fall outside the circularity to which a mechanical argument is subject.[25] A dynamic activity would not be prone, *by its nature*, to the charge of circularity. An interactional model does not view the "habit of obedience" as simultaneously creating and being created by the exercise of coercion. Postema points out the emphasis on collectivity in Bentham's theory. The will of the sovereign had to be collectively authenticated as "law". There had to be some communal recognition of the fact of sovereignty. Postema explains that Bentham's aim was to produce clear and publicly accessible signs which would enable the people collectively to infer a new customary rule. Violations of the boundaries constituted by these signs should easily be perceived.[26]

Bentham discussed various types of mandates which could limit sovereign power. In *Fragment* he argued that sovereignty could be limited by an "express convention" (a term which signified a treaty between two political authorities in a state or federation, or between a political authority in a state and the people of that state),[27] constitutional promises of self-limitations by an authority,[28] or by *constitutional laws in principem*, which were certain expressed volitions of which the sovereign, as opposed to the people, was the subject.[29] Postema concludes that, for Bentham, these signs were communal triggers, both formed by the existing state of expectations in the collective body of the people, and also operating to modify expectations in the collective body of the people.[30]

The argument in the rest of this chapter is that Bentham saw in sovereignty not only a criterion of authenticity and formal acceptance as advocated by Postema, but also an element of critical ongoing interpretation and justification

[25] Postema, *Bentham and the Common Law Tradition*, pp. 233–4.
[26] Ibid., p. 245.
[27] *Fragment*, pp. 488–9.
[28] *OLG*, p. 16.
[29] Ibid., pp. 64–5.
[30] Postema, *Bentham and The Common Law Tradition*, pp. 253–4.

of political authority. It is argued that Bentham's doctrine of sovereignty revealed that, in accounting conceptually for the normativity of law, there was a gap between a positivistic use of the term "authenticity" and an interactive model of custom. Legal positivists use this gap to generate a non sequitur, namely that that it does not follow from the fact that law is *influenced* by morality that it is *conceptually* identified with it. This logical fallacy of legal positivism could be exposed by acknowledging that it can only maintain the conceptual separation of law and morality by not capturing a more general critical historical discourse of interpretation (for Bentham, of course, *utilitarian* interpretation) of authority as essential to a proper (as opposed to popular) social use of legal terms. Legal positivists view the idea of "influence" as something which could only be spoken about as functioning outside an authentic validation and formal acceptance of rules. Such is their thesis about legal closure. I shall argue below that it is a mistake to adopt whatever conception of influence while maintaining the positivist thesis. This is the case even with regard to a less formal, more moderate positivist thesis which concedes some interpretative evaluative perspective in law to function side by side to legal closure. In other words, the use of the word "is" in a positivistic sense of "what the law *is*" would have to imply a judicial moral evaluation (not carried out exclusively by judges) at its foundation. Such an interpretative activity would conceptually incorporate whatever conception of influence (i.e. causal or systemic) one might care to use to justify a conception of law.[31]

III

This section aims to reinterpret the concept of sovereignty in Bentham's theory. It connects Bentham's understanding of "sovereignty" to the idea of the justification and normativity of the exercise of coercion in a social group. Generally speaking, any social observation would reveal that the query "why does a certain authoritative measure, or coercion, have normative force?" is potentially wide in scope. Social practices in themselves can, and often do, imply various degrees of superiority and subordination among people. Certain social "codes" often lead to behaviour which may not seem to be a result of a moral judgement arising from a process of reasoning carried out by some participants in the practice. However, it will be argued that Bentham's account of sovereignty showed that a pure exercise of coercion—an exercise of coercion without some critical reflection upon its legitimacy by another body—could not be an adequate description of sovereignty in a political society.

[31] On influence, see chapter 6, pp. 199–206 below. For the distinction between a causal and systemic conception influence, see G. Teubner, "How the Law Thinks: Toward A Constructivist Epistemology of Law", *Law and Society Review* 23 (1989) 727–52, and *Law as an Autopoetic System* (Oxford, 1993), chapters 2–5. See also M. King, "The 'Truth' About Autopoesis", *Journal of Law and Society* 20 (1993) 218–36.

A preliminary point should be made with regard to the various ways Bentham used the term "sovereignty". Bentham used this term to signify different ideas depending on the nature of the particular problem with which he was dealing. Sometimes he used "sovereignty" in the sense of power to legislate—what modern writers would classify as "legal sovereignty".[32] Sometimes he used it to signify a certain degree of superiority within the context of an abstract discussion of powers, in which the concept seemed to be detached from any specific political discussion altogether, and assumed a characteristic of endless relativity in relationships of superiority and subordination.[33] In his mature constitutional writings, he used "sovereignty" in relation to the right of the people to locate officials in their positions—or what modern scholars would call "political sovereignty".[34]

My argument is that there was a common denominator uniting these different senses of sovereignty.[35] This common denominator centred on an ongoing, socially dynamic, limiting communal interpretation which formed a part of the concept of sovereignty. In other words, an exercise of sovereignty necessarily involved *popular critical justification* of a given authoritative measure. This general meaning of sovereignty did not change, regardless of the context in which Bentham used the concept. Throughout this book the argument is that, throughout his career, Bentham retained the same general theory of "sovereignty", although the *use* he made out of it varied with the subject matter in hand.

The split nature of sovereignty

The common core of Bentham's definition of sovereignty is to be found in the first chapter of *Fragment*, in which he distinguished a political society from a natural one. The heart of the distinction stemmed from the fact that only in the former would the people habitually obey a common superior.[36] In *OLG*, Bentham replaced the idea of "habit of obedience" with a "disposition to pay obedience":

[32] For example, in *Fragment*.

[33] See, for instance, *OLG*, chapter 9, where Bentham discussed the generality of a law. The relativity of sovereignty will be discussed in chapter 3 below.

[34] A.V. Dicey, *An Introduction to Study of The Law of the Constitution* (London, 1959), pp. 429–32. See also ibid., pp. 41, 76–85, 406–14.

[35] Postema had the insight that, in his mature democratic theory, Bentham had not advanced a different theory of law, in which a conception of popular sovereignty replaced an earlier conception: see *Bentham and The Common Law Tradition*, pp. 260–1. Postema was responding to Hart's argument in *Essays on Bentham*, pp. 228–9.

[36] *Fragment*, pp. 428–32. Note that Raz delivers a comparable argument in his "social thesis" of authority. This thesis links the very existence of a political society with the fact that the people in it recognise a commonly perceived authority: see "Authority and Justification", in J. Raz (ed.), *Authority* (Oxford, 1990), pp. 115–41, at 118.

> "By a sovereign I mean any person or assemblage of persons to whose will a whole political community are (no matter on what account) supposed to be in a disposition to pay obedience."[37]

The difference between the notions of "habit" and "disposition" was that the former would be backward looking in that it was rooted in past practice, whereas the latter meant that people would have the inclination to obey the authority in the future.

Bentham thought of the "habit" or "disposition" to obey as a significant social process, something which would precede the actual action of obedience or disobedience. Bentham did not equate the actual *action* of obedience with the limits of sovereignty. That *act* of obedience, or disobedience, was the practical implication of reflection upon the collective social justification of authority. Social justification of authority meant for Bentham a collective judgement which conditioned obedience or disobedience. The present section will try to determine the precise nature of this collective judgement as well as the relationship it bore to the concepts of "sovereignty" and "law".

There appear to be two ways in which a "habit" or "disposition" could produce normative effects. The first would be through the normative force created by custom. On this interpretation, people obey because they infer rules from expectations, these expectations being the result of a certain existing practice. (This, essentially, is Postema's claim.) Hence the force of a custom *would be* the source by which power was authenticated, and seen to be validly exercised as a legal power. The second interpretation would give custom only a preliminary role. The interpretative, critical state of mind of a citizen would be much more important than custom. I shall explain why Bentham saw the notion of a rule which was inferred from a custom as forming only one element in a wider interpretative personal and communal process, in which citizens participated in order to assess the social justification of a specific authoritative measure. Bentham did not intend the concept of a "custom" and with it the concept of "authenticity", to capture the whole explanation of sovereignty, as Postema claimed.

The most important passages about sovereignty are in *OLG*. The purpose of this monumental work was to find a solution to a problem which had remained unresolved from *An Introduction to the Principles of Morals and Legislation*, namely the distinction between penal and civil law. This distinction was important for the establishment of universal principles for a system of legislation. Legislation was needed in order to fill the gap between the principle of utility as a principle of hedonistic psychology, and as a principle of moral evaluation. Legislation would aim artificially to unite people's duty and interest. In order to bring about such unification, offences would be constituted, each on account of the mischief that they caused. In order to be comprehensible, the classification and arrangement of individual laws would have to mirror the classification of offences, and, in turn, of mischiefs. Thus, in order to provide for a single

[37] *OLG*, p. 18.

offence, Bentham was required to individuate a single law.[38] The prevailing view defined offences as either "civil" or "criminal", but Bentham recognised that *any* offence would contain civil and penal elements. These elements would exist both in the criminal law, say, of murder, and in civil law, say, of contract. It seemed necessary to analyse their respective roles in each individual law. He therefore had to rethink the distinction between civil and penal law. While he was trying to grasp this distinction, Bentham got caught up in a problem, still one of the most controversial questions in analytical jurisprudence, namely what constituted a *complete* individual law, whatever its subject matter. The whole of *OLG* was written to answer this particular question.

In the course of defining an individual law, Bentham sought to establish the minimal requirements for an individual law to exist. Bentham argued that there were only two such basic requirements. These were an act, which would serve as the object of a volition of the sovereign, and some expression of will by that sovereign with regard to that act.[39]

As Hart pointed out, one of the problems involved in the process of individuation was to determine what would make this measure a "law", as distinct from any other coercive measure. Could his theory of sovereignty offer a clue? What made a certain person or body of persons into a sovereign who could promulgate individual laws? What was the point at which this body would no longer be a sovereign? Was a body simply "known" to be sovereign? Must it be accepted by a body in order to be considered sovereign? If so, by whom? What was the nature of this acceptance for Bentham?

These questions lead to an obvious difficulty. Under the simple definition of a law as an act and an expression of will with regard to that act, it was logically impossible for a sovereign itself to be the subject of a law. The notion of constitutional law, which in part is law dealing with the nature and limitations of validity of legislation, becomes incoherent. An escape from this logical impossibility might be attempted by saying that for a sovereign to be subject to a constitutional law, this law must be related in some way to a volition expressed by some other bodies. These other bodies would have to form a part of any analysis of the concept of a law, otherwise the legislature's volition would not itself be that of a true perceived sovereign, even for the purposes of ordinary legislation.

The ingredients of a law, namely an act and the sovereign's volition in relation to this act, would also exist in a constitutional law. Yet, what would be the characteristic mark of this law? It must be that this law would connote a certain tension which exists *as a part of* the concept of sovereignty. There would be a qualitative difference between a law which limited sovereignty and any other individual law, in that the former must be assumed in any validation of the latter. That is to say, any individual law presumes another individual law (the latter must possess all the minimal characteristics of a law).

[38] On "individuation", see M. James, "Bentham on the Individuation of Laws", *Northern Ireland Legal Quarterly* 24 (1973) 357–82.

[39] *OLG*, p. 93.

Thus, a way to avoid the conceptual problem of constitutional law under a command theory of a law would be to say that, in a sense, every law of the system would include two volitions, one of the legislature, and one of another body which expressed some volition having the first body as the subject of its volition. Both these types of laws would form an integral part of the concept of law if the authoritative foundation of a single individual law as the exercise of sovereign power was to be understood properly. Sovereignty seemed to be a dynamic concept which could be exercised at different levels. To what extent a legislature was subject, and to what extent it was sovereign, was the task of a theory of sovereignty to explain. This point would have to be addressed in any *description* of a law.

Bentham thought it would be a misuse of language to assert that the legislature could be *legally* limited:

> "In the definition that hath just been given of a legal mandate it follows that the mandate **of the sovereign** be it what it will, cannot be illegal: it may be cruel; it may be impolitic; it may even be unconstitutional: but it cannot be illegal."[40]

As has been said, *constitutional laws in principem* were a special kind of laws, the subject of which would be the legislature and not the people (as opposed to other laws *in populum*). These laws would limit sovereign power. These laws signified what "mandates [the sovereign] may or may not address to [his subjects]".[41] These laws, Bentham argued, stemmed from the sovereign. The subject of such constitutional laws would be some present political authority. However, the promulgation of such laws would serve as "recommendatory mandates" for any future authorities. Such a recommendation meant that the laws in question would have to be taken into account by that future political authority in assessing the limits of its competence.[42]

It was not clear why the sovereign would bother to bind itself in this way. As Postema noted, Bentham put a lot of emphasis on the idea of the expectations which such a law would create in the people. The force of these expectations would exert pressure upon political authorities to bind themselves. Moreover, the state of expectations would be so intense that the succeeding political authorities would have no choice but to adopt the law, or face a massive outcry or even a revolt.[43]

In the context of discussing the possible ways in which *constitutional laws in principem* could be given effect, Bentham paused to explain the import of the term "sovereignty". This is a key passage and hence it is quoted in full:

> "the truth of [the fact that the sovereign cannot be coerced by the political sanction] depends upon the idea annexed to the word *sovereign*. The case is, that supposing the

[40] Ibid., p. 16.
[41] Ibid., p. 64.
[42] Ibid., p. 65.
[43] Ibid. Discussed in Postema, *Bentham and the Common Law Tradition*, p. 253. This idea will be developed in Part 2 into a socially dynamic account of the relationship between ethics and politics.

power in the state to be [distributed so as to coerce the sovereign], there is no one person or body of persons in whose hands the sovereignty is reposed. Suppose two bodies of men, or for shortness' sake two men, the one possessing every power in the state, except that the other in case of public accusation, preferred in such or such forms, has the power of judging him; including such power as may be necessary to carry the judgement into execution. It is plain that sovereignty would not be exclusively in either: it would be conjunctively in both. Yet, in common speech it is probable that the first man would be styled *the* sovereign, or at least *a* sovereign: . . . if the narrow sense were to be given to the word *sovereign*, it is plain that the proposition above mentioned concerning the impossibility of the sovereign's being judged by anyone, would not be true. . . . Taking advantage of the inexplicit notions annexed to the words *superior* and *inferior*, he would perhaps assume for his medium this proposition, that it is impossible for a man to be superior and inferior to another at the same time: or perhaps in different propositions he would use the same word *sovereign* in two different senses: at one time in its strict and proper sense; at another time in its **popular and improper** sense, according to the distinction above taken. . . . It may occur, that the distribution of power above supposed is not an expedient one, or that it cannot be a lasting one. This may or may not be the case: but the expediency or the durability of such an arrangement are points with which we have nothing to do here. I consider here only what is **possible**."[44]

Elsewhere, when discussing the distribution of powers in any state, Bentham said that the power to legislate was inherently limited in terms of its functioning:

"[By] legislative power ordinarily so called, I mean the power of legislating *de classibus* even though it be supreme, can never of itself be **absolute and unlimited**. It can never so much as amount to the entire power of imperation: It will fall short of **being equal** to that power by so much as is contained in whatever powers of aggregation or disaggregation are established in the state."[45]

These two passages are very revealing about Bentham's formulation of the word "sovereignty", and despite their relative brevity they contain a complete argument. They convey in a concise way some key features which explain how the concept of sovereignty *ought* to be understood as opposed to how it is commonly understood.

The first point was that the term "sovereignty" in the sense of power to make laws, properly understood, *must* involve a relationship between two bodies. It had to be understood as an inherently "split" concept. It was like a sheet of paper which must have two sides to it. The word "split" signifies a tension pertaining to the concept of sovereignty. "Sovereignty" in its proper sense had to contain two interdependent dimensions. The two dimensions were any state of affairs signified by the word "sovereignty", and the terminology "split concept" is used here to connote this feature.[46] In functional terms the notion of a "split

[44] *OLG*, pp. 68–9, note n.

[45] Ibid., p. 91.

[46] When it is argued that such a "split" is inherent to the concept, a statement in universal theory is made: see chapter 1, pp. 13–20 above.

concept" means that there *must* be two bodies, the interaction between which constitutes sovereignty. One would *be* a sovereign so long as the other judges it to be so. This means that one body cannot be a sovereign unless there is another body which judges it to be a sovereign and if necessary gives effect to this judgement. To use Freeden's terminology, the relatively complex concept of sovereignty *ought* to be talked about as having a core structure of two concepts—"power" and "judgement"—contrary to what Bentham regarded as the popular way of talking about it as incorporating "power" only. "Power" and "judgement" deconstructed one another, hence bringing their respective ineliminable component to bear a fuller conceptual, though still minimal, meaning.[47]

This conceptual tension did not involve merely a *possibility* of limited political authority. This inner conceptual tension, or "split", portrays "sovereignty" as involving *necessary* limitations upon the exercise of power. Sovereignty in its very inception was to be understood as an exercise of a limited authority. The conventional association of Bentham with the idea of "might" was unfounded.[48] The interpretation of sovereignty denounces the idea of unlimited power to make laws. As will be elaborated upon below, and indeed in the rest of this book, no unlimited political authority could exist. Further, as will be argued shortly, the precise materialisation of social/historical manifestation of political authority out of this inner conceptual tension was a dynamic interpretative process.

Only on this basis would Bentham be able to assert that the sovereign might be bound and still remain sovereign. This peculiar feature of sovereignty would not ordinarily be obvious, but would become so only when constitutional problems were raised.[49] Only in the popular and misguided sense could sovereignty be seen as a concept involving just one body. Such a misguided view has been attributed to Bentham by his critics, but here he has shown that this was not his position, nor was it one that could be substantiated. One body was, for *most* purposes, superior, the other inferior. However, the very existence and extent[50]

[47] "Ineliminable" feature connotes an airy basis for the linguistic use of a term, for example, "absence of constraint" for the term "liberty". An ineliminable feature is itself created by a certain use of language. Elimination of such a feature would change the use of the term to such an extent that it would not matter whether another term was used. Ineliminable features constitute the most fundamental root of linguistic usage, the point of an unquestionable system of reference. They are merely preconditions for a given conceptual "talk". Being only "features" they do not amount to a full conceptual meaning of the term. The thickening towards a fuller conceptual meaning is carried out through a relational process of one term to another term. To continue the example, the term "liberty" would get fuller conceptual meaning only if related to another term such as "equality" or "power". Further, this type of analysis does not purport to justify one direction of thickening of a term. So, to say "this is the *right* way of talking about the term 'sovereignty' is itself contingent. Such contingency would amount to essential contestability of the concept, namely competing ways in which a term ought to be decontested: see M. Freeden, *Ideologies and Political Theory* (Oxford, 1996), chapter 2, esp. pp. 55–67.

[48] See N. MacCormick, "The Dialectic of Might and Right: Legal Positivism and Constitutional Change", *Current Legal Problems* 31 (1998) 37–63, at 31–5.

[49] See chapter 4, pp. 128–9 below.

[50] In Bowring, ii. 540–4, Bentham used the word "dominion" to signify the extent of sovereignty.

of the first body's superiority would be determined *by* a judgement of the second one.[51] In order for an exercise of coercion to be discussed in terms of "sovereignty", it must be an exercise of a legitimate authority. By "legitimate", Bentham meant the exercise of an inherently limited authority; an authority limited by a critical judgement made by the subjects of that authority.[52] The coercion must, if it was to be regarded as an exercise of "sovereign" power, logically operate, *to a certain extent,* in the context of a judgement by the coerced body as to the justification of the coercion. This feature of sovereignty would hold, it will be argued, even in the case of a pure monarchy.

Secondly, it is important to note how the relationship of superiority and subordination should be understood in the context of the "split" nature of sovereignty. Bentham clearly opposed the popular idea that a relationship of superiority and subordination provided a sufficient explanation of the concept of sovereignty. Such an explanation would be implausible if one were to assert that authority could be constitutionally limited. A more appropriate notion was that of mutual dependence, or interaction, or equality of power, which would characterise this "split". The judging, coerced body, would pass a judgement, the subject of which would be the very superiority of the coercing body. However, "split" sovereignty equally implied that the judging body must be ultimately superior, despite the assumption that in most cases it would be inferior. Hence the mutual dependence: nobody could be absolutely supreme.

[51] See also *Authority*, p. 12, where Raz argues that the idea of limited authority is sensitive to, and therefore is limited by, a judgement which relates to varying social, technological and cultural circumstances. Arguably however, Raz would not go as far as saying that *every* political authority *must* be limited by such a judgement.

The idea of sovereignty as a "split", or two-dimensional, concept, could be referred to through a normative structure of reasons in a Razian manner. There are some reasons which justify certain status of reasons as exclusionary. Such reasons which justify authoritative utterances having an exclusionary status could be referred to as "constitutive reasons". It is argued in chapter 4 that Bentham recognised a constitutional sphere which employs "constitutive reasons" for political authority. Constitutional thought is activated, and constitutional interpretation launched, when a social conflict reopens the "protected" status of some reasons for authority (see pp. 43, note 9 above) and a rift is recreated between conventionally unquestioned exclusionary reasons and other competing reasons for authority which mesh into first-order reasons. The account for such constitutive reasons may be incorporated under the conceptual umbrella of Raz's "normal justification thesis" for authority, namely that people accept authority for reasons which apply to them, reasons which override *direct* personal reasons, see, *The Morality of Freedom*, chapter 3, esp. pp. 53–7. Such a move on his part would be unsatisfactory, though, because it would blur the distinction and interpretative dynamism that exists functionally between exclusionary and constitutive reasons. Indeed, Raz seems not to choose this path and distinguishes in a positivistic manner between "operative" and "auxiliary" reasons for authority. This distinction is unsatisfactory: see further, pp. 70–1, below.

[52] The word "legitimacy" has hitherto been carefully avoided. Bentham did not like this word and mounted a host of objections to it in his mature constitutional writings. He saw "legitimacy" as a notion which could be utilised to support bad governments. Theories of legitimacy (such as the divine right theory) claimed that there was some sort of basic entitlement for a person or a government to be in power irrespective of its quality. The issue of legitimacy thrived on prejudices and as such the use of it in political vocabulary could persuade people to act contrary to their interests: see chapter 6, pp. 220 note 76 below, and *First Principles*, pp. 113–16. However, it goes without saying that Bentham would accept the idea of legitimacy not in an a priori way, but in the sense of limits to acceptable exercise of power. Bentham explicitly linked legitimacy to the limits of validity of the act of command: see *A General View of a Complete Code Of Laws*, Bowring, iii. 197.

Thirdly, Bentham went on to give a hint regarding the nature of the second, judging body. He made it clear that the body which judged the law-maker did so through a process of *public accusation*. This implied that the judging body expressed some public discontent which led to the process of judging or questioning the extent of the law-making body's superiority. It was quite clear that the public had the capacity to bring accusations. In order to make such accusations, the body of the people must be conceived as constantly engaging in the task of interpreting the limits of the lawgiver's superiority. This conception would hold good even if the particular judgement did not lead to the performance of a specific action. There was, therefore, a participatory dimension in the very conception of the term "sovereignty".

Although it is possible here to see that the "people" constituted this second "judging" body, it should be stressed that a democratic government did not follow directly from this requirement of social justification, although no doubt such a popular judging body was perfectly compatible with democracy.[53] Further, the requirement of some reflective judgement on the part of the people did not guarantee that their judgement was necessarily in their best interest. The people could arrive at a judgement contrary to their interests as a result of obstacles to communication, obstacles such as intimidation by the government, or prejudices.[54] Bentham did not attempt an evaluation of this judgement in these two passages, only an assertion that for a proper understanding of the term "sovereignty", there must be a reflective judgement by the people. The important point here is that the more interaction was facilitated between the people and the government, the more the political society in question engaged in reflection on the limits of coercion exercised within it. A good government would not be determined by a given ideal state of relationship between the two bodies but would be one which was socially dynamic in the sense of enabling this judgement of the body to be constantly operative and interacting with that of government.

When one thinks about an authority which commands, one immediately thinks about a surrender of moral autonomy. This is why a command operates in such a way as to exclude independent reasoning. But the greater the extent to which the questioning of the limits of authority or commanding is facilitated, the more legitimate the authority becomes. As will be argued, the idea of questioning the limitations of authority is compatible with the authority having very great powers indeed.[55]

Bentham's account in *OLG* was conceptual and aimed at describing how the notion of sovereignty ought to be understood. It showed that sovereignty embodied the notion of a legitimate government which meant a necessarily lim-

[53] The only way it would mean a democratic government would be to broaden the common understanding of the term "democracy": see chapter 4, pp. 121–2, and chapter 8, p. 297 below.

[54] This point will be discussed in chapter 6, pp. 220, note 76 below.

[55] See chapter 4, pp. 119–20, and chapter 5, pp. 143–5 below.

ited government. Bentham formulated a minimal, formal account of a legitimate (and therefore limited) authority which had the *right* to make laws, as opposed to a *de facto* power based purely on physical superiority and subordination. It was a formal account, because it did not advocate any particular system of exercising authority. It pointed at a minimal requirement for political authority. Every political authority, and therefore every government, however bad and cruel it might be, must ultimately be understood according to this criterion. This inherently "split" feature of sovereignty was the basic criterion for a socially justified exercise of authority, as opposed to a naked act of power. Without it there would be no difference between an order given to a dog and a law addressed to a human being.

This basic, formal, normative principle of constitutionalism—this minimal *conceptual* requirement in the shape of a critical attitude as to the extent of social justification of political authority—entails some necessary minimal capacity for adjudication as to the limits of sovereignty. For an authority to be socially justified, it must operate in a context wherein those subject to it have some sphere of moral autonomy which gives them the capacity to invalidate this authority. This minimal judgement could relate to the basic need for survival or security,[56] but, as will be argued below, could evolve into many other social instances which embodied some other social good (like, for example, an entrenched distribution of fundamental rights).

The inherent tension pertained to the concept of sovereignty is an important feature to grasp, in that it clarifies the nature of a constitutional government.[57] Even under forms of government such as a pure monarchy, based on apparently naked power, there would be some judgement which would make the exercise of power socially justified. This is not to say that these will be good forms of government. The formal requirement of sovereignty means that sovereignty implies an exercise of superiority which is judged by another body to be justified. Again, however bad a public judgement happened to be, whatever the role of fear and prejudice in it, this formal requirement would have to exist if sovereign power were exercised. In this sense, even an absolute monarchy would be a limited government. Even in an absolute monarchy there would be some

[56] This is reminiscent of Hart's minimum content of natural law in *The Concept of Law*, pp. 189–95. Hart's view was static in that he considered only the minimal moral *conceptual* ingredients of law. However, he did not allow for situations in which, in more developed societies, this *conceptual* (as opposed to merely influential) link between law and morality would be extended beyond these minimal domains.

[57] The conception of sovereignty as "split" concept does not simply mean that sovereignty *could* be divided in a state, in the sense of its being exercised by two or more different institutions at the same time. A division of sovereignty in this institutional way would be vulnerable to Postema's criticism that, if one accepted the division of sovereignty, at least a single law which had given rise to this division would have to be assumed: see Postema, *Bentham and The Common Law Tradition*, p. 234. It is clear from the dynamic understanding of the idea of sovereignty that some functional division, however minimal, must exist on a conceptual level. Having said that, institutional division may, but need not, follow from the conceptual one argued for here. This institutional type of division will be discussed in the next chapter in terms of the relative and plural nature of sovereignty.

limitations as a result of some judgement, a limitation which could be encapsulated in constitutional law and which would limit the monarch. This judgement, a judgement with regard to the social justification of authority, might not be readily observed. It might be more observable in one form of government, and more hidden in another. In some forms of government it might have no other means of expressing itself than through physical resistance. In short, the fact that in popular talk this minimal conceptual requirement of sovereignty may not make sense does not mean that it does not exist and function, however minimally. The split would be a part of the conceptual understanding of sovereignty. This point will become more apparent in the next section, and as the argument progresses.

The trust which constitutes political authority

When an authority promulgated a constitutional law, it would produce a sign (or piece of information) which from one perspective could be seen as its own will. This was because it would, strictly speaking, form the source of the command. Yet, if one accepts the inherently "split" nature of sovereignty, while still adhering to Bentham's basic definition of a law as an act and an expression of will with regard to this act, one must come to the conclusion that the act of the authority in question must relate in some way to a volition of another body. This other body would supply the motives for the legislature to limit itself, by means of a sanction which, of course, must be different from the legal sanction.[58]

In order to make sense of the precise nature of the communication or interaction between the "judging" body and the body which exercises coercion, attention must be paid to Bentham's conception of investitive and divestitive powers. J.H. Burns points out that in *IPML*, when Bentham discussed offences against sovereign power, he mentioned the fiduciary relationship between the government and another authority which could invest the government with, and divest it of, its powers. Burns's interpretation is that Bentham had recognised very early in his writings the importance of the *people* in which sovereign power originated, and that this might reveal democratic tendencies as early as the late 1770s.[59]

In *OLG* Bentham defined two types of powers in terms of the person by whom they might be exercised:

> "[The power] may be styled direct, when the acts in which the exercise of it consists are the acts of the very person by whom the power is said to be possessed: in this case it may be styled the power or right of occupation: it may be termed indirect, when

[58] For a discussion of the physical, legal, moral and religious sanctions, see *IPML*, chapter 3. As far as the sympathetic sanction is concerned, see chapter 6, pp. 209–13 below.

[59] J.H. Burns, "Bentham on Sovereignty: An Exploration", *Northern Ireland Legal Quarterly* 24 (1973) 399–416, at 403–5.

those acts though still taking their origin in some measure from his will, are not his acts but those of some other person."[60]

The indirect powers, continued Bentham, were of two sorts—investitive and divestitive. They were investitive when the *will* of one person was that another would exercise the act in question; divestitive when the will of one person was that another would exercise the act in question no longer.[61]

From the foregoing discussion of the idea of sovereignty, it would seem that a natural investment of power—one which simply happens, as in the case of the power of a parent over a child—did not capture fully the idea of sovereignty. "Natural" power would involve no interpretative reflective, constitutive judgement on the part of the coerced body and thus would involve a static understanding of authority. Instead, the coerced would simply receive, as well as act on, reasoned utterances. The reasons behind such utterances would replace *all* the independent reasoning on the part of the coerced body. This would be the case with any natural authority.[62] A natural authority would be unconditional, apart from the trivial condition that the utterance must in fact be made. The expression "natural authority" can bear meaning to sovereignty only in the sense of some convention the description of, and reasons for, which are accepted without question by a group of people. It would be possible (though highly inaccurate) to say, for example, that a given parochial culture embodies reasons to accept authority, reasons which are looked upon as "parental" and therefore "natural".

For Bentham, a political authority, however bad, cruel and absolute it might be, had to be related to some voluntary investiture. Some voluntary elements in investiture would exist even when they were latent in, say, an indolent or oppressed social group. There must be some judgements relating to certain conditions attached to the exercise of political authority. Again, it must be emphasised that these judgements might be based on misconception, or false consciousness. Fear and prejudice might give a certain direction to such judgements, but the judgements must exist nevertheless. The inherent limitations on the exercise of sovereign power were understood by Bentham as an interpretative, rather than as a natural, static, phenomenon. As such, his interpretative understanding of sovereignty could both accommodate cultural elements and go beyond those elements. Indeed, it is a central tenet of my whole argument that the utilitarian's conception of "nature" ought to be understood as entailing a socially dynamic interpretation, in which cultural elements play a large, but not an exclusive, role.

If sovereignty involved voluntary investiture, would the act of investing someone with sovereign power amount to a blank cheque? On the contrary, Bentham maintained that every investitive and divestitive event had to accommodate a

[60] *OLG*, p. 268.

[61] Ibid.

[62] On the connection between natural and political authority, see J.H. Burns, "Nature and Natural Authority in Bentham", *Utilitas* 5 (1993) 209–19, at 213–6; see also chapter 3, pp. 82–4 below.

condition understood at the point in time when the investiture took place. In a voluntary investiture, the body which had the investitive or divestitive powers would attach a condition for the investment.[63]

Bentham distinguished between two kinds of power according to the identity of the party which the power purported to benefit. In the first case, the power was intended to benefit the power-holder only, and was a beneficial power. In the second, the power was intended to benefit some other party, and was termed a "fiduciary" power. Beneficial and fiduciary elements coexisted in every exercise of political power.[64]

He elaborated on the idea of trust in his discussion of powers in *OLG*:

> "For the benefit of somebody [powers] must have been designed, so long as the legislator has acted with a view to utility, or in short with any view whatever. This party or parties must have been either the person himself to whom the power is given or some other: in the first case the power may be styled a beneficial power or simply a power; in the other case a fiduciary power or trust."[65]

In the latter case, added Bentham, the beneficiary could be an individual, some unassignable individuals, or the public at large. The fiduciary relationship, in the case where the public at large was the intended beneficiary, was called by Bentham a "public trust".[66] This concept of trust carried the notion of a limiting condition. To say "you are trusted" means that you are trusted for some purpose. There could be no trust in the abstract. Any trustee must be able to show that the purpose of the trust had been adhered to (adhered to in some sense, although it might not be the best sense).

It has been argued that the interaction between the two bodies gave the concept of sovereignty its social significance. The investing body would judge the body which, for most of the time, exercised the coercion. The condition which would, to some degree, be attached by the first, investing body to the investiture of power in the second body, would be that the authority thus created would pay regard to the utility of the investing body. The exercise of coercive power would be conditional, in that the authority would have to exercise its power to the benefit of the investing body. The reason for investing this power might be summarised thus: that some of the investing body's goals would be better achieved by investing (delegating) the power rather than by not so doing. Therefore, investing a body with authoritative power on trust would form an inherent limitation on the exercise of its powers. Public trust would form one

[63] *OLG*, pp. 286–7.
[64] Ibid., pp. 295–6.
[65] Ibid., p. 271.
[66] See also ibid., p. 86, where Bentham said:

> "When the right or power which is conveyed is one that is exercisable only on a public account, that is for the benefit of the public at large, the power of conveyance is a *constitutional* power, for public powers differ no otherwise from private fiduciary powers than in respect of the scale on which they are exercisable: they are the same powers exercisable on a greater scale."

ingredient of the definition of a law, namely a volition of the investing body.[67] This volition would be what Bentham called a "conditional command", as opposed to an "absolute command". A conditional command was where the addressee was not obliged in all cases to use the power conferred, but if he decided to use it, he would have to do so in compliance with the expressed condition.[68]

One characteristic of this act of investing power was that it would be a global expression of will. It would have no specific object apart from the general condition inherent in the power of investment. In manuscripts entitled *Preparatory Principles*, Bentham stated that the exercise of investitive power was unlike the ordinary exercise of legislative power, which necessitated an expression of volition and an object of volition:

> "The acts of the Legislative power are commands: But an act of this investitive power is not a command. To every command belongs a modal object: the act or the forbearance of the person who is the personal object of the same command. But of an expression of the investitive power there is no such modal object."[69]

Bentham in fact cancelled this passage in his manuscripts. However, the question which perhaps bothered Bentham was the precise difference between an act of commanding and an act of investitive power. He was clearly unsatisfied with a mutually exclusive definition of these two ideas. At first Bentham thought that the act of the investitive power could not be the same as a command at all. This, however, would not sit comfortably with the idea that a condition must be attached to investitive power which could serve as a general modal object of the volition to invest. A conditional command would therefore also have a modal object.

If we try to identify the common denominator between the view expressed in this cancelled passage and the notion of a conditional command as defined in *OLG*, it can be seen that both lack a specific object of volition. However, both have a general condition as a "suspended" object of volition. The idea of a political authority which is entrusted with powers by a conditional command would be equivalent to an investment of authority by employing an undecided expression of will. Bentham discussed in *OLG* certain legal mandates where the aspect of the will might be "undecided".[70] Permissions and non-commands could both be seen as conditional commands. These types of mandates express a wish in

[67] This will be discussed further in chapter 5, pp. 163–5 below.

[68] *OLG*, pp. 112–3, 296–7. This explanation of the trust by a conditional command has implications for Hart's argument in the last chapter of *Essays on Bentham*. Bentham envisaged the possibility of a command operating as CIPR only if the commander exercised it in a certain fashion. It was not necessary that a command excluded all independent reasoning by the commandee, only restricted that reasoning; see also chapter 4, pp. 128–9 below, where the immediate and categorical spheres of reflection upon coercive measures are discussed.

[69] UC lxix. 236.

[70] For an explanation of Bentham's idea of the logic of the will, see *OLG*, chapter 10; Hart, *Essays on Bentham*, pp. 112–5; and L.J. Lysaght, "Bentham on the Aspects of A Law", *Northern Ireland Legal Quarterly* 24 (1973) 383–98.

relation to a certain limitation on the exercise of power by a subordinate power holder. An example might be a mandate which aimed to protect some spheres of liberty. Bentham added:

> "In this case indeed the effect is produced not so much from the literal import of the mandate itself, as from another mandate which is so connected with it that if not expressed it may of course be looked upon as implied. I mean a mandate which in the form of a prohibition is addressed to subordinate power-holders in general restraining them from breaking in upon the liberty of the party whom the uncoercive mandate in question is meant to favour. Thus much must be inferred of course: to which may be added in some cases a law of a particular kind **including the sovereign himself under the same restriction.** It is easy to see that some of the **most important** laws that can enter into the code, laws in which the people found what are called their liberties, may be of this description."[71]

In the context of the relationship between the two bodies whose interaction constituted "sovereignty", this would mean that the authority could exercise its powers only on the basis of the implied mandate that it operated to the benefit of the investing power. There would be no justification for the authority's exercise of power outside the sphere of competence allowed to it by this mandate.

To recapitulate, it has been argued that sovereign power is inherently "split". This "split" could be characterised as a trust, namely as a fiduciary relationship. This relationship meant that there would have to be a body which would invest (or constitute) an authority subject to a conditional command, the condition being that power should be exercised for the benefit of the investing body. The importance of the "split", within the concept of sovereignty, was that the condition of investment of power would be the ground for a continuous evaluative judgement regarding the extent to which the existence of the authority benefited the investing body. This would remain the case no matter how misconceived this judgement might be, on account of, say, fear or prejudice. The benefit was characterised, generally speaking, by what Bentham called "original utility" in so far as investment was more likely to achieve some goal than non-investment.[72] Hence, the existence of socially justified authority involved a continuing process of evaluating whether the authority could ultimately serve its purpose.

Sovereignty, therefore, could be limited by a constitutional *law*. This was because the law limiting sovereignty would have the two components essential for a law, namely an act and an expression of will with regard to this act. *Constitutional laws in principem*, "express conventions" and the like, would have the role of focusing the investing body's attention on the justification of

[71] *OLG*, p. 99.

[72] "Original utility" connotes assessments of potential consequences which concerned the distributive choices suggested by the measure in question (considering the measure in its own right). "Expectation utility" relates to the consequences stemming from the effects of the measure on existing social relations. See also chapter 4, p. 114, below, and Postema, *Bentham and The Common Law Tradition*, pp. 148–83.

authority. Their importance lay in the manner in which they facilitated an efficient and effective judgement based on authentic criteria. However, these laws must not encompass the whole activity which the concept of "sovereignty" signified.[73]

An authority might be given licence to legislate on every matter whatsoever, without saying categorically what it could not do. Hence a legislative authority could be theoretically unlimited because all the signs of limitation relating to it would be of *prima facie* status and hence subject to a fresh moral judgement by the "trusting", investing body. In short, the theoretical illimitability of sovereignty is compatible with prima facie social limitations on it. Every legislature might try to coerce the population in a new way. In this sense it would be unlimited. However, each new attempt to extend such coercion would be subject to a judgement as to its necessity.[74]

An authority invested with power could not be legally limited. Yet, as it was shown, it had to be, at least to some minimal extent, to be constitutionally limited by a constitutional law. It could be argued that a written constitution was some kind of entrenched basic law which limited legislative authority. Such a written constitution would be a procedurally entrenched limitation on the exercise of coercion by the legislature. By accepting the existence of a written constitution, the need for Bentham's distinction between the sovereign's status as never being legally limited, and its being constitutionally limited by constitutional law, could be avoided.

Bentham would answer that, even if one identified some basic entrenched "sign" expressing the limits of sovereignty, ultimately the sovereign who made *this basic law* would face the same problem of being superior and inferior at the same time. Any attempt to explain constitutional limits would face the same problem of legal limitation upon the supreme authority which promulgated these constitutional laws. Any such attempt would therefore amount to no more than a shifting of the problem to a more general level; it would by no means eliminate the question of how a sovereign could be legally limited.

The nature of the investing body's judgement

What did Bentham mean by "judgement" of the investing body? Would the resolution of the investing body follow, as Postema argued, an inference of a rule arising from some practice—and thus be simply a matter of the authentication

[73] This point is discussed in chapter 5, pp. 162–5. below.

[74] Such a state of affairs will be referred to below as the "enabling rationale" for the exercise of governmental powers: see chapter 5, pp. 143–5 below. In *Constitutional Code*, when Bentham said that to the legislature's power there were no limits, only checks, he meant that there should never be areas where potential coercion was totally excluded, since there could be a need for such coercion. However, there would be a check to prevent the legislature from acting against the public interest, and this check would constitute the *moral* general limitation on the sovereign: see *Constitutional Code*, pp. 41–2.

of normatively accepted customary rules about sovereignty? Or would it follow a critical moral judgement, namely a judgement which would operate to justify, according to utility, a choice between some courses of action?

In the first place the necessity for the investiture of a power to legislate calls for some explanation. In providing such an explanation it is essential to understand what "desire" meant for Bentham. Bentham maintained that once a person wanted to bring about an event, this event became an object of desire—an object of volition.[75] However, it might happen that in the view of the person who had a certain desire, its fulfilment could only be realised through an action undertaken by someone else. Under such circumstances, the required action by this other person would become the object of desire. The person who had the desire could then communicate his or her volition to the other person, who could bring about the desired event.[76] At the point of time at which a desire was formed, there may or may not exist any expectations as to the manner in which the other person would bring about the desired event.[77] It would usually be the case that the desire to bring about the event would be influenced by existing patterns of behaviour or expectations. Utility, as the basis of evaluation, therefore, had to take into account any convention of understanding with regard to how things might be done.

In our context, such an analysis explains the primary motive for investing a centralised power of coercion in some person. This investment occurred because of the *belief* that an action was necessary in order to bring about a better state of affairs than that which already prevailed. This state of affairs could not become a reality without such an investment. Here lies the reason for investment—the moral basis of socially justified authority. Centrally, sovereignty was a two-dimensional term, which involved two persons. One person must have the desire that the other should be superior. It might be said, by way of historical justification, that the original act of investment *had to be* voluntary and not natural, in that it was the product of the will of an investing person, however unsophisticated the harm which was to be avoided by that investment. This will would constitute the political authority. Although there was no need to invoke notions like a "social contract", an act of constitution was nevertheless necessary, although the terms of the constitution would be the subject of continuous change.[78] This explains why sovereignty *must* be a "split" concept in the sense discussed above, and why a socially justified authority would be inherently limited.

This idea of desire helps to explain more specifically how a relationship of superiority and subordination originated in a social context, and how the ground for the exercise of power was formed:

[75] Bowring, viii. 329.

[76] Ibid., pp. 329–30.

[77] Social and cultural circumstances would of course be the context in which a person formed his or her desires: see chapter 6, sections II–IV below.

[78] See chapter 4, p. 106, note 19 below.

> "In respect of power, **regard being had to the particular occasion and purpose in question**, what is his situation in life in relation and comparison to mine? Is it that, **in my view of the matter, I have it in my power** to exercise a greater influence on his wellbeing than he has on mine?"[79]

This passage shows that Bentham characterised the relationships of superiority, equality and subordination of power in the same way. The "view" or imagination in question would always relate to a specific situation, or a specific goal, and would also depend on an assessment made by the person in question as to whether it would be in his power to bring about certain consequences. The decision to invest would mean that it was thought to be *better* that the invested person exercise the authority in question.

Such an assessment was the starting point of the existence of political society and so it logically preceded any customary rule, a rule based on expectations concerning how authority should be exercised. The specific context of the following passage, namely a time of war, should be seen in the broader context of Bentham's discussion, in *Pannomial Fragments*, of the origin and persistence of coercive authority. The impulse towards the first establishment of authority was some "lack" in a form which was conceived as harmful. The avoidance of harm by a delegated authority was at the heart of the establishment of the trust which led to its constitution. The origin and development of authority in a political society was motivated by the expected pain which would arise from its non-existence:

> "It is not the rights of man which causes government to be established:—on the contrary, it is the non-existence of those rights. What is true is, that from the beginning of things it has always been desirable that rights should exist; and *that* because they do not exist—since, so long as there are no rights, there can only be misery upon the earth—no sources of political happiness, no security for person, for abundance, for subsistence, for equality:—for where is the equality between the famished savage who has caught some game, and the still more famishing savage who is dying because he has not caught any?"[80]

It has been seen that a critical judgement would form the object of the "judging" or "investing" body. This judgement was an inherent ingredient of "sovereignty". In the long footnote quoted from *OLG*,[81] it was shown that this body could then bring accusations against the coercing body concerning questions arising from its judgement.

In the context of sovereignty, this judgement could consist in the inference of a customary rule, an inference founded on observation of the practice of the legislature. The legislature would be expected to behave according to certain conventions, but Bentham also said:

79 Bowring, viii. 330.
80 Pannomial *Fragments*, Bowring, iii. 219.
81 See pp. 52–3 above.

> "So great in short is the influence of all these [original considerations of expediency which had produced measures of self-limitation] when taken together, that in any tolerably well settled government the successor is as much expected to abide by the covenants of his predecessor as by any covenants of his own: **unless where any change of circumstances has made a manifest and indisputable change in the utility of such adherence.**"[82]

There would be a utilitarian judgement, *in addition to the custom,* which determined the limits of sovereignty, or more precisely the limits of the social justification for coercion. A judgement was, for Bentham, an opinion. It was a dictate of utility.[83] A judgement or opinion was an act which belonged to a faculty of the mind which Bentham called the understanding.[84] Sovereignty was something more than the mere authenticity of law. A moral judgement was immanent in a resolution which concerned the limits of sovereignty. Such a judgement would be arrived at after a discussion and assessment by the investing body, in response to the fact that an alleged transgression of a custom had taken place.

Bentham's theory of sovereignty purported to explain the way in which one might have a desire, based on whatever reasons, to establish a body which would be superior to oneself. It helped to explain why there existed the desire for the investment of power. However, it seemed also to be the case that this investment should cease to operate once the subject arrived at a judgement, based on an understanding, that some superiority over him was no longer morally justified. Sovereignty for Bentham was not only concerned with a test for the "recognition" of measures as "authentic law". Sovereignty also embodied an evaluation of the need for authority. A point which marked the limitation of authority, or a constitutional limitation,[85] must be rooted in a moral judgement of "original utility" (whatever the actual quality of the judgement).

Summary, and implications for Bentham's legal positivism

It is now possible to reconstruct Bentham's understanding of the nature of sovereignty. Sovereignty was inherently "split" in that the concept *presupposed* a dynamic relationship between two bodies. The relationship which characterised sovereignty was that of a trust. The trust would be exercised by an authority acting as a fiduciary towards the body which had invested it with power. This trust was not a legal concept, in the immediate sense of the word, because it was inter-

[82] *OLG*, pp. 65–6.

[83] UC lxix. 90.

[84] Bowring, viii. 320. The exact meaning of "understanding" in this context will be discussed in more detail in chapter 6, pp. 199–206 below.

[85] It might be argued in terms of terminology that "*constitutional* limits" conveyed the idea of a "constitutive" or "investing" body which conditionally "constituted" or "invested" a body with authority. Thus under the interpretation suggested here, limits of sovereignty and constitutional limits connote the same meaning.

nal to the concept of sovereignty, itself presumed in Bentham's *general*, as opposed to *minimal*, understanding of a law. Yet, once the minimal characteristics of a law were considered, namely an act and an expression of will with regard to that act, this trust could be regarded as constitutional *law*, which was a peculiar type of law.[86] Suffice to say, at this stage, that like any other law, constitutional law, in its bare essentials, was composed of an act of volition and an object of volition. The act of volition was the act of an investing power. The object of the volition was that authority should be exercised in the investing body's interest. This object of the volition was dynamic in that it could change over time, as a group developed. As the group reflected on its practices, sometimes in relation to other groups, the object of volition could become more concrete in certain respects, or more abstract in other respects. Communal judgements would be triggered once potential transgressions by the authority occurred. The judgement consisted of an inference of a rule of custom, an inference which was an exercise of opinion, and one whose normativity was derived from expectations. However, the judgement which constituted sovereignty, and hence, constitutional limits, could be modified according to considerations of overall utility. In the case of a prima facie case of transgressing a custom, the investing body could form an opinion, an obligatory opinion, which could either accept the transgression of a customary rule as a legitimate practice, or not. In the latter case, the judgement might generate a volition to exercise divestitive powers.

A convention was, for Bentham, a sign which announced the reasons and will of the public at a certain moment, and which the reasons and will of any other moment might revoke.[87] A convention was only of prima facie status, as the whole notion of "disposition" was a prima facie concept. If obedience was to constitute sovereign power, if the limits of sovereignty were the limits of obedience, there would have to be an extra critical stage through which a judging body must go, namely an evaluative judgement in relation to the utility of having the very power to enact a new measure, *which could accord with or transcend* an existing convention pointing to this or that course of action. Only then would the process of a critical judgement, intrinsic to the concept of sovereignty, be completed. Bentham said:

> "The true rampart, the only rampart, against a tyrannical government has always been, and still is, the **faculty of allowing this disposition to obedience**—without which there is no government—**either to subsist or to cease.** The existence of this faculty is as notorious as its power is efficacious."[88]

The decision whether to persist or not in the disposition to obey could not be explained by merely saying there is a "disposition to obey".

[86] The nature of constitutional law will be discussed in chapter 5, pp. 160–8 below.
[87] Bowring, iii. 219.
[88] Ibid., 219.

Arguably, this analysis of sovereignty suggests that it formed a central aspect of Bentham's conceptual analysis of law, which cannot in consequence be regarded as positivistic. The argument criticises legal positivism as involving artificial isolation of a field of enquiry in the conceptual discussion of law. Bentham's account did not merely imply that law is *influenced, censored*, or *disobeyed* because of moral considerations—a claim which is compatible with the conceptual separation of these moral considerations from legal validity. There was much more to Bentham's understanding of sovereignty than the epistemic "recognition", as well as formal acceptance, of a certain measure as "law".

Legal positivism attempts to formalise the idea of validity and acceptance of rules. It does so by turning conceptual analysis of law into arguments about "authenticity". "Authenticity" connotes a formal, epistemic account which is associated with the term "validity", and "normativity" of legal rules. Such a formal account of validity and acceptance enables, so legal positivists claim, to differentiate epistemically the "legal" from other possible normative structures. Thus, law is capable of identification and acceptance without resort to moral considerations. Legal positivism separates legal validity and moral worth.

Hart's argument in favour of legal positivism is based upon the claim that two undesirable consequences follow from fusing legal validity and moral worth. The first is that of anarchy. This danger exists if moral worth is fused with legal validity because moral disagreement would deny the recognition of the measure in question as law: "because this law is unjust it is not law for me". The second is the entrenchment of bad laws on the basis that they are valid: "because that law is valid it is also morally just". The first danger implies the loss of all order and security, the second implies totalitarian arguments for the persistence of bad laws and so the loss of moral criticism.[89]

Bentham's theory of law encompassed more than merely recognising a measure as an authentic legal measure. Evaluative considerations were conceptually linked in his account to the understanding of an individual law. This is not to say that pernicious laws were not laws according to Bentham's account. My claim is entirely compatible with the existence of an unjust, or as it is commonly called, a "wicked" manifestation of sovereignty, and as a result, of law. The compatibility can be sustained because Bentham understood "morality" partly as a historically contingent, utilitarian interpretation and evaluation, according to which a political authority could be justified and limited, and partly as a utilitarian interpretation which observed, criticised and transcended such historical contingency. In the same way that a given utilitarian judgement could be confined to the past, being observed from a contemporary perspective, it was possible to speculate and to look upon the justification of authority as being to some extent contingent with regard to *any* society. The fact that law ought to be understood as involving evaluative considerations could, but need not to, exhaust the *interpretative* question as to whether these considerations were just

[89] See Hart, *The Concept of Law*, pp. 203–7.

or not in relation to the most abstract harm that a given historically contingent social world could conceive. For Bentham, arguments/interpretations/evaluations of acceptance and validity involved an ideological system of reference. However and further, any transcendence of this historical/ideological contingency would mean that perspective which enabled evaluative considerations and which underpinned previous arguments about validity and acceptance of law, was modified or replaced. The important point was that under no circumstances would validity and acceptance of law be conceptually divorced from evaluative considerations.[90]

Let me explain in more detail what is involved in rejecting Bentham's theory as fully-fledged legal positivism. What I claim is similar in nature to modern accounts of natural law. Modern accounts of natural law, such as that of Fuller's desiderata which accounted for what he called procedural-natural law,[91] and Finnis's idea of the self-evident basic goods,[92] and even Hart's account of the minimum content of natural law,[93] are all compatible with the existence of wicked laws and legal systems. While admitting the existence of law (and this would, presumably, include interpretation and argumentation about true proposition of law) in a wicked legal system, all these accounts claim that there are some moral features of law which are an inherent part of its universal description. All these accounts differentiate between universal properties of law which *must* include moral postulates and historically particular manifestations of them (again, including argumentation about true propositions of law within a given historical period of a community).

These modern accounts of natural law locate the universal domain of law as containing different moral criteria. All of them maintain that because certain moral features are necessary for the fulfilment of some *fundamental purpose*

[90] See *Essays on Bentham*, pp. 262–7, where Hart claimed that there were two versions of conceptual fusion between legal validity and moral worth. The extreme version would claim that legal obligations were species of moral obligations. This would be refuted by the existence of wicked legal systems. The moderate view would be that a legal obligation included moral beliefs, true or false, sincere or pretended (the last distinction is referred to by J. Raz, *The Authority of Law*, p. 28), that justify it. The moderate view would be compatible with legal positivism and could confine its application to officials and judges. However, Hart questioned even this moderate version by pointing towards social situations in which officials were not engaged in moral reasoning, and so concluded that a "committed" attitude to legal obligations *could*, but *need not*, include moral considerations.

Yet, in the context of the argument advanced here, Hart had a narrow view of the meaning of "moral considerations". "Moral considerations" could include many kinds of mental operations in considering the justness of an action. For example, a committed attitude which stemmed from adherence to custom could form *a part* of a critical reflection upon a state of affairs. In other words, many of the social situations which Hart raised to refute the moderate version of a conceptual fusion between law and morality, might themselves be regarded *as* forming the basis for moral considerations which would operate to evaluate substantively the trust which constituted political authority. Much more will be said on this point as the argument progresses: See pp. 74–5, note 104, chapter 4, pp. 113–16, and chapter 6, pp. 191–222 below.

[91] L. Fuller, *The Morality of Law* (New Haven , 1969).

[92] J. Finnis, *Natural Law and Natural Rights* (Oxford, 1980).

[93] Hart, *The Concept of Law*, pp. 189–95.

of law, they must form an inherent part of a conceptual account of law. Accordingly, these moral features cannot be reduced to formal legal validity.[94] The fact of the law being unjust, or interpreted unjustly, is therefore rendered compatible with the *universal conceptual account* of law having moral features which relate to the purpose of law. Thus, we can differentiate two levels of theorisation, one a universal conceptual account, the other a historically particular manifestation of it. Irreducible moral features of law are interpreted differently in different communities in a different stage of their historical development. An argument such as Hart's, that all laws are validated by a master rule of recognition, which is incorporated into every other law, but whose validity is not legal but social, requires further magnification and analysis of in what the recognition of such a rule consists.[95]

Moderate positivists such as Raz have attempted to soften this separation thesis. Raz has even attempted to reconcile the fact that both adjudicative processes and acceptance of rules involve the resort to moral considerations with the epistemic closure of legal systems.[96] Arguably, however, Raz's theory of law, by conceptualising the basis for its authoritative nature, cannot be a complete analysis of law in this respect. Raz's account involves the underplaying of a purposive universal model, interpretative in nature, according to which the very fact of certain utterances having authoritative status is explained and justified. In adhering to the positivist thesis, namely identification of law without directly resorting to morality, Raz reduces an implied social complexity. In particular, Raz's theory formalises, and therefore does not accommodate, a model the derivation from which would endow a person or a body of persons with political authority. His separation of the statement: "this is in fact an authority" from the statement: "this is an account of reasons which makes *x* an authority" is too strong and too clinical. Raz's thesis that "authority exists for reasons" is a sufficiently stable formula for regarding the precise nature of the formation of these reasons as a non-question for the conceptual identification of authoritative, and in turn legal, propositions. However, by virtue of which conceptual model can we account for the fact that certain utterances acquire an exclusionary status? The question of "why have an authority?" is globalised into what Raz calls "auxiliary reasons".[97] How do authoritative utterances acquire the CIPR status? By not conceptualising certain types of reasons for the investiture and divestiture of political authority of its status as such, Raz underplays the conceptual connection that exists between a critical justificatory model which accounts for the constitutive role of political authority and the factual manifes-

[94] Reciprocity between officials and the population, involving moral considerations, has been included in a conceptual analysis of law by modern scholars: see R. Sartorius, "Positivism and the Foundation of Legal Authority", in R. Gavison (ed.), *Issues in Contemporary Legal Philosophy: The Influence of H.L.A. Hart* (Oxford, 1987), pp. 43–61, at 43.

[95] In *Natural Law and Natural Rights*, p. 21, Finnis stresses the need for further analysis of the rule of recognition.

[96] See, *The Authority of Law,* chapter 3.

[97] See Raz, *Practical Reasons and Norms,* pp. 33–5.

tation of this status in every case which involves authority and law. It is through this dramatic underplaying of complexity that Raz is able offer a positivist thesis of law which is allegedly sensitive to morality but which defends a legal closure at the same time. The question that one is left with when reading Raz's account is: given further magnification of the idea of authority, could we elucidate a model which would have to be assumed in every conceptual account of authority and law? This very much-needed model may include a description of a critical interpretative process, historical on many levels (history of the interpretation of an ideology, history of the breakdown of ideologies), which involves the basic investment of, and limitations upon, authority in a social group.

The problem that such a reductionist account causes is a normative puzzle with regard to the whole notion of exclusionary reason. Does the concept or exclusionary reason which evolves into the status of protected and pre-emptive reasons for action,[98] explain a level of reasoning which it can never exclude, namely a level which involves reasons to invest a body with, and divest it of, political authority? This never-fully-excluded level of reasoning can be presented as being a part of "exclusionary" force of the exclusionary reason only as a result of an artificial maintenance and sanctification of the positivist separation thesis. In fact, however, this level conditions the exclusionary status that reasons have, and hence must be different from it, though this does not mean that the concept of political authority could be convincingly accounted for by removing it from the field of enquiry and presenting it as "auxiliary". The relevance of this other level, though not the existence of it, to a conceptual account of law, seems to be a non-question for Raz. If there is such a conceptual model, what does it involve? Arguably, if a full conceptual analysis of authority is undertaken in relation to the conceptual analysis of law, authoritative utterances operate not only as protected and pre-emptive reasons (or as CIPR). The exclusionary function of authority meshes with, rather than merely being influenced by, another conceptual model. A severance of that model seriously undermines Raz's conception of law. It undermines it because it fails to identify and explore the deepest nature and function of a *judicial* (as being broader and more fundamental than an *adjudicative*) activity that forms a part of the normative structure of authority, a consciousness that any institutional, judicial, constitutional, interpretative processes are connected to.

So much for the arguable reductionism involved in legal positivism's separation thesis. This sophisticated model of legal positivism is today contrasted with an interpretative model of law advocated by Dworkin. Law for Dworkin, in stark contrast to the positivist thesis, consists of a moral argument. One cannot make sense of true legal proposition unless one makes a moral justificatory argument about why a certain proposition of law is true or false. There is no law

[98] For the difference between exclusionary protected and pre-emptive reasons for action, see note 51, p. 55 above.

to be "found" and beyond it to be "developed", "refined" or "created". There are only legal arguments to be made, and these are moral arguments about coherency of moral principles featured in a political morality of a community, itself an interpretative construct.[99] Dworkin denies the possibility of separating moral argument about law and any epistemic closure of law. Legal positivists are unable to account for a practice which shows that lawyers and judges used justificatory moral arguments which may embody different theoretical purposes for law, in order to justify true legal propositions in a given case. The threshold objection to positivism is that it is notoriously unhelpful in accounting for both the creativity and constraint which characterises legal argument. Positivism cannot explain what is going on in legal practice, namely the way justifications of true legal propositions are made and critically justified.[100]

It is difficult, and perhaps somewhat unhelpful, to locate precisely Bentham within this positivist/interpretative debate. However, as mentioned above, Bentham's understanding of sovereignty and as a result, his conceptual account of law, cannot be reduced to the positivist's separation thesis. Arguably, in this Bentham would also support an interpretative thesis. The analysis of sovereignty in this chapter offers a socially dynamic interpretative model about the limits to the justification of authority. This is a universal model which forms a part of both legislation and adjudicative interpretative processes in any particular community. To put it another way, anything universal which is said either about legislation or adjudicative processes must assume the socially dynamic interpretative model about the justification of authority argued for here. This model recognises a conceptual continuum between knowing the law and the critical acceptance of it. Bentham's attempts at codification may perhaps be seen as something which functionally assists this socially dynamic interpretative process, something which facilitates public communication and interpretation. However, it does not make him a legal positivist. Despite his lifelong attempt at codification, this model of sovereignty, which was essentially about the moral reasons involved in the investment of authority, did not merely state that some authoritative utterance existed as a matter of fact or, as a socially static description of a normative structure. It would involve a reduction to claim that at any given time of historical development law exists *as a matter of fact* because the justification of authority would have to be argued for and justified. As I shall argue below, political authority which carried authoritative status was understood by Bentham as an outcome of an ongoing interpretative process of social interaction between governors and governed. The outcome of this interpretation would constitute the co-ordinates according to which some moral argu-

[99] Raz objects to Dworkin's attempt to develop a theory of law *as* judicial interpretation and claims that it undermines the authoritative nature of law. Arguably, the very fact that Raz conceives a theory of "law as interpretation" as a "problem" is telling, because Dworkin's view is compatible with Raz's own normative structure though *not* with his maintenance of the positivist separation thesis: see "Authority, Law and Morality", *Monist* 68 (1975) 295–324.

[100] For a general view of Dworkin's theory, see his *Taking Rights Seriously* (London, 1977), chapters 2 and 4, and *Law's Empire*, chapters 1–7.

ments in a more particular level about the justification of coercion could be seen as better than others. Bentham's theory of law incorporated social interpretation but locates the communal hermeneutic thesis within a universal conceptual model of authority. He did not, of course, offer as developed a theory of adjudication as Dworkin's and in this respect his tackling of the explanation of legal practice is undoubtedly lacking.[101] However, despite the importance he attached to certainty and predictability, through a publicly accessible code of law, his broader theory of law is closer to an interpretative approach to law rather than to a positivistic one. His positive code for individual laws need not commit him to the separation thesis of legal positivism. His universal conceptual model which encompassed two-dimensional understanding of sovereignty could feature in any actual interpretative community which justifies coercion within it. In this sense, the social interpretation is to be presumed in any more particular, and hence ideal-orientated, adjudicative, interpretative theory of law. This model also explains the social change of that justification (and, with it, the ambit of interpretation) as a community changes. Having said that, Bentham would reject Dworkin's conception of law as integrity. "Law as Integrity" calls for the ongoing construction of moral coherence from the complexity that the practice of legal reasoning establishes. Under utilitarian theory of law, a socially dynamic, interpretative thesis of authority would mean that the unquestionably accepted, even ideological, framework which constrains interpretative creativity as to constitutional limits is itself understood as historically contingent and transient. Any conception of harm—harm to be averted by law—which constitutes an interpretative system of reference, within which one could always justify (and refute) a phenomenological, non-demonstrative (in other words "argumentative") coherence, would itself be transient. This would mean that law as interpretative integrity would not have a basis to arbitrate a theoretical disagreement between different conceptions of harm.[102]

IV

This section assesses the implications of the above reconstruction of Bentham's theory of sovereignty for both Hart's critique and Postema's interpretation. In relation to Hart's criticism of Bentham with regard to the normativity of law, it is conceded that a volition of *a sovereign* would on most occasions appear to operate as a CIPR. However, Hart (and Raz for that matter) did not allow any room for the socially dynamic and critical dimension which characterised the very concept of sovereignty, properly understood. This dimension meant that

[101] For an attempt to reconcile Bentham's positivism with a theory of adjudication, see Postema, *Bentham and the Common Law Tradition*, chapter 12.

[102] See chapter 7. Cf. S. Fish, *Doing What Comes Naturally: Change, Rhetoric, and the Practice of Theory in Literary and Legal Studies* (Oxford, 1989), chapter 16 and A. Marmor, *Interpretation and Legal Theory* (Oxford, 1992), chapters 3, 4, esp. pp. 73–82.

authority would be justified only to the extent that the investing body understood it to be morally expedient for it to operate as CIPR. Hart would probably treat such an argument as circular. Yet, the level of reflection about sovereignty was more general and latent than the apparent and immediate level of the operation of volitions as CIPR. A command would operate to exclude only immediate reasoning and would be peremptory and content-independent only to this "immediate" extent. The immediate exclusion of reasoning could be observed by any anthropologist who perceived the authority that the *law* actually has. However, categorical reasoning which related to the most general critical justifications of the institution of law could not be fully excluded by a political authority. The nature of such categorical reasoning could change from one social group to another. In some groups it could be made ineffective, for various reasons, but it could never be fully excluded. The split nature of sovereignty must operate, to some degree at least, in order to justify the authority in question. In short, there would be a constitutional, or categorical level, which will be discussed in more detail in Chapter 4, at which critical reasoning relating to the social justification of coercion could never be excluded by authoritative utterances.

Hart cannot consistently claim, on the one hand, that there is a customary social rule of recognition which operates to validate other rules, and, on the other hand, exclude the moral dimension which the existence and operation of such a customary rule would necessarily involve. Further, he cannot convincingly exclude from a universal explanation of "validity" the moral judgement of the governed, which would be triggered in every case of transgression of collective expectations, whether such a moral judgement was sound or based on misconceptions. This chapter has argued that Hart did not succeed in doing away with the concept of "sovereignty" (which, according to Austin's account, seemed to involve the existence of a de facto relationship of power), and replacing it with the idea of "recognition", which arguably better represented the normative dimension of law.[103] The idea of formal recognition and acceptance underplayed a tension which related to the exchange of reasons, the outcome of which was the volition of investing or divesting authoritative power. The idea of recognition was not a novel situation with which the concept of sovereignty could not be grappled. Properly understood, the concept of sovereignty encapsulated a dynamic, reasoned communicative exchange of expressions of wills, descriptions of actions and relationship of subordination and superiority.[104] Law is still a matter of fact under Hart's theory. The interpretation of

[103] The distinction between legality and validity in relation to Hart is discussed in chapter 5, pp. 168–72 below.

[104] An argument to the effect that notions of sovereignty and the normativity of law might consist of more than authenticity was first put forward by MacCormick in his analysis of Hart's "internal point of view". MacCormick claims that one should look more closely at the normativity of law and hence into the social manifestation of the "internal point of view". Normativity may not only concern authenticity (which would depend on a cognitive faculty), but may involve volitional elements on the part of persons who accept it. Even in what appears to be an uncritical reflection, these

Bentham's theory of sovereignty offered in this chapter has implications for the significance of the distinctions Hart drew between validity and effectiveness and validity and legality. The proper place to discuss them is in Chapter 5 when an analysis of constitutional law will be offered on the basis of the broad argument of the book.

Postema detected considerable similarity between Hart's and Bentham's accounts of sovereignty. Both Hart and Bentham saw sovereignty *as* an authenticity test by which coercive measures were categorised as law. Further, for both, Postema claimed, sovereignty connoted a normativity which would ultimately be generated by social facts or practices. However, he also argued that Bentham's theory was more sophisticated than Hart's. Bentham allowed people more participation in determining the limits of this authenticity test. More particularly, Postema firstly claimed that Hart did not emphasise the potential social effects which people's attitudes might have in determining the limits of sovereignty. Secondly and further, Postema's account implied that Hart did not elaborate sufficiently on the *normative* dimension of the epistemic test of ascertaining rules concerning legal validity, as far as the people, as opposed to officials, were concerned. As far as the second of Postema's arguments is concerned, it has been maintained above that Hart suggested that the people, even if not necessarily in possession of a critical, reflective attitude towards the rule of recognition, would, for various reasons, see authoritative utterances as peremptory content independent, that is as normative. In other words, contrary to what Postema's account implied, Hart did recognise that the test of recognition *is* normative for anyone, though such normativity could take many shapes. Arguably

volitional elements would include some judgements according to which the act of recognition would be founded on some perceived satisfaction of self-interest: see *Legal Reasoning and Legal Theory* (Oxford, 1978 (2nd edn. 1994)), pp. 290–1. Volition certainly seems necessary to the internal point of view. What MacCormick calls a volitional element would also involve a judgement upon which the volition should be based. Otherwise the volition would be an effect without a cause.

MacCormick's argument is refined in *H.L.A. Hart* (London, 1981), pp. 33–40, especially p. 35, where he argues that the "internal point of view" might consist of both cognitive *and* volitional elements. MacCormick goes further to explicate something akin to what Raz called a "detached statement" (*The Authority of Law*, pp. 157–9). MacCormick calls such statements "non-extreme external statements", in which people have the cognitive *but not the volitional* element in their attitude towards rules. One would need, MacCormick argues, only to assume a hypothetical "internal point of view" in order to describe legal phenomena in a socially sensitive way. Further still, it would be possible for people to argue critically about a basic proposition in regard to the acceptance of a rule as authoritative, without feeling any volition as a result of these critical judgements, that is without feeling "a commitment" towards them. In short, a critical judgement, in whatever form, need not lead to volition.

The argument in this chapter is that although some individuals may be purely conformists, and as such could hardly have any volitional elements in their acceptance of rules (or indeed, some of them *may* be critical without having any volition in relation their acceptance), the people as a "trusting body" would of necessity have a volitional element, based on a judgement or preference, however minimal this judgement might be. Under my interpretation of Bentham, both the volition and cognition of officials and "the people" as a trusting and judging body would be interpretative with regard to the social justification of authority. The distinction between "officials" and "people" in this respect would be one of degree only; see also p. 44 above.

also for Hart, a minimal requirement for the existence of a legal system—a recognition test applied by the people—would be normative in nature. Hence, only the first of the above claims by Postema is fully accepted here, namely that Hart underestimated the role people necessarily played in the general network of social interaction which determined the limits of sovereignty.

By not including the normative acceptance of the people, Postema rightly claimed, Hart could easily distinguish between the validity and the efficacy of the law. Hart's initial move was to explicate the term "recognition" as connoting authenticity. The next was to oversimplify this understanding of "recognition" by removing the people's participation in interpreting and shaping the criteria of authenticity. This Hart did at the expense of not explaining how official actions, of both judges and legislators, could be justified by reference to communal interpretation.[105] Having said that, Postema's own interpretation of the epistemic normative recognition conceives sovereignty still as a static and formal test for the "authenticity" of rules, coupled to formal acceptance of rules through the normative force of expectations. This interpretation does not capture fully the interpretative, justificatory and critical elements in Bentham's account of the concept of sovereignty. It is still too positivistic in approach and as such it is incomplete. Bentham's theory of sovereignty attempted not only to deal with the identification of authority, but also with the social justification of the exercise of authority, *despite his recognition that these were different notions*.

In one instance the authenticity of the authority and normative force from existing expectations might be identified with its justification. This instance was where expectations were created by a common customary recognition of such authority. Customary rules could, therefore, be seen as justifying this authority. However, this would be only a "weak" sense of justification. A "stronger" notion would also be present in answering the questions whether the authority in question was needed, and whether there would be occasions on which its existence could not be justified, despite its operation being within the criteria provided by the customary rules, and indeed vice versa. The point is that the common epistemic meaning of the term "authenticity" was insufficient to account for law in a socially sensitive way, unless its meaning expanded beyond the positivist thesis to include critical justification. An interpretative dimension of sovereignty was vital to the understanding of the authority of law although on many occasions it may not be immediately apparent.

I must caution again against a possible misinterpretation of the argument. It is not my claim that Bentham identified the issue of justification of authority with a view that authority did not exist if it did not act justly. People could, and often would, arrive at a misguided judgement as to the justification of the authority in their society.[106] What is claimed, however, is that the people, to

[105] Postema, *Bentham and The Common Law Tradition*, pp. 256–7.

[106] See the discussion of the senses of "ought" in Bentham's theory, chapter 1, pp. 13–22 above.

some extent, must regard the authority's existence as justified on the balance of utilities, *in addition* to any inference of a customary rule from existing practices. My argument is that although legal positivism, in conceptually separating legal validity and moral worth, attempts to provide a complete account of political authority, ultimately it fails to do so convincingly. It fails because it does not recognise an irreducibly, morally evaluative dimension in the justification of authority, involving the exercise of a collective moral judgement.

Postema attributes to Bentham an account of authenticity which is based purely on custom. Postema is correct to claim that a given customary practice would be the basis from which ultimate constitutional rules would be inferred, at least on a prima facie basis. Yet this account does not address Bentham's central concerns. Why did certain people have authority? What ultimate mischief could such an authority prevent? Must some belief exist about the possibility of such prevention, *however mistaken this belief might be*? Would there be a point where the danger of such ultimate mischief would cease to exist? Was a discussion of the notion of "sovereignty" exhausted by describing the normativity arising solely from past social practices?

Custom can have only prima facie status, and can only form a *part* of a doctrine of sovereignty. Bentham recognised this, and, in one of the passages quoted by Postema from *OLG*, he wrote: "the authority of the sovereign is founded *or at least in a great degree influenced* by custom and disposition".[107] It was clearly not Bentham's intention fully to identify custom with sovereignty, since, on his own account, custom only influenced sovereignty. Custom would not be sufficient, of itself, to explain the relationship between rulers and ruled. Why, for instance, is a transgression of a certain custom sometimes accepted by the people, and sometimes not? Could the answer to such a question involve something more fundamental than asserting that "the people's opinion *censures* the authority"? As has been argued above, when Bentham wrote about *constitutional laws in principem*, he argued that the recommendatory mandate from one sovereign to the other would, as a matter of expediency, in *most cases* be adopted.

Postema's account of custom is intended to be interactional. As has just been argued, Bentham claimed that custom would play a part in influencing the judgement about the justification of a coercive authority. However, the idea of "interactional custom" is incoherent. One should look more closely at the general meaning of the idea of interaction. If x's act contradicts y's expectations with regard to what should be x's act, to say that y would resist x's act would still be a mechanical, not an interactional, description. However, if y does not resist, something *other than* these expectations must cause him not to resist. This "something" which causes him not to resist is exactly the reason by which x influenced him, something which has to do with his understanding. Hence, by going beyond the notion of mechanical obedience, Postema should give us an

[107] Quoted in Postema, *Bentham and The Common Law Tradition*, p. 255.

account of the nature of this extra "something". This "something" cannot be explicated merely by stating that the custom is interactional. To argue thus would be stating the tautology: "*x* interacts with *y* because *x* interacts with *y*". In short, there is a logical gap between validity and interaction that Postema's account, or any positivistic interpretation of law for that matter, could resolve.

Where Postema quotes Bentham to the effect that the essence of the interaction is contained in a habit of commanding on one side, accompanied by a habit of obeying on the other, or on the one part in a disposition to expect obedience, and on other in the disposition to pay it, he arguably says very little.[108] He does not succeed in transforming the mechanical model of the relationship between rulers and ruled into an interactional one. In short, it is not clear that Postema's account is able to differentiate between two cases: first, where the sign constitutes a signal for resistance, because an act had transgressed expectations; and secondly, where the transgression of expectations would operate merely to *shape* future expectations. Hence, my claim is that Postema's account is unsuccessful in explaining Bentham's repeated assertion that sovereignty is constituted *by* the obedience of the governed. Postema's account still clings to the thesis of legal positivism and does not capture the socially dynamic interpretative process that characterises Bentham's theory of sovereignty.[109]

[108] Ibid., p. 255.

[109] Postema's view of the justification of authority (which gets closer to my reading of Bentham) is one of "constructive conventionalism", which arguably implies a critical judgement: see "The Normativity of Law", in R. Gavison (ed.), *Issues in Contemporary Legal Philosophy*, pp. 74–104, at 92–104.

3

The Relativity and Plurality of Sovereignty

> It is evident that in point of fact sovereignty over any given individual is a matter which is liable to much diversity and continual fluctuation. Subjection depends for its commencement upon birth: but for its continuance it depends upon a thousand accidents. In body he can be subject to but one at a time: but in mind, in reputation and in property he may be subject to multitudes at once.
>
> *OLG*, p. 20.

> That the quantity of these [possessions, such as, Reputation, Honour, Glory] which, in the situation of sovereign, it will be in a man's power to possess will be in proportion to the quantity of power in the international and in the national sense which he possesses—the power which he and his subjects possess with reference to the rulers and subjects of other nations and the power which he possesses with reference to and at the expense of his own subjects—is manifest enough.
>
> *Deontology*, p. 231

I

In this chapter two important features of sovereignty—its relative and plural nature—are discussed. In *OLG*, Bentham, as part of his initial definition of an individual law, noted that a law would be made in *a state*.[1] This appears awkward, because the aim of the book was to give a universal definition of an individual law, that is one which held for all places and at all times. The inclusion of a nation state was an odd step for Bentham to take, because many other forms of legal activity can exist without it. One can imagine the existence of various legal frameworks, some narrower, and some wider, than the nation state.

By "state" Bentham may have meant something very different from the popular understanding of it. The popular understanding of a nation state characterises it as consisting of an assignable territory, populated by assignable people, with a centralised regulative agency.[2] In contrast, Bentham, it will be argued,

[1] *OLG*, p. 1.

[2] For a definition of a state in international law, see L. Henkin, R.C. Pugh, O. Schachter and H. Smit (eds), *International Law—Cases and Materials* (Minnesota, 1987), pp. 229–30.

used this word to signify the crystallisation of some relationship of superiority and subordination in a social group which could persist over time. This general understanding of "a state" is more in accord with Bentham's account of a "political society" put forward in *Fragment*. In short, "political society" is a broader notion than a "nation state". At any moment in time, and *a fortiori* in historical processes, the social manifestations of sovereignty are liable to change. Sovereignty need not imply that institutions exist within the framework of a nation state. Sovereignty relates to the idea of "political community", of which a nation state is but one particular manifestation. As far as historical development is concerned, the nation state has been very important. It was vital that, to use Bentham's phrase, the "track of civilization" for a given society should reach a stage where political processes occur within what is usually understood by "a nation state", and should be realised in such a state in a manner which would achieve the greatest happiness. A stage of mature "statehood" was important, in that it facilitated the continuation of a process of self-reflection by the community on the desirability of the persistence of state-based coercion.

Bentham realised that an individual law was capable of existing in many more contexts than that of the nation state. He saw sovereignty both as a relative concept, and as one which could have plural applications in a social group. First, with regard to the relative nature of sovereignty, the possibility of flexible social manifestations of an individual law has generally been treated by Bentham scholars as involving the division of sovereignty.[3] However, the notion of a "division" of sovereignty cannot fully capture the way in which law is able to mirror the flexible nature of a "political community". The idea of "division" is static, and does not capture the dynamic, reciprocal influences of the various spheres of legal operation. Although the notion of division may convey the sense of a number of sovereign spheres (such as judiciary and legislature), it can hardly account for their interdependence. The language of "division" is the language of static facts. For example, to say, "In this community sovereign power is exercised by such and such agencies in this other matter, and by such and such other agencies in this matter", is to describe a "division" of sovereignty. The language of the relativity of sovereignty, on the other hand, captures the divided nature of sovereignty and to that extent overlaps with division, but in addition conveys the mutual normative influence and interdependence of the divided spheres. In other words, through the idea of "division", each sphere of legal operation can be described in isolation from the other spheres. The idea of relativity implies that each sphere *cannot be fully understood* without some reference to its relationship with another sphere. "Relativity" means that a particular legal sphere cannot be conceptually distinguished from the context in which it operates. The notion of relativity, unlike that of division, permits discussion of many spheres,

[3] See, for instance, J.H. Burns, "Bentham on Sovereignty: An Exploration", *Northern Ireland Legal Quarterly* 24 (1973) 399–416, at 406–7; Hart, *Essays on Bentham*, pp. 226–7.

all of which, *at the same time*, operate as contexts for other spheres, and within contexts of yet other spheres. In short, the idea of relativity conveys more adequately the social dynamism which exists between various spheres of legal operation.

The second point in this chapter concerns the plurality of sovereignty. In Chapter 2, it was argued that sovereignty was a two-dimensional, or a "split", notion, in that it involved both a coercive body, and another body which would both constitute and continuously pass judgement on the social justification of coercive measures. This conceptual discussion of sovereignty implied a unity of judgement on the part of a trusting, or constituting, body. However, as well as a legal philosopher, Bentham was a social theorist who also looked at actual social possibilities in assessing the plausibility of an analysis of legal concepts. He theorised that the actual function of "communities" in general, and "political societies" in particular, was constantly changing. The flexibility of his view of a "community" influenced his view with regard to what state of affairs could amount to "legislation" and "a law". Both his theory of legislation and his theory of an individual law formed parts of a legal philosophy which viewed law as operating on many social levels. Many actions which were not usually considered as "legal" in common speech would be embodied within such a theory. The existence of a multiplicity of "communities", within which sovereignty was exercised, will be referred to as the "plurality of sovereignty".

In acknowledging the multiplicity of "communities", it was important for Bentham to account for how the relative and the plural nature of sovereignty related to one another. He would maintain that it would not be sufficient for a socially sensitive legal theory to focus solely on the various social manifestations of legal operations (as manifested in the plural nature of sovereignty). Legal sociologists who call for a more extended view of what may be considered "law"[4] have tended not to focus on what ties together such a multiplicity of legal manifestations into a whole—into a united coercive enterprise.[5] Again, for Bentham, the relativity of sovereignty was a means of reconciling an underlying unity of legal phenomena with legal pluralism. On the one hand, there was the need to account for the diversification of legal practice. For example, legal operations took place at the levels of family, school and state. Further, regulations which characterised a particular ethnic group within the state, could be seen as "law" despite their having little or no connection to state-based law. On the other hand, a socially sensitive account of how these various spheres of legal operation were united in a legal order was an essential part of any conception of law.

[4] Such as E. Ehrlich, *Fundamental Principles of the Sociology of Law* (Cambridge, Mass., 1936), pp. 9–48, 71, 198–203, 346–9; see also R. Cotterrell, *The Sociology of Law*, pp. 25–8; see further G. Gurvitch, *Sociology of Law* (London, 1947), pp. 156–81, and his discussion of Ehrlich, ibid., pp. 116–22; see finally K.N. Llewellyn, "The Normative, The Legal and The Law Jobs: the Problem of Juristic Method", *Yale Law Journal* 49 (1940) 1355–400, at 1374–9.

[5] Cf. chapter 7.

It is not easy to combine in a single theory accounts of both the unity and the plurality of legal operations. To focus solely on unity as the main subject of analysis (as Kelsen did in his idea of law as a coercive *order*, or Hart in his conception of the idea of law as a *system* of rules, or even Dworkin in his account of law as "integrity", which has at its core a personification of interpretative communities) is to risk losing sight of the diversity of legal operations, as reflected in the diversity of the relationships of superiority and subordination between and within groups.[6] For example, when describing law in a given society, it could be argued that sovereignty was exercised by many agents at the same time, rather than by the monolithic, ultimately validating, state. A universal theory of law that placed the emphasis on the dichotomy of officials and citizens would risk describing law in too simplistic a fashion.

These ideas of "relativity" and "plurality" of sovereignty are functionally connected to, but should not be confused with, the two-dimensional nature of the concept of sovereignty. Relativity and plurality are social conditions which manifest themselves in a unique way in different groups. The conceptual split of sovereignty reappears at each level of the operation of sovereignty. However, it will also be argued in the final section that the different spheres in which sovereignty operates, or the different spheres in which a relationship of superiority and subordination exists, can influence one another. This influence might contribute to self-reflection in each sphere with regard to its scope *qua* sphere. In other words, mutual influences might give rise to critical reflection about the terms of the trust which constituted sovereignty, reflection which would take place within every social framework in which such a trust was in operation.

II

In *Fragment,* Bentham related the existence of a political society to the habit of obedience of the population to a common superior.[7] A "natural" society would not have this feature of the "habit of obedience". In the context of discussing the differences between natural and political society, Bentham made some comments, admittedly quite abstract ones, about the nature of political society. These comments show that he started to grapple with the complex social manifestation of sovereignty.[8] First, Bentham argued that there was a strict correspondence between the existence of "political" and "natural" qualities in a group, and the way in which the social group was structured. It would be too simplistic to conceive a society purely in terms of an institutional, centralised coercive authority, which would be habitually obeyed by a second body, gener-

[6] On the issue of unity, see P.M.S. Hacker, "Hart's Philosophy of Law", in J. Raz and P.M.S. Hacker (eds), *Law, Morality and Society—Essays in Honour of H.L.A. Hart* (Oxford, 1977) pp. 1–25, at 22–5.

[7] *Fragment*, p. 428.

[8] Ibid., pp. 429–34.

alised under the name of "people". Some relationship in a group could involve a habit of obedience to a centralised coercive mechanism, but no group could, in its entirety, be spoken about as being totally "political", or totally "natural".

Diversification within groups varied from one society to another. Anthropological observations would reveal every society to be a hybrid of the "natural" and the "political", according to the social manifestations in different frameworks of a "habit of obedience". Bentham discussed explicitly the variety of manifestations of a "political society". The query whether a society was "natural" or "political" could only be answered in relation to a given person, and as such could have many answers, depending on the specific relationship the person in question bore to other persons. A person could be conceived to obey habitually and *at the same time* not to obey with respect to different persons. Hence, the idea of "political" society was relative to the object of habitual obedience. The same person could be, at one and the same time, in both "natural" and "political" society, depending on the "object of obedience". This was important, because it hinted at the potential complexity of Bentham's conception of a political society, a complexity which he might not yet have fully appreciated at the time of writing *Fragment*. Any discussion of the concept of society, and *a fortiori* of political society, would be necessarily problematic. In short, it made no theoretical sense to make general statements about "society", though such statements were commonly made.

Secondly, Bentham's account in *Fragment* concerned the nature of this "habit of obedience". Bentham argued that a habit of obedience could have a variety of manifestations. It could exist, for instance, within a family. However, Bentham also argued that in order to qualify as a defining characteristic of political society, the habit of obedience would have to be of a continuous nature, and be capable of persisting indefinitely. A family, when looked upon in isolation, could cease to exist, when the parents died for example, and so it would be improper to characterise it as a "political society". It is important to note, in this context, that Bentham said neither that the "habit" needed to be homogeneous, so as to be practised by all people within the group in question, nor that the body obeyed must have the same characteristics all the time (for example, be a certain type of institution). No actual institutional framework, such as a "state", was mentioned. Not even an analysis of what "political" might mean was offered, except that it was related to an act of a person who governed. It was a very abstract discussion, which explained the minimal defining characteristic of a "political" society as a persistent "habit of obedience".[9]

The third point arises from the previous two. In *Fragment*, Bentham began to capture the idea of the relativity of sovereignty. He showed the importance of grasping the relative nature of political society, as opposed to the mere division of a certain organisation. There was no point in speaking about a family as a "political society" unless family activities could be carried out in the context of

[9] *Fragment*, p. 429.

some other social activity which would be more persistent.[10] The *context* of an act was crucial. A context of persistent social activity which was followed by a group of people gave a unity to many diverse, even private, manifestations of obedience, and embodied them in a *unified* legal discourse. Bentham was well aware of the inadequacy of common discourse, which was guilty of offering oversimplified statements about "society".

More particularly, social activity would give rise to diverse relationships of superiority and subordination. For sovereignty to be understood, the possibility of a habit of obedience which occurred simultaneously between numerous parties on different levels of generality had to be accounted for. Social descriptions were potentially complex, so if one wanted to assess whether a certain relationship between two parties ought to be characterised as "natural" or "political", another question may have to be asked, namely "in relation to which other relationship do the parties in question stand?" These other persons? The rest of humankind? In the presently discussed passages from *Fragment*, the relativity of sovereignty can be seen to be central to Bentham's understanding of social processes in general, and of authoritative relationships within a social group in particular. At any given point of time, one could see many individual situations as having the same normative status by virtue of their being performed within a wider social context of a power/habit of obedience relationship. For example, an individual's relationship of obedience in a family could have the same normative status as another's relationship of obedience at school. Their similarity of status would come about because both were manifested within a wider social context of habit of obedience, such as a local authority. One can see the dynamism of his account—an ever-changing relationship of superiority and subordination—which would embrace diversification as well as unity. The extent to which a person lived in a "political society" could change over time. A person might enter into a whole variety of social relations in relation to his group, or other groups. These relations might be of a "natural" or "political" nature. A person could be in a state of either "political", or "natural", society, in relation to his family, or indeed, in relation to other groups or communities, depending on the social context and the particular act in question.

Bentham completed this abstract discussion with an illuminating remark. On the basis of his abstract description of a political society, and its many manifestations within a social group, Bentham warned of the danger of oversimplification in talking about a "corporate action". He warned of the pitfalls of any simplistic model (the "social contract" might have been his target here) in speaking about general "consent" as a characterisation of a "political society". At this point he acknowledged the need to extend the discussion, but indicated that it would go beyond the design of *Fragment* to do so.[11]

[10] See chapter 2, p. 59 above (including Burns's discussion of the issue, referred to in note 62 therein).

[11] *Fragment*, p. 433.

Bentham again returned to the idea of the complexity of a social group in the context of his discussion of the relativity of sovereignty. He gave the example of the Dutch Provinces, where Spain was sovereign, to illustrate the possible varieties of sovereignty.[12] Further, he claimed that a "political society" might consist of a number of states, and include more general political unions, such as the German Empire. Sovereignty would be limited in any given state in cases where jurisdiction belonged to more extensive political bodies. Therefore, a person might belong to various political communities *at the same time*. To take a contemporary example, the question is not whether a person in the United Kingdom is subject either to "the sovereignty" of the UK or to that of the European Union. Rather, the question can only be answered precisely in relation to a certain matter, and in relation to certain persons. But if a generalised answer is sought, people are subject to the sovereignty of both communities *at the same time;* these communities are mutually inclusive rather than mutually exclusive.

The degree of relativity, and hence limitability and divisibility, of sovereignty in relation to a given people in each particular community would be determined by social observation.[13] There could be no universal jurisprudential account of a socially static and absolute sovereignty. People might regard themselves as being in a state of "political society" in relation to a state, but simultaneously, in regard to certain subject-matters, as also being in a state of "political society" in relation to larger or smaller political unions.

III

In *OLG* Bentham developed further the general idea presented in *Fragment* of the complexity of "sovereignty" and "community". He discussed the parties by whom a mandate might be issued:

> "according to the definition, the word *law* should be applicable to any the most trivial order supposing it to be not illegal, which a man may have occasion to give for any of the most inconsiderable purposes of life: to any order which a master may have occasion to give to his servant, a parent to his child, or of a husband to his wife."[14]

The field of legality was not confined to the general level of centralised institutions *vis a vis* a people. Law could be exercised in the private domain. Bentham argued that the idea of a *mandate*, understood as "some expression of volition of a constitutional nature", would be general enough to capture all the manifestations of legal activity. It would capture the complex social and inter-cultural activity with which legal discourse was associated. It conveyed a sense of the various *sources of law*.[15]

12 *Fragment*, p. 435.
13 Ibid., pp. 488–9.
14 *OLG*, p. 4.
15 Ibid., p. 15.

Bentham distinguished between legal and illegal mandates, in that the former had to emanate from a sovereign. Any mandate was capable of being acknowledged as a species of legal activity (in which case, the mandate would become a *legal* mandate). A *context* consisting in a *unified* pattern of superiority and subordination might transform specific mandates into "legal" ones. An example could be the mandate of a parent issued to his child, which, in itself, would not amount to an exercise of political authority. However, this parental mandate could, if issued in the context of a wider mandate which authorised its exercise (what Bentham termed "adoption" or "pre-adoption"), become a legal mandate. A particular act of superiority must be understood within such a context.

The idea of "adoption" conveyed the relative nature of sovereignty. "Adoption" had elements of validation and normative acceptance in it. "Validity" and "normative acceptance" were terms of relation. A socially sensitive analysis of the idea of validity and normative acceptance would acknowledge, on all occasions but one, at least two systems of superiority and subordination with regard to a single action. In order for an act to be valid and accepted, some authority would have to permit, or to "adopt" it. The exception was the ultimate link in a chain of validity and acceptance. The relationship between these two spheres of superiority and subordination was *volitional* in nature.[16] As such, an act of adoption was an imperative power of a constitutive nature. The unity between various particular mandates, which were created by the more general permitting, or adopting, context, might embody a natural parental mandate in a wider scheme of social activity.[17]

However, relativity was only one aspect of validity and acceptance. A further aspect of them was related to the two-dimensional (or "split") nature of sovereignty. This "split" was, as has been argued in the preceding chapter, essential to an understanding of sovereignty. In most instances, for the idea of validity and acceptance to make sense in a socially dynamic way, each person who took part in reflecting upon the social justification of coercion would have to participate in at least two levels of the hierarchy. For example, people in a state could acknowledge the adopting context of a federation. Yet, the same group of people would participate, together with the people of the other states in the federation, in determining the sovereignty of the federation. They would participate in both levels *at the same time* in critically assessing the social justification of the coercion exercised over them. Under Bentham's theory of sovereignty, the united order constituted by the hierarchy would be achieved when coercion was seen to be justified at every level of its operation.

In this context, the "split" nature of sovereignty would be most apparent at the top of a hierarchy. Here, the two-dimensional nature of sovereignty would supply the only criterion by which to assess the social justification of coercion.

[16] See chapter 5, pp. 163–5, 170–2 below.

[17] Bentham explicitly related the idea of adoption to the idea of "legal validity". He did so with respect to covenants, and explicitly said that such an adoption would be what made a collection of particular exercises of power into a system of law: *OLG*, pp. 23, 25.

Ultimately, any "adopting" relationship depended on a certain group of people, who formed a judgement with regard to a body which exercised coercion. Even the recognition of a level as being at the summit of the hierarchy would itself be a result of a social judgement. Legal validity would then amount to an assertion that, in relation to a certain matter, the people in a given group did not acknowledge any other superior, more general, adopting context. For example, if people in a state, for some reason, saw the state as the ultimate social group, sovereignty would not be related to any adopted context, because the people of that state would not participate in a more general social, and hence legal, activity. Thus the people in that state would be the only relevant reference point in resolving problems of sovereignty.

At this point, the distinction between vertical relativity and horizontal plurality of the social manifestation of sovereignty should be introduced. The first feature of the vertical relativity was its *hierarchical* nature. It consisted, in a series of hierarchical relationships, of superiority and subordination, each serving as an "adopting context" to another. The one example given in *Fragment* was, as has been mentioned, of federations. Bentham resorted to similar examples in *OLG*.[18] However, sovereignty could be exercised, and hence legal mandates issued, by subordinate power-holders, whether they belonged to the administration, or whether they were merely heads of families.[19] This hierarchy might begin with a parent, and move up through a local authority, a state, a federation, and ultimately a world government. The vertical hierarchy of sovereignty was dealt with by Bentham when he discussed "adoption". All, even the most trivial, transactions might be adopted by a wider socially recognised and justified context of superiority and subordination, and would thereby become legally valid in a unified way for all the people who acknowledged and accepted this adopting social context. This vertical relativity might include states as well. Nation states, though sovereign in a certain way, might be limited through belonging to a federation, which might or might not adopt their actions. One might belong to a number of political communities each at a different level in the hierarchy of sovereignty—the level of family, local authority, state, federation or the whole world.[20]

The second feature of the vertical relativity of sovereignty was its *potential artificiality*. Each level of the hierarchy could be artificial in that it could be subject to the investment of power for utilitarian reasons by a group of people who might be of various cultural orientations. Vertical relativity could be conceived in terms of a united *order* which was artificially crafted. It goes without saying that such an artificial unification could not become a culture in itself, a culture

[18] *OLG*, p. 29.

[19] Ibid., pp. 22–3, 27, 28.

[20] In chapter 9 of *OLG*, Bentham dealt with sovereignty and constitutional law in terms of the *generality* of the exercise of the powers of imperation. A universal theory which embodied the relative nature of sovereignty would claim that a doctrine of sovereignty manifested an aspect of such generality. An individual law could be seen as such only in relation to a more general context of imperative.

that could grow in an organic way like any other culture. The term "artificial" here connotes merely a political artefact. This order would be united because each level of it would be adopted by another, artificially established but more general, level.

However, Bentham's theory of sovereignty allowed for greater complexity than the manifestation of this vertical relativity. In his view, it was crudely reductionist to describe a "political society" solely in this vertical sense. Bentham differed from Kelsen and Hart, who saw law only as a manifestation of unity of norms which all had the same ultimate reason for their validity.[21] Bentham's socially sensitive approach led him to see the operation of law in a much more diverse way than this purely hierarchical idea of validation. Vertical relativity of sovereignty could not account for the plurality of allegiances existing at each level of the hierarchy.

Bentham recognised the potential difficulty of describing a "community", and the resulting difficulty of successfully portraying a "political society". A community was manifested in more than this hierarchical chain of validation, although, as has been argued, this chain did create some unity in a community. However, people could belong to several communities *at the same time*, not exclusively in this hierarchical, vertical sense. "Community" was a problematic concept in the same way that "people" was problematic. For example, it could be misleading to use the term "people" to refer exclusively to people subject to the same nation state or federation. A "people" might be bonded together by other means, for instance religion or some other cultural orientation. The bond which created a "people", and the social limitation to the justification of authority that this bond entailed, might possibly go beyond, or be contained within, an established artificial, centralised hierarchy.

This difficulty of defining what constituted a "people" had implications for what Bentham meant by a "political society". Law could manifest itself *within* this hierarchical, artificially established vertical domain of social validation in a complex way. A person might belong to different communities not only in the vertical sense, that is to a local community, a state, and a federation, but also, *at the same time*, to different political communities with regard to a given subject matter. This multiplicity of hierarchies could exist widely across each of these levels of the artificial, centralised and vertical one. Bentham discussed this manifestation of communities in *OLG*.[22] To follow Bentham's example, a Jew could be a citizen of the United States of America, but belong also to his religious "political community", which habitually paid obedience to another persistent superior, say a given Rabbi, as far as eating pork was concerned. The separate coexistence of "religion" and "state" could be accounted for in this way. A Jew would belong to several political communities, and in each could be a political superior in relation to some matters and some people and inferior in relation to other matters and other people *at the same time*.

21 See H. Kelsen, *Pure Theory of Law* (Berkeley, 1970), pp. 31–3.

22 *OLG*, pp. 18–19, note b.

This multiple manifestation of hierarchies, or multiple "sovereignties" across each level of the artificially, centralised and vertical hierarchy, will be referred to as the "horizontal" plurality of sovereignty. The manifestation of this plurality meant that there was a multiplicity of hierarchies cutting *horizontally across* each level of the vertical hierarchy. In a state, for example, one would observe a number of relationships of superiority and subordination within that state level, which mirrored the diversity in orientation of the people of that state. This would be the case despite the fact that all of them functioned under a united level of a given artificial, centralised and vertical hierarchy, namely that state. Further, all these various groups would relate to the collectivity (in this case, the "state" community), despite the relationship *between them* being more akin to a "natural" relationship rather than to a "political" one. The reason was that the engagement *between,* rather than *within,* these groups would be based solely on communication which did not necessarily establish any kind of a persistent "habit of obedience".[23]

It would be too simplistic to understand sovereignty and law as operating solely within a network bounded by the state, or any other form of artificially established, centralised, coercive institution. To treat any one group in the vertical hierarchy in isolation from any other group would be to ignore the plurality of social groups, as well as the potential complexity of their interaction. Social interaction might give rise to hierarchies of adoption which would extend horizontally within, as well as between, communities, and which in turn might give rise to a plurality of relationships of superiority and subordination. A universal definition of law and sovereignty must account for this horizontal plurality, and hence sovereignty has to be conceived as complex in this respect, as well as in the respect of vertical relativity.

The artificial, centralised and vertical hierarchy which gave rise to the relativity of sovereignty would impose *some* unity and identification in certain areas. On the other hand, the horizontal plurality would emphasise the complex nature of identity and "belonging", and would represent pluralism— pluralism at each level of the hierarchy. Thus, to capture fully the social dynamism which the concept of sovereignty connotes, it is necessary to account for the tensions between social unity and plurality. Bentham accounted for the tension between unity and plurality of sovereignty. However, never did he attempt to resolve substantively the tension. As is argued in the rest of the book, this tension resembles a dynamic formation and dissolution of conceptions of harm. Although unity and plurality could coexist in many situations, there were inevitable conflicts between them. *Some* account had to be provided to signify the demarcation between, on the one hand, sovereignty as a hierarchical unified process by a body of people who would be disposed to obey a given centralised person or

[23] It goes without saying that the relationship between groups in a state, for example, involved superiority and subordination. The issue of authoritative utterances which could take shape between people in the course of their communication belongs to the analysis of consensus formation, and will be discussed in detail in chapter 6, pp. 199–222 below.

body of persons, and, on the other hand, pluralism within any level of this hierarchy, be it the local community, the state, or the world.

IV

The implications of the tension between hierarchical unity, as manifested by the vertical relativity of sovereignty, and horizontal plurality of allegiances across each level of such a hierarchy, are far-reaching for the analysis of law and its points of contact with the justification of coercive distribution schemes. It would be an oversimplification in terms of microsociology and forms of sociality, and even in terms of "descriptive sociology", to employ Hart's terminology,[24] to speak about "a law" purely in Kelsenian, Austinian (both of whose accounts incorporate the idea of superiority and subordination), or even in Hartian (whose account incorporates a unified recognition of the validity of rules) terms. The artificial, centralised, unified, grouping of people could, as a matter of social fact, accommodate to some extent the cultural fact that people may belong to various "political" societies. The unifying characteristics of this grouping could function *together with social diversity*. I say "together" because one might otherwise have the impression that the utilitarian reasons for establishing the artificial, centralised community would imply the necessity of eliminating diversity in order to provide a homogeneous context for this beneficial social activity. The potential for conflict between a certain group's acceptance of centralised authority, and its particular cultural practices might, but need not, result in the suppression of those beliefs. It is true that some groups, for instance some religious groups, may, in fact, not be tolerant towards other groups. Nevertheless, Bentham would insist that, if law has to be accounted for, *some* congruity and therefore compromise would have to exist between the manifestations of the various cultures (including *their own* special manner of evolution), and demands for unity brought about through some artificial, centralised, hierarchical structure. Bentham spoke about horizontal plurality as a matter of fact—a fact of pluralism. Thus, the utilitarian, instrumental need for coordination, as well as *some* substantive co-operation in certain agreed areas, must be made compatible with horizontal plurality, the existence of which would *in fact* limit the disposition of people to build these hierarchies in the first place. *Some* solidarity which was effectuated by the constitution of a centralised authority would therefore have to account for differences in cultural identification. If the *de jure* solidarity does not match the de facto cultural differentiation, some oppression would result. An account of sovereignty should account for the socially dynamic process which would determine the borderline between actual cultural pluralism and unity, as manifested in the vertical relativity of sovereignty. A degree of despotism and violence would be the characteristic mark of

[24] See chapter 1, p. 5, note 11 above.

a society in which constitutional law stood at odds with social facts which pulled towards differentiation. For example, if Jews considered themselves not bound by the state's intervention in relation to some issues, while constitutional law, as a collective expression of the will of the state, ignored this differentiation, and refused to allow them to govern themselves in relation to these issues, then persecution would arise.

The nature of the harmony between cultural diversity and the unified, artificial, centralised hierarchy is the issue with regard to which the role of constitutional law should be discussed. Constitutional law, as will be argued, was determined as a result of communication in the public sphere.[25] In general, admittedly minimalist, terms, "constitutional" meant a communal expression of unity with regard to difference. As such, what is "constitutional" would obviously be ideology-dependent. Constitutional law would signify the *extent* to which people were recognised, in regard to certain subject matters, as belonging to an incompatibly different culture from, say, that which constituted a particular state. Constitutional law would result from a judgement which signified limits to the exercise of coercion. These limits, in turn, demarcated the extent to which containment of different identifications was to be maintained and justified.

Thus understood, constitutional law would itself be an expression of unified will to the effect that certain differences should be respected. Further, this expression of unity, or of communal obligation, would constitute an area in which the locus of obligation would ultimately lie within public communication, rather than being located in, and dependent upon, the decrees of a centralised institution.

Constitutional law must be viewed as emanating from the hierarchical artificial order. However, expressions of law, made by an artificially united, centralised "community", might bear reference to, and even constitute, other "political communities" within the artificial, centralised community. Hence, a major role of constitutional law (which could be fulfilled differently in different communities) was to determine the exact relationship between the vertical relative manifestation of sovereignty, and the horizontal plurality of sovereignties—between the centralised, artificial sense of "community", and a differentiation of "communities"—*at any point in time*. In short, the tension between unity and differentiation would be addressed by general communal propositions which would be the basis for constitutional law. There had to be some points regarding which different groups would have to interact in order to form a unified will, which in turn would give rise to a political expression, an expression of an artificial, centralised unity.[26]

In the previous chapter it was argued that the relationship between the two bodies which constituted "sovereignty" was one of reciprocal influence.[27]

[25] Constitutional law will be discussed in chapter 5, pp. 160–8, and chapter 6, pp. 232–3 below.
[26] The nature of that interaction will be discussed in chapter 6, pp. 199–222 below.
[27] The idea of "influence" will be discussed in detail in chapter 6, 199–206 below.

Applying the idea of influence to the question of the relativity and plurality of sovereignty, it seems that a relationship of superiority and subordination within any one level of hierarchy, or system of allegiance, might influence the interaction between coercer and coerced within any other such level or system. Self-reflection exercised by a "community" might be influenced, both horizontally and vertically, by any other "community". The vertical hierarchies of a community, and the multiplicity of possible communal allegiances within each level of a hierarchy, could mutually influence each other, to the extent that new propositions of constitutional law could be arrived at in each one of the hierarchies. An argument about the justification of a proposition of constitutional law could, for instance, determine that in a given area the state was the ultimate, validating level in the vertical, relative hierarchy.

Both vertical and horizontal influences would involve some authority, although only the former would involve influence by a political authority. For example, the people in a state community could be influenced by sympathy towards an ethnic minority. This would involve horizontal influence, which, as will be argued in Chapter 6, would work through an obligatory medium. However, the group which constituted a state, being part of an international community (another manifestation of artificial, centralised community), could also be influenced by international norms to the extent that it would feel sympathy towards how people in other communities in the world were treated. Both types of influence would operate to determine the extent of sovereignty within the level of the vertical hierarchy in question, namely the state, with regard to constitutional limits regarding the securities of minorities against excessive coercion.[28] Constitutional law, as a manifestation of the two-dimensional nature of sovereignty in that state, *could* be crystallised into a binding proposi-

[28] Bentham provided an example of how influence might operate on each and every state in his writings on international law. The object of international law was to subject sovereignty in every state to the influence of "a citizen of the world". In his analysis of "dominion", or "sovereignty", in these writings, Bentham suggested that adjudication by international institutions could generate an *international* public opinion which, in turn, could mobilise public opinion within states, to the extent that the limits of sovereignty in them would thereby be determined.

He claimed that the degree to which communication on a world scale could influence what went on within each state would be dependent upon the degree of the freedom of communication between ruler and ruled within each state. The perfection of each state in this sense could effectuate the establishment of a world system of superiority and subordination, one which would produce worldwide norms. Globalisation and statehood were expressions of unity on the part of the community of the globe and of the state respectively. The role of constitutional law as determined by an expression of unity, which in turn determined the borderline between unity and differentiation, also applied in international law: see Bowring, ii. 537–54; and also *First Principles*, p. 295 where he wrote:

> "But as nations are now connected, information to any one nation is information to every other, applying poison or obstruction to any one press is applying it to every other. Carrying on hostility in any one nation, and thereby against that one nation, is carrying on hostility against every other. The mischief produced by the suppression of information on the one side, on the side of the victims of misrule, while false and delusive information in support of misrule is let through, may spread itself over all nations, and continue in all times."

See further, ibid., p. 57, and *SAM*, p. 66. Finally, see *Deontology*, pp. 230–1, where Bentham discussed the operation of private ethics in the international domain.

tion which forebode the persecution of minorities. In this sense it *would* reflect a communal view that centralised coercion should not produce laws which persecuted minorities.

In *OLG*, Bentham made another statement of his universal theory, intended to be true irrespective of time and place:[29]

> "Why might not [this diversification of sovereignty in relation to different subject matters],(in point of practicability I mean) be **settled by law**,[30] as well as by an **inward determination** which bids defiance to the law?. . . . Let it be observed once more I consider here not what is most eligible, but only what is possible.[31]
>
> One great difficulty is to draw the boundary line betwixt act and act, betwixt such **classes of acts as the sovereign may, and such as he may not, take for the objects of his law, and to distinguish it by marks so clear as not to be in danger of being mistaken:** The plainest marks are those which are made by *place* and *time*. By place: for this is all that there is to distinguish the power of any one sovereign from that of another. By time: accordingly at Rome, even in a rude age, a man would be absolute for six months without any hope or chance of protracting his power a day longer, so in regencies, as we see every day, though the minority be ever so long. As to *place*, where that circumstance is the mark, the line is the stronger, in as much as the physical power terminates in great measure with the political. **But to examine these matters in detail belongs to the particular head of constitutional law.**"[32]

This is the appropriate point to summarise the argument. For Bentham, a theory of law and sovereignty had to account for the diversification which characterised legal operations. The concept of sovereignty, as manifested in constitutional limits and law, had to explain the nature of, and to account for, the tension between two features. The first was the vertical relativity of sovereignty. This relativity represented communal expressions of unity. This unity was manifested by an artificial, centralised, publicly accessible coercive order. Such unity was needed for some common achievement and promotion of utilitarian values, namely subsistence, security, abundance and equality.[33] A second feature for which a theory of sovereignty had to provide an explanation was horizontal plurality. This plurality was a characteristic mark of many social groups. Apart from determining the ambit of an artificial, centralised, unified hierarchy, sovereignty, and hence constitutional limits and law, reflected the areas where unity was imposed upon cultural plurality by institutional authority, according to some general communal conception of harm (or in Bentham's word, mischief). The mutual influence of the various communities rendered this communal

[29] See chapter 1, pp. 13–20 above.

[30] In *Essays on Bentham*, p. 233, Hart treated this expression as enigmatic. However, owing to his limited perspective, he failed to account for the role for constitutional law in Bentham's thought. For general criticisms of Hart's approach, see chapter 5, pp. 168–75 below.

[31] Note that Bentham had already used this expression in *OLG* in relation to his analysis of sovereignty: see chapter 2, pp. 52–3 above. This statement affirms that he saw his analysis here as part of a universal theory.

[32] *OLG*, p. 19.

[33] See, e.g., Bowring, ix. 11–15.

judgement which determined "harm" a dynamic, interpretative activity. Thus, constitutional law would be a temporal incarnation of how the community saw itself. The extent to which the values of tolerance and pluralism were appreciated by the members of a community would be mirrored in its constitutional law. By contrast, constitutional law might reflect the aspirations of a community which preferred to eliminate differentiation and create a strong sense of identification. Bentham was not suggesting what he considered to be preferable: as he said, he considered merely what was possible.[34]

[34] See N. MacCormick, "Beyond the Sovereign State", *Modern Law Review* 56 (1993) 1–18. MacCormick holds the view that one can account for a multiplicity of legal orders without reference to an ultimate, single, centralised authority. He further maintains that the formal idea of "recognition" can account for a plurality of legal domains, and that, therefore, the idea of "sovereignty", which is so often used in political debates, need not be relied upon. MacCormick seems to advocate a middle way between legal monocentrism and legal pluralism in this respect (p. 17).

However, a test of authenticity, or "recognition" is static. It will not account for the *socially dynamic interpretation and determination* of those points of conflict which can arise between competing claims for the limits of justified coercion. As has been argued, constitutional law, the basis of which is a communal obligation within each level of the vertical hierarchy, comes in to resolve these conflicts. Bentham's insight into the relativity and plurality of sovereignty, as well as the potential influences between spheres of superiority and subordination, goes some way towards accounting for the problem of how an expression of unity within each hierarchy can contain differentiation with regard to claims of validity. The borderline between unity and plurality of sovereignty can encompass the dynamic relationship between individual groups and states, between private and public domains, and between individual states, political unions and the world domain.

This paradigm of constitutional law, as manifested in the split, relative and plural nature of sovereignty, would, in its most abstract form be a demarcation of the boundary between unity (or "unified rationale for reasoning about law") and differentiation. Further, the idea of formal legal validity, as will be claimed in chapter 5, pp. 168–72 below, cannot fully replace the ideas of superiority and subordination, or "sovereignty". Therefore, it is argued that we cannot do without the concept of sovereignty as understood as a "split", relative, plurally manifested and, above all, socially dynamic concept.

4

The Role of the People in determining Constitutional Limits I—A Democratic Reading of A Fragment on Government

> Here we touch upon the most difficult of questions. If the law is not what it ought to be: if it openly combats the principle of utility; ought we to obey it? Ought we to violate it? Ought we to remain neuter between the law which commands an evil, and morality which forbids it?
>
> *Theory of Legislation*, p. 65

I

This chapter aims to provide a fresh reading of a well-known Bentham text. Together with the next two chapters it seeks also to develop, for the first time, a united, harmonious interpretation of Bentham's account of constitutional limits. Using the arguments about sovereignty developed in previous chapters as a foundation, these chapters will examine in detail the relationship between the two bodies whose interaction constitutes sovereignty. The present chapter investigates the central role which Bentham assigned to the people as the "judging body", and who determined and effectuated constitutional limits by interacting with governmental institutions.

In Chapter 2 it has been argued that sovereignty involved a trust. In *every* political society there was a delegated, and at the same time limited, political authority. This chapter will argue that whatever the institutional structure of a society and legal system, constitutional limits were ultimately a product of the relationship between the body of the people and their government.[1] Popular judgement was an inherent part of sovereignty, understood as a socially dynamic concept. *Any* plausible constitutional theory has to give an account of the relationship between two forces—the government and the people. It will be argued that in *Fragment*, Bentham discussed two broad themes in conjunction.

[1] It is important to note that "government" here has a broader meaning than the common conception of government as an institutionally-based coercive mechanism. It also includes communally-based coercion, or self-government. More will be said about this in chapter 6 below.

First, he discussed the limits of sovereignty and socially acceptable coercion as part of an analysis of the nature and persistence of political society. Secondly, and more particularly, he discussed the conditions for, and the signification of, obedience to law, a "habit of obedience" being the fundamental feature of every political society. Hence, in reading *Fragment*, the analysis of obedience to law is the key to understanding the relationship between the popular determination of constitutional limits and the effectuation of such determination through popular action.

In discussing obedience to law, the present chapter discusses the meaning of the phrase "a moral duty to obey the law" in the light of Bentham's epistemology and arguments in *Fragment*. In doing so, the chapter adds another dimension to the formal analysis of sovereignty offered in Chapter 2. This chapter discusses in much more detail the conditions for, and significance of, the activity of the "entrusting body", the activity of which was one of the two dimensions which characterised the "split" understanding of sovereignty. However, it does not give a formal analysis of the communication which enables such an "entrusting body" to take shape. Such an analysis is reserved for Chapter 6. Although the connection between the idea of legitimate authority and the duty to obey has not always been asserted,[2] it is my claim that there is a connection between the limits of the social justification for political authority (matters of sovereignty) and popular reflection and action. Since Bentham tied together the idea of sovereignty and the habit of obedience, constitutional limits and the duty to obey the law were intimately linked in his theory. In a nutshell, the argument is that, in *Fragment*, "the duty to obey *the* law" related to the social justification for the existence of law. Such a duty might be termed "the duty socially to justify the sovereign *as sovereign*".

II

Bentham's theory of obligations

What, for Bentham, was the precise nature of a moral duty to obey the law?[3] Initially, it is proposed to analyse the phrase "a duty to obey the law" according to Bentham's epistemology, that is, according to his theory of fictions. The reason for so doing is to discuss criticisms that the principle of utility is an incoherent basis for obligation in general and political obligation in particular.[4] It will be argued that Bentham in fact contended that the principle of utility could not serve as a basis for *any* particular moral obligation, and further, that the

[2] See K. Greenawalt, *Conflicts of Law and Morality* (Oxford, 1989), pp. 56–7.

[3] Postema mentions the issue only to say that the principle of utility would determine whether one should obey the law. He does not explain the nature of this utilitarian quandary: see *Bentham and The Common Law Tradition*, p. 248.

[4] See B. Zwiebach, *Civility and Disobedience* (Cambridge, 1975), pp. 31–7.

principle of utility could account only for the *expediency of obedience*, in particular historical circumstances. The resort to Bentham's epistemological theory supports the contention that Bentham provided, in *Fragment*, a flexible *social* account of how coercion could be exercised in a political society. This reading takes for its foundation Bentham's epistemological attack on abstract moral rights. Bentham's epistemological understanding of rights and obligations allowed him to present as dogmatic, and to refute on utilitarian grounds, *any* generally accepted justification of the ways in which a given political society was justified. Moreover, Bentham's epistemology enabled him to assume the position of an observer of the historical process of communal development, and to make generalisations about the universal nature of political society. *Fragment* was arguably written from such a speculative observational standpoint. Bentham could infer that one could never speak about a general moral duty to obey the law, despite the historical utilitarian expediency of such obedience at certain stages in the social development of a given community. It will be argued that the expression "a moral duty to obey the law" would be as incomprehensible to Bentham as the alleged existence of any other a priori moral duty. Bentham's epistemology enabled him to give an account of political society in *Fragment* which supposed no moral duty to obey the law.

What did the word "duty" or "obligation" mean for Bentham? How could the idea of a "duty" or an "obligation" be defined in such a way that two people would know that it existed in the same way? The concept of a duty was discussed in Bentham's *Theory of Fictions*.[5] According to Bentham's theory, which anticipated many late-Wittgensteinian features, fictitious entities (as opposed to "real" entities which could be physical or mental) like "duties" and "obligations" could be defined for the purpose of an inter-subjective communicative discourse *only* as long as they were paraphrased, and given a context in a sentence in such a way as to relate them to real entities. In other words, mutual comprehension of the persons communicating depended on the translation of fictitious entities into terms describing real entities. When an obligation was spoken of as *existing*, it meant that people saw some action as obligatory. They would feel some commitment to the content of the obligation. One of the "real" entities involved in the paraphrased definition of an obligation—pain—meant that *some kind* of a sanction would have to form a part of its definition.[6]

[5] For a version of Bentham's text, see C.K. Ogden (ed.), *Bentham's Theory of Fictions* (London, 1932), pp. 7–52, 86–91. For an illuminating exposition of the theory, see Harrison, *Bentham*, chapters 2–4; see also Hart, *Essays on Bentham*, pp. 128–30.

[6] Modern thinkers have also considered the role of sanctions. Raz presents an effective objection to too rigid a connection between the idea of a threat of a sanction and the existence of law. He argues that evidence is scarce for such a strong connection between the two: *Practical Reasons and Norms*, pp. 154–7. However, Raz approaches the idea of a sanction very narrowly. For him a "sanction" would amount only to what Bentham regarded as the political sanction. Raz does not speak about other types of sanctions, all of which can form part of an analysis of the obligatory status of a law.

Bentham insisted that the distinction between the existence of rights (or obligations) and arguments about rights had to be maintained. An explanation of rights and obligations had to be kept distinct from their justification. "Hunger is not bread", he wrote in *Anarchical Fallacies*.[7] Doctrines of natural rights could not maintain this distinction, and their subject matter, the substance of those rights, could not be meaningfully defined and thus made the topic of communication. Nobody could fully understand them, let alone censor them. Any one particular understanding of those natural rights was as good as any other.

The implication of Bentham's analysis of fictions in general, and of duties and obligations in particular, was that there could not be obligations which emanated directly from a moral principle. A moral principle, although a precondition of an obligation, could not be the direct source of that obligation. A moral principle and an obligation (a manifestation of will expressed through the propositional medium backed up by a sanction) did not stand in relation to one another as cause and effect. There had to be a proposition, backed up by a sanction, which existed at an intermediate level, that is between the moral principle and the person who inferred an obligation.

Not only were *natural* rights "non-existent", "fabulous" entities, but so were any imprescriptible moral, or utilitarian, entitlements. Hart acknowledged the point of Bentham's account in separating the existence of rights from their justification. He argued that Bentham, unlike Mill, had been logically consistent. Mill's account recognised some higher rights and obligations which stemmed directly from higher pleasures. His account led to utilitarian entitlements. The result of Mill's account was a non-utilitarian proposition, namely that there could be circumstances in which no conflict would be generated between utility and rights.[8] Moral obligations, for Bentham, were derived from popular prescriptive propositions which supplied the propositional medium backed by the moral, or (as will be argued below in Chapter 6) the sympathetic sanction.

Obligations, on the above analysis, could be subjective or inter-subjective, that is communicable in a group of persons, but only the latter would function as social norms. A social norm entailed an obligation which would bind the members of a group by the normative force it possessed. A normative force would operate where there existed a source from which pain *of some kind* could be anticipated. This pain would be inflicted where there occurred a transgression of the content of a prescriptive proposition. Such anticipation of pain could, for example, be a result of expectations regarding the recurrence of a certain practice,[9] or could be an anticipation of the pain of disappointment on the part of other members of the group in question, and, in consequence of the pain

[7] Bowring, ii. 501.

[8] Hart, *Essays on Bentham*, pp. 94, 97, 103.

[9] Or more precisely, it could result from a proposition inferred by people who would both participate in a practice and observe it. They would have to participate in it, but in order to abstract a proposition with prescriptive force they would have to put themselves in the hypothetical position of observers of themselves participating in it. They could not just "do things". There would have to be some degree of self-reflection in order to infer an obligation.

arising in any individual's mind as a result of his anticipation of criticisms likely to be made in the event of deviation from the practice.

Now, apart from explaining the idea of obligation, the above analysis is helpful in understanding what Bentham meant by the idea of a *moral* obligation. The mere fact that a prescriptive proposition was inferred constituted some part of its "morality". Our criticism of existing practices is influenced to some degree by the cultural "baggage" that we carry. This "baggage", which features in all utilitarian calculations, can amount to some abstract prescriptive propositions in relation to which a critical interpretation is undertaken on a more concrete level. Further, this "baggage" can amount to the motivational weight which pertains to the very existence of this abstract propositions when these propositions are reflected upon.

A utilitarian evaluation is also influenced by our imagination of possible future pains and pleasures, which could, for instance, be a product of our empathy towards other people.[10] However, for Bentham, the mere existence of the obligation, whatever its source, would form part of the utilitarian calculation in assessing its morality. Statements like "there is a legal obligation to pay tax", or "there is a prescriptive proposition that everybody should go to church on Sundays", are inferences of prescriptive propositions which are supported by sanctions arising from different sources. However, both propositions would generate expectations, and, as such, their mere existence, or "the fact of their inference", would itself give them moral weight in any future evaluation.

The status of a moral duty to obey the law

With this analysis in mind, we may discuss how Bentham would understand "a *moral* duty to obey the law". This expression could be interpreted as having two different meanings. First, it could mean that there was an obligation not to refrain from doing what the content of a given legal prescriptive proposition specified. Secondly, it could mean that we have a direct moral obligation to "obey the law". This meaning differs from the first in so far as it refers to the law globally, with a more remote and indirect reference to the content of its specific provisions. In this latter sense, there would be an obligation to obey because of the prescriptive proposition which formed a justification for having law. The reasoning in this more global sense relates to the existence of law, or to the question "what do we need law for?" It goes without saying that even the second, global obligation to obey the law might be influenced by the content of this or that specific measure that a legal system produced. In such a case, the argument about the content of law would be utilised at a different level of reasoning.[11]

[10] Empathy will be discussed in chapter 6, pp. 212–3 below.

[11] This more global level of reasoning is explained by Raz in terms of "second order reasons", which may operate as "exclusionary reasons" for action. See in this context chapter 2, p. 43, note 9, above. Essentially, exclusionary reasons suspend the reasoning process upon first-order reasons,

The first interpretation would imply that the force of the moral duty to obey was related to a calculation, determined by the threat of punishment attached to a volitional utterance. This would constitute an "immediate" obligatory medium which would, on most occasions, produce a duty to obey. If a person was asked: "why do you obey?", the answer would be: "because if I am caught not obeying, I will have to bear the punishment". This is a banal statement of the duty to obey. It is plausible, but unhelpful in cases where a person has personal reasons (or convictions) for not obeying.

The second interpretation, however, would imply that there was an obligation to obey the law for reasons which were ulterior to a person's own reasoning with regard to the law's content. These may be reasons to obey which stem directly from the social utility of law as an institution, for example its function in creating an artificial identification of duty and interest, or in the co-ordination of moral beliefs. On this understanding, a more global concept of the duty to obey would stem from a prescriptive proposition formed by reasoning which was not conceptually related to the content of the legal provision in question. There would be a prescriptive proposition of conventional morality which recognised this ulterior purpose of the institution of law.

However, the connection to the content of a provision need not be underestimated in the more global understanding of the duty to obey. Arguments which are related to the function of law as an institution could be weighed against, and on occasion be overridden by, other rules of conventional morality, which might themselves relate to the content of law. This would mean that the question of whether certain reasons functioned as second-order reasons or not would itself depend on the content of the provision and the first-order reasons which stemmed from it. For example, a prescriptive proposition could be argued to be pernicious, either because it had transgressed a deeply rooted social convention, or because of its very harmful consequences. In such a case, its content would serve as a second-order reason. The case for disobeying the law would amount to saying: "My reasons for objecting to that measure are so strong that they overcome its presumptive exclusionary status."

In the case of the first, banal type of reasoning, Bentham would insist that the question of the existence of an obligation to obey should be kept distinct from that of its justification. But on the premise of the impossibility of imprescriptible universal rights, as well as of utilitarian entitlements, where there was no obligatory medium, confusion between the question of the existence of a conventional obligation to "obey *the* law", and that of its justification, ought to be avoided. This avoidance holds even on the second, more global understanding according to which there might be a conventional duty to obey because of social advantages related to the existence of the institution of law as such.

disallowing ordinary calculation as to the balance of reason or advantages. For example, I may have a personal reason for disobedience, but the exclusionary nature of the second order reasons forbids me to consider it: see *Practical Reasons and Norms*, p. 41; and also *The Authority of Law*, pp. 16–26, 235–6.

Bentham would argue that no duty could stem purely from a utilitarian calculation, but only from a prescriptive proposition backed up by a sanction. The expression "a moral duty to obey the law" would be nonsense and incomprehensible *even if it related to the institution of law*, in the same way that any proposition of natural law would be nonsense. There could be no universal utilitarian consideration which would give rise to a utilitarian duty to obey the law. To assert the existence of such a duty would be to commit the error later made by Mill.

According to Bentham's analysis of the impossibility of utilitarian entitlements, there could be no moral duty to obey the law, or more precisely, there could only be a popular prescriptive proposition in favour of obedience to law. This prescriptive proposition would be based on a crystallisation into an obligation of a reflection which consisted of the most general social utilitarian assessment and justification of law as a social institution.

Part of the moral weight attached to this proposition would stem from existing conventional prescriptive propositions. Yet, the fact that a reflection about the expediency of obeying gives rise to a convention which advocates reasons for the obedience to the law, does not mean that there is a moral duty to obey the law. One could argue for the existence of a convention to the effect that: "the duty to obey exists providing that certain conditions are met". However, this would render the articulation of the duty to obey the law unhelpful in so far as "there is a duty to obey if it is expedient so to obey". Again, the fact that on many occasions it would be expedient to obey, and that, in consequence, a conventional moral rule to that effect would develop, does not imply that it is plausible to talk about "a moral duty to obey the law".[12] Bentham would recognise that a commitment, such as an obligation to obey the law, could be formed at various levels of abstraction, for instance at the "banal" sense of such a duty which is based on immediate expediency, or at the more general, social level. However, no such commitment could give rise to the existence of a moral duty to obey the law.

This argument leads to what I term *utilitarian-based anarchism*. It implies that a moral obligation to obey the law cannot be understood and justified in the abstract. The existence of a centralised coercive mechanism cannot be justified a priori, but only on utilitarian considerations, which are, of course, however global they might be, capable of modification. Even general obligations based on a "habit", or "disposition", which is based on conventional, or popular, reasons for obeying the law which relate to the institution of law as such must

[12] The fact that a speculative opinion would conclude that under certain circumstances people OUGHT to obey, does not imply the existence of a global moral duty to obey the law.

R.E. Flathman acknowledges that the answer to the question "should I obey the law?" depends on the circumstances of the particular situation. It is very difficult to assess each situation, and so it is difficult to answer the question in universal terms. The answer to the general question is culturally contingent, or, as Flathman says, it depends on time and place: *Political Obligation* (New York, 1972), p. 245.

always be understood in a particular social context.[13] People can generally justify obedience to the institution of law, for instance on the grounds of co-ordination and protection, but such justification is entirely compatible with a philosophical and critical claim that there is no moral duty to obey the law.[14] Bentham would warn against the acceptance of notions like "legitimacy", or "the duty to obey the law", all of which would be symptomatic of a social statism.

Utilitarian-based anarchism claims that under no circumstances can there be any global utilitarian justification for totally surrendering one's moral autonomy in the face of coercive volitional utterances, whatever the source of these utterances. This argument is anarchical because it precludes, even at the level of reasoning which relates to the law as a social institution, any a priori understanding and a priori justification of political obligation.[15]

[13] I should not be understood as advocating the existence of a prima facie duty to obey the law. The statement "there is a prima facie duty to obey the law" is a global statement to that effect and would make no sense in utilitarian terms. This is because it would be equally valid to say that there is a prima facie duty not to obey. The assertion of such a global statement, however, is different from saying that any formulation of the duty to obey would only have a prima facie status, a position which would be fully shared by any utilitarian. See M.B.E. Smith, "Is there a *Prima Facie* Obligation to Obey the Law?", *Yale Law Journal* 82 (1973) 950–76.

[14] The existence of an argument at a level of utilitarian reasoning which relates to the law as an institution may help to answer Greenawalt's query as to why utilitarians regard disobedience to law as a more severe violation of the general welfare than any other violation: *Conflicts of Law and Morality*, p. 116.

[15] This anarchism is autonomy based, and is philosophical in the same sense as R.P. Wolff's "autonomy-based anarchism". Wolff's argument assumes that political authority must necessarily curtail moral autonomy, and therefore one must choose between the two. (*In Defence of Anarchism* (New York, 1976), p. 71). However, Wolff admits that on some occasions it is expedient to obey the orders of government. What he objects to is obedience to law because it is law (Ibid., p. 14). He accepts that even without coercive centralised institutions, an all-embracing direct democracy might plausibly emerge in a human society of free, autonomous individuals. In such a society, individuality, understood as some combination of freedom and responsibility, would be interdependent in an optimal way.

The argument in this book is that for Bentham too, disobedience could be facilitated and would form part of the political aspect of a free society. However, while Wolff sees autonomy as an ideal, Bentham conceived a free society as one in which such autonomy could be realised on the balance of utilities, that is when the existence of state government would be more of an evil than the absence of it. Bentham's utilitarian anarchism enabled him to contemplate a society in which self-government would predominate. He could contemplate such a society despite the fact that political obligation could be justified, on utilitarian grounds, in manifestations of political society which were characterised by a great deal of institutional power. For Wolff, a just state, and therefore a justified political obligation, is a logical contradiction. For Bentham, by contrast, political obligation could be justified, but could always be questioned *as such* when the social situation demanded it. For Wolff, autonomy is an unattainable ideal. For Bentham, like Mill after him, it was a matter of social evolution, and, as will be argued in chapter 6, a matter for communal reflection and re-negotiation. "OUGHT" therefore could have meaning only within the realm of "CAN". An unrealisable "OUGHT" was simply a contradiction. A vision of autonomy in a group without reference to potential social circumstances, or to a stage in the group's development, was too implausible to be taken seriously. Bentham would concede that autonomy was in itself good, whereas authority was in itself evil. However, for instrumental reasons such as security, enhanced autonomy would not be an ideal worth pursuing in a social group not mature enough to make any good use of it. See also p. 104, note 17 below.

From which standpoint is this *utilitarian-based anarchism* developed? The assertion of the absence of a moral duty to obey the law would have to be made from the speculative viewpoint of a philosopher/observer, whose enterprise it was to try to discover the universal features of all political societies. The empirical fact that distinct, historical, socially dynamic processes, observable in different communities, corroborated the inference of the non-existence, or rather only the transient belief in the existence, of a moral duty to obey the law, conjoined the philosophical speculative insight of utilitarian-based anarchism.

From this point of view, utilitarian-based anarchism, as a theoretical position, would be entirely compatible with the transient expediency, and indeed abuse, of centralised coercion. If one adopted the point of view of this philosophical anarchism, derived from the epistemological basis of obligation, one might also say that although in certain stages of the historical development of a social group, a duty to obey the law was understood to exist because of its current expediency, this duty could not form a universal feature of the description of that society. Indeed, the absence of such a duty would be an essential characteristic of it. Over time, therefore, the philosopher/observer would say there was no such duty.

The utilitarian-based anarchistic claim would not take the form "under no circumstances should authority be justified", or "the only form of good society is that which does not have a centralised coercive authority". Further, it should not be associated with the chaotic social state potentially arrived at by the application of natural law theories. These theories posited that the authoritative status of utterances should be acknowledged *only* as long as they adhered to natural law, of which any one interpretation would be as good as the other. Bentham would criticise both these interpretations of anarchism; rather, utilitarian-based anarchism would be arrived at after observation of many historical evolutions of social groups, and would be derived from the epistemological basis of obligation which denied the existence of utilitarian entitlements.[16] So utilitarian-based anarchism can be seen as a speculative attitude about the transient nature of any justification of a particular manifestation of political society. As such, it should not be confused with the popular understanding of anarchism as simply a chaotic social state arrived at either from extravagant claims to moral autonomy, or from a reliance on natural law.

However, utilitarian-based anarchism should also be distinguished from another sense of anarchism. This other sense of anarchism would have a social

[16] Sartorius argued that in a *stable* polity people would presume that the laws were generally just. However, he maintained that this fact should not lead to the use of the terminology of a moral duty to obey the law. Once appeal is made to such terminology, the political union would be in the process of disintegrating: *Individual Conduct and Social Norms: a Utilitarian Account of Social Union and The Rule of Law* (California, 1975), p. 108. Sartorius described the nature of a relatively just political society in the context of a duty to obey. In doing that, however, he spoke about a particular application of a universal principle not about the universal itself, as far as the nature of political obligation was concerned; see also chapter 1, pp. 13–20 above, where universality in Bentham's thought is discussed.

or empirical orientation. Utilitarian-based anarchism could form the theoretical basis for the dynamism of social struggles upon which critical or empirical anarchism would be arrived at by a social group, though, of course, in a transient way. This materialisation of an anarchistic social group would be an account of a society critically justified under a utilitarian theory. In other words, utilitarian-based anarchism would be the theoretical basis which could help to maintain the social dynamism encapsulated in a utilitarian social and political theory, enabling it to accommodate an actual anarchistic society, which would embrace an anarchistic ideology. The philosophical, critical attitude of utilitarian-based anarchism about the basic justification of centralised authority in a social group could propel global reflection on, and, in turn, evolution of a political society, to the degree that it could eventually justify and embrace an anarchistic ideology.[17]

[17] The social, or empirical application of a philosophical anarchistic attitude within the framework of a utilitarian legal and political theory might be twofold:

First, as will be argued in chapter 6, Bentham, in a similar fashion to J.S. Mill, reflected extensively upon the histories of communities. Bentham advocated a continuous questioning of the global justification of political obligation. Secondly, an anarchistic ideology might form part of Bentham's utilitarian political theory. Such an anarchistic theory would be based on a political ideology, at the core of which would be harmony between individual and communal conception of harm. The gist of such a theory would amount, on the one hand, to a communal context of censure according to which individuality is oriented and evolved. This communal censure would give meaning to the *enhancement of individuality*, by being transparent to individual criticisms and pleas. Such a communal context would be sensitive to individual contributions, even to the extent that these contributions concerned the modification of the collectivity.

What constitutes a transient consensus about a conception of "harm" in such a community would be determined as a result of interaction between individuals and some communal entity, the latter being a product of communication: see chapter 6, sections II–IV below. Utilitarian political theory did not necessarily imply that "harm" would be "determined" by centrally-based state institutions. This idea of mutually-enforcing community and individuality would imply that only in the context of a community is it possible for individuals to communicate as well as to modify this context. Anarchism as "communal individualism" is developed in A. Ritter's *Anarchism: a Theoretical Analysis* (Cambridge, 1980,) pp. 4, 29, 32–7. For a general account of anarchism, see D. Miller, *Anarchism* (London, 1984,) pp. 2–29.

Bentham's methodology meant that in order to arrive at this philosophical and social communal individualism, he did not have to resort to over-optimistic assumptions about human nature of the sort usually made by theoretical anarchists. For Godwin, the capacity for individual utilitarian reasoning, which would be based on a capacity for understanding other people's similar reasoning, formed the foundation for a right of private judgement, around which, in turn, his case for anarchism revolved; see W. Godwin, *Enquiry Concerning Political Justice* (Harmondsworth, 1976). Bakunin argued that the capacity of individuals to "internalize" communal decrees, without institutional coercion, was the foundation for anarchism. See M. Bakunin, *God and the State*, G. Aldred (ed.) (London 1920). Kropotkin believed that the capacity for benevolence, and hence general reciprocity, as well as mutual aid, was the key factor in the success of the anarchistic enterprise. See P. Kropotkin, *Mutual Aid: A Factor of Evolution* (London, 1910). See also P. Marshall, "Human Future and Anarchism" in D. Goodway (ed.), *For Anarchism: History, Theory and Practice* (London, 1989), pp. 127–49, at 134–7. By contrast, for Bentham, human nature was neither virtuous nor evil. A human being as an evaluative agency was understood by him to be, to some extent, the constructive personal result of, and hence would be modified by, social circumstances (law being one of them), which could change as the collective identity of a social group developed.

Further, as will be argued in chapter 6, anarchists have typically been mistaken in claiming that in anarchistic communities virtues like "internalisation" or "benevolence" could function regardless

In short, utilitarian-based anarchism is a philosophical attitude which should not be confused with the possible actual, and not least, transient, *result* of the social evolution of a group, namely the existence of an anarchistic society.

Only the perspective of philosophical, utilitarian-based anarchism would equip a social theorist with a sufficiently flexible apparatus to observe social processes to the degree that an anarchistic society could be contemplated, and indeed justified on utilitarian grounds. This flexibility would imply that even a near-perfect government, one which produced generally just measures, would be temporal and transient, subject to social forces and conflicts, and so would not entail a duty to obey the law. The perspective of utilitarian-based anarchism enables the diverse manifestations of political society to be connected by a number of universal features, one of which is the absence of a duty to obey the law.

Finally, to stress the point again, it goes without saying that Bentham's theory could accommodate a conventional, customary duty to obey the law. This duty would stem from existing propositions, which could be inferred among members of a social group, and would be enforced by the moral sanction. Yet this would be different from saying that there was a moral duty to obey the law. It will be argued in the next section that Bentham's statements concerning the universal features of political society, including the absence of a moral duty to obey the law, are to be discovered in *Fragment*. It will be argued that in *Fragment*, as a practical consequence of his utilitarian-based anarchism, Bentham did not identify a moral duty to obey the law as a central feature of political society. The expediency of obeying did not imply a duty to obey the law.

III

It is now appropriate to present a reading of *Fragment* from a new perspective. Based on close reading of *Fragment*, the arguments in this section clarify the connections Bentham saw between the public sphere, constitutional limits and the foundations of political society. *Fragment* was a polemic against Blackstone's account of the origin of society and the nature and limitation of law-making powers. Bentham, however, also meant to offer his own account of how political authority, and the limits of political power, should be understood. The work contained many ideas which were not fully developed. Nevertheless, these themes were developed later by Bentham into a more complete legal and constitutional theory, remarkable for its consistency.

of the manifestation of the existence of obligations, and hence of sanctions, be those sanctions institutional or communal in nature: see A. Ritter, *Anarchism, a Theoretical Analysis*, p. 21. For Bentham, as will be argued in chapter 6, anarchistic communities would have different *kinds* of sanctions and obligations.

It must be left for other occasions to offer a detailed study of anarchism. It merely points towards the possibility of connecting the notion of constitutional limits as a social phenomenon to a philosophical anarchistic attitude.

Bentham attacked Blackstone's explanation of the origin and persistence of government. Blackstone rooted his explanation in the concepts of a social contract and natural law.[18] Bentham argued that the power of government, and with it what he called "political society", was characterised *by* a "habit of obedience" on the part of the people. The opposite state to obedience, Bentham called "resistance", "disobedience", or "revolt".[19]

He mentioned, untypically briefly, the idea of revolt, and distinguished between disobedience in *law* and in *fact*, and between *unconscious* and *conscious* disobedience. The most relevant category for the discussion which follows was conscious disobedience to the law. This type of disobedience could be either *secret* (fraudulent) or *open* (forcible). Bentham recognised that the most difficult form of disobedience to undertake would be *forcible conscious legal disobedience*, but he declined to elaborate, since he thought the length of the discussion would require a separate work.[20] The only remark he made on this occasion was:

> "This disobedience, it should seem, is to be determined neither by *numbers* altogether (that is of the persons supposed to be disobedient) nor by *acts*, nor by *intentions*: all three may be fit to be taken into consideration."[21]

This shows that Bentham assigned the same importance to the issue of disobedience as to obedience. If obedience was related in his thought to the social justification of authority, so was disobedience in marking the limits of this social justification. Bentham also attached importance to the *people*, who were to fulfil the role of a continuous judging body, which checked, that is determined, the limits of the social justification of authority. Further, in assigning the idea of intention to the subject-matter of disobedience, Bentham saw the act of the people as an act of will, which must have followed an act of understanding of some kind.

Bentham criticised the doctrine of the original contract as an inadequate justification for political obligation. He relied here on Hume.[22] Hume, however, was a conservative in the sense that reform based on utilitarian considerations was for him secondary in importance to the utility which arose out of stable, established conventions. Bentham, by contrast, put much more emphasis on the principle of utility as a critical standard for justifying reform in general, and, as will be argued, disobedience to government in particular.

[18] W. Blackstone, *Commentaries on the Laws of England*, R.I. Burn (ed.) (London, 1783), Book I, pp. 38–53 esp. 46–53.

[19] Bentham discussed the basis of political obligation in *SAM*, pp. 126–7, editorial note 2. Bentham condoned the idea of a "contract", but, and this is a crucial qualification, the contract had to be understood as socially dynamic, the terms of which might, *by mutual consent of both parties*, be changed *at any time*. This approach would answer many of the objections to "one-off consent" theories as the basis for political obligation: see Horton, *Political Obligation*, pp. 38–9.

[20] *Fragment*, pp. 435–7.

[21] Ibid., p. 436.

[22] See in this context, D. Hume, *A Treatise of Human Nature*, P.H. Nidditch (ed.) (Oxford, 1978), p. 539 (*Of the Source of Allegiance*); See also Hume's essay "Of the Original Contract", in *Essays Moral, Political and Literary*, E. Miller (ed.) (Indianapolis, 1987), pp. 465–87.

Because the principle of utility was the sole source of justification for political obligation, Bentham questioned the role of promises as the basis for political obligation. He denied that people were bound by compacts based on promises. A Lockean social contract was not capable of improvement, since it required society's dissolution before it could be renegotiated. Bentham attacked this stagnant, and hence potentially decadent,[23] feature of contractarianism. He argued that, "It is manifest, on a very little consideration, that nothing was gained by [the contract] after all: no difficulty removed by it".[24] The dilemma as to whether to obey or not would remain unresolved.

Bentham's attack on the social contract theory was founded not on an epistemological basis, but on a social, empirical one. A "one-off" contract would be incapable of meeting the new demands generated by the development of any social group. Only a government susceptible to continuous assessment of utilities would be worth advocating. Even if one tried to reformulate the substance of the original contract so that government undertook to be subjected to the law, Bentham enumerated *four* situations in which a government ought not to be obeyed on utilitarian grounds. The first situation would arise under a bad government, in which the whole rationale of the law would run counter to the happiness of the community. The second would occur where a government impaired the happiness of the people without violating any single law. Thirdly, Bentham argued that circumstances might change, in which case the greatest happiness might call for resistance to the law. Finally, Bentham made the important distinction between the expediency of obeying a law, and the expediency of obedience to "the law". No single law, even if it operated to diminish happiness, could render the people so unhappy as to make inexpedient the maintenance of the whole social arrangement based on the contract. One unjust law would not operate to outweigh the whole utilitarian justification of the political system. Some more comprehensive unhappiness would be required in order to justify the conclusion that there was no utilitarian justification for obedience to *any* of the measures promulgated by government.[25]

The question remains as to what role promises played in Bentham's theory of the origin and persistence of government (or political authority). In giving his account of the subject, Bentham based the persistence of government on the utilitarian calculation made by *the people* concerning whether or not to obey. Bentham repeated the same formulation many times throughout the essay. Bentham's style becomes an important issue here in reading the text.[26] The answer to the question of obedience was encapsulated in a short formulation. A nearly identical formulation was repeated *in a number of different contexts*.

[23] *Fragment*, p. 446.
[24] Ibid., p. 442.
[25] Ibid., p. 443.
[26] Style is important because some modern writers criticise Bentham's account in *Fragment* as being an oversimplification. They argue that Bentham had very little to say about the basis for political obligation: see A.J. Simmons, *Moral Principles and Political Obligations* (Princeton, 1979), pp. 47–52, and J. Horton, *Political Obligation* (London, 1992), pp. 56–60.

Each time the formulation appeared, it cast light on a different problem. Instead of introducing the formulation once and then explaining its nuances, Bentham repeated it over and over again. This procedure arguably helps to clarify his general understanding regarding the connection between popular resistance and constitutional limits, or the limits of sovereignty.

In his general formulation of the principle of resistance, Bentham referred to the "juncture of resistance" (hereafter referred to as "the formulation"). Bentham had already mentioned the future of resistence in *A Comment on The Commentaries* written in 1774–5:

> "This then, and no other, being the *reason* why men should be made to keep their promises, viz. that it is for the advantage of society that they should, is a reason that may as well be given at once; . . . Why they should obey in short *so long as the probable mischiefs of obedience are less than the probable mischiefs of resistance:* why, in a word, **taking the whole body together**, it is their *duty* to obey, just so long as it is their *interest,* and no longer. This being the case, what need of saying of the one, that *he* PROMISED so to *govern*; of the other, that they PROMISED so to *obey*, when the fact is otherwise?"[27]

This passage, in which the formulation is first introduced, discusses the formation of a popular *collective* judgement, which presupposes a standard upon which people could agree.[28] Bentham argued that, at a theoretical level, the principle of utility was the only standard upon which people could agree. It was not that people had some infallible means of calculating utility, but that the principle of utility would be the only standard with reference to which communication could take place. Communication might produce a utilitarian consensus regarding the possibility of resistance. The consensus so produced had to be conceived as a popular, communal, critical judgement, which, once formed, would be acted upon. Individuals would communicate with one another, with the subject of their communication being a joint communal judgement: "The people, no matter on what occasion, begin to murmur, and **concert** measures of resistance."[29]

Bentham conceived the power of the people to form a consensus and to resist as the very foundation of political authority in their society. He asserted that people were able to think in terms of communal utility. This would not involve a calculation of individual interests as such. Instead every member of the community would think in communal terms about the consequences of resistance. This point appears in a second version of the general formulation:

> "when, according to the best calculation he is able to make, *the probable mischiefs of resistance* (**speaking with respect to the community in general**) *appear less to* ***him*** *than*

[27] *Comment*, pp. 444–5.

[28] In *Fragment*, p. 481, Bentham attacked Blackstone for arguing that in every state there must be an unlimited power. Such an argument, Bentham contended, would serve as a justification for rulers demanding absolute obedience from the people. However, for the people themselves, such an argument would be no more than an abstract proposition in jurisprudence. Bentham looked for a principle which would also constitute a standard by which the people would be prepared to judge the action of rulers.

[29] *Fragment*, p. 483.

> *the probable mischiefs of submission*. This then is **to him**, that is to each man in particular, *the juncture of resistance*."

The following passage explains the point further:

> "A natural question here is—by what *sign* shall this juncture be known? By what *common* signal alike conspicuous and perceptible to all? A question which is readily enough started, but to which, I hope, it will be almost as readily perceived that it is impossible to find an answer. *Common* sign for such a purpose, I, for my part, know of none: he must be more than a prophet, I think, that can shew us one. For that which shall serve as a particular sign to each particular person, I have already given one—his own internal persuasion of a balance of *utility* on the side of resistance."[30]

This passage makes some important points. First, there could be no ultimate common signal for resistance other than considerations of utility, and any signal that could be conceived, such as "express conventions" or "*constitutional laws in principem*", would be of prima facie status only. These, and any other types of convention, would be common signals not for resistance, but only for individuals to begin to calculate on the basis of the principle of utility. Bentham recognised the usefulness of such common signals, but, very significantly, added that a transgression of them would sometimes lead to disobedience, and sometimes would not.[31]

The second point which arises in this passage might be said to expose an apparent incoherence in Bentham's argument. On the one hand, he argued for a *collective* judgement as to the possibility of resistance. He therefore relied on the capacity of the people to disobey when the time was ripe. On the other hand, he put the onus of the judgement on the *individual*. The judgement ultimately consisted in the internal persuasion of the individual when thinking communally. Communal judgement was derived from each individual's subjective internal persuasion.[32] Yet the incoherence is more apparent than real. Bentham's account relies on the communicative possibility that individuals might be able to form an inter-subjective consensus with regard to the utility of resistance. This inter-subjective consensus, achievable in a situation of free communication, would be facilitated by express conventions and other constitutional measures, which would stimulate the interpretative communicative process. Beyond having an express convention to facilitate inter-subjective communication, Bentham seemed to believe that the people might co-ordinate themselves by communicating about the probable consequences of resistance. Their calculation would naturally be influenced by their existing expectations.[33] The important point to emphasise is that the communicative activity, aiming at consensus

[30] Ibid., p. 484.

[31] Ibid., p. 490.

[32] This point will be discussed in detail in chapter 6, pp. 191–222 below.

[33] In the previous chapter it was argued that people need not be solely influenced by the express conventions existing within their own group, but might also be influenced by those existing within other political societies: see chapter 3, p. 92, note 28 above.

formation, would occur after the recognition of common signals, such as the breach of constitutional laws.

Another feature of the juncture of resistance was that it should offer theoretical guidance in resolving the dilemma of liberty and authority. If the people were to retain some moral autonomy to judge the acceptability of the limits imposed on the exercise of coercive power over them—if liberty to resist the unjustified exercise of authority was to be preserved—there would have to be a guiding principle pointing out the reasons why and the time when resistance was to be undertaken. This guidance, Bentham maintained, could not be furnished by Blackstone's contradictory account of an absolute authority on the one hand, and a freedom to transgress human laws which violated rules of natural law on the other. Such guidance could only be sought from the "principle of *utility*, accurately apprehended and steadily applied".[34]

The next occasion on which Bentham presented the formulation was in relation to the establishment of constitutional limits, which could never, for him, be solely institutional but were also necessarily popular in nature.[35] Constitutional limits were based on moral arguments and the crystallisation of popular, or moral, propositions about what these limits *ought* to be:

> "Grant that there *are* certain bounds to the *authority* of the legislature: of what use is it to say so, when these bounds are what nobody has ever attempted to mark out to any useful purpose; that is, in any such manner whereby it might be known beforehand what description a law must be of to fall *within*, and what to fall *beyond* them? Grant that there *are* things which the legislature *can*not do; grant that there *are* laws which exceed the *power* of the legislature to establish. What rule does this sort of discourse furnish us for determining whether any one that is in question is, or is not of the number?"[36]

Bentham was dealing here with the limits of sovereignty, or the limits to the justification of authority. A mere statement that the legislature was limited, argued Bentham, would be unhelpful in assisting one in ascertaining whether a given measure was within or outside these limits. The meaning of a void law was, therefore, not simply that the power to make this law and every other law was forfeited. Bentham wrote:

> "had [the people] arrived at the same practical conclusion through the principle of utility, they would have spoken of the law as being **to such a degree pernicious**, as that, were the bulk of the community **to see it in its true light**, *the probable mischief of resisting it would be less than the probable mischief of submitting to it.*"[37]

There was no point in speaking about law as legally void, irrespective of the interpretation of its social effects. These social effects would be the subject of a communal utilitarian calculation in relation to a future proposed coercive mea-

[34] *Fragment*, pp. 482–3.
[35] See chapter 5, pp. 152–7 below.
[36] *Fragment*, p. 486.
[37] Ibid., p. 487.

sure. Bentham emphasised that, beyond a certain point, a given measure might be seen to be so evil as to justify disobedience to it. This passage shows Bentham not as a lawyer, but as a sociologist of law who advocated social dynamism and popular judgement as the only foundations for justifying the authority of law. No constitutional limitation could exist, independent of a communal interpretation and judgement, and of an action which might follow this judgement. Bentham shifted the argument from the legal to the social sphere—from a simple view of power exercised by a coercive institution which was conceived or "recognised" as authentic, to a view of power resulting from an interaction between social forces and government.

The last passage raises another important point, one to which Bentham gave much more attention in his mature constitutional writings, namely whether the people were capable of seeing the issue "in its true light". For present purposes, the important point is that Bentham would not have spoken in the conditional tense had he not foreseen the possibility that some obstacles might exist to the people's seeing a coercive measure "in its true light". He acknowledged the damaging influence of fallacy. He recognised the possibility of false consciousness.[38]

This passage is illuminating in relation to the type of disobedience which is dealt with in *Fragment*. Bentham was not concerned with an act of individual disobedience stemming from an individual's calculation with regard to the likelihood of punishment, a threat of which would be attached to a given authoritative measure. Further, although his discussion overlapped with civil disobedience in the Thorleauan and Rawlsian sense, Bentham talked about a more fundamental disobedience of a constitutive nature. Civil disobedience would arise when a group of people, usually a minority, felt a deep sense of injustice in what Rawls called a "near just society". The aim of such civil disobedience, carried out by an aggrieved group, would be to persuade the obedient part of the population of an injustice produced by the near-just system. The disobedient group would accept the consequences of their actions and endure the attached punishment.[39]

Arguably, Bentham is focused only in part upon civil disobedience in *Fragment*. Surely a group which makes a point can be seen as a collectivity. However, the whole point of civil disobedience is to challenge, many times unsuccessfully, the extent to which the injustice to a given group can be captured as part of a bigger, collective, evaluative, communal public reason and judgement. Bentham did make remarks pertinent to civil disobedience in *Fragment*. He referred to the censuring of coercive measures, although merely censuring would not go far enough to establish a constitutional or social limitation on the authority in question. Civil disobedience effectuated the stimulation to all-out

[38] See chapter 6, p. 220, note 76, and p. 229 below, for a discussion of the obstacles which prevented people from seeing coercive measures in their true light.

[39] See J. Rawls, *A Theory of Justice*, pp. 363–8; see also H.D. Thoreau, "On the Duty of Civil Disobedience", in *Walden or, Life in the Woods and On the Duty of Civil Disobedience* (New York, 1965), pp. 251–71.

disobedience, but in itself did not exhaust the general collective disobedience which concerned Bentham. Civil disobedience might develop into something more fundamental, something which might reduce the social justification of an authority either in regard to all matters, or in regard to a single promulgation. Bentham's account in *Fragment* concerned the people, as the entrusting body, collectively challenging the social justification of the authority in their society.

The final context in which the juncture of resistance was mentioned addressed its precise content. To recapitulate, the utilitarian judgement concerned a communal calculation with regard to the possible outcome of resistance. Additionally, the juncture would be arrived at when an individual measure was so pernicious as to tip the balance of utilities in favour of resistance. It has been argued above that the transgression of conventions already established, whether expressed in writing or not, would only be a prima facie ground for disobedience. In a revealing passage Bentham went on to add a consequential ingredient to the communal judgement:

> "The footing on which [the principle of utility] rests every dispute, is that of matter of fact; that is, future fact—the probability of certain future contingencies. Were the **debate** then conducted under the auspices of this principle, one of two things would happen: either men would come to an **agreement** concerning that probability, or they would see at length, **after due discussion** of the **real** grounds of the dispute, that no agreement was to be hoped for. They would at any rate see clearly and explicitly, the point on which the *dis*agreement turned. The discontented party would then take their resolution to resist or to submit, upon just grounds, according as it should appear to them worth their while—according to what should appear to them, the importance of the matter in dispute—according to what would appear to them the probability or improbability of success—*according*, in short, *as the mischiefs of submission should appear to bear a less, or a greater ratio to the mischiefs of resistance*. But the door to **reconcilement** would be much more open, when they saw that it might be not a **mere affair of passion**, but a difference of judgment, and that, for any thing they could know to the contrary, a sincere one, that was the ground of quarrel."[40]

This passage is perhaps the clearest in showing that the whole idea of limitations to the exercise of authority would be a matter of communal consensus, arrived at after free inter-subjective communication and interpretation. The aim was to achieve *some* mutual understanding (consensus), and then to resist or accept the measure with one voice. Bentham realised that often, due to various obstacles in communication, people would assume a conflict all too hesitantly, even when no *real* conflict existed. The opposite was also true, namely that people were in the danger of assuming a consensus where there was none. This passage hints that the dimension of authenticity in public communication was close to Bentham's heart. False consciousness was therefore to be guaranteed against if people were to form an authentic utilitarian consensus about the justification and limits to centralised coercion in their society.[41]

[40] *Fragment*, p. 491.
[41] In this respect, see chapter 6, p. 220, note 76 below.

Two possible outcomes of a free and uninterrupted exchange of views were related to the issue of resistance. One was that a consensus would be arrived at concerning the probable evils resulting from resistance. The other was resistance by a part of the community, analogous to a general form of civil disobedience, with regard to the social justification of the authority which promulgated the measure in question. The juncture of resistance at the heart of these two scenarios was of the same nature.[42]

What becomes apparent in studying these formulations of the junction of resistance is the social use made of the principle of utility. Bentham described the dynamics at the foundation of every political society. People would apply utilitarian considerations once there was a free exchange of views and information among themselves, and between themselves and the government. Bentham seemed to believe that despite the fact that the authority in question was entrusted with indefinite power (and to the extent of this power, its actions would tend to exclude independent reasoning on the part of the governed), there would be a sphere in which people would retain some degree of moral autonomy. Bentham's account had real social significance, and as such was not plausible only as a theoretical premise. The extent to which a communal judgement could function effectively would depend on the degree of development of the social group in question. Bentham did not attempt to specify any more detailed substantive content pertinent to the utilitarian calculation which would fit a given social group. It was not the occasion for him to do that, because the purpose of *Fragment* was only to discern the main universal features of political societies.[43]

A sketch can be given of the application of the juncture in a society in which communication in the public sphere is fairly free and transparent. As a description, this sketch should not be treated as exhaustive and may not fit other stages of the development of a group.[44] The nature of the juncture never changes but,

[42] By acknowledging both possible diversity and concurrence between people, Bentham avoided explaining political obligations, or the limits of such obligations, by means of the artificial doctrine of a social contract. He arguably showed sensitivity to the fact that the minds of people have different complexions, and he would reject an approach which aspired to deduce certain metaphysically based principles of justice without sensitivity to the social context that made them: see Horton, *Political Obligation*, pp. 47–8.

[43] It is arguable that, beyond stating the general parameters in evaluating the dilemma of obedience, the question of why people ought to obey is not reducible to a single answer. A single foundation for political obligation, such as consent or gratitude, would not be general enough to capture most social situations. Thus, a general substantive justification for political obligation would be too inflexible and so unhelpful: see T. Macpherson, *Political Obligation* (London, 1967), pp. 62–5, 84–5. The utilitarian dilemma, on the other hand, could utilise noun-substantives such as consent, promise, or gratitude, all of which would signify certain cultural sources of pain and pleasure; see further pp. 116–7, note 50 below.

[44] Bentham did not, in *Fragment*, discuss the conditions for free communication. In a case where these conditions were hampered, the juncture of resistance would remain the same, but it would be inefficient in operation, and socially realisable only through violent revolution which would involve a total loss of security. In the absence of free communication, oppression would remain unchecked for a long period, not only in terms of the quality of centralised regulation, but also in terms of the degree of its exercise.

as will be argued in the next section, the *manner* in which it is socially realised could be different under a despotic and a free government respectively. The utilitarian considerations would be of such a nature that they would determine the extent to which *communal* benefit would be increased as a result of resistance. An assessment of the communal benefit of resisting could be arrived at *despite* individual agreements or disagreements.

Suppose a new coercive measure is introduced by the centralised authority. This measure transgresses the expectations of a group, causing them to experience the pain of disappointment. The transgression constitutes an apparent breach of constitutional limits. Once such an apparent breach has been identified, the process of communal judgement, in relation to that group, would be that which Bentham discussed in *Fragment*. From this moment onwards the measure would not be regarded as an authoritative measure (i.e. an expression of will that operated to exclude independent, immediate reasoning), but would amount to a recommendation, or a proposal. The measure at this point could trigger a different *kind* of reasoning.

Possible arrival at the juncture of resistance would now depend upon two processes. The first consists in an evaluation of the measure, and thus involves a critical discussion, that is an attempt mutually to influence opinions, carried on among members of the community, between minority and majority groups, and between the government and the community.[45] This discussion takes into account considerations of "original utility", that is assessments of potential consequences which concern the distributive choices suggested by the measure in question (considering the measure in its own right), and those of "expectation utility" which would relate to consequences stemming from the effects of the measure on existing social relations.[46] The outcome of this process is a critical opinion as manifested in the internal persuasion of each person.

People would reflect critically upon a communal conception of harm, the aversion of which both justified and limited legislative authority. Their communication could result in many levels of reflections. They could think that the measure is too offensive against some good the community held dear and as a result should not be regarded as authoritative. They could hold, in a second-order way, that the witholding of a generally disagreeable measure was itself harmful and, therefore, the unaccepted measure should nevertheless be regarded as authoritative. In short, people could assess various combinations of first- and second-order communal conceptions of harm. The second-order constitutions would be of a more co-operative nature than the first-order ones.

The second process is a "formal" one; "formal" because it does not relate to the evaluation of the measure's substance. The question instead concerns an *estimation of the degree of consensus* which exists with regard to the merit or otherwise of the measure in question or the degree of co-operation about harm

[45] The idea of influence will be extensively discussed in chapter 6, pp. 199–206 below.

[46] See chapter 2, p. 62, note 72 above.

in the face of disagreements on the substance of the measure. People would weigh the harm posed to the legal order from lack of co-ordination of moral beliefs, as against the first- and second-order considerations mentioned.

The utilitarian calculation of the juncture of resistance takes these two processes into account and weighs them against one another. The communal benefits and burdens of submission to the measure are seen in the global context of obedience—that is not in terms of the measure taken singly, but in terms of the social justification of the institution of law as a whole. Two elements therefore have to be weighed: the burden of the measure as seen by the community on the one hand, and the estimation of the degree of which a consensus has been formed, as seen by each member of the community, on the other. The latter element involves an assessment of the prospective damage to the law as a co-ordinating institution.

In this context, the distinction between civil disobedience and the type of disobedience currently under consideration should be stressed. Once the people encounter a co-ordination problem, and to the extent that they understand that in this concrete case they have such a problem, the only form of disobedience possible is civil disobedience in the Rawlsian sense, because the *communal* utilitarian consensus would not be in favour of resistance. Civil disobedience occurs when a group reaches the conclusion of its own utilitarian calculation, *despite the fact* that there has been as yet no co-ordination of moral beliefs in the community regarding the particular issue in question. As Rawls argues, the undertakers of such an action rely on a presumption of an abstract, shared conception of justice in the community, the relevance of which to the concrete case in question might not yet have become apparent. Civil disobedience might still be carried out, despite the existence of a good justification for authority. A smaller group would resist it, on their calculation of the balance of utilities, there was a case to do so, that is, if the issue was of fundamental importance to them.[47]

Having said that, the distinction between civil and constitutional disobedience is somewhat blurred here. The hope of people who embark upon civil disobedience could consist in a last-resort attempt to convince the community to renegotiate a communal conception of harm. If a social struggle about harm did not yield a re-negotiated settlement under a revised conception of harm, secession could result if the disobedient group felt strongly about the injustice done to them. Alternatively, they could back down.

What is important to note again is that for the full realisation of all these social processes, their operation should not be obstructed by communicative obstacles. Social/communal actions, and consensus formation, will *naturally* occur once there exists an opportunity for free communication around a

[47] Rawls discusses situations in which, although all the conditions are ripe for civil disobedience, people ought not to resist. He contemplates such a situation where damage will occur to the institution of law itself because of, say, the simultaneous effectuation of civil disobedience by some other groups: see *A Theory of Justice*, pp. 373–6. It seems that Rawls in effect considers here the juncture of resistance of a given small group in deciding whether to obey or resist.

common theoretical standard of pain and pleasure, or, in this case, the mischiefs of submission and resistance. It is also important to notice the significance of the role which Bentham gave, at such an early stage of his career, to the people, and to the public sphere (or communal collective thought), in determining the extent of their political society *as such*. Bentham firmly believed that in many cases people could agree on constitutional matters. People were able to form a consensus on the basis of the principle of utility, providing they were able to exchange views, and thus make an assessment of the probable consequences of coercive measures. They would be able to correct each other's past observations on similar questions: "Men, let them but once clearly understand one another, will not be long ere they agree."[48]

In a society where free communication was facilitated, this description of the juncture of resistance would account both for a situation in which a common agreement between the people emerged, and one in which an agreement was made between them to differ and if no consensus is formed about the value of containment, to separate the dissenting politically. Even a justification of authority which is based on co-ordination would be a result of consensus. As Bentham argued, even an agreement to differ would have some substance. People would discern the exact nature of the conflict between them. Even pluralism requires agreement that people are entitled to uphold different values (communication having had the effect that, to a greater or lesser extent, difference is not to be interpreted as causing "harm"). A consensus on pluralism could be entrenched and function as a constitutional limit.[49]

Bentham's understanding of the basis of political obligation has now been sketched, as has his understanding of the way in which power is limited through an application of the principle of utility by means of a communal judgement. Once the people have a focus of expectations, once there is some convention, this convention can operate as the basis for a successful communal, critical, utilitarian reflection, interpretation and judgement. Thus, Bentham understood "sovereignty", and the limits of sovereignty, in popular terms. It was the people who would determine and effectuate constitutional limits. There was no plausible, socially dynamic way of understanding the limits of political authority, or constitutional limits, other than by connecting them directly to a popular utilitarian moral judgement.

There have been modern attempts to construct a formal duty to obey the law. This duty has been understood as binding, irrespective of the substantive values that a given community holds.[50] For instance, Gans's thesis is arguably a restate-

[48] *Fragment*, p. 292.

[49] See chapter 5, pp. 186–90 below.

[50] Various foundations for a moral duty to obey the law have been laid. These have included the idea of gratitude (as argued for in Plato's "Crito": see *Plato—The Trial and Death of Socrates* (London, 1963), pp. 78–9), and the principle of reciprocal fairness (as developed in Hart's "Are There any Natural Rights?", *Philosophical Review* 64 (1955) 175–91, at 185, and in Rawls's *Theory of Justice*, pp. 342–50). Another foundation for the duty to obey is the duty to support reasonably just institutions as a part of a general duty to justice, also argued for by Rawls (*A Theory of Justice*,

ment of the Benthamic juncture of resistance, only involving a more complex terminology which is itself of dubious value. His formulation oscillates between what he calls the *limited obedience* thesis, and its logical complementary—the *near absolute obedience* thesis.

He explains the limited obedience thesis as involving the following considerations of expediency:

> "On the one hand [the decision whether to obey or not] depends on the **intensity** of the **damage** to the functioning of the legal system by the disobedience, **modified** by the factor of the level of enforcement that the system supplies the political morality and the **probability** that such **damage** will occur.
> On the other hand, it depends on the **intensity** of the damage facing the value due to which the law is objectionable, modified by the **factor of this value's importance** and the probability that such damage will occur."[51]

The *near absolute obedience thesis* means simply that in regard to matters where there is no ultimate value which mandates disobedience, disobedience cannot be justified. This would mean that if there was no shared political morality in a given social group, there would exist a justification for the surrender of moral autonomy because the inherent value of the institution of law would be more important. If a political morality were shared, the protection of more concrete entitlements *might* outweigh the co-ordinative rationale for the binding force of law as an institution.[52]

Utilitarianism, which has been explored in the reading of *Fragment* presented here, is at the centre of the moral thinking of individuals in Gans's scheme. His argument has all the consequentialist properties, as well as the elements of

p. 334). Soper bases the duty on the notion of respect to the interest of people who can be hurt in the case of disobedience ("The Obligation to Obey the Law", in R. Gavison (ed.), *Issues in Contemporary Legal Philosophy*, pp. 127–55, at 134, 150). Dworkin bases the duty to obey on what he calls "communal obligations", a notion which relates to his idea of integrity as a distinct political ideal, an ideal which is based on an interpretive process in which arguments about personified "communities" are constructed and justified (*Law's Empire*, pp. 196–9).

Arguably, none of these global assertions of the duty provides a plausible criterion which captures the interpretative dynamism *at the level of harm* which precludes any moral basis for the duty to obey the law. For example, when new circumstances produce change in the most general pattern of communal values it would be absurd to interpret and justify pre-existing communal obligations on those values. Similarly, a duty to obey just institutions does arguably depend upon a conception of justice which, if approached interpretively, is culturally and historically indexed. The problem of the duty to obey may well arise in the context of disagreements about justice. Thus, a duty to justice, if it is to avoid being a general circular statement devoid of real social significance, will be limited to circumstances under which arguments about injustice can be acknowledged *decidedly* by the public's conception of harm. Moreover, a general duty to justice runs the risk of being reactionary as it is built around the notion of "legitimacy", which would in turn be based on an acknowledgement and entrenchment of a given conception of harm. In short, all assertions of global grounds of obedience have to be understood as socially materialised, and thus only *as part* of a utilitarian calculation. Thus, all these grounds face the objection to the existence of a duty to obey as derived from utilitarian-based anarchism. They may develop certain parameters for obedience to law, but they will never be able to provide an epistemologically sound global moral duty to obey the law.

[51] C. Gans, *Philosophical Anarchism and Political Disobedience* (Cambridge, 1992), p. 125.

[52] Ibid., p. 127.

indeterminacy, which are found in the formulation of the juncture of resistance in its various contexts in *Fragment*. No formal construction of the considerations of obedience, some of which would transcend any particular group's (or generally, any cultural) view of justice and morality can sensibly pre-determine the outcome of the utilitarian calculation. Gans, in formulating the duty to obey, needs to address the epistemological objections to the *existence* of *a utilitarian duty* to obey the law. It would seem that his claim is not only entirely compatible with utilitarian-based anarchism, but must be overshadowed by it. Gans seems to be a utilitarian, and as such he ought not to accept a moral duty to obey the law.

IV

Although constitutional theory will be discussed in the next chapter, it is appropriate in the context of this reading of *Fragment* to introduce it in order to argue that already, in this diverse and essentially incomplete essay, Bentham went much further than engaging in a mere polemical dispute with Blackstone. He made a number of incursions into constitutional theory, an area that he developed much more fully in his later thought.[53]

As early as *Fragment*, Bentham developed a connection between the operation of the juncture of resistance (which was a communal utilitarian judgement), the idea of a free government, and a democracy. Further, if, as has been argued, the underlying philosophy of the arguments in *Fragment* can be characterised as *utilitarian-based anarchism*, the account provided there must be compatible with the transient existence of an anarchistic community, or a community based on communal individualism.[54] This would imply that the concept of a free government, and perhaps of democracy, was wider than that of representative democracy, which would still rely, at its heart, on the existence of centralised institutions. An individualistic community was, of course, not something that Bentham overtly discussed in *Fragment*.

Bentham's mature constitutional writings centred on the workings of a representative democracy. However, to indulge in some Benthamic constructivism, it could be argued that Bentham viewed representative democracy as a necessary stage of social and political development, a stage which, in his lifetime, no political society, with the possible exception of the United States, had reached. In so far as Bentham, observing social development from a particular historical vantage point, was sensitive to the dynamic nature of social interaction, it is not inconceivable that, in his view, the accumulated communal experience of a mature, stable democracy, might lead to the development of a communal consensus and, in turn, to the diminution in formal, centrally coercive, state institutions.

[53] See chapter 1, p. 6, and note 12 therein above.
[54] See p. 104, note 17 above.

Bentham argued that the criterion on which a public utilitarian judgement would be based could only meaningfully be described at a highly abstract level. This criterion would *be* the same, he argued, in a despotic and in a free government. Assuming then that the criterion for constitutional limits was the same, what, queried Bentham, still on the level of universal theory, constituted the difference between a despotic and a free government? The next passage is of crucial importance, and is therefore quoted in full. Bentham maintained that the difference between free and despotic government depended on:

> "the *manner* in which that whole mass of power, which, taken **together**, is supreme, is, in a free state, *distributed* among the several ranks of persons that are sharers in it:—on the *source* from whence their titles to it are successively derived:—on the frequent and easy *changes* of condition between gover*nors* and govern*ed*; whereby the interests of the one class are more or less indistinguishably blended with those of the other:—on the *responsibility* of the governors; or the right which a subject has of having the reasons publicly assigned and canvassed of every act of power that is exerted over him:—on the *liberty of the press*; or the security with which every man, be he of the one class or the other, may make known his complaints and remonstrances to the whole community:—on the *liberty of public association;* or the security with which malcontents may **communicate their sentiments, concert their plans,** and **practise every mode of opposition short of actual revolt**, before the executive power can be legally justified in disturbing them.
>
> True then, it may be, that owing to this last circumstance in particular, in a state thus circumstanced, the road to a revolution, **if a revolution be necessary**, is to appearance shorter; certainly more smooth and easy. More likelihood, certainly there is of its being such a revolution as shall be the work of a number; and in which, therefore, **the interest of the number are likely to be consulted. Grant then, that by reason of these facilitating circumstances, the juncture itself may arrive sooner, and upon less provocation, under what is called a *free* government, than under what is called an *absolute* one**: grant this;—yet till it *be* arrived, resistance is as much too soon under one of them as under the other."[55]

This passage is remarkable for, generally speaking, it discloses, albeit in an undeveloped way, Bentham's rationale for constitutional liberty. More particularly, this passage brings the following points to light: first, it shows that constitutional freedom did not depend on any a priori bounds to power. The actual extent of a government's power was not the factor on which the freedom of the constitution depended. This claim, however, should be distinguished from the claim that sovereignty, or the power to make laws, was inherently socially limited. Bentham showed that the limitability of sovereignty was related to the idea of constitutional freedom. In order to establish a government which was free, yet also, of course, socially limited (as *all* governments were), Bentham distinguished between "infinite" and "definite" limitations to power.[56] This distinction mirrors

[55] *Fragment*, p. 485.
[56] Ibid., p. 484.

what will be referred to in the next chapter as the "enabling rationale" for government.[57] Briefly, a distinction could be drawn between two ways of portraying limitations on power. On the one hand, such limitations could be portrayed as a priori, expressed by "you can or cannot do this" (a definite limitation of power, which Bentham criticised). On the other hand, limitations could be portrayed as inherent *social* limitations on sovereignty. "Corrective" or "checking", a posteriori limitations on power could exist by virtue of which sovereign power would never be infinite (a limitation of power approved by Bentham). The latter category of limitations would amount to an implied statement to the power-holder, embodying the concept of a "trust": "do as you wish but you must know that the body of the people retains some moral autonomy to assess the global social necessity, and thus the extent, of your powers". This was the kind of check on sovereign power which Bentham recognised.

This category of limitations on power *emanated from its exercise* and constituted an *enabling* rationale for the exercise of coercive powers, as opposed to a *disabling* one. A disabling rationale would lead to decadence, stagnation, and the inefficient regulation of an ever-changing social reality. The place of this passage, in the midst of Bentham's discussion of the utilitarian communal calculation, shows that he believed that freedom of communication—communication which would in fact promote the efficacy of collective opinion and action—would lead to the most effective, a posteriori, limitations of powers. This point is significant, because it implies that the logical dichotomy usually drawn between an "unlimited" and a "legally limited" government is inaccurate.

The second insight contained in this passage is that the degree of freedom would depend on the way in which the powers of government were divided and interacted with one another. This appears to be Bentham's earliest definition of constitutional liberty. Now much has been said about Bentham's idea of liberty.[58] Bentham has been interpreted as understanding the idea of liberty purely in terms of the "absence of coercion". On this understanding, "liberty" was a misleading idea in explaining the rationale of political coercive activity, such an activity being exactly the opposite from an "absence of coercion". For example, the protection of individuals by coercive measures was traditionally discussed under the heading of "civil liberty". Further, protection against bad government was traditionally discussed under the heading of "political liberty". Bentham preferred the term "security", which was for him the main noun-substantive to be used in relation to the justification of political power. He wrote about the idea of security in several forms, including security *of* property and *of* expecta-

[57] See chapter 5, pp. 143–5 below.

[58] Bentham's idea of liberty and security has been extensively discussed by F. Rosen, in his "Thinking about Liberty", inaugural speech, University College London, 1990, "Bentham and Mill on Liberty and Justice", in G. Feaver and F. Rosen (eds), *Lives, Liberties and the Public Good* (London, 1987), pp. 121–38, at 121–6, and *Bentham, Byron and Greece* (Oxford, 1992), pp. 33–38; see also Long, *Bentham on Liberty*.

tions (instead of "civil liberty") and security *against* misrule (instead of "political liberty").[59]

Despite his refusal to use the term liberty, there is in this passage what might be seen at first as an incoherent fusion of terms like "liberty" (liberty of the press, liberty of public association), and "free" (free government, free state) on the one hand, and "security" (security for the expression of complaint—used to explain the liberty of the press, security of communication—used to explain the liberty of public association) on the other. The point here is that if the term liberty were to be paraphrased in this context, it would mean that a free government was "a government in which there existed some 'absence of coercion' ". However, using "security" rather than "liberty" to characterise a free government would be much more consistent with Bentham's point of view. In terms of "security", such a free government, in which there was some "absence of coercion", would be regarded as "a government which would provide security for the people against misrule". In other words, people would have security against their being prevented from reflecting on how much security by rule (or law) they thought they needed. In this way, security and liberty, both of which are mentioned in the quoted passage, would signify the same state of affairs. Both would mean a guarantee, by law, of an absence of obstacles in the way of people's ability to determine the extent to which coercion should be exercised over them in the name of security by law. Where coercion was used, it would hamper the ability of the people to exchange their views, and collectively to act upon these views. The provision of free communication was thus an essential element of a free government.[60] In this passage, Bentham argued that the freedom of the constitution would depend on the smooth formation of a communal judgement. Means for people to discuss their discontents and aspirations, and to engage in any form of opposition short of revolution, would have to be secured in a free government. Again, emphasis is placed in this passage on the absence of restraint on any communication which might lead to the formation of a utilitarian consensus, and successful collective action.

Thirdly, this passage shows a close affinity in Bentham's mind between a free government and a democratic form of government. Bentham explicitly made the connection between a free government and democracy when he said that in a free government the interests of *the number* are likely to be consulted. Although he did not write about sinister interests here,[61] the possible antagonism between the interest of rulers and that of ruled was clearly contemplated. Further, by writing about the change of condition between governor and governed, and about the responsibility of the governors, and by highlighting the importance of the necessity of providing information for people in order to bring about

[59] See chapter 6, pp. 232–3 below.

[60] This thought may be the embryo of Bentham's more extensive discussions of the idea of a free government in his mature writings: see chapter 5, pp. 152–60 below.

[61] The term "sinister interest" is explained at chapter 5, p. 137 below.

accountability, Bentham demonstrated that he had in mind a clear connection between a free government and democracy.

Bentham's understanding of a free government contained a latent conception of democracy. Democracy was certainly a desirable normative application of the popular element in sovereignty. Yet, it seems that Bentham was democratic in a wider sense than devising a representative democratic form of government. As a part of the universal description of political society, Bentham saw that an inherently popular element in the exercise of sovereignty would exist in all political societies. Understood universally, the term "free government" was not only an evaluative but a relative term. "Freedom in government" could exist to some extent in a mixed monarchy. However, taking into account both the enormous participatory role assigned to the people, and Bentham's characterisation of a free government, the degree of freedom available under a government which was undemocratic would be very small indeed. In short, although the popular, and hence democratic, element of sovereignty was a necessary part of the description of what might exist in every government, a democracy appeared to be, logically, a *desirable* form of government.[62] It was free communication and exchange of views between people which *critically* justified, limited, renegotiated and, as will be seen, transcended, the political "togetherness" which meshed Bentham's conceptions of free government and democracy.

The final point of interest in this passage concerns the difference in the operation of the juncture of resistance in despotic and free governments. Bentham argued that under a free government the juncture of resistance would be arrived at with ease, and that even minor provocations could precipitate it. The freer the government, the more easily would people be brought to consider the utilitarian dilemma regarding the ambit of authority in their society. Conversely, an actual revolution would, to all intents and purposes, be unnecessary in a free government.

This apparent inconsistency can be accounted for. Bentham distinguished between a "political" revolution and a "legal" one. Both types of revolution would operate according to the same juncture of resistance. However, there would be a difference between the two concerning the manner in which this juncture was effected. A political revolution undermined *all* fundamental constitutional prescriptive propositions which gave at least prima facie authority to the machinery of government.[63] It would involve a loss of all order, and with it, security. Such a state of affairs was extremely undesirable. A legal revolution, by contrast, would be just as fundamental, but would leave security untouched. A legal revolution would mean that at the core of *every* alteration to the consti-

[62] A conception of democracy under a utilitarian theory would be wide ranging and would defend socially dynamic relationships between ethics and politics. This conception of democracy will be discussed in Part 2 of the book.

[63] Bentham gave the following example of a situation which could lead to a political revolution. Where the government was so bad in its inception that it fundamentally and flagrantly opposed any adherence to the universal interest of the community, the people might join forces and get rid of "the nuisance": see *First Principles*, p. 128.

tution would be a utilitarian argument about what ought to be the extent of the power of government. Such a legal revolution was fundamental because it would involve a contest in which the extent and limits of authority, *including the form of government itself* (assuming that radical institutional change could be brought about at one stroke), was challenged under the existing form of government. For example, any establishment of constitutional limits which signified a transfer of authority from representative institutions to the community would be seen as a legal revolution. Under a legal revolution, any change would be carried by the framework of the existing constitutional framework, which had established the old form of government. Further, the social justification of the authority of every *individual* measure of the government could be questioned in this fundamental, revolutionary way, without also destroying the social justification of the whole order. Thus, every political revolution would be a legal revolution, but not vice versa.

The relation of obedience to validity was given serious consideration by Bentham. An objection to the legal validity of legislative activity would consist of a social judgement, even if it related only to a single measure. It goes without saying that even the basic convention, which *prima facie* governed the distribution of power in a free government, would itself be susceptible to the same utilitarian test. Indeed, in this passage Bentham admitted that it was so susceptible. Yet, he would think it highly inexpedient and self-defeating, on most occasions, to oppose the constitution of a free government, whatever it might be.

Leaving this basic law aside, the execution of any legal, as opposed to political, revolution would be made not only possible, but easier in a free government. The application of any utilitarian consensus which had been formed, and which would determine constitutional limits, would be better facilitated in a free government. In a free government, the dilemma regarding whether to resist could arise very easily, although the actuality of resistance, that is the development of circumstances so bad as to provoke actual resistance, would be a highly remote possibility. Reconciliation both among the people and between the people and government could lead to the production of self-limitations on the part of the government. Such reconciliation would be the hallmark of a free government. Resistance would be less frequent in a free government, but could be arrived at very easily should the agents of the government suddenly produce a very pernicious law. In a free government, the threat of resistance would be maximised although the prospect of its actual realisation would be remote. The government would be more likely to listen to the public, or other institutions which interacted with it, and pursue reconciliation through re-negotiation or secession.[64]

The distinction between a legal and a political revolution would be highlighted in a free government, while in an absolute government, because

[64] The imposition and then withdrawal of the "Poll Tax" may serve as a good example of such a process of reconciliation.

resistance would take so long, and require so much provocation, any legal revolution would be likely to coincide with a political one.[65] In an absolute government any revolution would entail a loss of security and, therefore, the utilitarian consensus, *even when the people had a sense of their true interests*, would usually incline towards passive obedience.[66] This would be the case until the situation became so unbearable that, under the influence of opinion within the community, and possibly from other political societies, a collective act of resistance would be violently effectuated.

V

In this section the implication of the interpretation presented above, of the duty to obey, is discussed in relation to the debate about how the principle of utility would be used both by a central, regulative mechanism and by those subject to its regulations.

In the preface to *Fragment* Bentham said: "Under a government of Laws, what is the motto of a good citizen? *To obey punctually; to censure freely*."[67] In the light of the analysis of the nature of the duty "to obey the law", or lack of such a duty, and the popular nature of constitutional disobedience, there appears to remain a puzzle. The puzzle concerns the manner in which, thanks to this short motto, it seems that Bentham viewed disobedience as disagreeable. A good citizen would obey all the time. He must first obey, *whatever he thinks, and whatever he thinks others would think in relation to him*, even if the matter concerns the social justification of coercion (a justification which may relate to any given coercive measure). Disobedience seems something distinct from merely criticising the government. There appears, then, no possibility that at some point such disobedience could emanate from fundamental criticism of a government which produced a pernicious coercive measure.

What, then, was the point of Bentham's elaborating at length in *Fragment* about the irresolute, ultimate, theoretical basis for political obligation, while on the other hand advising citizens to obey punctually? What would be the point of conducting a sophisticated discussion of the irreducible moral autonomy of the people in deciding whether to obey or not, and then summarily dismissing such moral autonomy with a simple motto? It is argued above that the disobedience discussed in *Fragment* differed from mere censuring. Surely, where the condi-

[65] There does not appear to be a great deal of textual evidence to support this claim. However, in Bowring, ix. 38, Bentham seemed to imply that under a representative democracy, although there might be some violence and disagreement, tranquillity and security would be promptly restored.

[66] See chapter 6, p. 220, note 76, and pp. 225–6 (especially note 88) below.

[67] *Fragment*, p. 399. It is interesting that Kant wrote something similar in "What is Enlightenment", in *Foundations of the Metaphysics of Morals* (London, 1990), p. 89:

> "But only he who, himself enlightened, is not afraid of shadows, and who has a numerous and well-disciplined army to assure public peace, can say: 'Argue as much as you will, and about what you will, only obey!' ".

tions for collective resistance existed, *no* obedience would follow, and the existence of such conditions would be, as Bentham argued, facilitated under a free government.

An immediate response might be that Bentham was simply inconsistent on this point. It is a remote possibility, however, that a systematic thinker of Bentham's stature would commit such an obvious error within the framework of such a relatively short work, even allowing for the fact that *Fragment* contained several underdeveloped arguments.[68] A simple solution would be to read Bentham literally, and to say that he confined his motto of a good citizen to a situation "under the government of laws". This would imply that there *would be* many situations in which the citizen should firstly obey, and then censure. These would comprise situations in which the government did something worthy of criticism, but within the bounds of socially acceptable coercive measures. However, under this interpretation the motto would not hold in a constitutional dispute, where the social justification for an authentic expression of will was contested. Literally read, the motto would not hold in a situation where the government transgressed a crystallised, communal, moral view with regard to the consequences of such a transgression.[69] In short, this literal interpretation is inadequate in debating the status of laws *qua* laws, that is in debating the limits of sovereignty.

However, the attempt to provide an adequate explanation goes to the very heart of the operation of the principle of utility as a moral principle. The operation of the principle has been the subject of a subtle debate in Bentham scholarship.[70] Kelly describes two extreme ways in which the operation of the principle of utility may be explained. The first is direct utilitarianism, in which an "individual ought to do what in each case results in the greatest happiness". The second is indirect utilitarianism, which holds that, although the principle remains the standard for judging right and wrong, "These judgements (of

[68] Long, referring to Bentham's passage on free government quoted above, claims that a free government would be characterised by a "perfect balance between punctual obedience and free censure": *Bentham on Liberty*, pp. 94–5. It is difficult to make sense of Long's argument. Punctual obedience and free censorship can exist perfectly together. Long puts it as if there needs to be a balance between them. But if punctual obedience were *balanced* against free censorship, it would no longer be punctual. The real dilemma is how to reconcile this motto with cases in which punctual obedience was undesirable.

[69] There is also the question of how the motto can be squared with utilitarianism, and with Bentham's epistemology. A utilitarian direction to obey punctually would be a contradiction. Hare tries to give an account of such a utilitarian obligation. He argues that there is a utilitarian general duty to obey the law. It would be useful, he maintains, to have such an "unbreakable" general principle. This general principle would derive from each person's thinking in terms of all other persons affected by his action, and not solely in terms of his own benefit: see R.M. Hare, "Political Obligation", in T. Holderich (ed.), *Social Ends and Political Means* (London, 1976), pp. 1–12. Hare's view can be criticised on the ground that he falls into the trap of recognising utilitarian entitlements which, by the supposition, cannot be utilitarian. In consequence, he fails to conceive a social situation in which people could question, and if necessary reject, on utilitarian grounds, the necessity of the law as an institution.

[70] See especially, Postema, *Bentham and The Common Law Tradition*, and Kelly, *Utilitarianism and Distributive Justice*.

utility) are not the direct source of obligation, or authoritative reasons for action."[71] I shall call these two extreme characterisations of the operation of the principle of utility "pure characterisations".

The most recent interpretation of Bentham's theory as direct utilitarianism was offered by Postema. Postema analyses the operation of the principle of utility in the context of Bentham's theory of legislation and law. He shows that Bentham did not argue for an extreme act utilitarian theory, whereby everybody would be left to make their own calculation regarding the maximisation of social well-being. One of the most important components of social well-being was, for Bentham, security of expectations, and this security could not be provided for under a doctrine of extreme act-utilitarianism.[72]

The task of law, Postema argues, was to provide a regulative mechanism which co-ordinated moral beliefs, and hence provided security both for expectations and against bad government. Through law, a sphere was determined within which individuals could conduct their plans of life.[73] Postema argues that the basis of political obligation was indeterminate, *despite the necessity for co-ordination*. Obligations did not operate wholly as exclusionary authoritative reasons for action, but would always be conditional upon an application of the principle of utility. This indeterminacy was the corollary of Bentham's attempt to combine security and flexibility, and was a considerable improvement on the stagnant Humean notion of political obligation.[74]

Accepting many of Postema's arguments, Kelly claims that the principle of utility did not specify individuals' obligations. He goes on to argue that had the principle done so, it would have undermined the instruction to "obey punctually" in the motto of a good citizen, as it appeared in *Fragment*. Had the principle been the direct source of obligation, notes Kelly, surely there were conceivable circumstances in which obedience would not be warranted.[75] Further, direct-act utilitarianism could result in the impossibility of central regulation to protect some very basic rights, such as the right to life.[76] In this context, Kelly refers to Rawls's criticism that in such a pure, direct utilitarian theory a convergence is presumed between what is "good" and what is "right", with the assumption that individual entitlements will give way to utilitarian calculation when these calculations are proved to promote greater good.

[71] P.J. Kelly, *Utilitarianism and Distributive Justice*, p. 60.

[72] Postema, *Bentham and The Common Law Tradition*, pp. 160–1.

[73] Ibid., pp. 164, 174–5.

[74] Ibid., pp. 323–4. Elsewhere Postema discusses Bentham's insight into the public character of law. Postema claims, arguably in all too positivistic a fashion, that law, for Bentham, created a sphere in which individuals could exchange/communicate views for the purpose of evaluating the law: see "Bentham on the Public Character of Law", *Utilitas* 1 (1989) 41–61, at 46. The central question which the judge asked was, "What rule can I expect, through my decision and my reasoning for it, to attract recognition by my colleagues and the people in general?" Any authentic "legal" proposition could serve as a co-ordinating measure which would enable individuals to focus on it and hence ask themselves the above question. Law, in short, would enable collective action: ibid., pp. 46–8.

[75] Kelly, *Utilitarianism and Distributive Justice*, p. 50.

[76] Ibid., pp. 60–1.

Kelly agrees with Postema on the need for co-ordination. However, because he interprets Postema as also viewing the principle of utility as the "ultimate decision principle", Kelly disagrees with what he takes to be Postema's more moderate version of an unacceptable direct utilitarianism. Kelly criticises what seems to him to be internal inconsistencies in Postema's account. The inconsistencies are revealed by comparing Postema's recognition of the need for co-ordinative measures on the one hand, with his questioning of their unequivocal obligatory status by portraying them as subject to utility, on the other. Kelly concludes that Postema cannot account for the obligatory status of co-ordinative measures, while simultaneously repudiating their obligatory status by allowing the individual agent to be guided in his conduct by direct utilitarian calculation.

However, Kelly also objects to the pure characterisation of an indirect theory of obligation. He criticises Hart's pure indirect model. According to Hart's argument, Bentham would distinguish between an unacceptable conception of the principle of utility as a direct source of moral guidance for individual conduct, and an acceptable conception of it as a standard for the critical evaluation of such conduct. In addition, Kelly relies on Hart's interpretation of Bentham's epistemology, which has already been referred to at the beginning of this chapter. Hart's claim was that an obligation could not emanate directly from a moral principle. The understanding of an obligation was conditional upon the medium of a proposition which signified an expression of will backed by a sanction.[77] Hart could not, Kelly argues, be entirely right in his formulation of a purely indirect explanation of the operation of the principle because Bentham recognised circumstances in which individuals ought to guide their conduct in a manner which would be beneficial to the whole community.[78]

Kelly then proceeds to offer his own, subtle conception of the operation of the principle of utility.[79] Kelly's explanation runs as follows: because Bentham had a sanction theory of duties, that is to say, because the principle of utility could not constitute the direct source of an obligation, one should differentiate between two "ought" statements. One sense of "ought" derived from a prescriptive proposition, and hence would only be directly influenced by consideration of the pleasures and pains provided for by sanctions. Another sense derived directly from the principle of utility, and would amount to a general moral "ought"—an attitude of self-reflection that one ought to behave in a communally beneficial way. Kelly terms the latter a "weak", non- conclusive ought, which could function alongside the former "strong" and "conclusive" ought, or obligation.

For Kelly, Bentham's moral theory functions as a hybrid theory, employing the principle of utility both directly and indirectly. Indirectly, utility was promoted by adherence to co-ordinative measures, but what turned these measures

[77] Kelly, *Utilitarianism and Distributive Justice*, pp. 66–7, referring to Hart's introduction to *IPML*, p. xlviii.

[78] Ibid., p. 67.

[79] Ibid., pp. 67–9.

into conclusive obligations was that they were backed by sanctions. The direct pursuit of utility could never become obligatory in this sense, but remained a general critical attitude, which would be arrived at by self-reflection that one ought to behave in a way which would promote the maximum happiness of one's community. So, differing from Postema, Kelly argues that obligations become conclusive only when they exclude moral autonomy by means of some sanction. The non-conclusive moral attitude would be the foundation from which people *commented on*, or censured, the co-ordinative measure. However, this critical attitude, and the degree of moral autonomy implied by it, would exist alongside unquestionable obedience to law, however bad a particular law might be. In this way, Kelly seems to explain the motto of a good citizen in the preface to *Fragment*.[80]

Both Kelly's and Postema's interpretations are subtle and illuminating. However, it will be argued that both interpretations contain incoherences, the resolution of which would diminish the differences between them. I will first give my account of the function of the principle of utility, and then argue that the distinction between the views of Hart and Postema which Kelly discerns does not, in fact, exist. Further, I will argue that Kelly fails to provide an account which differs significantly from that of either Hart or Postema.

A functional distinction which has been identified in the current reading of *Fragment* relates to sovereignty as a "split" concept.[81] On the basis of the earlier analysis of the concept of sovereignty, it is now possible to discuss the reasons to pay "obedience to a prescriptive proposition", as operative within a *straightforward* or *immediate* level of obligation. This is to be distinguished from "an obligation to have an obligation" to which obedience is related to reasoning which is more global in nature, and which may be termed the *categorical* or *constitutional* level of obligation. This is the level at which, according to my interpretation, *Fragment* was written. This level may be regarded as a global, self-referential, level of "an obligation to have an obligation", because the utilitarian considerations involved at this level require an exercise of moral autonomy relating to the limits of the social justification of authority. This sphere would question the very status of this communication as "prescriptive".

However, it would be too strong, and reductionist, to argue that the existence of these two levels implies adherence to legal positivism. It would be wrong to claim that certain obligations either "existed" at an immediate level *as a matter of fact* in a legal positivist manner, or "criticised" according to some kind of an "inconclusive" reference to the principle of utility. The two levels—the immediate and the constitutional—despite being distinguished here, should be understood as belonging to the same *interpretative* continuum, namely the justification of authority. The signification of one level as being "immediate" does not amount to an assertion of a factual positivistic statement nor does the

[80] Kelly, *Utilitarianism and Distributive Justice*, p. 69.
[81] See chapter 2, pp. 52–8 above.

term "existence" amount to such a statement. The signification is rather that certain reasons for the assertion of given prescriptive propositions are taken for granted.[82] To put the point another way, positivism does not arguably follow from the inability of the principle of utility to serve as a direct source of obligations. It does not follow from the necessary mediating role of a prescriptive propositional medium that direct interpretative reliance on the principle could not be made in justifying the statement that there "existed" a true prescriptive proposition in a given case.

At the constitutional sphere of operation, as has been argued, any obligation to recognise an obligation would operate on a prima facie basis, and would be rebuttable by a direct application of the principle of utility. The criticism would doubt the existence of the obligation in the first place. Thus, an obligation could be said to function solely as an exclusionary reason only in the immediate moral sphere, in which the obligation would not be questioned as such. But if the categorical level of reasoning is engaged, the very justification and inference of an obligation at the immediate level would be subject to higher, or second-order, utilitarian reasoning.[83] The transition to this categorical level of self-reflection would be similar to a situation where a person understands in his dream that he dreams and then he wakes up because he reflects upon his experience *as* a dream.[84] It would be absurd to suggest, on this reading of *Fragment*, that Bentham wished people to obey regardless of the consensus they came to regarding the limits to authority. The general task of co-ordination would not be impaired if people refused to recognise the authoritative status of an individual measure. Kelly's interpretation implies a notion of passive obedience, which, as will be argued in the next chapter, Bentham condemned in his later constitutional theory.[85]

[82] See chapter 2, pp. 68–73 above.

[83] See chapter 2, p. 55, note 51 above. The categorical level is recognised in Flathman, *Political Obligation*, pp. 107–8. Flathman finds it impossible to reconcile "must be performed" and "free not to do". However, distinguishing between levels of reasoning goes some way towards resolving this problem.

[84] The social process which leads to the transition from the immediate to the categorical levels of the operation of the principle of utility is discussed at chapter 6, pp. 203–5 below.

[85] If one accepts the existence of different levels of reasoning, or utilitarian calculation, one must emphatically reject the distinction between what is commonly referred to as "act" and "rule" utilitarianism. A general criticism against this distinction is that rule utilitarianism either collapses into act utilitarianism, in circumstances in which the violation of a rule would be more beneficial, or that it ceases to be distinctively utilitarian if obedience to rules is required in circumstances where the result is not beneficial: see D. Lyons, *Forms and Limits of Utilitarianism* (Oxford, 1965), pp. 143–60, and N. Simmonds, *Central Issues in Jurisprudence* (London, 1986), pp. 35–6. This criticism is most evident at the constitutional level, where the utilitarian merit of rules *qua* obligatory prescriptions is questioned.

The criticism would also present a similar difficulty for Kelly's direct/indirect account of the operation of the principle of utility, under which the principle of utility allegedly does not require the direct actual maximisation of well-being by rulers. Kelly's argument cannot resolve the utilitarian dilemma with regard to the global justification of rules made by the utilitarian legislature *qua* rules. It is not plausible to discuss solely an indirect approach, confining a direct approach only to the process of "improvement" of rules. This dilemma, and with it, the difficulty for Kelly's account become very acute in regard to constitutional problems, for which see chapter 5, pp. 186–90 below.

What are the implications of this analysis for the debate under consideration? It seems that the dichotomy Kelly introduces between Hart's view and Postema's is more apparent than real. Kelly's erroneous move is to derive a positivistic reading of Bentham's utilitarian enterprise from the impossibility of the principle of utility to serve as a direct source of obligations. However, it is my argument that Bentham's theory was *interpretative* and not positivistic. The principle of utility cannot, *on epistemological grounds,* serve as a direct source of obligation. A prescriptive proposition was needed in order to *know* an obligation. However, the need for a propositional medium did not preclude the interpretative use by the people in justifying disobedience at the categorical level, a level at which doubts might be cast on the existence of the status of an obligation *as such*. This interpretative approach would mean that some other obligation could be argued for to be true as a result of a popular interpretative process.

Postema would probably concede the epistemic point. He would not argue that the principle of utility could serve as a direct source of obligation. However, he *could* argue that the principle of utility functioned at two levels of abstraction, as suggested by his groundbreaking interpretation of Bentham's theory of sovereignty.[86] He *could* argue that there would always be some sphere which would allow for a residuary moral autonomy, by the exercise of which moral obligations could be formed. These obligations would have prima facie status. This status could be ascribed to any sort of obligation, be it a legal obligation (an interpretation of the reasons for a prescriptive proposition contained in a code of laws), or a moral obligation (a reasoned convergence of inferences of prescriptive propositions as a result of communication between people). Certain further communal beliefs could be formed which, as has been argued, would strengthen the justificatory force of these prima facie obligations, or would replace those obligations with better ones.

It is my argument that the adjective "direct" should not be taken to mean that the principle of utility would coincide with the description of the constituents of an obligation. These amount to a prescriptive proposition and a sanction. A "direct" reliance on the principle of utility would mean that there would always be a sphere of moral autonomy which might generate an alternative interpretation in the light of which a prescriptive proposition would be justified as true or false. This alternative interpretation would, and ought to, override the justification for the assertions of an existing obligation as true or false. In any case of disobedience, either at the immediate level (individual or civil disobedience), or at the categorical level (constitutional, collective disobedience), the obligation which overrode the existing one would stem from the re-interpretation and formation of a prescriptive proposition arising from a source other than the institution in question. This source for the re-interpretation of new prescriptive propositions could be an individual, a small group, or the whole community.

[86] See chapter 2, p. 45 above.

Postema's vagueness is accounted for by his statement that the advantage of Bentham's theory was the manner in which obligations were not understood automatically as exclusionary reasons for actions. With regard to this point, Postema's account is unable to determine whether an obligation operated to exclude subjective reasoning or not. Postema could be interpreted as recognising the principle of utility as a direct source of obligation, but this would be incorrect. He simply recognises that the principle of utility might have implications for actual behaviour, *despite the existence of legal obligations or any other communal obligation*, and that as such it might retain its status as an ultimate decision-making principle. Postema does not provide an analysis of the way in which the two levels, at which the principle operates, relate to each other. For him, it is only when individual calculation indicates that disobedience would result in the maximisation of social well-being that the political obligation is not seen to be binding.

Postema goes astray when he claims, equivocally, that legal rules merely add new reasons for the subject to follow the rules.[87] This position hovers between positivistic and interpretative approaches to Bentham's utilitarian enterprise. There need not be *new* reasons. Instead, two levels of reasoning are involved in establishing a reasoning continuum. One level at which the legal or political sanction, punishment, as well as the stated reasoning for a prescriptive proposition enters as part of the utilitarian calculation, and a second, constitutional, categorical, level, at which inter-subjective social communication leads to more global utilitarian reasoning. It is important to note that even at the immediate level, "disobedience" also requires a utilitarian calculation which leads to the formation of a prescriptive proposition different from the one prescribed by the institution in question.

Kelly claims that Postema overstates his case, in that he allows individual utilitarian calculations to override institutional co-ordinating obligations. However, Postema cannot be criticised for overstatement here, because the justification of any obligation could be evaluated by the direct application of utility at all levels of argumentation. Disobedience which followed criticisms in the categorical sphere would be totally compatible with the co-ordinative nature of the social enterprise and the existence of a code of law. The existence of an institutional, co-ordinating measure would not *annul* the possible application of the utility principle by citizens, in order to form a different prescriptive proposition, again at the level of the individual, group or community. Again, the fact that a direct application of the utility principle does not make that principle the *creator* of an obligation, but only an evaluative principle which gives rise to the *justification as true* of alternative prescriptive propositions, should not be overlooked.

To address Kelly's own hybrid argument: it is very difficult to understand the exact nature of the *ought* which Kelly describes as resulting from the

[87] Postema, *Bentham and The Common Law Tradition*, p. 324.

obligatory–inconclusive, direct operation of the principle of utility. It may mean that the principle ought to be used as a critical standard in censoring a prescriptive proposition, that is an act of the understanding corresponding to the statement "this obligation is bad" or "this obligation is good". Alternatively, it may mean that the principle ought to be used directly in order to generate an alternative prescriptive proposition, that is an act of the understanding corresponding to the statement: "this new obligation increases the happiness of the community", or "this new obligation reduces the happiness of the community". It is not clear that Kelly succeeds in establishing a non-conclusive normative medium, which is not the equivalent of one or other of these two alternatives. If an allegedly inconclusive normative statement like "one ought to promote the greatest happiness of the community" represents a requirement for the possession of a critical attitude, then its inconclusiveness amounts to no more than saying that the attitude of censorship ought to exist although this attitude has not yet crystallised into an obligation. The inconclusiveness in such a case would merely emphasise that to censor and to be obligated are not the same thing. The difference between the banal statement "the principle of utility is the standard of right and wrong" (the fact that utility is a critical principle), and the statement of the non-conclusive ought, namely that "one ought to promote the greatest happiness of the community", would be negligible indeed. Likewise, the difference between the conclusive statement "this new obligation is better" and the non-conclusive *obligatory* statement that "I ought to act in a manner which promotes social well-being" would also be negligible. A global obligation to promote utility is thus not a significant addition to the uses already made of the principle of utility.

If such is the case, and assuming Kelly has failed to create a third normative medium, it does not appear that his position differs significantly from that of either Hart or Postema, whose interpretations of Bentham, it has been claimed, are not the opposed "pure characterisations" which Kelly portrays them to be. Both Hart and Postema argue that a propositional medium, backed by a sanction, must occupy the space between a moral principle and the existence of an obligation. This propositional medium might be supplied by a convention or a written provision in a code, and could appear at various levels of abstraction. This is an *epistemological explanation* of an obligation. However, it does not follow from the epistemological point that the principle of utility, on the accounts of Postema, Hart and indeed Kelly, could not be understood as operating directly in an interpretative, rather than positivistic, fashion. The sphere of *justification-as-true* always involved a direct relation to utility, and did not entail a factual, positivistic existence of obligations. All those three accounts ended up with a positivistic reading of Bentham's enterprise and could be criticised for that.

Why should it be assumed that where institutional direction was absent there would be no obligation in the fullest sense of the word? After all, a convention (a prescriptive proposition which is backed up by the moral sanction) could give rise to a popularly conceived obligation. Kelly argues:

> "Bentham provides for the possibility of moral obligations within his theory, by relying on the moral sanction as a means of giving effect to these obligations. However, there is no necessary connection between the requirement of the moral sanction and the requirement of utility unless the conventional morality is also an explicitly utilitarian morality, whereby the moral and social pressures which create moral obligations are informed by the principle of utility."[88]

It can be argued that there was some functional connection in Bentham's thought between the quality of communication which gave rise to public opinion and what was right. However, Kelly is correct to stress the divergence between conventional and utilitarian morality. It would only be in a democratic government, where free communication was established, that what was considered popular would start to converge with what was right. From a participant in the practice's point of view, conventional morality *would be* prima facie the requirement of utility. However, Kelly's argument in this respect is *entirely* compatible with the existence of a constitutional sphere in which moral obligations which determined constitutional limits would operate.

In sum, Kelly fails to distinguish between the operation of the principle of utility at the immediate level and at the constitutional level, and hence fails to provide for the direct application of the principle in the development of an obligation which may justify constitutional disobedience. The operation of the constitutional level means that a prescriptive proposition, and hence an obligation, would be inferred without any reference to an intermediate institutional agency, such as a parliament or court. Its source would be communication within the public sphere. Also, on Kelly's interpretation of the motto of a good citizen, the idea of constitutional limits, or limited sovereignty, is difficult to explain. Kelly discusses the operation of the principle of utility from a positivistic perspective, namely as if there already existed as a matter of fact a legislature's constraining act in this or that way. In other words, he assumes the *existence* of some indirect level of background reasoning to "law", coupled with general critical reference to the principle of utility. He explains neither the nature of the foundation of this law which is arguably interpretative in a direct utilitarian manner rather than positivistic, nor the limitations to make law which is the core issue of this direct utilitarian interpretation. As it stands, Kelly's argument fails to make sense of Bentham's legal writings.

The utility which stems from co-ordination would always, under Kelly's interpretation, justify obedience. This is plainly incorrect, because in the name of co-ordination any communal opinion might be suppressed without provoking disobedience. So, although Kelly's argument is subtle in that it offers an interpretation in which Bentham's moral theory operates in a hybrid (direct/indirect) way, his interpretation of Bentham's constitutional theory is socially dynamic only in respect of constitutional and legal *improvement*. As far as constitutional *limits* being determined and effectuated by the community are

[88] Kelly, *Utilitarianism and Distributive Justice*, p. 66.

concerned, however, Kelly's account presents Bentham as positivistic and disappointingly static. Under the interpretation suggested here, the motto of a good citizen, in fact, only has a prima facie status and is only applicable to the immediate level of utilitarian reasoning. This is the central point of the argument in *Fragment.*

This direct/indirect hybrid interpretation leads Kelly to what is arguably a serious misinterpretation of Bentham's argument. He writes:

> "the individual agent is required to act in accordance with rights and duties because of the imposition of sanctions, *irrespective of his judgement of the utility of such obedience.*"[89]

This creates a general difficulty for Kelly's own project, namely the full accommodation of Bentham as a liberal. If Kelly is correct, Bentham might as well have torn up *Fragment.* Kelly's interpretation sees Bentham as intent on providing individuals with security, and ready to invade their constitutional moral autonomy to the maximal extent possible in the name of security.[90] This is because the only moral autonomy which Kelly allows individuals is at the immediate level, in areas where there is no coercive intervention. There is no further sphere where individuals can question the very necessity for an obligation to be imposed on them.

[89] Ibid., p. 69.

[90] Criticisms of Kelly's largely indirect approach will continue on a more general level in chapter 5, pp. 186–90 below, where the importance of the argument advanced in this book is discussed in relation to Rawls.

5

The Role of the People in determining Constitutional Limits II—Mature Constitutional Theory

This then in a word is the perfection of government: that all rulers should be subjects: rulers only to certain purposes, subjects to all others: in that case subjects can not suffer but they must suffer with them. But if there are any rulers who are not on any occasion subjects, then all suffering is on the side of subjects, no suffering, in so far as it is in their power to prevent it, on the side of rulers.

First Principles, p. 136.

All power depends upon opinion. Any kind of limitation is as capable of being set to it as any other. All that is requisite is that the limitation be intelligible.

On The Efficient Cause and Measure of Constitutional Liberty, UC cxxvi. 10.

What good effect is it that the contrivers could have had in view? Giving stability to the constitution?—vain pretence. On what depends the stability of the constitution? Upon a form of words? Upon the acquiescence of the nation under a pretension equally pernicious, groundless, presumptuous and absurd? Upon the surrender of all feeling on the part of the people and of all claim to common sense on the part of their pretended rulers? No: but upon the approbation of the people continually bestowed upon the constitution, upon the general sense and spirit of it.

Necessity of Omnipotent Legislature, UC cxlvi. 29.

I

This chapter continues the examination of the role of the people in Bentham's legal and constitutional theory. It discusses constitutional limits in Bentham's mature constitutional writings, and shows that Bentham's legal and political enterprise provided for a constitutionally limited government. It argues that Bentham's mature constitutional writings are consistent with his earlier legal and political ones in their analysis of constitutional limits.

Bentham scholarship has tended to take a limited, partial view of his endeavours, entertaining the view that there were two "Benthams".[1] Arguably, however, there was, from a theoretical point of view, only one "Bentham". On this view, Bentham merely changed the perspective from which he considered the same problem, namely the construction of social arrangements capable of achieving the greatest happiness of the greatest number in the group concerned. There is no theoretical point in making a conceptual distinction between "*legal* sovereignty"—that is the nature of, and limitations on, the power to make law—and "political sovereignty"—that is the power of the people in a representative democracy to "locate" and "dislocate" officials.[2] Both these "types" of sovereignty, involving concepts in legal and constitutional theory respectively, converged within Bentham's theory of legislation, and within his analysis of an individual law, especially a constitutional law. It is the argument of this book that Bentham showed remarkable consistency in his utilitarian enterprise, and that scholarly divisions have led to the development of certain preconceptions which misrepresent his theory.

II

In this section, the least controversial points of Bentham's constitutional theory are sketched. There is no need to give an elaborate exposition of the subject given the thoroughness of several other accounts.[3]

The ultimate end of Bentham's constitutional theory was to establish and to maintain a good government, and to prevent the formation and persistence of a bad one. The goodness or badness of all the laws, civil and penal, including laws imposing constitutional limits, depended on the quality of the government. A bad government would have the propensity to institute a penal code which would tend to increase the wealth of rulers at the expense of the community.[4]

The intimate relationship between the quality of the constitution and the end of the laws appeared in Bentham's writings as early as *OLG*. There, Bentham devoted a chapter, albeit a short one, to the subject of "the end which a law might have in view". He argued that the intended, as opposed to the eventual or

[1] See chapter 1, pp. 6–7 above.

[2] Bentham used the terms "location" and "dislocation", and not "appointment" and "dismissal". He thought that the word appointment could be misleading in cases where the opposite would be "disappointment": see Rosen, *Jeremy Bentham and Representative Democracy*, pp. 76–8. On subordination as a central constitutional principle, see ibid., pp. 8–12.

[3] A detailed account of Bentham's constitutional code can be found in Rosen, *Jeremy Bentham and Representative Democracy*, chapters 2, 4, pp. 83–92, 93–101 and 106–10; see also his *Bentham, Byron, and Greece*, pp. 40–92. For an exposition of some aspects of his theory, see P. Schofield, "The Constitutional Code of Jeremy Bentham", *King's College Law Journal*, 2 (1991) 40–62, and "Bentham on Public Opinion and the Press", in D. Kingsford-Smith and D. Oliver (eds), *Economical with the Truth, the Law and the Media in Modern Society* (Oxford, 1990), pp. 95–108. See further, Harrison, *Bentham*, chapter 7, and Hume, *Bentham and Bureaucracy*, chapter 4.

[4] On the relationship between penal law and constitutional law, see pp. 165–8 below.

actual, end of a law was a matter of design. Adherence to the proper end of a law could be considered both in relation to a subordinate law-making body, or in relation to the sovereign itself. Further, Bentham already recognised that ensuring that the persons in power would adhere to the interest of the community was problematic. The badness or goodness of a law would depend on whether the conflict of interest which would inevitably exist in the rulers' minds, between their own and the community's benefit, could be resolved.[5] Maintaining the goodness of law was a task, indeed the paramount task, that Bentham set for a form of government to achieve.

Bentham first had to define what it meant for a government to be "good". The proper end of government was the promotion of the "universal interest"—the interest of the greatest part of the community in question. The actual end of government was the promotion of the government's own interest, which would amount to the self-regarding interest of the rulers.[6]

The aim of a constitution was to make these two ends, the proper and the actual, coincide. This would be achieved by the means-prescribing, or junction-of-interest prescribing, principle.[7] If they did not coincide, and the actual end predominated over the proper one, the result would be a government which would promote its self-interest, at the expense of the universal interest. The interest of rulers *in such circumstances* was termed by Bentham a "sinister interest".[8] Misrule would result from the predominance of a sinister interest.[9] Instead of the idea of "constitutional rights", Bentham provided for constitutional "securities against misrule". These securities were designed to prevent the formation of sinister interests, and to ensure the promotion and perpetuation of the universal interest.

The subordinate ends through which the identification of the interests of rulers and subjects was to be achieved were firstly, the maximisation of official aptitude, and secondly, the minimisation of expense. The discussion of expense in this respect was an original contribution by Bentham to constitutional theory.[10] However, aptitude will be the main area of focus in this chapter, as Bentham's analysis of aptitude was directly connected to the way in which Bentham conceived constitutional limits.

In order to achieve security against misrule, that is security against the formation and persistence of a sinister interest, Bentham devised securities for the appropriate aptitude of officials. His most general assumption was that if

[5] *OLG*, p. 31; see also Bowring, ix. 2.

[6] See *First Principles*, p. 232. Bentham saw self-preference as a predominant property of human nature. He conceived it as *necessary* for the survival of the species. The precise nature of the "universal interest" will be extensively discussed in the next chapter.

[7] Ibid., p. 235. For a further account of a "good" and a "bad" government, see ibid., p. 245.

[8] Ibid., p. 270.

[9] Ibid., p. 151. On the subject of "interest", see Rosen, *Jeremy Bentham and Representative Democracy*, pp. 29–33. The distinction between the "universal" interest and a "sinister" interest turned upon the number of persons, or the proportion of the community, to whom the interest belonged: see *First Principles*, pp. 235, 246–7.

[10] Rosen, *Jeremy Bentham and Representative Democracy*, pp. 93–7.

morally apt and intelligent people were put in government and maintained these qualities during their time of office, a good government would be the result. Bentham believed that as long as officials possessed appropriate aptitude, they would not develop a sinister interest, and would administer a government which would adhere to the universal interest.[11]

Bentham divided aptitude into three branches. The first and the most important one was moral aptitude, which referred to the tendency, or the inclination, of the possessor of power to adhere to the universal interest. This would mean that as far as the official was concerned:

> "the end to the accomplishment of which his endeavours are directed is the promotion of the universal interest, whatsoever may be the effect with regard to his own personal or any other particular interest."[12]

As has been argued, Bentham believed that the predominant motivation of each human being was self-interest—indeed this was the basis for his psychological theory. Bentham assumed that self-interest, or self-regarding interest, was predominant in human nature. This assumption would apply also to officials.[13] Bentham thought that the interest of officials was bound to become sinister, unless they were prevented from pursuing their own interests except through their share in the universal interest. The only way moral aptitude could be maintained was to enforce a variety of sanctions which would make officials inclined to direct their self-regarding interest towards the service and maintenance of the universal interest. In short, the only way to identify the actual and the proper interests of officials was through the threat of sanctions. The coincidence of interests could only be achieved by making adherence to the universal interest *obligatory* for them.

However, in order for the sanctions to operate effectively, officials' actions had to be made accountable. Furthermore, institutional means for administering sanctions had to be created and made efficient. Only then would securities for appropriate moral aptitude be effective. These two conditions, and in turn, security for moral aptitude, could be achieved by various methods.[14] In order to achieve accountability, single-seatedness, whereby each official's responsibilities and actions would be clearly defined and known, was necessary. Single-seatedness would make it possible for a superordinate official, or a member of the public, to judge the quality of an official's performance, and to form an opinion with regard to it. Another way for attaining accountability depended on the principle of subordination. Every functionary would be subordinate to another functionary, who would be able to punish him. Every official would be watched by his superior and be liable to immediate dislocation. Accountability to the public at

[11] For Bentham's summary of his understanding of aptitude, see *First Principles*, pp. 4–5, 151.
[12] Ibid., p. 16.
[13] Ibid., p. 13.
[14] For Bentham's account of the securities for appropriate moral aptitude, see *First Principles*, pp. 30–59, 276–288.

large would be achieved through total freedom of speech and association, publicity and the elimination of official secrecy within the machinery of government.[15]

However, the most important method for securing appropriate moral aptitude was the establishment of legal and moral responsibility. The efficient operation of these responsibilities lay at the heart of Bentham's broad aim of good constitutional design. Legal responsibility referred to what may be seen as akin to the classical Dicean understanding of the rule of law. Officials' actions would be subject to the substantive law, that is penal, civil, and constitutional law. Officials, like anyone else, would be subject to legal procedure which aimed to give execution and effect to any provision of substantive law.

Popular or moral responsibility was directly connected to the form of government itself. Its effective operation implied a democratic government as a starting point. There would have to be an efficient means for the public to form an opinion, and to exert what Bentham called the "moral or popular" sanction. This sanction ultimately relied upon the public's ability to remove the functionary in question. Bentham's code provided for annual parliaments, and for the possibility of the immediate dislocation of officials by popular petitions.[16] It also relied upon the fact that the reputation of an official might be damaged, and thus his prospect of re-election. Thus democracy was the precondition for a good government, because it was the only way of identifying the official's interest with that of the community.

Another security for appropriate moral aptitude was to be brought about by the minimisation of the money available to officials. This would deny them the means either to carry out sinister tasks or to corrupt others. In this way, officials would be denied the means to tempt others to succumb to sinister interest. The final security for the attainment of moral aptitude was the exclusion of factitious dignity. Factitious dignity was an award (such as titles of honour) given to the functionary, but divorced from any real merit.

The second kind of aptitude which officials should possess was intellectual aptitude, which consisted of appropriate knowledge and judgement. This aptitude was secured, *inter alia*, by the examination of prospective officials.[17] The beneficial effects of intellectual aptitude depended on the official's possession of moral aptitude. However intellectually apt an official might be, it would have no useful consequences if he did not have the propensity to use his intellect in a way which promoted the universal interest.[18] Finally, the third aptitude was active aptitude. It required the physical presence of officials in their place of work (such as Parliament) during their working hours. Officials' presence was an obvious condition for the performance of their duties, and was to be secured by attendance-related pay.[19]

[15] On the importance Bentham assigned to publicity, see *PT*, pp. 29–41, 143–7.

[16] Ibid., pp. 57, 137.

[17] Ibid., pp. 77–86.

[18] Ibid., p. 179.

[19] Ibid., pp. 87–94.

The principles of single-seatedness, subordination, moral and legal responsibility, and other securities for appropriate aptitude were to be incorporated into the institutional design. I shall focus on the main institutions of government, as it is in regard to them that important patterns of continuity can be identified between Bentham's earlier legal and political writings and his mature constitutional theory.

As has been shown, Bentham argued in his earlier writings that the basic feature of political society was interaction between people and government. In his constitutional writings, Bentham continued to recognise a central distinction within political society, namely between supreme constitutive power and supreme operative power. The relationship between them was one of subordination, in that the supreme operative power was subject to the supreme constitutive:

> "Considered in respect of the nature of its functions, all power in a Government is either *operative* or *constitutive*. *Operative power* is that in the exercise of which the business [is] done: *Constitutive power* is that by the exercise of which it is determined who the person or persons are by whom the operative power shall be exercised. Constitutive is therefore such with relation to the operative."[20]

The people were to have two institutional roles. The first role would be to exercise a power of location and dislocation in relation to officials. This could be done by elections and, in periods between them, by popular petitions.[21] In this capacity, the people would function as members of the supreme authority in a political community—the constitutive authority. The prime object of this authority, to recount, was to exercise an act of will—to locate and dislocate officials. This act of location and dislocation would be an exercise of the "moral" or "popular" sanction.

However, there was another role for the people in their capacity as members of what Bentham called the *Public Opinion Tribunal* (POT). Some of the features of this institution should be mentioned here.[22] In *Constitutional Code*, the POT had judicial powers,[23] and was the means by which the constitutive authority could exercise its supreme constitutional powers to locate and dislo-

[20] Ibid., p. 6. The meaning of the word "government" in *Fragment* was arguably broader than in *Constitutional Code*. In *Constitutional Code*, Bentham elaborated on the various powers of government, including the **legislative and the executive**, the latter consisting of the judiciary and the administrative authorities. The administrative and the legislative would constitute the **"government"**. The executive and the legislative made up the "operative" power. The executive would be subordinate to the legislative (*Constitutional Code*, p. 27). According to this exposition, it would seem that judicial powers were, strictly speaking, not considered a part of the "government". In *Fragment*, by contrast, Bentham wrote about the government and the people. The essential division there was between official (governmental) and popular powers. It seems that because Bentham spoke globally about "political authority" when he referred to a government, the account in *Fragment* assumed that the judicial power belonged to government.

[21] If one fourth of the population signed a petition for the removal of a functionary, he would be dislocated: see *Constitutional Code*, p. 33.

[22] The next chapter will analyse in more detail Bentham's account of this institution.

[23] *Constitutional Code*, p. 35 (section 4, Art 1).

cate officials. This tribunal was a "fictitious entity". By "fictitious entity", Bentham meant that there was no formal institution which could be seen to be working under such a name. In other words, such a fictitious institution was conceived by Bentham in contradistinction to real entities such as a "parliament" or a "court", whose jurisdiction, personnel, place of meeting, and procedure were established by law and could be perceived as such. The term "Public Opinion Tribunal" was invented by Bentham to convey the idea that the public could arrive at a collective opinion through communicating upon governmental business. This body consisted of people who had an interest in a given subject-matter.[24] It was described by Bentham as having a structure of "sub-committees", which were formed by any group of interested citizens in relation to some particular subject-matter of public concern. A necessary precondition for its effective operation was the removal of any restriction on publicity, and in particular the removal of the cloak of secrecy from official activity. The POT resembled in many ways an official judiciary. It gathered evidence in the place where a public event occurred, for example a court's gallery. On the basis of the evidence, it formed an opinion and a judgement.[25] The theatre of this tribunal was the public domain, and among the most important sources for its supply of information and comment were newspapers.[26] The tribunal's main aim was to assess whether transgressions of the universal interest of the community had taken place, and by doing so to detect potential misrule. It was the source of the moral sanction, which would manifest itself, *inter alia*, by a sharp decline in the popularity of the government, with the threat that if the government did not change its ways, it would be replaced.[27] It will be argued below that the POT also had a crucial role in determining and effectuating constitutional limits.

Bentham saw all the powers of government, that is both the power to make laws and to execute them, as ultimately constrained by popular judgement. The supreme power in the state would be "judicial" rather than legislative or administrative in nature, and would communicate its judgements to the supreme constitutive power. In fact, one might see the public as a large court in which the operative power would be no more than one party. The constitutive authority could use the ultimate weapon (the dislocation of officials) where any transgression of a constitutional limit took place. However, it was the continuous role played by the POT, rather than the regular but abrupt interventions of the constitutive authority, which determined and effectuated constitutional limits between elections. The relationship between the POT and the government would mostly be one of persuasion and argument, as in a real court. Members of the POT would act as judges between two parties as far as constitutional limits were concerned. The POT would judge between the public interest as presented by the operative power on the one hand, and another public interest on the other.

24 *SAM*, p. 28.
25 Ibid., p. 56.
26 Ibid., pp. 62–3.
27 Ibid., p. 29.

Public opinion would act as a continuous "check" against abuse of power. If necessary, public opinion would culminate in an act of will and in a manifestation of collective disobedience. Indeed, the connection between an abuse of power and an act of collective disobedience marked a significant element of continuity between Bentham's earlier and later writings. However, public opinion might be altered and modified by arguments put forward by government, so that instead of resorting to an act of will, involving disobedience, or dislocation of officials, it accepted the government's action. By providing for continuous interaction between the government and the people, Bentham was able to reconcile *limited sovereignty* with *an omnicompetent legislative power* on which there would be no a priori limits.

Arguably, the nature of the relationship between the supreme constitutive and the supreme operative was crucial to the maintenance of the proper end of government. I shall, therefore, concentrate in the next section on this relationship, and not on all the complex relationships of subordination between functionaries at other levels of the administration. As far as the supreme constitutive was concerned, Bentham saw no problem in making its interest coincide with the universal interest of the community. As long as all the individuals who constituted the political community in question reflected on the best means to promote their own interest, the result of their interaction would inevitably be in accordance with the universal interest.[28] However, the predicament would be different with regard to the supreme operative power. In its case, the task of constitutional design was to ensure that its interest would coincide with the universal interest. As will be seen, no a priori limitations to power could curb the tendency of the operative power to try to promote its own interest. The operative power would be subject to public checks, but not to definite limitations. In Bentham's words:

> "[operative power] requires to be applied to it the strictest limits which in any direction can be applied to it, consistently with its retaining amplitude sufficient for its giving accomplishment to that same end."[29]

Finally, it should be mentioned that Bentham objected to the doctrine of the separation of powers.[30] The details of his criticism must be reserved for another

[28] A more detailed discussion about the nature and formation of the universal interest will be undertaken in the next chapter. In the last section of the next chapter it is argued that if free communication is facilitated and conducted, the collective judgement of the people would always be in accordance with the universal interest.

[29] *First Principles,* p. 134.

[30] For a general discussion of the meaning and the end of this doctrine, see M.C. Vile, *Constitutionalism and the Separation of Powers* (Oxford, 1967), chapters 2, 3, esp. pp. 13, 115; see also J.L. De Lolme, *The Constitution of England* (New York, 1792), pp. 62–3, 149–65, Baron De Montesquieu, *The Spirit Of The Laws* (New York, 1949), books XI, XII, esp. pp. 75–80, 151–9, A. Hamilton, J. Madison and J. Jay, *The Federalist On the New Constitution* (Oxford, 1948), no. 10, pp. 266–7, *Marbury* v. *Madison*, 5 U.S. (1803) 1 Cranch., 137 (the theoretical rationale for this case appeared in *The Federalist,* No. 28, p. 392).

occasion.[31] However, the gist of his criticism was that such a doctrine could not prevent the formation and persistence of a bad government. Such a doctrine did not allow for the dynamic, direct involvement of the public in constantly checking the government. It relied on a complicated, and, in effect, inactive, self-paralysing institutional network, to prevent any one interest in society becoming dominant. It placed very little faith in direct democracy to resolve any conflict of interests. Based on inaction as well as on promoting the waste of time and resources, the doctrine enabled corruption to flourish behind a complex web of institutions. Ultimately, a government based on this doctrine would become non-transparent to the public. However, Bentham might be understood as advocating the establishment of mutually-checking powers, although not one which entailed "checks and balances between institutions". He often referred to the popular or moral sanction, administered by the POT, as a *counterforce* to that of the government.[32] Bentham's idea of mutually-checking forces was socially dynamic. This idea should be distinguished from checks and balances designed to provide institutional equality of power, which was socially static and involved inaction, and therefore the destruction of government.

III

The role of the people in Bentham's thought unites his early legal and political theory and his mature constitutional writings. This section will focus on their role in *determining*, and *giving effect* through an act of will, to their own resolutions about constitutional limits. Several "patterns" of continuity between Bentham's early and mature thought will be discussed, all of which are related to the question of constitutional limits. These "patterns", which all involve themes found in *Fragment*, are as follows: the enabling rationale for government; the conceptual fusion between the quality and the quantity of the exercise of powers; the relationship between constitutional limits and securities against misrule; the determination of constitutional limits by popular judgement, and if necessary, by an act of collective disobedience; and the recognition of collective judgement, and if necessary, disobedience, as a prime value in a free government.

The first point of continuity between Bentham's earlier and later writings is his endorsement of an enabling rationale for government. This rationale was identified in *Fragment*.[33] The enabling rationale meant that government could be a priori unlimited yet be constantly subject to public inspection. The reflection arrived at as a result of this inspection would constitute a social constraint

[31] For Bentham's objections to the doctrine of the separation of powers, see *The Book of Fallacies*, from an unfinished paper, by a friend (London, 1824), pp. 24, 248–50, *On the Efficient Cause and Measure of Constitutional Liberty*, UC cxxvi. 8–18; cxxvii. 4, 5.; clxx. 168, *SAM*, pp. 121, 231–3, *First Principles*, pp. 22–5, 101–7, 138–9, 193–5, 208–9. See further, *PT*, pp. 24–9.

[32] See, for instance, *First Principles*, p. 279.

[33] See chapter 4, pp. 119–20 above.

on the government's powers. It is necessary to grasp this enabling rationale in order fully to appreciate how a presumptively unlimited government could still be constrained by the collective attitude of the population. Bentham's statement in *Constitutional Code*, that to the powers of the legislature there were no limits but only checks,[34] should be understood in the light of this enabling rationale for government.

In his writings at the time of the French Revolution, which prefigured his mature writings on constitutional theory, Bentham saw the enabling rationale for government as the heart of any good constitutional design. His account in these writings followed that in *Fragment*, in arguing that a priori limitations on legislative power did not adequately characterise a free government. The enabling rationale for government is summarised in this passage:

> "If there were a proposition in government more self-evident than any other, one should think it would be that at every period there should be some one authority competent to do every thing that may require to be done by government, and that authority should extend to every case whatsoever."[35]

Clauses of invalidity would be detrimental as they could encourage a hostile attitude on the part of the people. Such clauses could serve as the pretext for rebellion.[36] The legislature should be left to work out its policies under the direct influence exerted by the people. The "enabling rationale" suggested that the relationship between government and people would be based mainly on influence and persuasion by reason, rather than by an exertion of will over will.[37] Although ultimately disobedience (a decisive and explicit act of will) might be exercised, constitutional limits were founded on a reasoned communication between people and government. Governmental power should be presumed to exist in every field of action, subject to public discussion, and the formation of the ever-dynamic social constraint—public reason and opinion.[38]

The following passage illustrates the "enabling rationale" as presented in Bentham's later constitutional theory, although he admitted that it was too crude a description of the relationship between the two main forces in the constitution—the operative and constitutive powers:

> "In regard to the possessors of the supreme operative power, the general description of their power must be that their power extends to every thing—is all-comprehensive—that in virtue of it they are at liberty and have been empowered on all occasions to do whatever they please in relation to all persons and all things appertaining to the community in question. But on the other hand, to confine the exercise of this power

[34] *Constitutional Code*, pp. 41–2.

[35] *Necessity of an Omnipotent Legislature*, UC cxlvi. 19; see further T.P. Peardon, "Bentham's Ideal Republic", in B. Parekh (ed.), *Jeremy Bentham—Ten Critical Essays* (London, 1974), pp. 120–44, at 127.

[36] *Necessity of an Omnipotent Legislature*, UC cxlvi. 45–6.

[37] This is an overgeneralisation. A more detailed account of "influence" will be given in the next chapter.

[38] *Necessity of an Omnipotent Legislature*, UC cxlvi. 47.

within the limits corresponding to the universal end, an adequate counter-power or counterforce must be established: this is the power reserved or given to the creators of their power, the possessors of the supreme constitutive power, to be the annihilators of it whenever they please."[39]

The second pattern of continuity to be considered relates to the meaning of the phrase "abuse of power". As far as etymology was concerned, Bentham, in his writings at the time of the French Revolution, pointed out that *Arbitrium* meant "decision" or "will". Therefore, he said:

> "The meaning of the phrase as soon as it comes to have any can therefore be no other than this: viz: that where arbitrary power subsists the decision of questions relative to the exercise of all power depends on the will of those invested with it not only in the first instance but definitively, howsoever it be with the will of the body of the people. What follows? That it is on the opportunities possessed by the people of manifesting their will that the freedom of a constitution in reality and immediately depends, and not upon any other circumstance such as that of the division of the general mass of power into three independent branches."[40]

It would seem that *Arbitrium* was involved in the exercise of any sovereign power. However, on the basis of this literal and trivial understanding of sovereign power, Bentham maintained that if the phrase "arbitrary power" was to have any meaning, a distinction had to be made between a government whose powers were limited by popular will, and one whose powers were not so limited. Hence, Bentham went on to define "arbitrary power" as power exercised without any reference to *popular* will. His response to the threat of such power was to recommend all measures which could facilitate the formation and expression of that popular will. Defence against oppressive government depended not on the division of governmental power but on the enhancement of opportunities for public communication, discussion and action.

This passage is reminiscent of the long footnote in *OLG* discussing the "split" nature of sovereignty.[41] As a matter of universal theory, *any* exercise of sovereign power involved interaction between two wills, that of the government and that of the people. Thus, *to some degree*, no sovereign power would be totally arbitrary. However, in terms of the normative application of this universal theory, power would be exercised arbitrarily in a government under which there were hardly any formal opportunities for the expression of popular will.

How did Bentham conceive of "abuse of power"? Bentham identified within the notion of abuse of power the two ideas of the "quantity" of a power and the "quality" of its use. Abuse of power, in the sense of the exercise of *too much* power, merged into the question of *how* power was exercised. In short, the question of "how much power is used?" could not be divorced from the goodness or

[39] *First Principles*, p. 134.

[40] *On the Efficient Cause and Measure of Constitutional Liberty*, UC cxxvi. 10–11.

[41] See chapter 2, pp. 52–3 above. The passage quoted on the previous page about the enabling rationale for government also echoes the "split" nature of sovereignty.

badness of its use. Because Bentham saw constitutional limits in social terms, that is as a concretisation of communal interpretation and judgement, he did not accept the notion that there were a priori limits to what the legislature might do, at least as long as the public were able to pass judgement on its (proposed) actions. An abuse of power would therefore amount to a bad measure, whether produced by a generally good or bad government.

Bentham would acknowledge that the question of the quality of a government was more wide-ranging than one concerned merely with the quantity of its powers. Therefore, "quality" would encompass the question of whether a government had used too much power (or had "abused" its powers). In other words, an abuse of power would consist in the production of a bad measure under a particular government. It would follow that a judgement that an abuse of power had taken place would amount to censorship or criticism of the government.

There were many channels through which a government might be censored. The quality of its measures might be criticised by the public through the press, while members of the legislature could be faced with the prospect of not being re-elected, or even of facing dislocation by petition and majority vote between elections. But criticisms of a measure might be so great and so widespread as to raise not only the issue of quality as such, but also the issue of the *ability or disability* of the legislature to deal with certain matters. In this case censorship (of the quality of the use of power) might signify constitutional limits (limits to the extent or quantity of power which government might properly use.[42] Censorship with regard to the quantity of power would be consistent with the enabling rationale for government discussed above, because it implied no a priori limits to government, but only constant "checking".[43] So, constitutional *limits*, which concerned the quantity or extent of governmental power, were related to the notion of the goodness or badness of government. Further, constitutional limits were compatible with the enabling rationale. However, because Bentham explicitly discussed "unlimited" powers for government, and because he did not specifically discuss constitutional limits in his constitutional writings, most scholars have wrongly assumed that his preferred form of democracy would not include such limits.

The third pattern of continuity to be discussed here is the relationship between constitutional limits and securities against misrule. This pattern of continuity is an implication of the two previous patterns. This pattern is built around the following argument. Bentham's agenda in his constitutional writings

[42] The relationship between the "quality" and "quantity" of the exercise of power is directly related to the discussion of both Bentham's theory of sovereignty and his legal positivism: see chapter 2, pp. 46–7 and 68–73 above. The point there was that any attempt to divorce conceptually the idea of the justification of law (the quality of it which might lead to censorship) from the limits of legal validity (which related to the quantity of power used, the ability or disability of the power-holder, and constitutional limits) would make sense only at the price of an unacceptable reductionism. Such a divorce would imply a failure to give a conceptual, yet socially dynamic, account of law.

[43] The fusion of the quality and quantity of the exercise of governmental power is also connected to an element of "permissibility" which is inherent in an account of "validity": see pp. 169–77 below.

was to provide for securities against misrule. In providing for securities against misrule, Bentham returned to an issue with which he had been preoccupied in *OLG*, namely the character of laws which amounted to self-limitations on the part of a legislature. In the context of such limitations he stressed the importance of people being familiar with governmental business. The laws which contained self-limitations would be prompted by a collective judgement of the people, itself made possible by the notoriety of governmental measures. In a nutshell, in his mature constitutional writings, Bentham continued to develop his analysis of constitutional limits based on a popular collective judgement.

In *SAM* Bentham proposed substantive constitutional securities for Tripoli. He called them, "Securities, given by the Sovereign, to the people of [Tripoli] *Against Abuse of Power and Forever*".[44] In an important passage, Bentham suggested that a declaration of natural rights be replaced with a declaration of securities against misrule.[45] The language of natural rights would call into question, in a hostile way, the legal sovereignty of the government, whenever there arose a fresh claim that a right had been violated. This language of hostility, and the prospect of chaos between subjects and government, would obscure the real issue, namely whether a particular constitutional arrangement gave the members of a political society some security against misrule (security against bad government). Bentham argued that a declaration of rights would tend to suggest that only the question of the quantitative exercise of power was at issue, whereas what such a declaration *ought* to do was something radically different, namely to prevent bad government. Once again, Bentham rejected the notion that the questions of the quantity of the power exercised, and the quality of its exercise, could sensibly be divorced. Further, Bentham made his familiar criticism of natural rights. This argument, derived from his epistemology, was that there could exist no rights which were not related to a real instrument of coercion: "To any such word as *right* no clear conception can ever be attached, but through the medium of a law, **or something to which the force of law is given**".[46]

It is noticeable that Bentham did not object to the idea of constitutional rights derived from constitutional law. Constitutional law, although it might be described as "law" would also have an extra-institutional dimension. Reading these passages together it seems that, for Bentham, constitutional rights received their force from coercive measures in which they were declared. However, constitutional rights should be understood *as* securities against misrule, and not as a priori limitations on the powers of government.

Bentham went on to make a move which at first sight looks like a change of agenda. This move highlights a puzzle which embraces the whole of his legal and political enterprise. Despite Bentham's lengthy discussions in his early legal

[44] *SAM*, p. 74.

[45] Ibid., pp. 23–4 and note a; in this context, see Rosen, *Jeremy Bentham and Representative Democracy*, pp. 56–8.

[46] Ibid., p. 23; see also J. Waldron, *Nonsense Upon Stilts: Bentham, Burke and Marx on the Rights of Man* (London, 1987), pp. 29–46.

and political theory of sovereignty and constitutional limits, he composed this footnote in *SAM* in order to avoid a discussion of constitutional limits. Bentham was objecting to a constitutional arrangement, the value of which would be explained in terms of natural rights and predetermined limits to sovereignty.[47] A proper interpretation of this passage is therefore crucial for understanding the extent to which Bentham's legal theory served as the context for his mature constitutional enterprise generally, and more particularly for his mature account of constitutional limits. Two main interpretations might be put forward. In the first place, it might be argued that, in his later constitutional writings, Bentham embarked on a quite different project from the one he had pursued in his legal theory. This would mean that in this passage Bentham abandoned, or left undeveloped, his account of limited sovereignty found in Chapters 2, 6 and 9 of *OLG*, and in *Fragment*.

However, there is a second, constructive interpretation, arguably a more plausible one, which makes a better sense of Bentham's enterprise as a whole. According to this interpretation, Bentham did not abandon his earlier analysis of limited sovereignty or constitutional limits. The reason for Bentham's change of terminology was not at all a change of agenda. Limits of sovereignty, or constitutional limits, carried exactly the same meaning in this discussion of securities against misrule as they had in his earlier writings. It would be wrong to assume that because he replaced the terminology of "limited sovereignty" with "securities against misrule", he abandoned his concern for constitutional limits, or the establishment of a legally limited government. Bentham merely thought that it would confuse the issue to speak of constitutional arrangements as being concerned with the protection of natural, imprescriptible rights, which implied some abstract and incoherent limitations on sovereignty. The point of this passage is to emphasise that the only way to maintain a plausible, socially orientated, discussion of constitutional limits, was through the language of securities against misrule. The idea of constitutional arrangements in the shape of "securities against misrule" was much more intelligible, and therefore more conducive to a proper understanding of constitutionally limited government. Thinking in terms of securities against misrule would convey the notion of a sanction—some fear of evil by which self-imposed obligations (*constitutional laws in principem*) might be enforced.

Here lies a continuity of objective. In *OLG*, when discussing *constitutional laws in principem*, Bentham wondered whether it would be plausible to conceive of a government limiting its own powers by imposing on itself this type of law. Why would a legislature tie its own hands? Bentham recognised that self-limitations could be fully effective only in a good government. They might be partially effective in a bad government which was responsive to some aspects of the universal interest. This would be the case, for example, in a mixed monarchy. In order to reach a situation where government began to be responsive, the

[47] *SAM*, p. 24.

constitutional design would have to give some effect to securities against misrule. Bentham ended this passage saying precisely this:

> "That, otherwise than by fear of evil, a Sovereign can be **brought to consent knowingly to tie up his own hands** is generally speaking too much to expect. But what without such fear he may perhaps consent to do, with less reluctance at least, is to tie up in the way in question the hands of his Agents: in which case matters may be so managed, as that without knowing it he may thus be made to throw obstacles in the way of his own steps in so far as they proceed in a sinister direction."[48]

It was through the establishment of securities that a coercive authority might tie its own hands. This argument was yet another manifestation of the enabling rationale for government. This rationale, having public communication and interpretation at its heart, was entirely compatible with a constitutionally limited government. It was apparent that *a priori* rules which tied the hands of the government would have no place in any constitutional arrangement entitled to the description "free". It was improper to characterise a free government in a positivistic way, namely as operating within the range of pre-established constitutional rules.

Elsewhere in *SAM*, Bentham discussed constitutional promises made by the sovereign, or what Bentham called "concessions of the sovereign".[49] As has been argued, Bentham believed that the rationale for a constitutional arrangement should be an enabling one. Hence, constitutional limits should emerge from an understanding on the part of the law-making authority that it ought to limit itself. Constitutional limits should emerge from dynamic social activity. As has been argued in previous chapters, although a constitutional law could be instrumentally described as an act of will of the law-making authority to limit itself, the nature of constitutional law encompassed a public will, the recognition of which would prompt the legislature to impose limits on itself. Bentham linked *limitations* of legislative power not to a priori limitations, but to a continuous check made by a collective public judgement, or public opinion. The efficiency with which the check on power operated would depend on "the spirit, the intelligence, the vigilance, the alertness, the intrepidity, the energy, the perseverance, of those of whose opinions Public Opinion is composed".[50] Concessions of power would take the form of promises.[51] It is noticeable that here there was a continuation in terminology from *OLG*, in which Bentham also talked about constitutional "promises" as self-limitations of legislative power: "Every thing that he can do on his part amounts, I say, to the giving of a promise, nothing more".[52] Even a constitutional arrangement providing for the election of representatives would amount to no more than one of these promises. In a properly

[48] *SAM*, p. 24.

[49] Although Bentham referred here specifically to the Pasha of Tripoli, it is clear that he understood "sovereignty" to have a wider meaning, namely the power to legislate.

[50] *SAM*, p. 139.

[51] Ibid., p. 138.

[52] Ibid; see also chapter 2, p. 47 above.

constructed constitutional arrangement, acts of oppression would be immediately *notorious*. They would be *detected* and *understood* as oppressive by the public. *Constitutional laws in principem* would be signs which would aid public judgement on the matter, but which would, by no means, be decisive. Only under such circumstances was there any possibility that the legislature would be disposed to impose self-limitations. Notoriety might lead to eventual dislocation.

The concept of notoriety requires explanation. Notoriety referred both to what the public knew about governmental operations, and to what the government knew about what the people thought of its operations. Notoriety was the precondition for any interaction between public opinion and the government; and that interaction was central to the understanding of the idea of "sovereign powers". Notoriety was thus related to the intellectual aptitude of the public, not only to that of officials.[53] Notoriety had two aspects. First, there had to be some knowledge of the ordinance in question, in this case the constitutional promise, or *constitutional law in principem*. Knowledge of the ordinance would be a point of focus for the public.[54] The second aspect related to the conditions in the public domain affecting reflection upon a given measure. For notoriety to exist in this sense, it had to be possible for the public to form a prompt judgement with regard to the effect of the ordinance in question. The public would have to be in a position to consider whether any action had taken place which was unacceptable given prevailing opinion.[55]

The absence of notoriety in the latter sense would imply the presence of obstacles to communication in the public domain. In consequence, the public would not be able to co-ordinate measures for resistance, because each person would not know and appreciate what other individuals thought about the measure in question, and about the possibility of resistance. Further, obstacles to communication could lead to false consciousness. Thus, as a result of such obstacles, each individual, and hence the public, could lack the will to resist, despite their knowledge of the content of the measure in question. In such a situation people might passively obey despite a measure being pernicious. The status quo would be perpetuated.

Notoriety would not be enhanced in a constitution which had as its foundation a priori limitations on law-making powers. Such a constitution would be socially static because there would be no requirement for the public to be involved in determining the ambit of these limitations. For example, in constitutions which adopted the institutional doctrine of the separation of powers as an a priori limitation, there would be no reason for the people to debate and, if necessary, modify, other a priori limitations. The institutional complex network would be trusted for this task. When people were not allowed to, or could

[53] *First Principles*, pp. 142–5.

[54] *SAM*, pp. 27–9.

[55] See chapter 6, p. 220, note 76 below, in which obstacles preventing the public from arriving at such a judgement are discussed.

not, for various reasons, form a judgement on constitutional limits, abuse of power would be the result. In the following passage Bentham objected to a constitutional arrangement which included an a priori principle demanding obedience to the laws. Such a principle, in effect, would remove the most effective remedy against the violation of constitutional promises—a prompt and effective collective judgement which could be followed by acts of disobedience:

> "every one would in the first instance, and unless taught to the contrary by experience, entertain the expectation and hope of seeing it [the promise implied in the ordinance which incurred self-limitation] observed: and in pursuance of such hope, individuals **might** rise up **with one accord and concur** in opposing effectual resistance: individuals into whose conceptions, **but for such ordinance**, no idea but that of unreserved obedience, active or at least passive, would have ever entered."[56]

The point of this passage is that promises would promote resistance in suitable cases. These promises would also focus expectations. The reverse however would also be true. The crystallisation of certain rules by the public would prompt the sovereign to promise adherence to constitutional self-limitation.

Many of the securities which Bentham thought might be introduced in Tripoli took the form of promises made by the sovereign not to disregard certain liberties of the subjects. These securities resembled *constitutional laws in principem*. Bentham, in effect, gave a list of constitutional limits which he thought it desirable for a liberal constitution to contain. These securities included, for example: "Security against National gagging: or Security for appeal to Public Opinion and the power of the law on the conduct of all persons whatsoever",[57] habeas corpus measures,[58] securities against illegal imprisonment, as well as many other personal securities.[59]

However, the most important feature of these securities was that they were to be understood in a socially dynamic way, despite entrenched social attitudes which acknowledged their fundamental nature and importance. These securities always acknowledged a "counter-security". This counter-security was a rule of interpretation which would comprise some circumstances in which the main security could not be maintained. For example, if some infringement of security was necessary in order to give "execution and effect to the law", the infringement would not "be made beyond what such necessity requires".[60] The underlying rationale of all these securities was some proportionality which was based on utilitarian calculation. However, it was assumed by Bentham that once certain self-limitations had been conceded and an expectation generated that these would be respected, it would be difficult for a legislature to transgress them. The very existence, as well as the concrete application, of these

[56] *SAM*, p. 140.
[57] Ibid., p. 80.
[58] Ibid., p. 84.
[59] Ibid., pp. 88–102.
[60] Ibid., p. 85.

self-limitations would be subject to a utilitarian threshold, however general this calculation might be, and however deeply these self-limitations were rooted in the community concerned. However, their utilitarian rationale did not preclude their being fundamentally rooted in a given society. This fundamental "rooting" would raise the threshold for the social justification of any attempt to transgress them.

Having argued for the continuity in Bentham's thought in relation to constitutional limits, let me go into more detail in relation to a fourth pattern of continuity—the means by which constitutional limits were determined and effectuated. In previous chapters, three main ideas concerning Bentham's universal theory of sovereignty and constitutional limits have been discussed. One idea concerned the limits of sovereignty, or the social limits for the justification of authority. The second idea, found in *Fragment*, concerned the way in which the limits of sovereignty were determined and effectuated by a collective judgement made by the people. The people's collective judgement, with reference to the social justification of authority, could operate in relation to a single measure undertaken by a generally good government (this has been termed a legal revolution). A third idea, also in *Fragment*, concerned the normative application of the second one. This idea concerned the extent to which a government could be called "free". It was here that the democratic tendencies in Bentham's largely otherwise descriptive account emerged. In *Fragment*, it has been argued, Bentham made a connection between the goodness of government and the ease with which disobedience to a socially unjustified, and therefore unconstitutional, measure could be effected. In a free government it would be easy for the people to arrive at the juncture of resistance. Such resistance would not necessarily entail an undermining of the whole institution of government.

It is in the connection between these two ideas, namely that sovereignty is determined and effectuated by popular judgement and, if necessary, disobedience, on the one hand, and that such judgement and disobedience were facilitated in a free government, on the other, that the continuity between Bentham's early work and his mature constitutional writings consists. In all of his mature constitutional writings, Bentham continued, in various contexts, to relate the idea of constitutional limits to a collective judgement of the people with regard to a given legislative measure. If necessary, disobedience to that measure would follow. Further, he even spoke about the ease with which these processes were carried out as the characteristic sign of a free government.

In *SAM* Bentham wrote about "ordinances". An "ordinance" was an entity akin to "a law". Popular opinion in a free government was embodied in the suffrage, in which Bentham saw the means to interpret and to remedy the transgression of ordinances committed by the legislative authorities. However, in *SAM* there are several passages in which Bentham identified the transgression of ordinances which signify limits to authority with misrule. Such ordinances were general in nature, and concerned the very nature and extent of the power exercised by officials:

> "Note that in the number of the members of this same tribunal [POT] is included the number of all those on whose obedience [depends] as well the effect of the several general ordinances by which vexation is prohibited, as also of any particular acts or particular ordinances in consequence of which any acts of vexation and oppression are exercised in violation and transgression of those same general and salutary ordinances."[61]

This passage illuminates two main points. The first is that there were assumed to be in existence "general" and "salutary" ordinances which had the general aim of preventing vexation. Secondly, Bentham attributed the persistence of such ordinances to continuous obedience on the part of the members of the POT. The pattern of continuity between Bentham's early and mature thought which related obedience to the limits of authority occurred repeatedly in his discussion of the operation of the POT. This pattern was another context for the operation of the POT which was generally designated merely as the chief "informer" of the constitutive authority, that is the people, in their capacity to locate and dislocate officials. Thus, because of his aversion to language which encouraged hostility and which, as has been seen, caused Bentham to reject the terminology of natural rights, he came back again and again to the terminology of his earlier legal and political writings. Collective judgement, and, if necessary, resistance and disobedience, were the means to determine and effectuate limits to the powers of government.

In his writings at the time of the French Revolution, Bentham again wrote about the relationship between constitutional limits and the obedience of the people. He qualified his objections to the doctrine of the separation of powers by stressing that the separation of governmental functions was a guarantee of accountability. Yet this statement was true only as long as this separation did not lead to an institutional balance of power. Such an institutional balance would be divorced from a direct reliance on the *obedience* of the people. The separation of powers only had any value so long as the official authorities interacted directly with the people, or competed for the obedience of the people.[62] Such a competition might exist, for example, between judicial and legislative authorities. Only under such circumstances would any constitutional liberty worth the name exist.

These passages from Bentham writings do not necessarily demonstrate that Bentham intended the people to use disobedience as a constitutional tool. They can still be interpreted to mean that he intended the POT to utilise disobedience only in the extreme case of an all-out revolution. However, in subsequent passages, he seemed not only to be sympathetic to the possibility of disobedience, but also to see its facilitation as a prime constitutional and democratic value in a free government.

[61] *SAM*, p. 30.

[62] *On the Efficient Cause and Measure of Constitutional Liberty*, UC cxxvi. 11.

It is important to emphasise again the relevance which Bentham placed on the subordination of government to the body of the people. This subordination persisted not only in terms of the location or dislocation of officials, but also in the context of the very obedience of the people to the government, obedience which reflected a collective, popular judgement about the proper extent of governmental power:

> "The degree of inclination [of officials to promote the universal interest] will be in exact proportion to the **dependence** of the governors on the governed: to the **dependence** of the persons intrusted with the power, on the persons by whose obedience the power is constituted: to the **dependence** of men in power on the body of the people."[63]

Subordination might be effected, *inter alia*, by means of a collective judgement which would have as its object the very creation of the powers of government.[64] In addition to their fundamental power to locate and dislocate officials, Bentham allocated to the people a continuous, participatory role. The link with the early political writings consists in this continuing reference to popular judgement which was the feature by which constitutional limits to obedience were effectuated. At this point of his argument however, the facilitation of constitutional disobedience was presented as a virtue of constitutional design. Communal participation was of inherent value in relation to any constitution, whether it occurred among the people or between the people and the government. It would be wrong to assume that once officials were elected they would be given a blank cheque. Again, an enabled government would not mean a constitutionally unchecked one.

In *SAM* Bentham continued to use the language of *Fragment* and *OLG*:

> "Power on the one part [the power to promulgate ordinances] is **constituted by** and **is greater or less in proportion to** obedience on the other. It is in the direct ratio of the obedience, and in the inverse ratio of resistance."[65]

This shows that the ability or disability of the government to promulgate certain laws, as determined by popular opinion, and the potentially general disobedience which might follow from such opinion, was explicitly envisaged by Bentham, and was seen by him as an important element in the attainment of securities against misrule, or of the guarantee of good government. The idea of constitutional limits, or limits on sovereignty, and the determination and effectuation of them through participation, and, if necessary, resistance, continued to play a major role in Bentham's rationale for his constitutional code. In an essay entitled "Constitutional Code Rationale", in discussing the moral sanction as the "counterforce" which could bring rulers to book, Bentham referred again to the power of rulers as directly proportional to the degree of *obedience*. It is the argument of this book that the moral sanction should not only be under-

[63] *On the Efficient Cause and Measure of Constitutional Liberty*, UC cxxvi. 12.
[64] Ibid., UC cxxvii. 5.
[65] *SAM*, p. 30.

stood in terms of popular discontent which might result in not re-electing officials, but also in terms of the determination of limits on the power of government *between* elections. Bentham said in this context:

> "What for the present may suffice for bringing [the force of the moral sanction] to view is the phrase *public opinion*: . . . In the opinion thus denominated stand included all those by whose obedience the power of the Monarch, be he who he may, or of the rulers, be they who they may, is constituted. Let this opinion take a certain turn, obedience ceases on the one part, and with it all power on the other. Accordingly in every government but a Representative Democracy, the idea of this sanction is of all ideas that are capable of presenting themselves to a ruling mind the most disagreeable, the most hateful and afflictive."[66]

This passage shows, moreover, that Bentham did not merely understand constitutional limits as directly correlated to collective judgement and disobedience. He also expressed his belief in the practical possibility of a prompt social reaction on the part of the collective body of the people to a ruler's activity. Bentham saw in democracy more than just the institution of elections, frequent as they might be, and of censoring the government between elections. He saw as an advantage of democracy the possibility of establishing constitutional limits by prompt, popular collective action.

Bentham's whole conception of constitutional limits is shown once again to be based on a socially interactive activity. People in power would be made to respond to socially dynamic forces rather than to acknowledge a priori limits to their power. Popular determination and effectuation of constitutional limits would be hampered by,

> "schism in the power of public opinion, and by means of a party formed for the purpose partly to corrupt and misdirect, partly to debilitate, the force of that original most efficient, or rather only, security against misrule."[67]

Such a schism might involve an attempt on the part of rulers to debilitate the public by preventing it from detecting an attempt to transgress constitutional limits. A good constitutional arrangement would be responsive to such schisms.

Bentham called on the public to resist public mischiefs. He acknowledged that despite provisions for ensuring appropriate aptitude on the part of officials at the time of their location, it was still possible for an article of the *Constitutional Code* to be disregarded, whether explicitly or by what he called "forced interpretation" by the legislature. In such a case, the people could either resist the act of the legislature, or they could accept it. In the latter case, the mischief would not be averted, and the process of enlightening the community would be retarded. Were the people to accept evil measures, the existence of unnecessary subjection might take years and years to detect, let alone to resist successfully. Even frequent elections might fail to bring to attention examples of

[66] *First Principles*, p. 279.
[67] Ibid., p. 280.

unnecessary subjection, as long as the public did not possess sufficient intellectual independence.

The whole institution of government would become mischievous if the people were unable to resist it quickly. If the people accepted an apology by the legislature, despite the maintenance of the mischievous measure, they would reveal themselves to have become indifferent to its content. It would mean that their judgement was clouded by prejudices. Bentham clearly showed a connection between the state of the public's intelligence and the protection afforded by constitutional law against the abuse of power by government. In constant public observation and reaction, Bentham saw the heart of the rule of law as a constitutional idea:

> "in a word as no security can be afforded by the laws any farther than the words of which they consist are faithfully interpreted and observed, by perverting the importance of words [people's acceptance of an apology on the part of the legislature] undermines and destroys whatever security can be afforded by the laws. . . . a people struggling with the diseases inseparable from the infancy of a constitution, and struggling without a remedy without a hand to help them: an only physician appointed, and he without power to prescribe."[68]

Bentham argued that in a representative government there could be hostility between the two main forces in the constitution—the government and the people. This hostility he termed fundamental constitutional disagreement, and characterised it as civil war. He mentioned again the relationship between the constitutive power and the obedience of the people. Security against misrule achieved through resistance would result from the collective application of the moral or popular sanction.[69]

In a number of passages in the Bowring edition of the first book of *Constitutional Code*,[70] Bentham spelled out what he meant by the different branches of law—the penal, the civil, and the constitutional. Here, Bentham gave the clearest evidence for the continuance of the rationale of the determination and effectuation of constitutional limits through a collective public judgement and, if necessary, disobedience. Bentham clearly saw the possibility of abuse of power despite the democratic location and dislocation of the functionaries of government. However, it would not be easy for the legislature to ignore the whole body of the people. He argued:

> "With power thus unlimited, might not the legislative body exercise their power upon the members of the constitutive body, individually taken, in such sort as to prevent the exercise of the dislocative power in question over the members of the legislative body?
>
> No: for in the case here supposed, the members of the constitutive body, on whose co-operation the giving execution and effect to the supposed ordinances of the leg-

[68] *Necessity of an Omnipotent Legislature*, UC cxlvi. 24, 25.
[69] *First Principles*, pp. 281–2.
[70] Bowring, ix.

islative body depend, would forbear to give it: if some used their endeavours on that side, a greater number would use theirs on the opposite side.

Upon their compliance or non-compliance, all power, as has been seen, necessarily depends. **On any occasion towards producing, on their part, non-compliance, all that can be done by a constitutional code, is to give them the invitation.** If by such invitation, power is not limited, by nothing else can it be limited."[71]

The context of this extraordinary passage is clearly a discussion of abuse of power. In this passage Bentham explicitly welcomed the possibility of disobedience, or non-compliance with ordinances, viewing it as a prime constitutional value. The aim of a free constitution would be to give the people the capacity, the cognitive and the instrumental means, of resisting pernicious measures undertaken by their government.

Can this passage be interpreted as suggesting that Bentham identified disobedience solely with an all-out revolution, with an overthrow of the government? Does the "invitation" spoken of in this passage refer exclusively to the dissolution of the government? The answer surely is no. Bentham acknowledged non-compliance to a single "ordinance" as an important constitutional value. Moreover, he continued:

"In any case in which it appears likely that, by the proposed ordinance in question, the members of the supreme constitutive will, in any considerable number, be likely to **regard it as a violation of their rights—rights naturally so valuable in their eyes,** the great probability seems to be that a majority of the legislature will not hazard the enterprise."[72]

Here Bentham puts the seal on his understanding of how constitutional limits should be determined and effectuated. The whole point of having a responsive legislature was to encourage it to anticipate the limits of acceptable social coercion. The legislature would have to reflect on what, in the opinion of the public, would be an unacceptable exercise of coercion. The legislature would have to think about the potential interpretation of the public to the proposed measure. This passage is crucial in revealing Bentham's understanding of the establishment of constitutional limits. It shows the central role of communication between government and people, and among the people themselves. Only as a last resort would disobedience in the sense of actual hostility be employed.

Reading this passage in the context of the general argument pursued here, it can be argued that Bentham found no difficulty in discussing constitutional limits in terms of fundamental rights (as opposed to natural imprescriptible ones), which placed boundaries on law-making powers in any form of government, and a fortiori in a democratic one. The argument shows that the idea of fundamental rights is consistent *both* with Bentham's epistemology, and with his theory of law. His only caveat would be that the idea of "fundamental" should always be interpreted within a communal conception of harm, the most general

[71] Bowring, ix. 120.
[72] Ibid., p. 121.

characteristics of which could self-reflect and change. As an ethical critical principle, utility was sensitive to moral pluralism. However, from a utilitarian perspective, one could also appreciate that fundamental moral thresholds derived from a communal conception of harm, were metaphorised and prescripted as "rights". These cautiously fundamental moral thresholds marked the extent of people's identification with some common ethical common view. The existence of a right-based morality was therefore a matter of course for utility, although it was silent as to what harm would determine a given distribution of rights. As I shall argue in the next chapter, entrenched, communally prescpriptible, fundamental rights reflected a communal conception of harm which was entrenched in people's deepest moral intuitions and hence utilitarian calculations. Generalisations about harm were carried out from public communication into a more generally recognisable, though ever-transient, pattern. The conception of harm which gave effect to a given distribution of rights was never imposed in an a priori way. Understood as such, issues arising from any concrete interpretation of such fundamental rights, namely fitness between abstract and concrete instances of them and fitness in their relative weight in different fields of human relationships *would*, for Bentham, revert back to the form of a general conception of harm.

Thus, Postema is inaccurate in portraying Bentham as having some principled hostility to the idea of fundamental rights for the reason that they are not based on "genuine public justification". In this context, Postema attributes to Bentham the argument that rights cannot be demonstrated to be determinate, and hence they conflict with the principle of publicity which was a necessary condition for the efficient operation of a democratic government.[73] Such a criticism of Bentham is proper only to the trivial extent that it interprets Bentham's argument as saying that no democracy can be established unless some general propositions, based upon *some* commensurability between people's views, are published. However, Bentham's argument was that a democracy could not be based on Natural Law theories. The metaphor "natural" could only be dissolved within an actually-presumed conception of harm. Beyond that conception of harm, and the sense it made of fundamental rights, there *was* literally *nothing*, though this nothingness did not preclude utilitarian re-evaluations of communal conceptions of harm.[74] Once this condition of some commensurability between people's views is met, it is arguable that a utilitarian theory can easily accommodate fundamental rights in a democratic government. As soon as rights come into being they will feature in people's intuitions and argumentations, albeit in a socially dynamic way.[75]

[73] G.J. Postema, "In Defence of 'French Nonsense': Fundamental Rights in Constitutional Jurisprudence", in N. MacCormick and Z. Bankowski (eds), *Enlightenment, Rights and Revolution* (Aberdeen, 1989), pp. 107–33, at 115–25.

[74] This point will be discussed in much more detail in Part 2.

[75] This idea is much developed in chapter 6 and Part 2 below.

The reconstruction of Bentham's constitutionalism attempts to show why fundamental rights must be seen as an integral part of a communicative activity, which would make them determinate at some general communal level. Bentham recognised the fact that certain limitations on law-making power could be entrenched within a code of law. He therefore recognised the possibility of rights, as well as the reasons why certain cultures might judge them to be necessary for their general well-being. Bentham, indeed, saw public debate over rights as democratically valuable, even allowing for the ultimate modification of some of them. Such a modification could be exemplified in a transition from rights which were based on a rationale of some neutrality between conceptions of good, into ones based on some common substantive conception of good, and vice versa. This issue will be discussed in the second part of the book.

In summary, it may be seen that Bentham continued to conceive of constitutional limits in his mature constitutional writings in the same way as in his early legal and political ones. He saw limits, as determined by a collective judgement of the people, which could be effectuated, if necessary, by disobedience. Further, he conceived that such disobedience might be of prime constitutional importance. The role of the people in determining and effectuating constitutional limits was one of the most important parts of his theory of securities against misrule. Bentham's concept of sovereignty, properly understood in social terms, was consistent throughout his legal and political writings. Sovereignty implied an oscillation, an influential interaction between the people and their government, or between the POT and the Supreme Operative. Conceptually, Bentham saw no distinction between legal and popular sovereignty. Popular sovereignty would be exercised all the time in order to determine the limits on law-making powers. In a democratic government, this exercise of popular sovereignty would of course include the most important constitutional limit of all, that of giving to the people the constitutive power of the location and dislocation of officials—what is usually referred to as "political sovereignty". Thus "political sovereignty" was itself an expression of constitutional limits, that is a particular application of the popular element involved in any exercise of sovereignty in its "legal" sense.

Therefore to portray his theory as developing in the direction of popular political sovereignty, in the sense of the people merely locating and dislocating officials, though a valid interpretation of Bentham's view, would be to miss the point. Instead, his theory of limited sovereignty, or constitutional limits, should be understood in terms of the dynamic relationship between officialdom and popular opinion. Popular participation was, from the very start, included in his conception of political authority. This dynamism was to be accommodated in his vision of democracy.[76] For Bentham, democracy did not merely mean the election of the most apt people, morally and intellectually, to office. Further, it meant more than the existence of procedures for dislocation if officials became deficient in point of

[76] M. Walzer also discusses the connection between a socially dynamic understanding of harm and democracy in "Philosophy and Democracy", *Political Theory*, (1981) 379–99. See also chapter 4, pp. 121–2 above.

aptitude. Although such democratic procedures were a precondition for any further improvement, by no means did they mark the limit of his democratic vision. Arguably, his democratic vision under the auspices of utilitarianism allowed the progression and regression of a popular perspective of harm from which coercive actions could be interpreted as transgressing constitutional limitation. The popular constraint, according to which legislative acts could be interpreted as transgressing constitutional limitations, was provided through the determination and effectuation of constitutional limits by the members of the POT.

Bentham provided for a "panoptic democracy". His whole aim in establishing constitutional limits was to facilitate the operation of the panoptic principle as effectively as possible. In other words, the gaze of the potential inflictor of the popular sanction—the potential disobeyer and dislocator—was fixed on every official in the most intensive way possible. The watching body of the people could act promptly and, if necessary, disobey what it considered to be an unconstitutional measure. However, it could also act as a censor, informing the constitutive authority, which in turn could exercise its power of location and dislocation.

Instead of advocating a socially static view based on an assumption that neither the public nor the political process, as a matter of social fact, could discriminate between calculations of maximising general welfare and adherence to fundamental entitlements (an assumption on which the rationale of natural rights was based), Bentham claimed that a utilitarian theory could accommodate fundamental entitlements which would function as constitutional limits. Moreover, he advocated a system of government at the heart of which was social dynamism. He wanted to provide the conditions for free communication in the public sphere, as well as for a responsive government to the changing conception of harm which would characterise this sphere. The quality of interaction between the people and officials in such a socially dynamic system of government would be such as to discriminate between proposals involving the transgression of basic communal beliefs which would operate to diminish the general well-being of the community, and proposals for the maximisation of well-being which did not transgress against such beliefs. Bentham was a political and constitutional thinker who believed in the value of an independent public. The only effective way to maintain constitutional limits was through a vibrant and independent public opinion. An analysis of consensus formation by the people will be the subject of the next chapter.

IV

This section discusses further a point left somewhat undeveloped in Chapter 2, in the discussion of constitutional law.[77] It is in constitutional law that a con-

[77] See chapter 2, pp. 62–3 above. It has been argued above that Bentham understood constitutional law in terms of constitutional limits. Thus Bentham's occasional discussion of constitutional law as having the role of determining the distribution of offices and personnel should be read as a portrayal

ceptual link can be made between Bentham's legal and constitutional theory, that is between his theory of law and his theory of representative government. The notion of constitutional law also connects the legal and popular elements which constituted his understanding of the concept of sovereignty. Bentham wrote about constitutional law on many occasions.[77] He thought of constitutional limits in terms of law. However, any idea of legally limited government would create an incoherence in his thought. On the one hand, he saw a dimension of "legality" in the phenomenon of constitutional limits, that is in acts which would be considered "unconstitutional". On the other hand, he seemed clearly to differentiate between what was "illegal" and what was "unconstitutional".[79]

Presenting "constitutional law" as something which could not signify illegality but could signify unconstitutionality was a very novel move indeed. The task of this section is to make the best sense, *on the basis of the argument so far*, of the problematic issue of constitutional law in Bentham's thought, a problem which he did not attempt directly to resolve. The main question which will be discussed is the extent to which the ideas of illegality and unconstitutionality are mutually exclusive.

Some scholars have tried to explain the incoherence of constitutional law within Bentham's thought, but they have either presented a conceptually insufficient account of constitutional law, or argued that Bentham was simply incoherent in attempting to explain how a legally limited government could be accounted for under the command theory of "a law". An example of the latter group of scholars is Hart, whose criticism of Bentham's theory of sovereignty and the normativity of law led him, as has been seen, to the conclusion that Bentham's command theory of "a law" could not account for the idea of legal validity, nor in turn for the idea of a legally limited government.[80]

Hume's account, on the other hand, places him in the former group. He recognised that the concept of constitutional law related to the idea of a public trust, and that it would cover the designation of persons invested with legal powers, as well as the extent of the powers with which they would be invested. Hume rightly maintained that constitutional law necessarily possessed both penal and civil aspects, and that it would be integral and uniform like all the other types of law.[81] However, he neither confronted the problematic nature of sovereignty, nor, in turn, of constitutional law, within the command theory of "a law". Even Postema who, as has been maintained, presents some very important insights in regard to Bentham's theory of sovereignty and the social operation of the principle of utility, does not confront directly the dilemma which

of constitutional limits in these respects: see UC lxix. 235; *IPML*, pp. 281, note a, 307–11; and *First Principles*, p. 3.

[78] See, for instance, *IPML*, p. 281, *OLG*, pp. 19, 64–6, 80, Bowring, ix. 1–3, 9–11, and *First Principles*, pp. 1–5.

[79] *OLG*, p. 16.

[80] See chapter 2, pp. 41–4 above, and pp. 172–5 below.

[81] Hume, *Bentham and Bureaucracy*, pp. 77–81.

arises in regard to constitutional law: how could constitutional law be "law"? How could a mandate of the sovereign be unconstitutional but not illegal?

Constitutional law as part of a system of legislation

In *Constitutional Code* Bentham wrote,

> "Public Opinion may be considered as a system of law, emanating from the body of the people. If there be no individually assignable form of words in and by which it stands expressed, it is but upon a par in this particular . . .with . . . *common law*. To the pernicious exercise of the power of government it is the only check; to the beneficial, an indispensable supplement. Able rulers lead it; prudent rulers lead or follow it; foolish rulers disregard it."[82]

Bentham saw constitutional law as forming part of a system of legislation, within the familiar scheme of his hedonistic psychology and moral theory. Constitutional law had several functions as part of a system of legislation. First, at its most general level, constitutional law belonged to the system of legislation like any other branch of law. The only thing that differentiated it from any other branch of law was its subject, namely officials, as opposed to private individuals. Constitutional law was concerned with the identification of officials' duty to promote the universal interest with their self-regarding interest, which on certain occasions could become sinister.

Secondly, the identification of duty and interest on the part of officials could have a particular application in the field of constitutional limits. Constitutional law was that part of a system of legislation which aimed at assigning limits to the extent to which centralised, institutional coercion by a government was permitted. Thirdly, the body of constitutional law was itself a system of moral obligations, a communal code which provided firm prescriptions concerning how, by whom, and to what extent, centralised coercion should be exercised. The degree to which every citizen and official was able to use it in his own prudential calculations would depend upon the degree of freedom of communication, both within the public sphere, and between the public sphere and the government. In the language of sovereignty, constitutional law would involve the entrusting body, the people, being able to specify certain moral obligations (which would also be sympathetic ones). Such obligations would give substance to, or gradually modify, any object of volition which formed the basis of the trust which constituted political authority. This trust was understood by Bentham as involving a critical social justification of coercive measures.[83] Constitutional law, in this sense, would serve as a system of moral rules which indicated the degree of communal development. As such, it was a system of legislation which gave effect, to a greater or lesser

[82] *Constitutional Code*, p. 36, Article 4. See in this context Ehrlich, *Fundamental Principles of the Sociology of Law*, p. 22, suggesting that public opinion should be considered law.

[83] For a discussion of the modal object at the basis of this trust, see chapter 2, pp. 61–2 above.

extent, to the trust of the people in *any* type of government. This system of moral obligation, backed by the moral sanction, would be able, to a certain extent, to tie the hands of the legislature.

In short, constitutional limits would be the product of an interaction between private and public obligatory media. Constitutional law, like every other law, would aim to prevent the commission of offences. In the same way that every law was a security against mischiefs,[84] every *constitutional law in principem* would provide security against misrule, or public mischief. In terms of Bentham's classification of offences, misrule was a "public offence", directed against the community of non-assignable individuals.[85]

An analysis of an individual constitutional measure

How could constitutional law be analysed in terms of the conceptual framework put forward in *OLG*? The problem in seeking to account for constitutional law as part of a command theory of law, was that constitutional law could not be identical to any other legal measure. However, it could have the essential characteristics of law—an act and an expression of will with regard to that act.[86] It could also possess the force of law through the moral and sympathetic sanctions. As a phenomenon, constitutional law would be "split" in the same way that sovereignty was. The understanding of a constitutional law would have to incorporate two dimensions, both of which were necessary for a full account of it as a social phenomenon. Although a *constitutional law in principem* could be referred to as a unified constitutional law in a simplified sense, to present constitutional law exclusively in such a way would be to distort its socially dynamic nature and signification.

Constitutional law would necessarily have two interdependent dimensions—one social and one institutional, each of which could be accounted for as an individual law. The first would involve a popular expression of will with regard to a certain proposition in relation to a certain action. This individual "moral law" would amount to a new condition placed upon the trust that had been bestowed by the people on the centralised coercive mechanism. In other words, the trust would operate as a conditional command, the condition being some proposition backed by the moral and, will be seen, by the sympathetic sanction.[87] An individual constitutional law would involve a single expression of will by the public, with regard to a particular constitutional limit. It would be a moral (and as

[84] Bentham classified mischiefs in *IPML*, pp. 143–5. Primary mischiefs would cause pain directly to the object of the act. Secondary mischiefs, danger and alarm, could affect people other than the immediate object of the act.

[85] See *IPML*, p. 203. In penal terms, breaches of constitutional law might also be classified as offences against sovereign trust, or as offences against sovereignty: see in this context, Burns, "Bentham on sovereignty: An Exploration", pp. 403–5.

[86] *OLG*, p. 93.

[87] See chapter 2, pp. 58–63 above.

will be seen in the next chapter, sympathetic) "law", and would have all the essential aspects of a law. Bentham's *OLG* was sufficiently general conceptually to accommodate such a popular manifestation of constitutional law.

The second dimension of constitutional law, the institutional, would come about as a result of the social process, as the legislature was influenced by the public. The popular or moral obligation could lead to the expression of a self-limitation on the part of the legislature. This self-limitation would be manifested by a *constitutional law in principem*, the apparent breach of which could trigger communal reflection and interpretation. The sanction which would (or would not—depending on whether justified by utilitarian calculations) enforce such a *constitutional law in principem*, would be the moral or the sympathetic. However, the expression of constitutional limits in the code would also help the judge, when assessing public opinion, to pass a judgement to the effect that a given act of the legislature was anti-constitutional.[88]

"Anti-constitutional" would mean "contrary to constitutional law". This expression, in turn, would have two aspects. First, an anti-constitutional act would be interpreted to be contrary to a "sign" in the penal code. In this sense it would be "illegal", because it would be contrary to the penal code. Secondly, the term "anti-constitutional" would confirm that the legislature was subordinated to certain basic communal beliefs. These beliefs would have arisen from communication between the legislature and the public on previous occasions, and would also arise after the appearance of the proposed coercive measure. This *interpretation* of unconstitutionality reconciles, on the one hand, the impossibility of a mandate of the sovereign being "illegal", and on the other hand, its being "unconstitutional", that is contrary to constitutional law. Two wills, and therefore two "laws", were involved in the full exposition of constitutional law—that of the public and that of the legislature—and both would give expression to constitutional limits after the social process of mutual influence had occurred. In some cases, even when *constitutional law in principem* was interpreted as being transgressed, this transgression would be justified in the eyes of the public, and thus not as a breach of duty towards them. Once the process of interaction had taken place, a new or modified constitutional law would be established. A popular proposition backed up by a sanction would be presented as a new constitutional obligation and would be embodied in the code.[89] The necessity of an interactive process between the public and the government meant that a transgression by the government of an obligation contained in a constitutional "sign" need not in all cases establish a constitutional offence in the eyes of the public. It was possible for the legislature to convince the public

[88] See Bowring, ix. 484. The judge would be able in such a case not to punish disobedient citizens: see *SAM*, p. 140, and Bowring, ix. 121.

[89] There is some theory presumed here between public reasoning and the wording of the law. This enquiry must be reserved for another occasion.

that despite this infringement, no action had taken place to the detriment of the public interest.[90]

To sum up, a constitutional law had to be understood as being a resolution of an extra-institutional interpretative process. It had an element of "legality", in that it complied with the conceptual requirement of a law. From the point of view of "descriptive sociology", it would make more sense to give an exposition of constitutional limits as the synergy of two constitutional "laws". The first of these "laws", communally-based moral law, would be reflected in and interact with the second, a correspondent institutional *constitutional law in principem*.[91] This socially dynamic manifestation of constitutional law would also reflect the social dynamism which characterised the concept of sovereignty.

The relationship between constitutional law and other branches of law

What was the relationship between constitutional law and other branches of law, namely civil, penal and procedural? Bentham claimed that the quality of the other branches of the law would depend on the basic interests from which they stemmed and which they endeavoured to protect. Constitutional law would determine the aptitude of the people in power and would constantly check their interest. Bentham said in this context that although the supreme operative[92] would be the body whose laws were immediately apparent:

> "Still however it is the constitutional branch that is the most important of the two as being that on which the other depends for all its qualities and all its effects, as an effect upon its proximate cause."[93]

Constitutional law was the most important branch of law, because of its two dimensional nature. It was legislation about legislation.[94] It would determine which interests would determine all other legislation. Constitutional law would ensure that the whole system of penal law accorded with the universal interest. It would determine the end in view of any individual law.[95] This end would of

[90] Burns discusses manuscripts, dated between 1783–8, entitled *Projet d'un corps complet de droit*. In these materials Bentham discussed constitutional laws as mirroring certain broad privileges (which themselves incorporated certain fundamental freedoms). These laws were ultimately enforced by popular discontent, and if necessary, revolt. Further, these constitutional laws would be essentially incomplete, or imperfect, in that their execution and effect would depend on penal and procedural law: "Bentham on Sovereignty: An Exploration", pp. 409–11.

[91] Bentham accounted for the crystallisation into a "habit" of a pattern which signified a synergy of communal and institutional obligations: see *Deontology*, pp. 183, 205.

[92] For a discussion of this term, see pp. 140 above.

[93] *First Principles*, p. 37, editorial note 2.

[94] In *First Principles*, p. 3, Bentham referred to constitutional law as the *remotely* operative branch of the law, in contradistinction to the penal and civil branches of the law which were *immediately* operative (which is reminiscent of the distinction between the immediate and constitutional spheres of public reflection and the operation of the principle of utility).

[95] Bowring, ix. 3. As has been argued above at pp. 36–7, the end of law was the question in relation to which every individual law ought to be analysed.

course incorporate constitutional limits, transgression of which would *expose* a flagrant breach of the universal interest. For instance, under a monarchy, treason and general political offences such as seditious libel were likely to be significant features of law. Torture would be common, while confiscation, inheritance rules, and the entire substance of the penal law would be geared towards the protection of the sinister interest of the monarch. The presence of royal gestures such as "pardon" and "mercy", as well as a cultivated belief in "legitimacy", would indicate a systematic protection and promotion of sinister interest.[96] A monarch would use these penal securities in order to avoid any *independent* reflection on the part of the public about the necessity to introduce a better form of government, one which would better adhere to the universal interest.

As has been seen, in *SAM* Bentham distinguished between a primary set of promises of self-limitation, and another set of promises which would give execution and effect to these primary promises.[97] Although constitutional laws could appear as constitutional provisions in a constitutional code, penal law and procedural law would be needed to turn breaches of them into offences. Penal law would constitute this "other set of promises". The provisions of penal and procedural law would give expression (which would lead to notoriety), as well as execution and effect, to constitutional law. Assistance from penal and procedural law was very important, especially in so far as defending *individuals* against misrule was concerned. In order to get protection, individuals would have to resort to procedures which entitled them to protection. Protection for individuals against misrule would be akin to individual constitutional rights in that it enforces a distributive pattern of entitlements. In *SAM*, Bentham argued that constitutional law would protect individuals against oppression in the same way that it would protect the public at large. It would be for the penal code to give execution and effect to a constitutional law which provided individuals with securities against oppression by rulers, for example against injurious confinement and banishment.[98]

In *First Principles*, Bentham argued that it would be difficult to understand constitutional promises as merely publicly orientated moral obligations. Moral "laws", made by the public, would need to become part of the penal law. They would need to be mirrored in self-imposed obligations which would then form part of the penal code. However, their introduction into the penal code would be enforced by the moral sanction. Even when the legal sanction was applied to constitutional "law", it would constitute an effectuation of the moral sanction.[99] In the following passage the fusion between the social and the legal, or the institutional, is most evident:

[96] Bowring, ix. 36.

[97] See pp. 149–50 above.

[98] *SAM*, pp. 132–4.

[99] The relationship between the legal sanction and the moral sanction, as far as the idea of punishment was concerned, was that the moral sanction could react against a broader range of mischiefs. In *First Principles*, p. 291, Bentham said: *cont.*

"The efficiency of the popular or moral sanction, with its Public Opinion Tribunal, can not be strengthened, but the efficiency of the law, in so far as its force is employed in augmentation of the happiness of the people, is also strengthened. In so far [as] a misdeed, which by reason of its detrimental effect on happiness is *vicious*, and thereby exposes the agent to punishment at the hand of the Public Opinion Tribunal, is moreover *criminal*—an act of delinquency against the law exposing the agent to punishment at the hands of the law. . . ."[100]

The formal part of constitutional law could be part of a penal code. A *constitutional law in principem* could become a part of the penal code. Bentham defined the penal element of constitutional law. This penal element was a scheme of offences ("you shall/shall not do that" backed by punishment). Some expository matter could be attached to these penal provisions, as to any other individual law.[101] The penal element of constitutional law would have, as its objective,

"The giving a description of a particular class of crimes, and of means employed against them, in the character of remedies. But that the thread may not be interrupted, convenience recommends the placing what belongs to these crimes, in company with what belongs to others, in the penal code."[102]

Bentham argued that the penal part of constitutional law would relate to making rulers liable as offenders. Moreover, and more importantly, these constitutional offences would necessarily be connected to facilitating the public detection of the abuse of official powers. In the following passage, Bentham connected the determination of constitutional limits by popular judgement, with their effectuation, if possible, by concerting measures for resistance:

"[The constitutional arrangement would be designed so that] acts done in resistance to, or for prevention of, misrule, and thence productive of more good than evil, to such acts, of whatever penal denomination they may appear susceptible, **no such punishment, if any, shall be allotted**, as might, with propriety, be allotted to them, if the application of them to the prevention of misrule had no place."[103]

Bentham related constitutional law to both the penal and procedural codes. Adherence to constitutional law could be guaranteed by permission given by procedural law to judges to refrain from punishing people who had disobeyed on the ground that they were disobeying an act of misrule.

Bentham's Constitutional Code was a single individual *constitutional law in principem* which would mirror a law "enacted" by the public. Its exposition in

"Punishment as applied by the legal tribunals—punishment applied under the name of punishment—attaches to such evil acts alone the mischief of which has place as well in a shape sufficiently determinate, as in a quantity sufficiently great, to warrant the application of evil in the shape and in the quantity in which it is so denominated. Punishment as applied by the Public Opinion [Tribunal], applied as it is in effect without the name, attaches itself to mischief in all shapes in which the hand of man can, without special and sufficient justification, be instrumental to the production of it."

100 *First Principles*, p. 291.

101 On expository matter, see *OLG*, pp. 198–9; see also Hart, *Essays on Bentham*, pp. 118–22.

102 Bowring, ix. 9–10.

103 Ibid., p. 10.

the *penal* code might be something like: "powers of government shall be exercised in accordance with what is provided for in the constitutional code". This comprehensive *constitutional law in principem* would exist alongside other constitutional limits which could appear both in the constitutional and penal codes. Under Bentham's system, the constitutional code itself would include penal elements and definitions (expository matter), more akin to civil law.[104] Bentham decided to include both penal and civil elements in a single, separate, constitutional code, although all the provisions in this code *could be* theoretically divided between the civil and the penal codes. It goes without saying that in Bentham's proposed penal code, individual *constitutional laws in principem* would not be mentioned. Constitutional limits would be mentioned as public offences in the penal code, although their full exposition would be given in the constitutional code.

Effectiveness and validity/legality and validity[105]

"Effectiveness", in Bentham's legal and political enterprise, had a wider meaning than "receiving obedience". The expression "habit of obedience" encompassed popular reflection, interpretation and judgement, both of which were elements in Bentham's concept of sovereignty. A coercive measure had "effectiveness" when it had a certain impact on social attitudes. As has been argued, such an impact would involve a reflection which related not only to existing conventions concerning limits to legislative power, but also lead to social reflection on the potential consequences of the measure in respect of such limits. "Effectiveness" was not simply a question of whether a given measure was obeyed or not, as Hart portrayed it.[106]

In *SAM*, Bentham said that there could not be a situation in which the violation of a constitutional promise by the legislature could be seen as having no legal effect. When a new coercive measure had been promulgated, neither a citizen nor a judge could deny that, in point of fact, there had been an authentic enactment of a coercive measure by the governmental authority. However, clinging to ideas like "authenticity" or "recognition" in a positivist manner would be to miss the point. Under Bentham's system, the constitutional significance of the wording of such a measure would be interpreted and reflected upon in the context of significance of the wording of the constitutional promise. The subject of reflection would not be authenticity or recognition but about utilitarian justification for coercion. A socially sensitive understanding of "validity" could not be complete without accounting for such a reflection. The people might decide to disobey the measure. "Effectiveness" here had a wider sense of "permitted by the people", rather than mere obedience to the law. This permis-

[104] The distinction between penal and civil law is discussed in *OLG*, chapter XVI.
[105] See also chapter 2, pp. 66–75, and chapter 3, pp. 85–7 above.
[106] Hart, *Essays on Bentham*, p. 234.

sion, which implied reflection and acceptance by the people, could not be successfully distinguished from validity. To press the distinction too hard would involve social reductionism. Effectiveness, or "permissibility", would be based on *public reflection*. Public reflection would consist in a general moral evaluation of the coercive measure in hand, and as such might lead to the measure being accepted *as* a legal measure. At this point, legal validity and effectiveness (or now, permissibility and acceptance) would no longer be conceptually distinguishable.[107] Disobedience amounted to a statement that the measure ought not to have been enacted. In the same way, a declaration made by a court that a measure was anti-constitutional amounted to holding the measure *ultra vires*, which was to say that the measure should not be seen as a legal mandate.[108] The limits of sovereignty could therefore be spoken of as being created and modified *by* the public reflection which prompted the disobedience. It has been argued above that in *OLG* Bentham saw the critical ability of the populace to *reflect upon* the limits of acceptable coercion as a necessary element in the concept of sovereignty. In *SAM* he developed this theme further.[109]

This understanding of "effectiveness" in a wider sense than mere "obedience" leads to a consideration of the distinction between "invalidity" and "illegality". What was "valid" and what was "legally permissible" could not be different in kind. As has been argued, in terms of the exercise of powers, the "quality" (a fictitious entity which makes sense in the context of a utilitarian judgement) and "quantity" (a fictitious entity emanating from claims about the limits of competence) of the exercise of power were seen by Bentham as strongly connected.[110]

Postema acknowledges that Bentham did not always keep clear in his mind the distinction between legally permissible and legally valid. The latter seemed to have been lost in the former.[111] However, Postema argues that Bentham had accounted for what would be socially "conceived as law", and that Bentham saw sovereignty as an epistemic test of "recognition". Hence, Postema claims, Bentham ultimately accounted for legal validity. In other words, Postema maintains that popular recognition of the authenticity of a coercive measure is very similar to what Hart referred to as "legal validity". In arguing this, Postema brings Bentham's idea of sovereignty into line with Hart's. It has been argued in Chapter 2 that this interpretation of Bentham's account of sovereignty, merely as a test of "authenticity", is inadequate.[112]

Arguably, there was no pressing need for Bentham to distinguish conceptually between validity and legality. As has been argued, any formalism whether related to epistemic tests or to formal normative acceptance did not fully

[107] In Hart's terminology, the measure in question had transgressed the boundaries of the social practice which gave rise to the rule of recognition, a rule which formed the basis of validity and normativity for any legislative measure.

[108] See the discussion of "adoption" in chapter 3, pp. 85–7 above, and note 17 therein.

[109] *SAM*, pp. 139–40.

[110] See pp. 145–6 above.

[111] Postema, *Bentham and The Common Law Tradition*, pp. 257–8.

[112] See chapter 2, pp. 66–75 above.

capture Bentham's conception of law and constitutionalism which was interpretative and socially dynamic. In a constitutional dispute, for example, a declaration by a court that a measure was, to use Bentham's term, anti-constitutional,[113] would mean that this measure was contrary to constitutional law. This would mean that *despite being authentic*, it would be interpreted as constitutionally, and hence legally (in the sense of a constitutional law), *impermissible*. For Bentham, the difference between the legally *permitted* and the legally *valid* could be significant only to the extent to which the element of "permissibility", and hence "legality", were commonly spoken about as referring to different laws. For example, it might be that what made a contract valid was a certain statute or court's ruling whose permissibility was interpreted as relating to the adoption of certain dealings between individuals. This could be distinguished in common speech from the permissibility by another law which rendered certain contracts illegal. However, both types of seemingly different type of "permissibility" were linked through an interpretative argument concerning the factors which determined the ambit of constitutional permissibility to enter into contractual relations.

"Legal validity" referred to permissibility based on the interpretation of certain constitutional laws.[114] These laws were "adopting" laws, in that they would assign spheres of powers to certain actions and relationships, in contradistinction to laws which were based on prescriptive propositions which simply permitted or forbade certain action in a more direct way. As has been argued in Chapter 3, as far as sovereignty at the top of any social hierarchy was concerned, there needed to be an extra-institutional coercive measure which would "permit" and delegate legal powers to governments.[115] Bentham's statement that a mandate of the sovereign could not be illegal was true as a matter of logic, given the supposition on which sovereignty was based. Yet a mandate of a sovereign legislature could certainly be constitutionally illegal as a matter of social practice. Hart's theory was deficient in that it was socially static: for him, constitutional law was a limitation on government which was legally validated by the rule of recognition, the latter being normatively accepted one way or the other *as a matter of static facts*. Hart failed to show that constitutional law was also a social process, of which the people's continuous checking and *permissions* as an investing body were an inherent part. Understood in such a socially dynamic way, the idea of "validity" coincided *conceptually* with some expression of will (commands, prohibitions, permissions, permissions to forbear), which was a result of some judgement. It is overtly reductionist to describe validity merely as authenticity and formal acceptance. An act of "recognition"

[113] See Bowring, ix. 484.

[114] See *OLG*, p. 28, where Bentham mentioned the idea of "validity" of mandates in the context of his discussion of adoption.

[115] Sovereignty would always be "split" and relative in nature: see chapter 3, pp. 85–90 above.

of a measure as a valid law was the *result* of a justificatory, and hence "permitting", process.[116]

For Bentham, the idea of something being contrary to law, or illegal, could be applied also to the *competence* of every subordinate authority in a state:

> "The supreme authority in a state is that on the will of which the exercise of all other authorities depends: insomuch that, if, and in so far as, by any other authority the will of the supreme authority is contravened, **the constitution** by which the several powers are allotted to the several authorities is violated, and what is done is **contrary to law**."[117]

A dimension of superiority and subordination, and hence of "permissibility" and "duty", should be attributed to "constitutionality". The entities to which Hart called "power-conferring rules" could not be fully conceptually distinct from "duty-imposing rules" as far as constitutional limits were concerned. A conceptual fusion between "duty-imposing" and "power-conferring" would be a characteristic of *any* act of delegation, or indeed a conferment, of a sphere of competence. Whenever a sphere of competence was delegated or conferred, it was arguably limited by a constitutional law which imposed some constitutional duty. This fusion between "duty imposing" and "power conferring" would hold good for any act of "adoption" or "pre-adoption" effectuating either a delegation of some authority to make law, or a conferment of competence to enter into binding contractual relations. To see something *as* being within a sphere of competence implied a more general constitutive "volitioning", permitting, duty-imposing activity.

Any presentation of a chain of validation, of the sort Hart put forward in *The Concept of Law*,[118] as an epistemic test of "recognition" of a purely "power-conferring" nature, is incomplete and misleading. Hart was right in claiming that, for Bentham, permissibility was a key concept. However, it was wrong for Hart conceptually to differentiate permissibility from legal validity. The criteria which differentiated "social validity" from "legal validity" would also have to embody a dimension of permissibility. A rule which permitted a transition from the "socially valid" to the "legal valid" was a constituting rule.

One drawback of Bentham's account might involve the fact that, because legal validity and efficacy were connected, constitutional limits could be counter-intuitive. Bentham's ideas make immediate intuitive sense only when the investing body (as it has been called in Chapter 2) can actually be perceived as engaging in a constitutional judgement as to the limits of justified authority.

[116] Curiously, Postema also seems to concede the necessity of an element of permissibility at some point despite his general claims to the contrary. He argues that, quite often, the ideas of "duty" and "disability" go hand in hand. He gives an example to the effect that a moral "duty" is always attached to any disability which is manifested in a Bill of Rights: see *Bentham and The Common Law Tradition*, p. 259; see also ibid., p. 257, in which Postema affirms that Bentham saw limitations on sovereign power as a kind of duty to the people.

[117] Bowring, ix. 96.

[118] Hart, *The Concept of Law*, pp. 102–4.

It is harder to account for constitutional limits when the judgement of the body of the people is stagnant or latent. Hart exploited this weakness. However, he did so at the expense of neglecting to account for the socially dynamic nature of social recognition. Bentham saw the question of the ultimate authority and validity of law as an *interpretative* question to be answered in a popular fashion (within the limits of the actual transparency of communication which characterised the community in question), rather than as a dryly descriptive one about formal bounds to validity and acceptance. Therefore, as has been argued in Chapter 2, his theory takes the analysis of legal phenomena into the realm of a popular, utilitarian, critical interpretation of a socially dynamic trust. As such, his account of law contains irreducible moral features, and arguably cannot be regarded as fully committed to legal positivism.

V

The argument advanced up to this point provides a unified understanding of Bentham's legal and political project. As a result of the failure to recognise the continuity between Bentham's legal theory and his constitutionalism, Bentham's constitutional thinking has been exposed to criticisms by constitutional lawyers on the grounds that his theory did not have a strong enough conception, if indeed it had any conception at all, of constitutional limits. As has been argued, there is no theoretical reason for such a non-unified approach to Bentham's enterprise. It makes no sense to treat Bentham's legal theory, including the notion of constitutional limits, apart from his constitutional theory. Bentham did not alter his views on the nature of political society. He was consistently loyal to the greatest happiness principle, and sought to construct a society which would operate to promote the greatest happiness of all its members. The relationship between constitutional limits (in law) and constitutional theory should, in general terms, be stated as follows: for the greatest happiness to be achieved, there must exist constitutional limits according to some communal conception of harm, and there must be an institutional structure which ensures adherence to such limitations. This *theoretical* claim should then be translated into institutions. This is the light, it is argued, in which the theoretical basis for Bentham's radical mature constitutional writings should be approached and analysed. In short, this is the light in which the theoretical principles and the practical reforms he proposed in his constitutional code should be evaluated. Bentham's constitutional theory should be approached as continuous with, not as separate from, his theory of law and sovereignty.

Hart's position has already been criticised in Chapter 2. There, it was argued that Hart's interpretation of Bentham's theory of sovereignty, as based on the "habit" or "disposition" to obey, was misguided. At the present juncture, it may be added that Hart did not capture the comprehensive nature of Bentham's account. As has been shown, Bentham envisaged an active participatory role for the people as early as *Comment* and *Fragment*. Bentham's description of sovereignty was not a dry assertion of a social fact that "what makes sovereignty is a habit of obedience on the part of the people", although the minimalistic style in which this description was presented might well have given this impression. Rather, this statement contained a commitment to an active role by the people for determining and effectuating constitutional limits on the government. This was the heart of Bentham's theoretical position on sovereignty and constitutional limits, and it did not change significantly throughout his career.

As has been argued in Chapter 2, Hart failed to see that although Bentham had a command theory of "a law", he did not advocate a command theory of "law", but a utilitarian social theory of law. This mistake led Hart to overlook the symmetry of Bentham's theory. This symmetry carefully created a utilitarian balance between security achieved through a rule and security against misrule. As has been argued, Bentham's constitutional theory might be described as *IPML* in reverse. Whereas in *IPML* the subjects were to be made to promote the universal interest by sanctions, in *Constitutional Code* the sanctions were applied to officials.[119] Bentham's constitutional theory was a theory of legislation for constitutional law, in relation to which officials would be subjects.

Hart did not appreciate the role of the people in *Fragment*, and further omitted to consider Bentham's constitutional theory in his critical discussion of Bentham's theory of sovereignty. He did not produce convincing reasons for so doing. The only point he made was that Bentham's constitutional theory constituted a different **theory of law**, because constitutional law was no longer regarded by Bentham as a command of the sovereign but as a customary rule which happened to be in force.[120] As has been argued, Bentham's theory of law and sovereignty remained basically unchanged throughout his career. As a result of his considering only Bentham's legal theory, Hart's view of Bentham was very limited. His relatively minor and technical points about the inadequacy of the nature of a "habit" and a "disposition", either of the courts or of the people, and of "command", as a full explanation of sovereignty, constitutional law, and the normativity of law, overlooked the broad scope of Bentham's argument. Hart did not capture the full meaning of Bentham's theory of sovereignty, constitutional limits and the normativity of law. The central point missed by Hart was that constitutional limits had to be accounted for in a socially dynamic way.

His limited approach led Hart to misunderstand Bentham's position in relation to the constitutional role of judges. In *Constitutional Code*, Bentham envisaged that judges would, *inter alia*, provide a legal check to any action by the

[119] See *Colonies*, pp. 35–6.

[120] Hart, *Essays on Bentham*, pp. 228–9. Postema was the first to comment on Hart's mistake on this point claiming that Bentham's constitutional theory was a normative application of his legal theory of sovereignty: see, chapter 2, p. 49, note 35 above. However, Postema did not look in detail at Bentham's constitutional theory, and as a result overlooked the continuity of the role of the people in determining and effectuating constitutional limitations.

legislature which potentially transgressed the limits of justified coercion. This legal check would also constitute the means of giving execution and effect to constitutional promises made by the legislature. Bentham thought that the judges could declare a legislative act anti-constitutional. The effect of such a declaration would be that resistance to it should be lawful and not punishable. Judges were entrusted with the power not to impose a punishment in the most severe cases of misrule, the most severe transgression of the universal interest, which is to say, in the event of what Bentham would term an unconstitutional act.[121]

Hart argued that the "habit of obedience" could not be imputed to the *courts* when refusing to punish disobedient citizens. This was so, Hart claimed, because if constitutional limits were created *by* the court's *habit*, the court logically could not refuse to punish the disobedient citizen in the first instance in which the legislature enacted an unconstitutional measure.[122] A "habit" would presume some past practice of the court to that effect. The role of judges, in the context of the argument advanced in this thesis, was far more extensive than Hart admitted. Hart did not give sufficient consideration to the role of the *people* in the *courts*, a role which was designed both to create and to give effect to constitutional limits on the power of government. Further, "obedience" could, in a certain sense, be imputed to the court, and thus the interpretation survives Hart's logical objection. Hart did not consider the precise nature of the proceedings in which an issue of constitutional limits would be raised for the first time. During such proceedings, despite the fact that a constitutional issue was being considered *for the first time*, the court would be able promptly to assess the extent of social discontent with a newly proposed coercive measure. If transparency of communication was achieved, the court would be able to detect a change in the "habit of obedience" immediately after such a change had taken place.

Arguably, Hart was preoccupied with his general objective in *Essays on Bentham*, namely to produce a more sophisticated defence of *The Concept of Law*, which attacked Austin's command theory of law, by considering instead Bentham's *OLG*. In doing so, Hart used Bentham as a means of defending his interpretation of law as a system of primary and secondary rules. He refused to admit either that Bentham's theory of law and sovereignty might involve anything more than just "a fact of a command", or that such a theory conceived sovereignty as more than just a habit of obedience or a disposition to obey.

Hart criticised Bentham's enterprise according to his own methodology of discussing *legal* concepts in the context of their social use. In doing so, he in fact explicitly borrowed his methodology from Bentham's's theory of fictions.[123] Ironically, the social context in which Hart described legal phenomena was a narrow one, namely a legal theory built on the common understanding of the

[121] See *SAM*, p. 140 and Bowring, ix. 121.
[122] Hart, *Essays on Bentham*, pp. 235–8.
[123] See H.L.A. Hart, *Essays in Jurisprudence and Philosophy* pp. 26–35.

concept of a rule. Because the terms "validity" and "authoritative" were, for Hart, confined to a test of authenticity and formal acceptance, by reference to a master rule of recognition, he failed to give a socially dynamic conceptual account of authority or sovereignty. He also failed to see the inherent connections between the popular determination and effectuation of constitutional limits, and the limits of legal validity. Hart's methodology of "descriptive sociology" was sound, but the social context in which this methodology was applied was far narrower than Bentham's.

It is not enough to advance a practical argument against Bentham's socially dynamic understanding of sovereignty. For instance, one might argue it would make more sense to lawyers to say that interpretation of constitutional limits could exist regardless of what the population actually thought about them. However, this does not mean that it would not make sense for a social theorist to insist that the ultimate basis for law and authority must somehow be related to the collective, popular, critical attitude of a social group. Hart's theory has indeed been subjected to criticism on these grounds by Postema[124] and Fuller.[125] The core of these criticisms is that Hart's theory did not account for the role of the people in establishing and maintaining political authority.

The main focus of this section is another partial reading of Bentham, this time with regard to Bentham's constitutional theory. This reading is "partial" for two reasons. In the first place, it treats Bentham as being either a legal "reformer" or a political "radical". In the second, it excludes consideration of his legal theory from an interpretation of his constitutional theory, that is it treats Bentham's legal and constitutional theories as distinct and unconnected.

The most comprehensive work on Bentham's *Constitutional Code* is Rosen's.[126] In very much the same way that Hart overlooked Bentham's constitutional theory, Rosen virtually ignores Bentham's legal theory. Rosen examines *Constitutional Code* in relation to Bentham's early political thought, and with regard to the practical aim of his legal theory, namely the production of a complete code of law.[127] However, although he mentions *IPML* and *Fragment*, Rosen does not attempt a comprehensive reading of Bentham's constitutional and legal theory as developed and elaborated in *OLG*. He does not make a connection between the limitation of legal sovereignty, that is limitations of the power to legislate, and the existence of a democratic government.

In his chapter on sovereignty, Rosen does not address the issue of legally, or more accurately, constitutionally, limited government, and its relation to Bentham's constitutional theory. There is no discussion as to how *constitutional laws in principem* or constitutional promises, concepts which Bentham discussed extensively in *OLG*, relate to Bentham's mature writings. Rosen's only

[124] Postema, *Bentham and The Common Law Tradition*, pp. 256–7. For a critique of Postema's own account, see chapter 2, pp. 75–8 above.

[125] Fuller, *The Morality of Law*, pp. 139–41.

[126] Rosen, *Jeremy Bentham and Representative Democracy*.

[127] Ibid., p. 2.

treatment of this issue arises in a discussion of Hart's account of Bentham's provision for a divided and limited sovereign.[128]

A major problem with Rosen's account is that he fuses the issue of the locus of sovereignty in Bentham's thought with the nature of it. By "locus" is meant the determination of where sovereignty resides. By "nature" is meant a conceptual understanding of sovereignty. Rosen argues that Bentham saw the locus of sovereignty as changing depending on the form of government. Bentham understood that in absolute governments all power would be located in the hands of one man. The locus would change in a democratic government from the legislature to the people. Therefore, Rosen argues, "Bentham's commitment to democracy requires him to separate sovereign power from the power to legislate."[129] And also, "For the most part sovereignty means for Bentham the authority to make laws. However, once Bentham in the *Code* places sovereignty in the people, he can no longer see sovereignty in this light."[130]

Rosen bases his argument on two passages in Bentham's *Constitutional Code*. In the first, Bentham clearly located sovereignty in the people: "The Sovereignty is in *the people*. It is reserved by and to them. It is exercised, by the exercise of the Constitutive authority."[131] The other passage Rosen relies on concerns the powers of the supreme legislative:

> "The Supreme Legislature is omnicompetent. . . . To its power, there are no limits. In place of limits, it has checks. These checks are applied, by the securities, provided for good conduct on the part of the several members. . . . The power thus unlimited is that of the Legislature *for the time being*. To no anterior Legislature belongs any power, otherwise than by confirmation given to it by the Legislature for the time being."[132]

The argument which Rosen seems to advance here is that the locus of sovereignty, whether residing in the government or the people, and the nature of it, whether legal sovereignty, that is "power and the limits of power to legislate", or political sovereignty, that is "power of location and dislocation of officials", are interdependent.[133] A change from sovereignty residing in the government to sovereignty residing in the people requires that "sovereignty" changes its *meaning* completely, from being a power to legislate, into a power of locating and dislocating officials. A change in locus would involve a change in nature. This

[128] Rosen relies on H.L.A. Hart, "Bentham on Sovereignty", in B. Parekh (ed.), *Jeremy Bentham, Ten Critical Essays* pp. 145–53, at 147.

[129] Rosen, *Jeremy Bentham and Representative Democracy*, p. 41.

[130] Ibid., p. 44; see also p. 47 where Rosen writes:

> "It was perhaps inevitable that once Bentham favoured representative democracy, he would have difficulty combining the association of sovereignty both with the power to legislate and with a supreme directing power in the state."

[131] *Constitutional Code*, p. 25.

[132] Ibid., pp. 41–2.

[133] The distinction between legal and political sovereignty was drawn by Dicey in *An Introduction to the Study of the Law of the Constitution*, pp. 285–6; see also chapter 2, p. 49 above for a discussion of the different senses in which Bentham discussed "sovereignty".

implies a fusion between locus and nature: a change in one would entail a change in the other. From the connection which Rosen makes between the locus and nature of sovereignty, it follows that once Bentham changed his position, by locating sovereignty in the people, he *could no longer* mean by sovereignty a power to legislate.

This is a misinterpretation on Rosen's part. It is true that Bentham might be charged with speaking inconsistently about the term "sovereignty", but this should not rule out an interpretation which makes the best sense of his theory, despite the apparent inconsistency. Rosen fails to see that popular and legal sovereignty were *both* essential parts of the concept of sovereignty. Once Rosen is committed to the view that the nature of the concept changed from the legal to the political (from legislative to constitutive power), because of the change of its locus, he sees no need for any further discussion of legal sovereignty. For Bentham, constitutional limits operated at the level of legal sovereignty, but because Rosen effectively ignores legal sovereignty, he has no means of explaining constitutional limits. Rosen's interpretation, therefore, excludes the possibility of accommodating within Bentham's theory constitutional limits on the powers of government. In this identification of locus and nature, Rosen in fact neglects the discussion of the limitation of sovereignty and constitutional limits found in Bentham's legal writings.

Rosen treats Bentham's constitutional writings as if Bentham wished to avoid discussing the issue of sovereignty, in the sense of power to legislate. Rosen does not confront the problem: if Bentham saw sovereignty (in the sense of power to legislate) as potentially limited and divided, as Rosen himself recognises,[134] how was it that he provided for an unlimited legislature in *Constitutional Code*? According to Rosen, Bentham solved this problem by adopting the term "omnicompetent", which replaced the term "sovereign" as far as power to legislate was concerned. However, this does not resolve the problem about the limitation of the power to legislate. Whatever words Bentham used to signify the power to legislate, the problematic fact remains, that he provided in his legal writings for limited sovereignty in the sense of the power to legislate. The term "omnicompetent", if substituted for the idea of legal sovereignty, must still account for the limitations imposed by the social justification of authority, which formed a subject of considerable importance in Bentham's legal writings. So, either Bentham was inconsistent in his use of the word "sovereignty" (meaning sometimes power to legislate, sometimes constitutive power), or Rosen has failed to make sense of his legal and political writings. In view of the argument presented in the preceding chapters, it is arguable that Rosen's explanation of Bentham's theory of sovereignty in general, and in *Constitutional Code* in particular, is incomplete, because it takes into account only what Bentham wrote in *Constitutional Code*, while passing over the earlier discussions of the concept.

[134] Rosen, *Jeremy Bentham and Representative Democracy*, p. 44.

Sovereignty, for Bentham, was the product of an interactive activity between the people and the legislature. This account holds good for *Constitutional Code*. By locating sovereignty in the people and by introducing the term "omnicompetent", Bentham simply implemented his enabling rationale for governmental power, according to which the sovereign would not be subject to a priori limits, although by the very fact of being "sovereign" it would be limited. Rosen's failure to incorporate Bentham's legal theory into his constitutional theory has implications for the accuracy and ambit of his subsequent discussion of related themes, both in *Representative Democracy*, and in his later book, *Bentham, Byron and Greece*. In the first place, as a result of the confusion of the locus and nature of sovereignty, Rosen clearly fails to grasp the centrality of the people in Bentham's enterprise in the determination and effectuation of constitutional limits. When Rosen writes, "The people are not making legislative decisions, reading some higher consensus, or expressing a general will", he is correct, since Bentham recognised that there had to be delegation to some authority.[135] However, Rosen continues:

> "[The people's] task is **simply** to choose their governors and remove them if they are not satisfied with them. The role is a limited one and must be understood in terms of the relationship between agents or representatives and the people."[136]

Despite his extensive discussion of the continuous role of the people as members of the POT,[137] as far as the exercise of popular sovereignty was concerned, Rosen interprets Bentham as allowing the people only this simple elective role. Even the role of the POT is seen by him as wholly subservient to the function of the people as the constitutive authority. This view is an oversimplification. As has been argued above, the people could exercise sovereignty between elections in determining and effectuating constitutional limits. This was a checking or negative power, of a judicial nature, over the extent of legislative power in a political community. The second implication of Rosen's failure to consider the unified nature of sovereignty in Bentham's legal and political thought, arises in relation to the minimisation of power. In *Bentham, Byron and Greece*, Rosen claims that Bentham did not advocate the minimisation of power. Bentham could very easily become committed to minimisation of power, Rosen argues, because as a utilitarian he thought that all authority was inherently evil. This presumption would incline towards minimal authority. However, Rosen contends, Bentham did not pursue this line of argument. Rosen relies on a note

[135] Bentham argued that power had to be delegated, or to use his word "deputed", because people would have difficulty in governing. He argued that people would not have sufficient time to make all the enquiries necessary for arriving at a proper judgement. Most of the people would have to labour for their own subsistence and hence would not be able to find sufficient time for investigation: see Bowring, ix. 95, 117. The people would also lack intellectual aptitude in relation to certain functions: see *First Principles*, pp. 119, 144. Further, it would be impossible for the whole electorate to act in concert, as one would expect from a decision-making body: see ibid., p. 238.

[136] Rosen, *Jeremy Bentham and Representative Democracy*, p. 50.

[137] Ibid.

Bentham wrote in 1827 claiming that "power maximized so as securities against abuse be so too".[138] First, minimisation of power in the hands of officials would be bad for the public interest because the authority in question would be constrained in what it could do to further the public interest; and secondly, there would be no point in arguing for the efficacy of a popular check over such minimal power.[139]

Although the criticism of the minimisation of power appears correct, this argument remains incompatible with the attitude of general scepticism to authority which Bentham wanted to cultivate in the population. The fact that, from a utilitarian perspective, an authority was regarded as a potential source of evil, meant that checks were required not only on *how* power was exercised, but on whether the power was needed in the first place. On the interpretation put forward in this book, what Rosen refers to as Bentham's objection to the minimisation of power was simply the restatement of the enabling rationale for government, namely that government ought not to be a priori limited. Minimisation of power meant, for Bentham, a priori limitations on legislative power. However, Bentham's position with regard to a priori limitations was entirely compatible with his critical attitude towards legislative power, namely continuous checking as to whether a certain power was needed in a given instance. This was the only way in which Bentham could provide for efficient government, which would also be checked efficiently by the people, without being accused of maintaining an authoritarian theory.

The third, and most important, difficulty which stems from Rosen's non-unified view of the concept of sovereignty is that he understands "omnicompetence" as a synonym for "unlimited power to legislate". Relying on the passage quoted above[140] with regard to the supreme legislature, Rosen reads it literally, at the expense of not making sense of the unity of purpose between Bentham's legal and constitutional theory. This reading leads him to the same conclusion that Hart reached, namely that Bentham did not provide for a constitutionally limited government.[141] Indeed it is not clear from Rosen's account to what extent *Constitutional Code* encompassed the idea of the rule of law as a constitutional principle. He writes:

> "Within the one-year period of office, the legislature may enact any law. If the legislature passes a law severely restricting, for example, freedom of speech and the right of

[138] Rosen, *Bentham, Byron, and Greece*, p. 74.

[139] On the subject of minimisation of power, see *First Principles*, pp. 30–5. In this context, "minimisation" meant not enabling government to do more than those functions required for the attainment of the universal interest. Further, it meant making the operative power subordinate to the constitutive. These senses of "minimisation" are entirely compatible with the enabling rationale for government; see also Bowring, ix. 119.

[140] See p. 176 above.

[141] However, his failure to consider constitutional law does not prevent Rosen from attaching the word "legal" to constitutional concepts; for example "the *legally established* Public Opinion Tribunal", in *Jeremy Bentham and Representative Democracy*, p. 56.

assembly of citizens, there is no Supreme Court to declare such a law unconstitutional and no President to veto it as is the case with the American constitution."[142]

Rosen goes on to argue that there would be no constitutional limits on the power of a legislature even with respect to a law which would abolish the constitution. The checks on sovereign power which Rosen does discuss—annual elections, promises in the legislator's inaugural declaration, and the institution of the Legislation Penal Judicatory—are attempts to provide securities against bad government.[143] However, these attempts were all minor and in any case insufficient, because none of them fundamentally address "constitutional limits" in their true sense. Nowhere does Rosen discuss the *legal* status of *Constitutional Code*. Rosen's non-consideration of Bentham's theory of law results in a further misinterpretation. He argues that under Bentham's system security against misrule was only effectuated if the majority of the people joined together in establishing certain opinions with regard to the government. Any Bill of Rights would have to be seen as a collection of principles agreed by the majority. There was no protection for individuals or minorities in the sense that they could initiate a legal process to protect their rights.[144] As has been argued, Bentham saw public judgement as the means of providing for a utilitarian consensus with regard to constitutional limits. Under Bentham's theory, the concessions made by the legislature would be obtained as a result of fundamental norms established in the community.

Rosen fails to account for the manner in which Bentham's understanding of constitutional arrangements incorporated law-making power and limits to it. His explanation of Bentham's constitutional theory cannot accommodate constitutional limits, or constitutionally limited government. Relying on a passage in *First Principles*,[145] Rosen argues that,

"The relationship between operative and constitutive power was a complex one. On the one hand, the holders of operative power **might easily destroy** constitutive power and thereby destroy **constitutional rule** in the process. On the other hand, constitutive power could only be enhanced by variations in the arrangements of operative power. In principle, operative power, the power of government, **was unlimited**. But it was **necessarily limited** by a constitution and the way it was organized as, for example, in the distinct arrangements for a legislature, executive, and judiciary."[146]

It is difficult to understand how operative power could be unlimited and limited by a constitution at the same time. Further, it is difficult to see how it could be possible to limit operative power on the one hand, but easy to destroy this limitation on the other.

142 Rosen, *Jeremy Bentham and Representative Democracy*, p. 61.
143 Ibid.
144 Ibid., p. 64. Rosen has recently modified his interpretation of Bentham's view on minorities: see chapter 6, p. 230, note 101 below.
145 *First Principles*, p. 135
146 Rosen, *Bentham, Byron, and Greece*, p. 66.

Rosen refers to the metaphor used by Bentham in *First Principles* in which the relationship between the constitutive and operative powers was compared to that between a spring and a regulator in a watch. Each part needs the other to work in a properly controlled way, and only together can the spring and the regulator perform the required operation. If the spring stands for the operative power, and the regulator for the constitutive power, what would the regulation consist of? Rosen is aware of this problem because it seems to him unclear that the act of regulation by the constitutive power would only consist in electing and dismissing officials.[147] Rosen does not furnish any explanation of what this regulating force might consist in, although he recognises the need for such an explanation.

The crucial question becomes, as Rosen acknowledges, who was the "watchmaker"? And Rosen answers—the legislature.[148] However, adhering to Bentham's metaphor for a moment, the interaction between the regulator and the spring would be governed by the principles of physics which would exist independently of the particular configuration of the regulator and the spring. The application of the principles of physics to the common operation of a specific regulator and spring would take place in some context which might be referred to as their "mutual operation". This context, which would give rise to the particular watch in question, would be the "watchmaker". Yet, according to Rosen's argument, one part of the "spring", namely the legislature, which was part of the operative power, would also *determine* (rather than influence) the prime parameters of the regulator. This must be wrong. The basic "principles of physics" in the instance of the government would be none other than the principle of utility, which would be the basis for communication and influence between the two main bodies of the constitution—the people and the government. The nature of this "watchmaker" would depend on some consensus achieved among the people, and between them and the government. This consensus would serve as a negative check on an empowered government. Hence the parameters of regulation would *depend* on this consensus, and would not be *determined* by the legislature. The effectiveness of the "watchmaker" would depend on the degree to which the constitution allowed freedom for the principle of utility to determine the interdependent operation of the constitutive and operative powers.

Rosen assigns too much importance to the legislature, and sees it as the ultimate power in a political society. He writes:

> "Bentham **did not** believe that any interaction between constitutive and operative power advanced the public interest. The **enlightened** legislator **should** see the object of a constitution as identifying the interests of operative power with the universal interest via a constitutional democracy."[149]

[147] Rosen, *Bentham, Byron, and Greece.*
[148] Ibid., p. 67.
[149] Ibid., p. 68.

Again, *everything* is entrusted to the enlightened legislator. It is true that Bentham wanted to ensure, as far as possible, the enlightenment of the legislature, and indeed saw it as necessary for a good government that the right people serve in it. However, the fact of securing good people in government could hardly explain what constitutions were all about. Rosen does not emphasise the crucial point that there could be no such thing as an "enlightened" legislature which existed independently of the universal interest. Rosen's dismissal of interaction as a means of advancing the public interest amounts to a crucial misinterpretation of Bentham's account. It was precisely the interaction between the legislature and the people which would create the universal interest, and would continuously help to determine what its ambit would be. The universal interest would not be promoted without interaction among the people themselves, and between the people and the government.

But, to stress the point again, there would be no such thing as an automatically enlightened legislature. There was instead a legislature consisting of officials who might potentially possess the characteristics (appropriate aptitude) which enable them to be enlightened. So the quality of interaction, or communication, between the legislature and the people would advance understanding of what the universal interest with regard to any given matter actually was. Enlightenment of the legislature would result from social interaction between it and the people.

Rosen then proceeds to the final part of his argument, in which he makes an excursion into legal theory. Rosen admits that the relationship between rulers and ruled was not of a simple "vertical" nature, but does not elaborate. He argues that in Bentham's theory, the holders of operative power could place themselves "above" the law. This is a further mistake on Rosen's part, because clearly, both in Bentham's legal theory, where *constitutional laws in principem* and constitutional promises could exist, and in his constitutional theory, where rulers could be brought to court and punished, there were constitutional limits on government which had the characteristics of law. *Some* part of Bentham's constitutional theory must therefore overlap with his legal theory. Rosen argues:

> "The interaction of constitutive and operative power is based on rules and generates further rules as to the arrangements for appointing and dismissing holders of operative power. Bentham's account not only provides for the continuity of sovereign power **but also for continuing change and variation in the exercise of that power.**"[150]

Rosen's argument here becomes incoherent, and his excursion into Bentham's legal theory is incomplete. On the one hand, he seems to feel, rightly, that the regulating force of the people involves something more than rules regarding the location and dislocation of officials. Yet, on the other hand, he does not look beyond location and dislocation in discussing Bentham's theory of law.[151]

[150] Rosen, *Bentham, Byron, and Greece*, p. 67.

[151] In comparing Bentham's constitutional theory with what Hart said about constitutions in *The Concept of Law*, Rosen equates the interaction between the constitutive and the operative power

Next comes a passage in which Rosen's argument becomes extremely confused, as he struggles with the difficulties of his own interpretation:

> "It is of interest that Bentham did not identify the exercise of constitutive power with a constitution. He did not do so partly because he was attempting to answer a different question, that is, one about the nature of a constitutional system rather than one about a legal system. Bentham was sufficiently realistic not to argue that it was the constitution itself which defined the constitutional system. While not denying that a constitution provided answers to questions about the validity of laws, Bentham would argue that this was neither its most important function nor its most characteristic one. Constitutions, for Bentham, were concerned primarily with offices and power and with the principles which governed their distribution. In the interaction between constitutive and operative power one sees the dynamic operation of a constitutional system."[152]

This passage is incoherent. It is not clear whether the status of constitutions in general, and the *Constitutional Code* in particular, is in any respect "legal". What is a "constitutional system" in this context, and in what way does it differ from a legal system? Is it true that Bentham had not been interested in the question of the limits to law-making powers in the *Constitutional Code*? If a constitution were concerned with "offices and power", how could it be divorced from questions which were peculiar to the *legal* system? A given distribution of offices and power was no more than the substance of a given constitutional law, which marked the limits of justified coercion and with it the limits to legal validity. Rosen attributes to Bentham's thought a divorce between issues which are conceptually linked. All these ideas—a constitution, a constitutional system, a distribution of offices and power, the limits of legal law making powers—are conceptually connected issues. That which is presented by Rosen to be a different entity, the constitutional system or constitution, *was* meant to circumscribe the limits of legal validity, or the limits of sovereignty, or the limit of the power to legislate. Any constitution which provided for a given distribution of power must include a *constitutional law in principem* to that effect. *Constitutional Code,* as has been argued above, was no more than a grand, detailed law, which itself specified the limits for law-making powers. In Bentham's language, *Constitutional Code* was no more than an all-encompassing *constitutional law*

with Hart's idea of the rule of recognition. He argues (rightly) that the rule of recognition stood for legal validity, but goes on to argue (wrongly) that Hart had equated the rule of recognition with constitutions. This was clearly not true, because the rule operated as a customary social rule which validated even the constitution and hence could not be identical to it. It was an ultimate rule of validity which could also be seen as a social fact about the legal system, including its constitution: see *The Concept of Law*, pp. 102–4.

[152] Rosen, *Bentham, Byron and Greece*, p. 68. This passage echoes another in *Jeremy Bentham and Representative Democracy*, p. 24, in which Rosen treats the issue of constitutional limits separately from legal theory. Relying on a passage from *Constitutional Code*, p. 36 (Chapter V, S.4, Art. 4), Rosen comes to the following conclusion: "Bentham does not say that **law, the rule of law, and constitutions** are the main checks to the pernicious exercise of power. Public Opinion **and not law** plays this role." In this passage Rosen in effect does away with constitutional law.

in principem. Constitutional Code was an extensive, self-imposed, limiting framework on the part of the legislature, the arguments in relation to the justification of which would serve as a recommendation to future legislatures.[153]

Hence, there remained a conceptual link between what a constitution was, and the limits of legal validity. It is true that Bentham did not emphasise this link in his constitutional writings, but it was very much there. *Constitutional Code* was an instrument of limitation to the power to make law. It was a detailed expression of volition, a self-limiting volition by the legislature to the effect that if laws were to be made constitutionally, they would have to be made in accordance with the distribution of offices and power in the code. The interaction and interpretation between the operative and the constitutive power was part of what Rosen calls "the constitutional system", which not only ensured that good people were in government, but determined who would be considered a good official, or even "an official". Institutions were only one aspect or dimension of this constitutional arrangement. A scheme of institutions was a subject matter with regard to which interaction between the government and the people could be conducted, having for its object the determination of the limits of law-making power. An argument over constitutional limits necessarily involved an argument which embraced questions about the constitutional system. In short, the object of arguing about constitutional systems and constitutions was to understand them as specific provisions for constitutional limits, or the limits of socially justified coercion. Constitutional systems were simply particular interpretations of the limits to the utilitarian justification of coercion.

The common denominator between the legal side of constitutional law and constitutional theory was that both were concerned with securing the greatest happiness in the community. They were only two different *aspects* of the same problem, namely the way in which a political society *ought* to be organised. Each assumed the existence of the other—neither was possible without the other. Constitutional limits were related to the general happiness, in the sense

[153] In a recent article Rosen argues that the principle of utility, and the maximisation of happiness it demands from legislators, was understood by Bentham in a distributive, rather than as an aggregative, way. The general criticism of utility, namely that it does not take seriously the distinction between persons, is wrong, Rosen argues, precisely because it takes the principle to allow a sacrifice, through law, of some vital interests in favour of the aggregated happiness. Such a criticism does not hold, says Rosen, because:

> "If one is a legislator and one's task is to promote happiness in the public sphere, one's concern is not with the perception and aggregation of private pleasure, but with the extension of pleasure throughout society. Hence, in its public sense, which is the sense in which Bentham mainly employed it, the principle of utility is concerned with the distribution of happiness and the extent of that distribution"—F. Rosen, "Individual Sacrifice and the Greatest Happiness", *Utilitas* 10 (1998) 109–43 at 139.

Again, Rosen seems to presume an enlightened legislator in terms of him reading correctly some public conception of happiness which is to serve as a constraint to immediate private aggregation of pleasure. Rosen does not give an account of how constitutional *limits*, which concern a critical threshold of happiness—one which is logically prior to a rule-bound maximisation of happiness through distribution of rights and resources—are arrived at and reflected upon. See my discussion of Kelly's argument in the next section.

that to coerce the population beyond what was socially acceptable would operate to diminish the general happiness, *both* because it would have a devastating effect on expectations, and also because it would be widely unpopular. This understanding of constitutional limits may be regarded as the substantive moral assumption from which the general happiness of a political society, even in the most basic form of such a society, should be accounted for. Constitutional theory might give rise to a particular constitutional arrangement which made provisions for constitutional limits to a greater or lesser extent.

However, such a morally-based theory of constitutional limits would be meaningless if the society did not adopt a constitutional system which was designed primarily to secure the non-transgression of the limits of acceptable coercion. Constitutional theory should provide the specific institutions through which the substantive idea would be realised, and that was precisely what Bentham tried to do in his writings at the time of the French Revolution, in *SAM*, and in *First Principles* and *Constitutional Code*. All of these works included both a description of institutional forms *and* a normative grounding of such forms.

In sum, the gist of this critique of Bentham scholarship is that it has so far failed to perceive the unity between Bentham's political and legal thought, as well as between his early and late political thought.[154] As has been argued, Bentham had a much broader philosophical view than Hart in understanding the foundation and limitation of political authority. Bentham claimed the position of an observer, a point of view which enabled him to give a universal account of the everchanging relationship between rulers and ruled under the dictates of utility. Bentham had a general critical attitude to authority, and provided for a constant, sharp, social policing of its limits. Bentham understood authority primarily in its psychological and social context. In so doing, Bentham was more of a social than a legal theorist. His understanding of political authority and its limitations always reverted to popular critical justification and action. He wanted to implement the popular, interpretative and critical dimensions of his understanding of the justification of political authority in his mature constitutional writings. As a result, his legal and political writings give a more comprehensive view of sovereignty and constitutional law than does Hart's account. The only exception to this failure by the scholarship to capture the unity in Bentham's thought was Postema, who clearly saw some connection between Bentham's early and later writings, but who did not develop his insights fully.[155] Bentham's *Constitutional Code* did not imply a rejection of the command theory of "a law". Further, his *Constitutional Code* did not neglect the question of the limits of legal validity or the limits of sovereignty. The common denominator between his legal and political theory was the people, through whom constitutional limits, of which *Constitutional Code* was an example, were

[154] Another scholar who fails to appreciate the fact that Bentham provided for legally limited government is R. Harrison: see *Democracy* (London, 1993), pp. 109–12.

[155] See chapter 7, pp. 243–7 below.

determined and effectuated. There is no doubt that in Bentham's mind democracy, characterised by the capacity of the ruled to get rid of their rulers, *and by the limits of legal validity which such a democracy would create to this end*, was a precondition for achieving many other features of a free government and society. However, in order to achieve a free government, it was necessary to allow the people to form a consensus on the question of constitutional limits, and to encourage disobedience to the law in cases where an individual or group felt that some fundamental communal sentiment was transgressed by a proposed coercive measure. Democracy should also operate between elections, by allowing the people a direct participatory role in determining and effectuating constitutional limits. Once determined, these limits could, but would not have to, persist beyond a given government. Constitutional law would be socially entrenched by focused expectations, *whoever might be in power*. However, Bentham always saw constitutional signs, such as *constitutional laws in principem*, as ultimately contingent upon utility, for the reason that the community might always change its most abstract distributive patterns as a result of certain contingencies. Therefore, even basic communal beliefs would be subject to the dynamism of social change. Constitutional law was, for Bentham, a mirror of a community's basic understanding of itself. The description of constitutional law was part of Bentham's universal jurisprudence.[156] The manner in which a community saw itself depended on its stage of development, its cultural heritage, and its ideology, at a given moment in time. Constitutional limits were a temporal reflection of a group's basic communal beliefs. In this sense, the concept of sovereignty would remain, first and foremost, popular.

VI

What are the implications of not incorporating constitutional limits into Bentham's thought? According to Kelly's recent revisionist interpretation, Bentham's writings contain a theory of distributive justice.[157] Bentham's theory is said to accommodate liberal values. A sphere of individual inviolability exists within a realm of secured expectations. These expectations are secured by a regulative mechanism. Within this sphere, each person is able to pursue his or her own conception of the good. The common theme of Kelly's and Postema's work[158] is that by providing for security through publicly accessible rules, Bentham has laid the foundation for each individual to live his life according to his or her own preferences.

However, neither theory discusses the most general sense in which antagonism exists between liberty and authority, namely between security achieved by the enforcement of rules and security against too much rule, or misrule. In other

[156] See chapter 1, pp. 13–20 above.
[157] Kelly, *Utilitarianism and Distributive Justice*.
[158] Postema, *Bentham and the Common Law Tradition*.

words, these theories do not address the antagonism which exists between individual security, and the invasion of individual spheres in the name of security. Such an antagonism, to which Bentham referred as early as *Fragment*,[159] can be understood only if Bentham's enterprise is considered as a whole, that is in both its legal and constitutional aspects. The resolution of this antagonism within utilitarian theory involves the social process of formulating and interpreting a conception of harm in the context of the group in question. This antagonism and the socially dynamic interpretative process it entails, is the critical context in which Mill's "Harm Principle" should be understood.[160] *The whole point* of seeing constitutional limits as a socially dynamic concept is to develop a social, culturally-based, yet historically contingent, conception of harm. Any conception of harm is to be understood as culturally contingent, both arising out of, and feeding back into, the ongoing global utilitarian calculation concerning the limits of justifiable coercion. For example, in a relatively undeveloped group, "harm" could simply refer to threats to individual survival, and the avoidance of such harm could be achieved by a provision for the security of persons. As has been argued above, discussion of harm might enter in relation both to the substance of a proposed coercive measure, and to the estimated degree of co-ordination of moral beliefs in the community, as far as judging a coercive measure was concerned.[161] A conception of harm would have to function as an element of the utilitarian calculation about the limits of the social justification of authority.

In order to defend a utilitarian theory which can accommodate this method of justification for coercion, one has to answer one of Rawls's criticisms of the principle of utility. Rawls criticised the principle of utility for treating a social body, a community, in the same manner as an individual. Rawls claimed that the principle of utility had to operate by assuming an allegedly "impartial spectator", who would decide on a dominant conception of the good to which all individual conceptions of the good would have to be aligned. Once a conception of what would maximise social well-being was determined, "society" would have to be organised in such a way as would maximise that well-being. Such an approach would be potentially insensitive to a just distribution of rights, for example. It would lack commitment to any particular type of distribution. Its only commitment would be to decide a communal conception of the good to be maximised, and then go on to maximise it. An imposition of the majority's opinion could be justified in such a way. In other words, in attempting to discover a *collective* conception of well-being, utility would have to presume an *allegedly* "impartial spectator", because, in fact, any "spectator" would necessarily be a partial one, and would dictate a dominant conception of the good to a social group, which, according to *his* intellectual and sympathetic power, would

[159] *Fragment*, p. 480.

[160] See, "On Liberty", in *The Collected Works of J.S. Mill*, J.M. Robson (ed.), vol. 18 (Toronto, 1977), p. 223.

[161] See chapter 4, pp. 113–5 above.

represent something, the maximisation of which would further well-being in that community. In short, Rawls's point is that a utilitarian would adopt for society as a whole what was the principle of rational choice for a single individual.[162]

Kelly has forcefully argued that on Bentham's account, the legislature would operate indirectly, in so far as it would not be concerned with a direct provision of individual well-being. Kelly overcomes convincingly a significant part of the charge that utilitarianism must assume an alleged "impartial spectator". By providing a realm of security, or a given distribution of property or rights, within which individuals could pursue their own conception of the good, Kelly provides an account which is sensitive to the existence of spheres of individual inviolability, under the law. In this manner, some degree of neutrality is accommodated within the operation of a utilitarian scheme of government. According to Bentham's theory of justice, if a more egalitarian distribution were required, it could be made if full compensation were given for the disappointment which would be caused by violating expectations existing under the prevailing realm of security. This was the only way in which security, which was a prime utilitarian value, could be reconciled with equality.

No criticism of Kelly's portrayal of Bentham's theory of justice is intended here. Rather, the argument which follows is the implication of an earlier criticism of Kelly's portrayal of the operation of the principle of utility.[163] What can Kelly mean by the "indirect" operation of the legislature, other than the acceptance of an alleged "impartial spectator" unquestionably interpreted as justified? Does Kelly's account explain constitutional limitations upon the indirect operations of the legislature? In Kelly's account, the sphere within which acts of the legislature operate is taken as "given", and as necessarily maximising utility by virtue of their conduciveness to security. Despite these acts being susceptible to gradual reform through changes in social attitudes, Kelly's account does not show how the powers of legislation in themselves could *already be limited* through direct utilitarian interpretation by such social attitudes. Constitutional limitations seem to be a non-question in his reading of Bentham. Kelly's account does not accommodate *constitutional* reasoning which would justify and limit the constitution and persistence of any "given" pattern of security. At most, his positivistic account could be extended to explain constitutional limitations in a socially static way. Such an explanation could be given through customary rules which would limit the sphere which is operated upon indirectly by the legislature. However, even such a socially static explanation on a positivistic line shows that something other than an indirect approach and utilitarian "reform" is in operation here. Such a positivistic account of constitutional limits would have to show that securities against misrule could encompass positivistic limitations to the exercise of power in a *direct* reference to the people.

[162] J. Rawls, *A Theory of Justice*, pp. 26–7.
[163] See chapter 4, pp. 124–34 above.

Kelly's account does not show how the parameters of a secure realm of individual inviolability could be modified, and its ambit limited, by communal interpretative process. The "indirectness" of his account either marginalises or blurs under the all-too-general heading of gradual social criticism, an important part of the operation of the principle of utility. This important part explains how communal interpretation can *limit*, by a direct appeal to the principle of utility, the potentially arbitrary, reactionary, and hence socially unjustified conception of the harm, the prevention of which would be guarded against under any manifestation of indirect operation. There is a fine line to chart here between popular censorship and a distributive reform on the one hand, and an interpretation which relates to the nature of the thresholds by which political authority is justified and limited on the other. The people, in entrenching constitutional limits, can ensure that the authoritative (and hence partial) spectator will not legislate beyond what is absolutely socially justifiable, and, in particular, will not be able successfully to commit undue suppression of spheres of individual inviolability.

Because, as has been seen in Chapter 4, Kelly assumes that actions of resistance have an automatically harmful effect in terms of utility—an assumption resulting from his narrow interpretation of Bentham's theory of obligation—he cannot fully answer Rawls's criticisms. My argument is that the maximisation of utility by an indirect, regulative mechanism was itself to operate within a more categorical obligatory context.[164] Kelly's indirect and positivistic account, which allows for the direct operation of the principle of utility only in the context of "criticism" and "reform", overlooks the new limitations upon legislative power whose entrenchment was the potential social result of each reform. My argument, which is closer to Postema's, is that in determining who the "spectator" might be, Bentham's constitutional theory tried to make the legislature or "spectator" not only ask what would best characterise the community (which it had to do were it to provide a means of co-ordination, for example), but also to reflect upon what actions would be regarded by the community as amounting to an excessive use of coercion, and thus condemned as misrule. This self-questioning by the legislature could only be grounded on a utility calculation which related directly to obligations imposed on the legislature by the community. The legislature must be capable of forming a judgement regarding the limits of acceptable coercion.

Both the immediate and the categorical spheres of the operation of the principle of utility were important for Bentham. The immediate sphere was constitutionally uncritical and as such could be seen as involving an indirect operation of the principle of utility. However, a direct utilitarian constitutional interpretation would govern the ambit of the area in which indirect utilitarian operation by the legislature could be critically justified.

A full answer to Rawls's criticism would admit that there existed a partial spectator (the legislature), but that its field of operation would be no more

[164] With regard to the immediate and the categorical (constitutional) spheres of the operation of the principle of utility, see chapter 4, pp. 128–9 above.

extensive than necessary. The legislature's field of action could *be limited* to a certain pattern of distribution of resources and rights, but a pattern susceptible to communal reinterpretation and judgement. The role of constitutional law in Bentham's theory was to make sure that the legislature (or the immediately observed spectator) would not be allegedly "impartial", but would *actually be impartial*, by mirroring a communal judgement about the social justification for such coercion in a transparent way. It was free communication which led the public to form an impartial, albeit transient, conception of harm. Social dynamism is what Bentham hoped impartiality would come from. Constitutional law would determine who the spectator would *be*, and in what manner, as well as to what extent, his power should be exercised to reinforce, or to diminish, neutrality between individual conceptions of the good. Constitutional law, for Bentham, was aimed precisely at providing for the social dynamism which avoided the need to posit a merely *presumed*, and hence potentially dogmatic, pattern, according to which the legislature would be said to be partial. The real and ultimate spectator was the people. The *allegedly* "impartial" spectator which Rawls attributed, justly, to a socially static, largely indirect utilitarian strategy, would be replaced by a *truly* impartial one which is open to transparency of communication with the public. Arguably, Rawls's approach to justice could itself be accommodated into a utilitarian scheme. As I shall argue in Part 2, it is not the utilitarian legislature, but the dogmatism of the Rawlsian legislature which should be the subject of criticism. The heart of this process would be a determination of the balance between the utility of authority and the utility of imposing limitations on it. Under a universal utilitarian account, Rawls's criticism does not operate to curtail the proper operation of the principle of utility. His own conception of distributive justice could become an entrenched ideology, which would limit the operation of the legislature. Rawls's description of the methodology of utility is correct. However, his inference from it, regarding utility's inevitable curtailment of a just distribution of entitlements, is incorrect. Rawls, in effect, advocates a certain ideological application of utility. His theoretical preoccupations are very different from Bentham's. Bentham aimed at a universal explanation of what was possible. Rawls aims at an ideological justification of what is desirable.

6

The Public Opinion Tribunal—an Analysis of Consensus Formation and the Evolution of Communities

Rights corresponding to and derived from correspondent obligations of the perfect kind are not derivable from any other source than law.

Of these legal rights shall they, and in what manner, on the several occasions in question, make exercise? Such are the questions for which it belongs to deontology to find the solution.

Deontology, pp. 171–2.

Suppose not only no extravasated factitious honour, but no superiority by power, no superiority by opulence, to have place, sympathy and esteem, thence free and spontaneous service in all its shapes, would attach itself to superiority in the scale of genuine moral virtue: of effective benevolence in harmony and alliance with self-regarding prudence: and thus it is that these same instruments of felicity, attaching themselves in the character of reward to that same moral virtue, operate towards the encrease of it, by furnishing inducements to the practice of it. This order is disturbed by power. . .

First Principles, p. 321.

I

This chapter analyses in detail the theme of a utilitarian consensus which, as has been argued in Chapters 4 and 5, dominated Bentham's *A Fragment on Government,* and persisted in his mature constitutional writings. Bentham believed that people could arrive at a collective judgement, approving or disapproving, of a given coercive measure. More specifically, it has been argued that, in *Fragment* as well as in his mature constitutional writings, Bentham understood constitutional limits as determined and effectuated by a popular collective judgement. In this chapter, the nature of, and the conditions for, the formation of public opinion will be considered in much more detail. The nature of a utilitarian consensus will be discussed, and particular attention paid to Bentham's understanding of the ideas of influence, or "interaction", and human motivation. The main purpose is to show that Bentham saw the formation of an independent public sphere as beneficial.[1] The efficient formation and execution of public opinion needed to be facilitated if it were to act as an effective check on the legislature.

It might be objected that constitutional limits cannot properly be understood in terms of a consensus formed by the public. Constitutional limits might exist regardless of public attitudes or expectations.[2] Thus, to equate constitutional limits with what the public *actually* thought or expected would be a mistake. However, as a social theorist, Bentham would not accept this objection. He would explain constitutional wrongs, and evil-doings on the part of government generally, in terms of a "functional deficiency", arising, for example, from the false consciousness of the public. Notions such as "constitutional limits", and "public opinion", had to be explained on the basis of the general parameters of the functioning of societies, whatever the quality of the actual conditions for this functioning might be.

For Bentham, there would always be some degree of public involvement in any comprehensible account of constitutional limits. In oppressive regimes, communal judgement would be distorted, but would still operate. For Bentham, oppression did not mean a discourse *without* public judgement, but a discourse in conditions which prevented the public from forming a proper judgement, or prevented the people from making effective any proper judgement once formed. An analysis, such as Hart's, which conceptually divorced what the people critically thought about legal validity from a formal account of such validity, would *itself* be a result of a communicative misconception on the part of various agencies which participated in the formation of public judgement.

This chapter consists of four parts which bear similarities to Habermas's argument.[3] The first examines the main features of the Public Opinion Tribunal in Bentham's mature constitutional writings. It discusses the independent nature of public opinion, or the collectivity, and the manner in which public opinion facilitates what has been termed above a "panoptic democracy".[4] The second examines the nature of what Bentham calls the "universal interest". A detailed discussion of the way in which a consensus might be formed in society is undertaken. The notions of "influence" and "sympathy" are analysed, relying substantially on *Deontology*,[5] and the unpublished writings written at the time of the French Revolution. These two sections overlap in that they analyse the same theme, namely the way in which the relationship between an individual and the collectivity might lead to the formation of a consensus. The two sections are

[1] The meaning of "independent" in this context is discussed at p. 220, note 76 below.

[2] In *Essays on Bentham*, pp. 233–4, Hart argued that constitutional limits existed whether a law was popularly obeyed or not.

[3] See J. Habermas, *Between Facts and Norms* (Cambridge, 1996), pp. 360–6.

[4] See chapter 5, p. 160 above.

[5] *Deontology* was Bentham's mature work on ethics. He distinguished between political deontology, which involved law and politics, and private deontology, which involved moral instruction between individuals—an extra-political activity. He presented a less-developed version of deontology in chapter 17 of *IPML*, especially at pp. 282–3.

structured so as to move from the general to the particular. "Public opinion" is initially discussed at a general, abstract level, then more concretely through the idea of "influence", and finally through a detailed analysis of consensus formation on the basis of the characterisation of human motives and the application of various sanctions.

In the third section, an account of the relationship between Bentham's accounts of universal theory and history is suggested.[6] I shall argue that, notwithstanding the unchanging nature of the universal concepts utilised in his legal and political theory, such as pain and pleasure, law, and sympathy, Bentham envisioned a significant change of emphasis in their operation within a social group as this group advanced in its history, as well as transcending its own cultural and historical contingency through communication. The fourth and final section will summarise the argument of the chapter, and will give the broadest account of constitutional limits defended in this book. This account will portray constitutional limits as a critical reflection which implies more and more communal constitutional limits on the operation of centralised institutions and even a possible and gradual change of locus of certain obligatory spheres, from central institutions to the community at large.

II

The Public Opinion Tribunal (hereafter POT) was a public court.[7] It was a fictitious entity.[8] Bentham had to use the language of fiction because the POT was not an institution whose membership was known in advance. The POT was a committee composed of all the citizens who took an interest in a given matter. The effect of the tribunal's judgement would be real, despite its fictitious nature,[9] and the fluctuation of its members. The tribunal's judgement could be discerned "as if" it really existed. It was by publicity, and hence notification, or "notoriety", that the POT's operation was enabled.[10] Bentham constantly portrayed the POT as an *independent body*. The POT could form a judgement and attach a correspondent *will* to it. The judgement and its execution could be applied in relation to the determination and effectuation of constitutional limits. Unlike a typical court, the POT would not be limited to a given code of law for its subjects of reference (or sources). It could take notice of all public matters, and would consider all sources of information it regarded as relevant in discussing any single matter.[11] Its ability to consider issues of public interest would

[6] See chapter 1, pp. 13–20 above.

[7] For a description of the main features of this tribunal in Bentham's democratic institutional scheme, see chapter 5, pp. 140–2 above.

[8] With regard to the meaning of fictitious entities and Bentham's theory of fictions, see chapter 4, p. 97, and note 5 therein above.

[9] *SAM*, pp. 28, 54.

[10] Ibid., p. 29. On "notoriety", see chapter 5, p. 150 above.

[11] *SAM*, p. 67.

be much more flexible than that of any official machinery. It would also have the potential to arrive at an establishment-independent judgement, based on communication between people, before its deliberations were communicated to central institutions—whether adjudicative or legislative.

However, Bentham did not only conceive the POT as a court,[12] but also as a legislature which would create moral obligations.[13] He argued that one of the advantages of the POT over a normal legislative chamber would be that, in the deliberations of the latter, because of the rigidity of procedure, there would be no immediate opportunity to point out contradictions. By contrast, while public opinion was forming, public deliberations would not be subject to rigid procedures which might hamper the flow of debate. Further, communication would be carried on without being influenced by considerations of power, which could hamper proper evaluation.

But what did Bentham mean by the term "public opinion"? By the idea of a "public", Bentham understood a group of people who happened to be interested in an issue, and hence would communicate about it. These people would exchange opinions with one another.[14] On many occasions during his career, Bentham seemed to refer to the impossibility of speaking about a community as an independent entity. The idea of community was only comprehensible as an aggregate of persons.[15] However, with reference to the POT, "aggregate" seemed to take on a particular signification, although it goes without saying that it would not be possible to talk about the POT without presuming the independent existence of the individuals who composed it.

The idea that public opinion arose from "summing up" individual opinions, though not entirely wrong, fails to capture the complexity of the social operations involved in its formation. Summing up individual opinions implies treating every person as an autonomous, already opinionated, being. The majority of such autonomous people who hold an opinion about a given matter are taken to represent "public opinion".

Such a description of the social process of "adding up" (although what is done in elections can be described in this way), cannot account for the complex communicative social process which would arguably take place prior to the stage at which such opinions were "added up", a process which may be quite distinct from such addition. According to Bentham's theory of fictions, a fictitious entity like the POT is understood by means of connecting it to real entities—to people who communicate with one another, and to pain and pleasure. Although the

[12] See chapter 5, pp. 140–1 above.

[13] See *Deontology*, p. 72, where Bentham wrote:

"The legislator *creates*, of himself, new interests. To the deontologist it belongs, of himself, to bring to view existing interests, and even, in proportion to the influence of his authority, to apply the force of the moral or popular sanction to the creation of new interests."

[14] For Bentham's idea of "communication", see *Chresthomathia* (CW), M.J. Smith and W.H. Burston (eds), (Oxford, 1983), p. 165.

[15] See, for instance, *IPML*, p. 11.

POT as a whole was fictitious, it was comprehensible as a product of communication which would result in a real social effect. As has been mentioned, Bentham referred to it as a committee. This committee was the group of people who took an interest in a given matter, and so would communicate on it. Bentham used paraphrasis in order to give a communicable and real meaning to the fictitious entity:[16]

> "The best course therefore will be to consider it as acting by a Committee—in this case all fiction **may** be excluded. That which is real being thus explained, the explanation may afterwards be applied with advantage to the **mixture of the real and the fictitious.**"[17]

The most important feature of the POT was its *operational autonomy*—its independence from the individuals in the community. Although its judgement could be *influenced* by individual opinions, it consisted of a collectivity of opinions. This collectivity would be the result of communication, and *as such* would be able to influence each individual member's opinion. The question was, to what extent could a distinct collective judgement function in the mind of each member of the social group, when he made up his own judgement?

When Bentham discussed situations in which "an official shall do/refrain from doing something because doing otherwise would result in a moral sanction imposed by the POT",[18] or when he wrote "this is what the public thinks", what did he mean? How could a public "have an opinion"? Although, technically speaking, the POT had no existence outside the individuals communicating upon a given issue, its judgement would be operationally independent, in that it could direct and limit individual preferences in a given direction. This collectivity, once formed, could alter individual judgements, in that individuals would be able to imagine what its judgement might be (to construct future possibilities), and this view of its possible future judgements might in turn influence their own judgements. The relationship between the "real" (individuals, committees) and the fictitious (communicative fictitious entity) would not be based on "aggregation" in the simple sense of "adding up".

This imagined collective judgement of the POT would function on a temporal basis in the mind of each individual. By "temporal", I mean that the individual in question would *remember* what past judgements of the collectivity had been, and would *foresee*, or *imagine*, possible future judgements, when he came to form his own opinion. It will be argued below that the moral and the sympathetic sanctions were the means by which the collectivity might exercise its influence over the individual. The process of forming public opinion was much more complex than adding up individual opinions. The fictitious POT would form the background to, and would operate prior to, any "adding up" process. Bentham envisaged a *separate and independent tribunal*, which would act on its

[16] On paraphrasis, see chapter 4, p. 97 above.
[17] *First Principles*, p. 70; see also Bowring, ix. 41.
[18] See, for instance, *First Principles*, pp. 56–9.

own, and would gather independence and momentum once a channel of communication on a given issue had been opened up. The POT would be independent from individuals, in the sense that a construct of its judgement might influence their own judgement. It would function as a distinct moral agency in each individual mind. In short, although its existence would depend on individuals, its judgement could become operationally independent from the individuals who constituted it.

It is very important to be clear on this point. The tribunal did not exist "out there". It was generated by individuals. As a result of communication it could be constructed by each individual's imagination and memory. As such, the judgements of the tribunal, although able to influence an individual judgement with regard to a given matter, were not identical to it.[19] The opinion of the POT, though fictitious, nevertheless had real consequences, since it would influence the thinking of each individual. In Bentham's words, the judgement would be a "conscience", formed in the mind of all the members of the community who took part in communication on the matter. It might be that the judgement would be given explicit expression in a newspaper, but

> "by others in an incalculable number by whom no judgment is expressed, a judgment on the subject—the like judgment suppose—is in mere conscience formed. But the judgment being formed, though no expression is ever given to it, a correspondent will, as above, is naturally formed."[20]

Public opinion would exist in the mind of each individual. It could not be given concrete expression, but everybody would be able to come to some conclusion as to what its judgement might be, despite the absence of any formal expression of that judgement. Not only citizens, but also officials, would be able to make an assessment of its content. It would be a communicative product, with regard to which everybody could know what it had contained in the past, and assess what it might contain in the future. Public opinion would be formed by the participation of each person, but each person would also be influenced by whatever generalisation he made on the basis of information which other individuals presented to him.

The POT was a communicative enterprise which literally "watched" every citizen and official who participated in its proceedings. This was the only way in which Bentham could speak sensibly about a threat of punishment "at the hand of the POT", in the case of an official performing some action or other. There would be a social context, constituted by the POT, in which each individual's mind operated. The judgement of the POT would enter the calculation of each individual/official within a social group. It is in the light of this idea of "conscience", which would be "formed" in the minds of individuals, but to which it was possible that no explicit expression was given, that Bentham's

[19] For a discussion of Bentham's understanding of the temporal function, see p. 209, note 52 below.

[20] *SAM*, p. 63.

democracy can sensibly be referred to as "panoptic", since a similar "watching entity" would operate in Bentham's prison house—the panopticon. "Conscience" would act like an inner voice within each individual, which on the one hand would watch him, but on the other hand would be constructed by him. An official would never see a real public tribunal actually watching and checking him. He would have to imagine this "observer". Because this "observer" could not be seen, only imagined, it would be constructed out of communication between people concerning what its judgement might be. This communication would have to be generalised, by imagination and memory, creating a would-be or hypothetical "ordinance" of the "observer" in the mind of the official. The full power of the POT stemmed from the very fact that although it was a communicative product of which each person could conceive, it could never be said really to exist in terms of the possibility of perceiving it. Its only existence, *real* existence, would be in the mind of a real person, be they an official or a citizen. The official would imagine a public judgement upon what he did. The individual citizen would imagine what his fellow citizens might think about what he thought or did. *The official* would imagine an all-embracing collective public opinion, an ongoing public inspection of his activities, and hence the imagined would *become real,* in the sense of exercising a direct influence on those activities. The official or citizen would generate his own observer. Everyone would create their own mentor. The power of the invisibility of this "observer" would be such that each official would, via communication, "make up" the public conscience in relation to a given matter.[21] In this way, public conscience would be in effect real *for the official,* despite its fictitious nature.

It would in fact be detrimental to the effectiveness of this tribunal if its judgements could be really ascertained by all people and officials, in the same way that a judgment of a court might be ascertained. A real entity would not produce an effective sanction because once its operations were fully known, they could easily be evaded.[22] Were the POT to be formally constituted, its flexibility, its independence, its operational efficiency, and thus its capacity to serve as a tool for popular self-reflection and enlightenment, would all be lost. This was the essence of the POT: its judgements arose from the random exchange of individual sentiments and opinions, yet were regarded as the judgements of a collectivity.

In short, the POT was a communicative entity which could not be perceived by the senses, but could be inferred and shaped by people, whether they were citizens communicating on governmental measures with their fellow citizens, or officials pondering a collective public judgement on a given matter. It was

[21] For the general discussion of an observer's "gaze" in Bentham's panopticon, see Bozovic's introduction, *The Panopticon Writings*, M. Bozovic (ed.) (London, 1995), pp. 1–27.

[22] On the other hand, the POT's judgment could be interpreted as being weak, because it did not have the full characteristics of a judicial tribunal. However, the POT would have a real effect, because each individual would be afraid of a force that he himself constructed in his own mind. Arguably in this sense, the POT's effectiveness might be stronger since it penetrated further into the psyche of individuals than those of real, formal institutions.

independent, in that its judgements could follow a certain discernible pattern which would develop in a given society at a certain moment in time. This pattern was not identical with, and could be to a considerable degree autonomous from, the development of the individuals who constructed it. However, as will be argued below, the attachment of sanctions to the tribunal's decrees could very much influence individuals' psyches. Thus, this communicative pattern which constituted the tribunal could play a role in the construction of individual judgements. It would serve as an influential *obligatory context* for individual deliberations. The POT could be seen as a "person" in its own right, deliberating on a given matter, *despite* the fact that its *existence* was entirely dependent on the existence of real communicating individuals.

III

Bentham argued on many occasions that the judgement arrived at by the POT would give expression to the "universal interest" of the community.[23] The aim of this section is to explain how the universal interest was formed as part of a continuous, communal, enlightening process. In short, it analyses the idea of consensus formation. A consensus should not be understood, especially in the writing of so radical a thinker as Bentham, as being associated with the maintenance of the status quo. *Some* status quo was, for Bentham, always a starting point, hence his belief in the importance of the security of expectations. There could be no alternative substantive starting point as far as any given group was concerned. This explained why the notion of the static social contract was not functionally convincing. The agreement between the people and the government would be subject to constant change. An agreement would be shaped by constant interactive activity involving a coercive mechanism which would influence, and be influenced by, public opinion.[24]

What did Bentham mean when he said in *Fragment* that he believed that once people were left to discuss matters under the auspices of the principle of utility, it would not be long before they agreed?[25] How was the universal interest formed? The nature of the calculations which people would have to make has been discussed in Chapter 4 above. An analysis of the social process which would bring about such a consensus will now be attempted.

[23] *On the Influence of the Administrative Power over the Legislative*, UC cxxvi. 3.

[24] See chapter 4, p. 106, note 19 above, which points to Bentham's explanation of "political societies" as a continuous, socially dynamic contract between the people and the government.

[25] See *Fragment*, p. 492, and p. 483:

> "It is the principle of *utility*, accurately apprehended and steadily applied, that affords the only clue to guide a man [in his judgement whether to obey or not]. It is for that, if any, and for that alone to furnish a decision which neither party shall dare in *theory* to disavow. It is something to reconcile men even in theory. They are at least, *something* nearer to an effectual union, than when at variance as well in respect of theory as of practice."

The idea of influence

This subsection attempts to explain the activity which has thus far been termed "interaction". It does so through an analysis of Bentham's concept of influence. Bentham distinguished between two types of influence. The first was that of will over will; the second was that of understanding over understanding. The former was concerned with an expression of will, the latter with forming a judgement, or an opinion, on a given matter. The former implied a relationship of superiority and subordination, that is of authority, as opposed to advice and recommendation. Influence of understanding over understanding, on the other hand, assumed a relationship of equality, and implied discussion and persuasion.[26] This initial distinction requires elaboration, and, as we shall see, some constructive reinterpretation. Although the faculties involved are the understanding and the will, the relationship between them is more complex than is implied by this simple distinction.

"Influence" was defined by Bentham as "a result produced by power applied indirectly and to a purpose collateral to the obvious end of its institution".[27] This definition might easily lead to confusion. First, it is not clear what Bentham meant by "collateral". The definition might be applied, for example, to a law, the obvious end of which was to prevent mischief, but the collateral purpose of which was to induce people to act in a certain way. Alternatively, the definition might be interpreted to encompass the use of power allegedly in order to promote the universal interest, while in fact promoting a sinister one. Secondly, this definition does not account for the many manifestations of influence which do not involve power. In short, this definition of "influence" does not cover the common usage of the term influence, namely as an application of power or argument (be the application of power of argument sincere or pretended) in a way which operates to modify a judgement.

The phenomenon of influence forms an inevitable part of the social activity within a group. Bentham thought that a proposition made by a few influential people must eventually influence the understanding of the many. Although an improvement in material conditions might lead to more leisure time, the natural differences between people in terms of intelligence, or what Bentham called in his constitutional writings intellectual aptitude, would necessarily lead to a temporary domination of the ideas of a minority within a social group.[28]

The relationship of influence could arise in two ways. First, a person could be influenced by another, because the influencing act would communicate information which would cause the recipient to see that to pursue a given act would be in his interest. This would be "passive influence", because all that was exchanged was an argument, communicated by the influencing party. This

[26] See *Deontology*, p. 111; see also Raz, *The Authority of Law*, pp. 14–16.

[27] *On the Influence of the Administrative Power over the Legislative*, UC cxxvi. 1.

[28] Ibid., UC cxxvi. 2.

mode of influence would be akin to influence of understanding over understanding. If some people discussed and exchanged views, the mere hearing of a view by one person, whether this view was directed to him or not, might cause him to see the situation in a different light. This might occur through the receipt of new information which had not been known before the exchange, or by the application of new arguments to information already known. Such a manifestation of influence would have the effect of "adding considerations", rather than being a form of manipulation towards a certain outcome. Such influence would amount to seeing one's own situation in a truer light, to be enlightened, to be more authentic. Such influence would result in a change of perspective and the consideration of a wider range of outcomes for each party to the exchange, that is in better "coverage" of the situation:

> "When one man acts for many it may be justly required of him that he pursue as well as comprehend the interest of the whole. But when all act each for himself all that can be wished for is that each man pursue his own interest and either comprehend it himself or act by the judgment of one who understanding better what is for his interest, is not in pursuit of any which clashes with that of his consulter."[29]

Here, it is the "information" which influences the judgement. Such an influence would lead to a judgement generated *solely by* the internal persuasion of the influenced party. There is no inducement involved. There is no obligation to arrive at a certain outcome.[30]

Secondly, influence could be "active". Here there would be some external inducement to make the influenced party act in a certain way. Some degree of force would be involved, with or without the utterance of an argument. This inducement could be the threat of a sanction (or the promise of a reward).[31] This mode of influence would be akin to the influence of will over will. The influence of will over will operated where a benefit could be conferred, or cost imposed, upon the influenced party, according to the pleasure or the interest of the influencing party.[32] It would signify a relationship of power, in which the interest of the party which had greater power would dominate the exchange.

However, this general distinction is insufficient fully to characterise influence. A further distinction can be made here between the pure influence of will over will, and the influence of will over will through the medium of the understanding. The former operates to the exclusion of the understanding, amounting to pure conformism, or unreserved obedience, on the part of the influenced. If *G* said to *J* "do this", the influence might be such that *J* would follow that utterance, adopting *both* the state of the understanding of *G*, which led *G* to utter the volition, and *G*'s will. The cognitive chain on *J*'s part in this case would be: You understand, you will, *therefore I have an obligation* to understand what you

[29] *On the Influence of the Administrative Power over the Legislative*, UC cxxvi. 3.
[30] See also Bowring, ii. 439.
[31] *Deontology*, p. 175.
[32] *On the Influence of the Administrative Power over the Legislative*, UC cxxvi. 5.

understand, and then to will what you will. The crucial factor is that there is only *one understanding* in operation. The addressee's understanding is passive in that it unreflectively imitates the addressor's:

> "As my will is necessarily governed in preference by the prospect of my advantage so is your will by the prospect of your advantage: if therefore in opposition to the dictates of my own will I follow those of yours, my interest is sacrificed to yours. If I conform to your will only because it is conformable to mine the case does not come within the supposition: it is then only your understanding that I conform myself to and take for my guide. The influence of will on will necessarily supposes the sacrifice of one man's interest, of what that man supposes at least to be his interest, to that of another."[33]

This type of influence can be characterised as a relationship of absolute authority, in which an obligation operates on reasons which fully exclude *independent reasoning* on the part of the addressee coupled with some inducement, institutional or communal, to give these reasons normative *force*.

However, influence of will over will did not have to operate this way. It could operate merely as a dominant, not an exclusionary, reason for action. The force would be generated by some inducement, and would be accepted as authoritative on most occasions. Yet, there would be a residual moral autonomy whereby the addressee could interpret and reflect not only on whether conforming in the instance was in his interest, but whether the *very existence* of the obligation was so, all things considered. This is to say the addressee could reflect on, and interpret afresh, second-order reasons, some of which might well relate to a more general justification for the authoritative utterance. Influence of this type would amount to the exercise of a "reflectively justified" (as opposed to the potentially dogmatic and unreflective "legitimate"—a term that Bentham deplored) authority. The cognitive sequence on the part of the addressee here would be: You understand, you will, therefore I have an obligation, I understand the existence of this obligation to be in my interest all things considered, therefore I will. This mode would be the influence of will over will through the medium of the understanding. A first-order obligation is involved, but a second-order obligation might be arrived at as a result of a more global reflection, which would question the status of the first-order obligation *as such*. Under such influence, the addressee might respond: "I know that I am under an obligation, but nevertheless I criticise its obligatory status", or even "I am not going to fulfil it". The main feature of this third characterisation of influence is that although a relationship of will over will is involved, which is to say that some obligation is involved, the ultimate superiority is that of understanding over understanding. The will operates "in the shadow" of the understanding. In an instance of pure influence of will over will, the utterance operates as what Raz calls an "exclusionary reason". In this third category, that is influence of will over will through

[33] *On the Influence of the Administrative Power over the Legislative*, UC cxxvi. 3. Note *The Book of Fallacies*, p. 405.

the medium of the understanding, the authoritative utterance operates as a dominant, but not as an exclusionary, reason.

There is some room, which will be elaborated upon below, for a further distinction in relation to an influential act. An act of authority might be explicit, or implicit. An example of an explicit act of authority is a straightforward, expressive imperative, familiar in the field of law. An implicit act of authority is related to an inducement, that is a sanction, which does not necessarily arise from an explicit act of will. An implicit act of authority might easily be confused with the influence of understanding over understanding, since there is no actual imperative utterance in either case. An explicit act of authority could be seen in law, where some expression was uttered by a sovereign. An implicit act of authority could be seen where the process of communication between people led to a crystallisation of prescriptive propositions backed up by the moral or sympathetic sanctions.[34]

In his writings at the time of the French Revolution, Bentham discussed the application of these distinctions. He saw the operation of the influence of understanding over understanding as salutary, and thought that public discussion would more easily find itself on the right track when the influence of will over will was suspended. Notification of public measures would lead every man to consider for himself in what the public interest might consist, and this consideration would be the basis for public discussion. Bentham argued that only when the influence of understanding over understanding was freed from that of will over will, would public opinion be properly formed. Influence of will over will was potentially destructive of free public communication. Bentham aimed to liberate the public sphere from the influence of will over will. An external will injected into public discussion would serve as an obstacle to free public dialogue, and hamper independent consensus formation.[35]

However, Bentham's position appears, at first glance, to be incoherent here. It does not make sense to exclude completely the idea of influence of will over will. The total exclusion of will over will was surely neither essential, nor socially possible. It did not make sense to exclude obligations, or propositions enforced by sanctions, from public discussion. It was ridiculous to assume that only "understanding" would be involved in people's interaction with one another. So what did Bentham mean when he said that the best government would be that based on the influence of understanding over understanding? The answer, in a nutshell, is that Bentham wanted to prevent the domination of public discussion by certain general patterns of official institutional influence of will over will (whether involving the understanding or not).[36] He did not object to the influence of will over will which would crystallise during the process of public communication. Further, he did not object to the influence of pure under-

[34] A sympathetic obligation was, as will be argued below, a proposition specifying behaviour to which the sympathetic sanction could be attached.

[35] *On the Influence of the Administrative Power over the Legislative*, UC cxxvi. 1–2.

[36] For example, corruptive influence, delusion and intimidation: see p. 220, note 76 below.

standing over understanding, even where the source of that influence was official or institutional. In short, he wanted to make sure that the influence of will over will, exercised by centralised institutions, would be confined to an immediate obligatory sphere. This meant that such influence would not hamper public censorship in general, and public reflection in the constitutional sphere in particular.

This answer requires a detailed explanation. As has been seen, there were three essential modes of influence: one of pure understanding, another excluding independent understanding, and a third combining understanding and will. This analysis of influence continues an argument advanced in Chapter 4, regarding the cognitive division of the faculty of the understanding of a people in a political society, between the immediate, and the categorical or constitutional spheres.[37] Bentham's confidence in the success of law was based on the effectiveness of the legal sanction in manipulating people's motives and artificially unifying their duty and interest. There would be an "immediate" medium, in which the law would operate to exclude independent reasoning on the part of the population. However, as far as the understanding was concerned, the exercise of coercion, and hence the existence of legal obligation, could never preclude a judgement concerning the legal obligation *qua a legal obligation*. Every legal obligation had to be justified as such. Individuals should be able and prepared to question that justification.

Now, the question is, socially speaking, at what moment would the transition from the "immediate" sphere, of acting under a legal obligation, into the "categorical" sphere, of questioning the social justification of such legal obligation *as such*, occur? In terms of social interaction, or influence, how did self-reflection, or enlightenment, take place? There had to be a moment at which reflection took place, consisting in the critical examination by the understanding of the justification for a pattern of obligation. There had to be a possibility of reflection, involving the memory and imagination of each person, stimulated by the exchange of ideas between people, on the extent of the benefit resulting from the existence of an obligatory pattern. Such a reflection, of course, would not be possible under the second type of influence, that is of pure will over will.

The social process of influence that is the focus of this section worked through both the first mode, that of pure understanding over understanding, and the third, that of will over will through the medium of the understanding. In terms of the third mode of influence, a social situation which could bring about a transition from the immediate to the categorical sphere would involve the generation of obligations in the community. Communal obligations would be both moral and, as will be argued, sympathetic. The social process which created these moral and sympathetic obligations would make it possible for the people critically to reflect upon, say, the primacy of a given justification of a legal obligation.

[37] See chapter 4, pp. 128–9 above.

This social process would lead to enlightenment by means of a conflict about the basis for a justification of obligations. People would have competing justifications for obligations. Such a conflict would result in an enlightened intellectual state, in which people's thinking would move into the constitutional sphere. People could come to question their justification for obligations as such. Such obligations could be justified either by a particular interpretation of a conception of harm, harm which these obligations try to avert, or by a construction of an alternative to the very interpretative framework carved by the conception of harm which people had traditionally followed. This enlightening process would begin with public discussion. It would then evolve, perhaps, into a judgement of the POT, which might then be enforced by the moral sanction. Moral obligations within the community, generated by such a discussion, would be brought into conflict with other previously existing moral obligations. In short, reflection would take place in the constitutional sphere in which the most abstract conception of harm in a community would evolve that is, either refined or rejected.

Let us now consider this shift of obligation, and the way in which obligations might be generated by the community, in more detail. The influence which would bring about this shift would arise from people's discussion and exchange of ideas, in other words from relationships of pure understanding over understanding. In the first instance, people would learn what other people thought, perhaps becoming convinced by their views. Such mutual discussion could, in turn, crystallise into an obligation, sympathetic or moral, in such a way that would make each individual in the community reflect on his previously "coerced" understanding with regard to crystallised, communal, moral obligations. The oscillating process between influence of pure understanding over understanding and the crystallisation of understanding into communal or interpersonal obligations, would enable people to reflect on legally-based obligations *as such,* and even to reflect upon new communal obligations as they were formed. This social process could take place regardless of whether a *prima facie*, socially unjustified ordinance had already been promulgated. The people of the community could be influenced by other members of their community, or by members of other communities. In other words, influence, within the public, and between the people and the government, would consist of a mixture of the first mode of influence—of pure understanding over understanding—and the third one—of will over will through the medium of the understanding. The former would predominate, since through the exchange of ideas between the government and the people, and among the people themselves, there would exist the possibility both of creating sympathetic and moral obligations, and of contesting the primacy of existing obligations.

This was what Bentham meant when he said in his writings at the time of the French Revolution that the dominant influence was that of the understanding over understanding. Although there would already exist a pattern of obligations, there would always remain some possibility for the *free* exchange of views. Although such an exchange has been referred to in relation to Bentham as "censoring" the existing content of an obligation (involving a separation between the acknowledgement of the validity of the obligation and the moral approbation of it), it would in fact interpret the social justification for the existence of an obligation, that is its social acceptability *as an obligation* (involving a unification of validity and approbation). The free exchange of views could emancipate the imagination, so that reflection at the constitutional level would become possible. As far as a political society was concerned, influence would operate *in the constitutional sphere* both among the people, and between the government and the collective body of the people.

As far as influence among the people was concerned, the domain of influence would be affected according to existing patterns of superiority and subordination between themselves. These patterns could vary from one social group to another. Bentham argued:

> "Thus far, as between suffrage and suffrage, it makes no difference which was the result of a self-formed opinion, which of them the result of an opinion derived from the influence exercised on the mind in question by that of some other member, exercised whether on will or on understanding, or on both together."[38]

As between the government and the collective body of the people, influence might also be exercised by understanding over understanding, but to the extent that a relationship of will over will was involved, the ultimate superiority lay with the collective body of the people. In the final analysis, it was the people who could resort to an explicit act of will—disobedience—in order to divest the government of its power, whether globally, or in relation to a single measure.

A word may now be appropriate with regard to the transformation of acts of understanding into acts of will. The significant domain, as has been argued, in which the POT functioned, was that of the *understanding*, a domain which involved judgements and opinions. However, Bentham conceived of a transformation of these opinions, in certain instances, into acts of will, of disobedience, in cases where government had infringed certain fundamental securities.[39] Bentham described a state of the mind which he called "valleity". He understood this term as a fusion of will and understanding. Valleity was the stage at which an opinion concerning the balance of pain and pleasure with regard to a particular question became so determinate, that it became a volition, of which an action would be the immediate consequence. The length of time required for this to happen could vary from one instance to another.[40] The role of the POT should be understood as *determining* (by the crystallisation of opinion involving will and understanding in the manner described above) and *effectuating* (by an act of will executing the judgement) constitutional limits.

[38] *SAM*, p. 31.

[39] See chapter 2, pp. 58–63 above, where it has been argued that the trusting body's opinion might be transformed into an act of divestitive power.

[40] *Deontology*, p. 94.

In sum, elements of both understanding and will joined together in the formation of public opinion. It should be emphasised that, notwithstanding the influential activities which took place within the public domain, it was also the influence of understanding over understanding (a free exchange of ideas) exercised between the government and the collective body of the people, which would enable the people to determine when unjustified obligatory patterns were being imposed on them. The extent to which the exchange of ideas was facilitated would signify the degree to which a political society could be characterised as being under a free government.[41] Hence, the medium of understanding would ultimately be the mode of influence under a free government. In a political society under a free government the exchange of arguments would lead to an enlightened reflection concerning the justification of obligations, whether legal, sympathetic, or moral. The next subsection will look in more depth at the volitional obligatory element, which operated between members of a social group, and between the group and the government.

The sympathetic sanction, probity and consensus formation

This subsection discusses in detail how Bentham envisaged the process of consensus formation, or the formulation of public opinion, on the basis of his theory of human motivation, and his understanding of the moral and sympathetic sanctions. It therefore constitutes a detailed analysis of the notion of influence in respect of both motives and sanctions. It discusses the creation of moral and sympathetic obligations. A consensus about checking the social justification of authority, could be formed both among the people who made up a social group, and between the government and the people, or in other words, between the supreme operative and the POT.[42] The manner in which the POT would operate *vis à vis* any member of a social group will also be explicated.

I shall begin by discussing consensus formation among the people, although, as will be seen, the account of consensus formation between the body of the people and the government does not differ in kind. I shall argue that a consensus could be formed by the operation of the sympathetic sanction, which would generate extra-regarding motives among the members of the political community. This consensus could lead to a transient determination and effectuation of constitutional limits. Bentham saw a lot of potential in the idea of communal sympathy, which would determine what people regarded as their best interest.[43] This subsection proposes a new interpretation of Bentham's conception of the relationship between individual and community, as well as of his view of the relationship between private ethics and legislation.

[41] See chapter 4, pp. 118–22 above.
[42] See chapter 5, pp. 140–2 above.
[43] *SAM*, p. 30 and p. 31, editorial note 1.

Bentham saw in sympathy a force capable of generating certain communal beliefs as well as of interpreting those beliefs in concrete instances. Adherence to those beliefs would operate as a common object of desire and identification.[44] Further, once sympathy had crystallised to a certain extent, it would operate in a very similar fashion to the moral sanction. In a well-developed community, people would take into account in their utilitarian calculation and interpretations what other people might think with regard to their pursuit of a given action. In the following passage, Bentham spelled out the levels of interaction both among the people, and between the people and government. The end of this interaction would be the maintenance of the universal interest. Bentham argued that;

> "For the accomplishment of the universal end in the case of the possessors of the supreme constitutive power, the provision made can not be well-adapted otherwise than **in so far as facility** is left or given to each individual to make what in his eyes is **the best provision possible for his own individual interest**: in the case of the possessors of the supreme operative power, unless **in so far as the utmost difficulty is opposed to his endeavours to make what in his eyes is the best provision possible for his own individual interest, to the detriment of the interest of the other individuals of that same community**, that is to say **in so far as mutual incompatibility and competition have place,** making provision for his own interests to the detriment of theirs."[45]

This passage forms the rationale for Bentham's general view of consensus formation as part of his constitutional theory. First, the universal interest could be regarded as the aggregate of every person's own interest. The predominance of self-regard in each individual's mind was the precondition for consensus formation.[46] The second feature of consensus formation was that each individual should, in calculating his own course of action, think about how his action would affect others. The first part of the passage describes the way in which the universal interest could be attained. The context in which individuals formed their own opinions as to what would be the best course of action *for them* would involve social considerations. This social context was the sphere in which influence would operate. This social context would involve freedom to exchange opinions, which would lead to the formation of communal obligations. The degree of freedom to exchange opinions within the community would vary from society to society. It was very important for Bentham to ensure that this social context, in which individuals formed their self-regarding judgements, was

[44] *Deontology*, pp. 92–3. Bentham related the idea of will to the idea of desire. Once there was an object of desire, there would be a motive and, as a result, a will to achieve it.

[45] *First Principles*, pp. 133–4.

[46] *Deontology*, p. 196; see also Bowring, ix. 63, where Bentham related the formation of a consensus to the mutual understanding of people of both their own self-interest and the self-interest of others. A communication based on the predominance of self-preference would lead to a consensus, because under the conditions of free communication people could see the importance to their own interest of accommodating other people's self-preferences. Functionally speaking, if a person opposed every other interest, then no one would join with him. This "joining" together, and the facilitation of free communication, were cardinal features of a free society.

formed *independently* of any dictated context (free from coercion, which would cause fear, or delusive arguments promoted by a government, for example).[47] Only where there was no dictated context could people reflect upon the true nature of the interest of their community. The existence of deficiencies in public judgement, whether arising from the actions of centralised authority, or from the preconceptions of the people, would hinder that open-mindedness which was so essential to a successful exchange of opinions. The quality of the social context, that is the degree of freedom of communication, and the nature of the self-regarding calculation by individuals, were interdependent. Governments, or operative powers, could put obstacles in the way of communication which would amount to a dictated context for the interdependent relationship between the social and the self-regarding interests. As a result, the self-regarding and the social interests would not be able to influence one another in a free way.

For Bentham, social interests were embodied within self-regard:

> "But the pleasure I feel at the prospect of bestowing pleasure on my friend, whose pleasure is it but mine? The pain which I feel at the sight or under the apprehension of seeing my friend oppressed with pain, whose pain is it but mine?. [The agent's] own well-being ought **on every occasion** to be the **sole** object of pursuit to every man, what I mean by it is that the conduct of him who on every occasion takes his own well-being for the object of his pursuit is approved by me: approved by me in so much that, if it depended upon me, his pursuit should not on any occasion have any other object."[48]

An objection might be made here. A contradiction would arise in that either individual interests embody existing, possibly pernicious, social interests, or they are independent of, and may seek to change pernicious communal beliefs. An individuality conducive to utility must be supposed to be independent of a context that is unacceptable from a utilitarian viewpoint and as a result would shape or accept a different context if necessary. However, if existing social interests are embodied in individual self-regarding interests, the latter cannot be independent of such context.[49]

This objection does not go as far as it seems to. The existence of evil tendencies in governments and society was commonplace. However, as long as members of the public were able to exchange their views, there would be some asymmetry between the attempt to place obstacles in the way of communication (to create a dictated context which hampered the formation of an independent consensus), or an attempt to transgress basic communal beliefs, and public opinion. From this asymmetry an enlightening process with regard to a given political society could emerge. Social dynamism and the independence of public opinion would lead to the formation of new social interests which are based upon a revised conception of harm (or revised interpretation of an existing conception of harm), and hence of new communal obligations. In short, the objec-

[47] See p. 220, note 76 below.
[48] *Deontology*, pp. 148–9.
[49] This aspect is taken further in chapter 7 when disinterestedness is discussed, see pp. 270–3 below.

tion is answered because a dynamic, random relationship between individuality and community could lead to the exposure of fallacious and pernicious social contexts.

But how could consensus formation be explained on the basis of human motivation? How could people have motives which would result in collective action? The explanation of consensus formation, or "public opinion", and hence the formation of constitutional limits, is to be found in the apolitical realm of private deontology. A collective public opinion would be formed by extra-political activity. This did not mean that there was no role for sanctions in helping the public to form such opinion. It meant only that in the context of consensus formation, sanctions would be of an apolitical nature. There would be a shift in locus, from a centralised coercive mechanism to communal-generated coercion, by means of communication between people:

> "Where the sanction is non-political, the pain or the pleasure may be considered as resulting or apprehended from the action of the human being in question considered as a member of a community of human beings having mutual intercourse and judging and acting, though without political power, with community of opinion and action; or as separately from, and without intercourse on the subject with, any other."[50]

Sanctions would facilitate the creation of collectivities. In *IPML*, Bentham discussed four kinds of sanctions, namely (1) the physical, (2) the legal and political, (3) the moral/popular and (4) the religious.[51] The moral sanction would operate to enforce any obligation promulgated by the POT.

However, there were two sanctions additional to the four discussed in *IPML*, namely the retributive and the sympathetic (or its opposite, the antipathetic)—which, it will be argued, would facilitate the operation of an effective moral sanction. The source of the retributive and the sympathetic sanctions was the individual, and hence Bentham called them "individually-operating" sanctions. The sanction was "retributive" if its source in an individual was the consideration of actual pain which had already been inflicted on another individual. If no such consideration existed—if a source of the sanction was the individual's own view with regard to future pain or pleasure—the sanction would be sympathetic (if pleasurable), or antipathetic (if painful).[52] In the discussion which follows, both what Bentham called "sympathetic" and "antipathetic" sanctions will be referred to as the "sympathetic" sanction.

[50] *Deontology*, p. 176.

[51] See *IPML*, chapter 3.

[52] Ibid., pp. 176–7. The source of pain and pleasure could be immediate by them being instantaneously experienced physically or mentally. However, to a large degree pains and pleasures were derived from memory and imagination. In fact it would be hard to interpret any immediate experience not of a physical nature as "painful" or "pleasurable" without reference to other pains and pleasures which would derive from memory or imagination. Therefore, it would not be the immediate pain or pleasure which would be the most important, but expected pains or pleasures derived from the culture that the person lived in: ibid., p. 90. Further, Bentham argued that an idea could attach itself to the mind only in a temporal way. The idea would have to relate to a past event (some memory function), or to a future event (the imagination of possibilities): ibid., p. 258.

Bentham argued that sanctions could be distinguished according to their nature, or to their source. In a letter to Dumont, Bentham confined the discussion of the nature of a sanction to the question of whether the sanction bestowed pleasures or pains.[53] Sanctions could also differ in terms of their source. For example, the moral sanction would originate in the community, the sympathetic in the mind of the individual who carried out an action which warranted the sanction. This distinction will be further developed in order to make Bentham's account of sanctions consistent with his account of motives in *Deontology*.

The sanction of sympathy was similar in *nature* to the moral sanction. Both would operate on the mind of individuals as a result of some already existing prescriptive context which would be external to the individual in question. This in fact was true of all sanctions. In this respect, the difference between the operation of the moral and the sympathetic sanctions was one of degree only. A moral sanction would be wider, in that its context might be a prescriptive proposition arrived at by a whole group. A sympathetic sanction could be seen as operating in the context of a prescriptive proposition arrived at between individuals, or between two individual communities. A second point follows from the first. The *source* of the sympathetic sanction was not merely the individual in question, despite its original definition. A person could feel sympathy, could expect to feel pleasure (or pain), only when his action was carried out in the context of some social whole, or in the face of the operation of some other agency external to himself.

Thus, *in a group*, the sympathetic sanction which operated between individuals consisted of an application of the moral sanction to what was taking place between those individuals. In other words, the moral sanction, attached to a proposition, would precede the feeling of sympathy in the mind of an individual towards another. The existence of a moral sanction would make it possible for the individual to interpret the potential consequences of his actions *as* bearing the pleasure or pain associated with sympathy.

These two arguments can be summarised as follows: the similarity in nature of the sanctions' operation implied that a full description of their respective sources would include both the individual who inflicted pain or pleasure by his actions, and an external agency which served as a prescriptive context for it. Thus, it would be too compartmentalised and incomplete a view (though not entirely a *wrong* one) to see the sanctions' sources as entirely discrete. I say "not entirely wrong", because there was a functional distinction between the final source of the two sanctions. This distinction was that in the case of the sympathetic sanction, there would be an additional application by an individual of a proposition, backed up by the moral sanction, to the specific situation between himself and another individual. In this limited sense the individual can still be seen as the final source of the sympathetic sanction. However, in both the moral and the sympathetic sanctions, the operation of an external agency

[53] *Correspondence* vol. x., p. 444; see also *Deontology*, pp. 175–6.

and the individual upon whom the sanction would be inflicted would be interdependent.

To repeat, this analysis of the similarities between the two sanctions asserts that their operation was interdependent. A change in propositions backed up by the moral sanction could change propositions backed up by the sympathetic sanction. Conversely, interaction between individuals could lead to the establishment of new general patterns of "sympathies", which could operate to modify existing propositions backed by the moral sanction.[54] In other words, an evolution of social relationships which gave rise to an operation of the sympathetic sanction, could extend the operation of that sanction across more and more people. This extension could lead to the development and crystallisation of new propositions by a collectivity (or to the modification of existing ones) which would be backed up by the moral sanction. Both the sympathetic and the moral sanctions were a part of a dynamic cultural phenomenon, in the context of which some pain or pleasure could be felt in the mind of the individual. The sanctions' similarity in *nature* might lead to a social situation in which the prescriptive context of the sympathetic sanction (which might consist in a prescriptive proposition which was originally established between two individuals) was embraced by the whole social group.

The implication of this argument is that any proper account of either of these sanctions might well refer to the other. Further, the strengthening and broadening of both would signify the concretisation, albeit a transient one, of a community. The more concrete the community, the tighter the functional interdependence of these two sanctions would be. The more developed a society, the more apparent the bond between the operation of these two sanctions would be. In a less-developed society, the functional connection between the two would be less apparent, with the result that sympathy would be much more limited. In such less-developed societies, actions sanctioned by sympathy would involve only small local groups. Sympathy would still have some force in less-developed communities, because of the existence of at least some collectivity, which could operate a "collective" moral sanction with regard to the individuals who composed it.[55] As will be argued in the next section, the more that sympathy is generated between individuals, as they develop collective norms in the course of their communication, the more force the general collectivity will have. To put it another way, as sympathy grows between certain individuals or groups, so does the force of the collective moral sanction, which in turn homogenises potential patterns of sympathy in the minds of individuals.[56]

[54] In terms of their social function, these patterns and their crystallisation into moral obligations would function as fundamental rights in the minds of individuals: see chapter 5, pp. 157–8 above.

[55] This argument relates to the issue of the flexible manifestation of "community" as discussed in chapter 3, pp. 88–90 above.

[56] Although this is not equivalent to a process of homogenising the community according to some uniform way of life: see p. 230, note 100 below.

Let me spell out in more detail this argument concerning the affinity between these sanctions. It is important to grasp that the sympathetic sanction would arise purely as a result of an interactive process among people. Further, sympathy would grow in force as the force of the moral sanction between members of a social group grew. A person could interpret others' pain as "painful" to himself, only to the extent that he reacted to potential actions by some kind of external agency, or, more specifically, to potential actions by a person or a group of persons.

The fact that a person feels pain as a result of considering his prospective actions can only be the result of an effort made by him to understand the repercussions of his actions for other people. He must make an empathic effort. The sympathetic sanction would rely on an understanding that the consequences of a person's actions would be "painful" to others. In other words, Bentham maintained that the sympathetic sanction depended on the possibility of an effort, or, as Bentham called it, an "affection" or a "desire for amity" among the members of a social group. Each individual could conceive (memorise and imagine) for himself what others might have thought or might think in relation to a given action. This he would do on the basis of communication with them. This empathic effort would be the first stage at which the social context conditioned the state of mind of each individual. This empathic effort implied that individual minds could "meet" (*as opposed to being the same*), which meant that one person was able to imagine, to empathise with, the pain which would be caused to another by his own actions or inactions. The sympathetic sanction would result in some conception of harm which forms the object of the sympathy, but which does not necessarily presume a full understanding of the other person towards whom the sympathy is felt.

But why should affection cause a person to alter his motives? Sympathy would be the result of a further stage in the contextualisation of individual actions. On the assumption that empathy was possible, the pain of sympathy might be produced in the mind of an individual as a result of contemplating the effect of his actions or inactions on another individual. The conception of harm according to which utilitarian interpretation and evaluation takes place will reflect this individual's empathic effort and sympathetic affection that results. Sympathy would be the interpretation as "painful" or "pleasurable" for the agent of the consequence of carrying out his action, an interpretation arrived at *as a result of* an empathic effort by him.[57]

[57] It is important to note that empathy may transcend any communal conception of harm that consolidates certain patterns of sympathy. Because empathy is a broader concept than sympathy it does not require a full articulation of a common conception of harm in the way sympathy does. A transcendence of a common, sympathetic conception of harm may lead either to the further re-negotiations and generalisations of those patterns of sympathy and the conception of harm, or it may lead to the breaking up of the community because no communal pattern of sympathy can be reasoned about. The issue of transcending a communal pattern of sympathy and a conception of harm is discussed in Part 2.

What was the nature of this pain of sympathy? The sanction manifested itself as bad conscience in the agent's mind, or what we might refer to as guilt. Bentham noted that getting drunk might generate pain for a parent or a partner of the drunk, and even in the mind of the drunk himself, resulting from contemplating the disapprobation of his fellow men.[58] "Bad conscience", however, required more than the expectation of disapprobation, in order to account for the full manifestation of the sympathetic "sanction". A person needed also to recognise the disapprobation by an external agency as "painful" to himself in the specific situation at hand, and as producing sufficient pain to cause him to alter his behaviour. The main point is, however, that for sympathy to exist, there would have to exist an external agency, the approbation of which would function as an object of desire for the individual agent. The moment his actions failed to conform to the actual or potential standards of the external agency, "bad conscience" could result. At its core, "bad conscience" (or guilt) was a social/cultural phenomenon, created when individuals exchanged their views on a subject over a certain period, with the effect that each person could, in his memory and imagination, generate a prescriptive proposition in relation to which he could feel "bad conscience". "Bad conscience" was a feeling of pain generated by the recognition that by his action the individual would cause pain to another person. The pain caused to that other person would give rise to some disapprobation of an external agency against the individual undertaking the action in question. This disapprobation could be applied by the agent to the specific situation at hand. In short, the sympathetic sanction was effectuated through a process in which causing pain to others was interpreted by the agent as painful to himself. This interpretation could only be accounted for in the context of the disapprobation of some external agency. Thus, in most situations, the moral sanction would generate the context in which any "individually-operated" sanction would be manifested.[59]

Between the people and the government, communication would be of exactly the same kind as among the people themselves. This communication would be based on the mutually operating sympathetic and moral sanctions.

[58] *Deontology*, p. 199; see also ibid., pp. 84–5.

[59] Ibid., pp. 206–7. A counter-argument against Hart's criticisms of the command theory of law, and the distinction he draws between "being obliged" and "having an obligation", in *The Concept of Law*, pp. 18–25, might be advanced here. The two phrases would be treated by Bentham as signifying obligations which arise from different *sources*. The expression "having an obligation" is a semantic artefact, signifying no more than what Bentham would see as a feeling on the part of the individual concerning the potential threat of the "moral sanction". This threat would be created by the normative force of expectations, and the potential pain of disappointment. Pain of disappointment may lead to the sanction being inflicted on this individual. Hart exploits the general hostile sentiments against a bank robber to conclude that one is not under an obligation in that situation. However, he does so at the price of mystifying the concept of obligation and narrowing it to the specific context of its manifestation in a social group. See in this context R. Moles, *Definition and Rule in Legal Theory: a Reassessment of H.L.A. Hart and the Positivist Tradition* (Oxford, 1987), pp. 53–5, who argues that Hart did not elaborate on his own idea of "obeying", or complying with, a social rule.

The moral and the sympathetic sanctions would influence which motives determined individual interests and dispositions, and accordingly, the way in which each individual would see the interest of his fellow men as part of his self-regarding interest. The sanction of sympathy would affect a whole range of motives. Bentham understood "virtue" through the idea of motives. The idea of virtue related to an object with regard to which a judgement of consequences would be made. Motives could relate either to the moral agent in question, in which case they were self-regarding ones, or to other moral agents, in which case they were extra-regarding.[60] An action was rendered virtuous if it was undertaken with the aim of promoting the welfare of others, rather than simply that of the agent undertaking it.

The first motive connected with the sympathetic and the moral sanctions was *self-regarding prudence*. Prudence meant for Bentham a choice about which course of action to take. Prudence involved a calculation concerning the happiness of the agent and was thus self-regarding.[61] It was a motive to perform an action which would benefit the agent himself. This motive was the predominant one in the human mind. As will be argued, while this motive played a major role in Bentham's understanding of virtuous acts, it could not provide a full account of them.[62] There had to be other motives, which would incorporate themselves into the self-regarding, before virtue could be said to emerge.

The other two motives were benevolence and probity. These two were extra-regarding and virtue could be understood in relation to them. Benevolence was the motive arising from the desire to contribute to the well-being of other people. An action which resulted from such a motive was termed "beneficent". Beneficence, and therefore benevolence, could be either positive or negative. Positive beneficence described an action based on a disposition to do good to other people; negative beneficence, on a disposition to abstain from doing evil to them.[63]

Probity, however, is of most importance in the explanation of consensus formation. In *IPML* Bentham described negative beneficence as resulting from actions based on the motive of probity.[64] However, in *Deontology*, Bentham distinguished between beneficence and probity, the latter being an act of beneficence carried out under an obligation. By obligation, Bentham meant here a prescriptive proposition which would be enforced by any one of the legal, moral, or sympathetic sanctions.[65] The distinction between benevolence and probity was important because it implied that beneficent action was not, *conceptually speaking*, in conflict with acts based on self-regarding prudence, and in cases where such a conflict was absent, no obligation, and no sanction, would

[60] *Deontology*, p. 191; see also ibid., pp. 122–6.
[61] Ibid., pp. 210–11.
[62] Ibid., p. 178.
[63] Ibid., pp. 183–6. For a similar view, see *Correspondence*, vol. x., pp. 443–4.
[64] *IPML*, p. 284.
[65] *Deontology*, p. 211.

be necessary to effect a benevolent action.[66] However, as will be argued below, Bentham believed that it would hardly be possible, socially speaking, to account for a case where a beneficent action would be effected without any sanction and, in turn, without any obligation. To speak about purely social motives would be conceptually plausible, but socially meaningless.

The account in *IPML* is perfectly compatible with the meaning of probity in *Deontology*. On such a construction, probity would imply an obligation not to do evil to other people. However, it is clear that the meaning that Bentham gave to probity in *Deontology* was broader than that given to it in *IPML*. In the former, he recognised circumstances in which positive beneficence stemmed from an obligation. An example could be any communal obligation, the fulfilment of which had the effect of contributing to the well-being of others. Virtuous motives might be enforced by sanctions such as the sympathetic and the moral. Probity with regard to a positive beneficent act would require a specific obligation (a proposition enforced by the sympathetic and/or the moral sanction), which would have the effect of contributing to the well-being of others. The recognition of such an obligation on the part of individuals, as argued in the previous subsection, was a cultural phenomenon. As such, to disregard it would give rise to the pain of "bad conscience" in the mind of the individual who caused pain to others. It was in the motive of probity that self-regarding prudence and extra-regarding benevolence were united into a single action of moral judgement.

The world of self-regarding motives, that is of *pure* self-regarding prudence, represented a hypothetical "atomistic" world of the individual. In many situations it would hardly make sense to speak about *obligations* of any kind, were only this atomistic world to be considered. Any meaning attached to the idea of "obligation" would have to presume an external source of pain and pleasure, that is a source *other than a purely self-regarding source*, which could enter into the calculation of any agent. The idea of obligation assumed some agency other than an individual which would influence the calculations of that individual. Because of the necessity for a sanction, an element of will was required, which would introduce the idea of obligatory influence. Such influence could have for its basis any of the three sanctions, in so far as some *social context* is assumed. The idea of obligation implied an identification between the consciousness which calculates and some conception of harm, however transient, which would be held by an external agency.[67]

Probity was related to the idea of "obligation". As such, it was entirely compatible with, and indeed complemented, self-regarding prudence. What made

[66] See in this context ibid., p. 185, where Bentham discussed the distinction between benevolent actions which could be exercised with no need for self-sacrifice, and those which could not.

[67] This is not to say that hypothetical, atomistic, purely self-regarded consciousness could not be conceived. As will be discussed in the next chapter, one could think about "obligation to oneself" which in some circumstances may well call for both the rejection and identification with and within the perspective of an external agency, and the recreation of, and identification with, other external agency.

prudence possible, socially speaking, was a group context, as opposed to the hypothetical, purely atomistic context of prudence. Were the individual alone in the world, prudence would only need to be exercised in relation to the physical sanction. This would be purely a matter of survival. However, once ideas of benevolence and negative beneficence came in, prudence could be exercised only in the context of some obligation imposed by an external agency with some cultural affiliation, that is by the moral or the sympathetic sanction *even when prudence required an interpretation of, or a challenge to, the conception of the harm which gave rise to those obligations*.[68]

The group generated a sanction, and hence an obligation, be it a legal, moral, or sympathetic obligation. In the absence of some sanction, and hence obligation, there would be *virtually no point* in talking about prudence, that is self-regarding prudence, at all.[69] Prudence had meaning only in the context of something that would make one act prudently—either with regard to the physical world, where one would say that there was an obligation to be careful—under threat of the physical sanction—or the social world, where one would say, however critically, that there was an obligation to act legally, morally or sympathetically. Arguably for Bentham, apart from "natural obligations", there was no self-regarding prudence worth the name without a social context to supply some obligatory medium. In most situations, in order to give meaning to the idea of prudential choice of action, or prudence, there would have to be some obligatory medium (legal, moral, or sympathetic) which would supply the necessary context for prudence. It was through probity, a motive brought about through an obligatory medium, that self-regarding prudence would embody extra-regarding considerations.[70] Indeed, it was precisely because of the predominance of self-interest, that any obligatory medium would have any effect on the individual mind. More specifically, in terms of consensus formation which might come about *purely as a result of transparent communication between people*, an obligatory medium based on the moral and sympathetic sanctions would perturb self-interested considerations in such a manner that a benevolent judgement might be contemplated.

This analysis bears reference to the explanation of the idea of pure influence of understanding over understanding, because self-regarding prudence must be accounted for before influence can be accounted for. The influence of pure understanding over understanding, i.e. an exchange of arguments which leads to an understanding of what one thinks it would be in one's own interest to do, would also involve some enlightenment, in that the exchange would influence

[68] The religious sanction would be included here as well.

[69] See note 71 below regarding the next chapter.

[70] It is important to stress again, however, that "probity" did not refer merely to the legal sanction. Probity on the part of rulers could be secured by moral obligation, that is a prescriptive proposition backed by the threat of the moral sanction. Bentham wrote: "To this same denomination—viz. bringing the less principal interest into accordance with the more principal interest—is referable whatsoever in private trusts is done in the view of securing probity on the part of trustees": *First Principles*, p. 242.

one's already existing prudential considerations. As has been seen, prudence implied some idea of obligation. Thus, it could not make complete sense to claim that a person was suddenly convinced by an exchange of ideas that something was in his own interest. In addition to the fact of his being informed of some argument, there would have to be some formation of prescriptive propositions which were crystallised as a result of the exchange, and which would operate to alter his previously existing prudential calculations.[71] All that pure influence of understanding over understanding could do would be to give a different perspective to one's prudential considerations. In short, the notion of individuality, including individual contributions to the exchanges of ideas, would make little sense in the absence of a culturally-orientated and historically-contingent obligatory medium as its interpretative context. The obligatory element could not be excluded by prudence, although prudence could challenge an obligation's content, for example through the reinterpretation of some traditional obligatory patterns.

Here lies the gist of the argument. A relationship of influence which was based purely on argument, as in the case of pure understanding over understanding, the influence which would make the public sphere critical, could initially operate only within an already existing community, which already had some obligations at its core, whatever the sanctions on which these obligations were based. The operation of the influence of understanding over understanding must therefore be preceded by the influence of will over will through the medium of the understanding. A critical argument would always start from an existing, obligatory, cultural set-up. Probity gave a social meaning to prudence, which in turn preceded, and indeed enabled the influence of understanding over understanding. Some obligatory context would have to exist before one could be influenced in whatever direction. There would have to be some communal norms, which would constitute a facilitating, interpretative horizon for these discussions, and would provide prudence with some grist for its mill. As will be argued in the next section, the nature of ultimate obligations in a community would differ according to the stage of its historical development.

In short, the extra-regarding motive of benevolence would be socially meaningful only if it related to self-regarding, prudence via the idea of obligation, or probity. What "appeared" to be free-standing, extra-regarding motives were in fact incorporated into the most basic motive of all—self-regarding prudence, either through an artificial legal obligation, or through a communal obligation (a phenomenon which would be regarded by any member the community as "natural"), that is through a moral or sympathetic obligation. Some prescriptive proposition was necessary, whether prescribed by law or by communal culture, which would supply the motive for self-regarding prudence to produce a beneficent action. Only

[71] Again, it goes without saying that the source of openness to the formation of new prescriptive propositions would stem from some openness that exist in the mind of the agent in question in the form of "obligation to oneself". See the next chapter pp. 265–73 for a more detailed discussion of the topic.

the *source* of obligation could vary as prudential calculations were influenced either by the realm of legislation (political deontology), or by the realm of private deontology. The operative principle was identical. All obligations were backed up by either the legal, the moral or the sympathetic sanction.

The following statement by Bentham should be understood in the light of the above interpretation:

> "The field which by its actual exercise the virtue of beneficence is capable of occupying and filling with efficient services rendered to the whole of humankind taken together is, even when taken at its simplest, extremely narrow: much more narrow must be that part of it which can apply and confine itself to the demands of any single individual or particular assemblage of individuals.
>
> Self-regarding prudence concurs, therefore, with probity and indeed suffices of itself, within the field of its dominion, to set limits, and those comparatively very narrow ones, to the exercise of the virtue of beneficence."[72]

Both self-regarding and extra-regarding motives could join together in the faculties of prudential judgement and volition in the context of an obligatory medium, or, generally, probity.[73] It was a matter of an individual judgement what it would be in one's interest to do.[74] Yet it was the medium of obligation,

[72] *Deontology*, p. 226. Rosen claims that, for Bentham, self-regarding prudence was compatible with effective benevolence, but offers no detailed analysis of the relationship between them: *Bentham, Byron and Greece*, pp. 84–9.

[73] In Bowring, ii. 537, in discussing international law, Bentham argued that probity could exist between nations in the same way that it could exist between individuals: see in this respect the argument about the relativity of sovereignty, chapter 3, p. 92, note 28 above.

[74] This might lead to a reconciliation between what seem to be the different positions taken by D. Lyons, *In the Interest of the Governed: A Study in Bentham's Philosophy of Utility and Law* (Oxford, 1973), and J. Dinwiddy, "Bentham on Private Ethics and the Principle of Utility", *Revue Internationale de Philosophie* 36 (1982) 271–309. The crux of the debate concerned the degree of integration between private and public ethics. Further they differed on the extent to which this division mirrored another division in an individual's mind, namely between pursuing their own interest and that of the community.

In his interpretation of *IPML*, Lyons claimed that individuals were required by public ethics to pursue the communal interest, and that this eventually would be united with their private interest. The self- and the extra-regarding would become, in the long run, united. The role of legal punishment was to correct apparent conflict between communal and individual interest.

Dinwiddy, on the other hand, claimed that self- and extra-regarding motives remained distinct in Bentham's thought, and that punishment was needed precisely because they were in conflict. The self-regarding (without punishment) would be in permanent conflict with the extra-regarding. The self-regarding and the extra-regarding were two distinct classes of motives.

On the current interpretation, Bentham argued that any utilitarian calculations, whether of self- or extra-regarding orientation, would be governed by self-regarding prudence. Further, it has been argued that their unification was explained by probity. In probity, self-regarding prudence becomes united with extra-regarding benevolence. Probity does not relate necessarily only to private deontology, but also to political deontology, or law. In the case of law, the extra-regard would, on many occasions, have to be worked out indirectly by a delegated authority. Thus, the unification of the self- and the extra-regarding in the mind was achieved by obligations backed by any of the five sanctions.

On the analysis offered here, there is no real conflict between Lyons and Dinwiddy. There are indeed two kinds of motives which operate on the human mind. But the cognitive act is solely based on self-regarding prudence. Lyons seemed to talk about the way these two functioned in the mind, while Dinwiddy seemed to emphasise their different nature.

See also in this respect J.B. Stearns, "Bentham on Public and Private Ethics", *Canadian Journal of Philosophy* 5 (1975) 583–94.

whether legal, moral, or sympathetic, which would lead to the formation of the will needed to produce a virtuous action. Benevolence, and especially positive benevolence, involved acts of will requiring a special effort—the effort to cause pain to oneself. If one bought a loaf of bread in order to have it for dinner, the motive would be pure prudence—the prudence of survival—but,

> "Suppose, when I have got the loaf, observing a man who, being in a famished state, has more need of it, I give him the loaf and so go without my dinner: here too is usefulness. But besides usefulness, here is virtue: for to subject a man's self to pain in any shape, as I by the supposition have subjected myself to it in the shape of hunger, requires an effort, and this effort I have made."[75]

The analysis offered here of the way self- and extra-regard joined together in probity has a temporal implication. A beneficent action cannot occur prior to a prudential judgement. There can never be an act of will, a special volition involving an "effort", which is not based on one's own judgement. This means that the understanding must first judge an action to be in one's own interest all things considered, and then and only then would it be possible to form a will, based on this understanding, to confer benefit on, or abstain from doing evil to, one's fellow men—to perform, that is, an action which was also beneficent. However, this understanding, based on prudential reasoning, could never precede an obligatory context, whatever its source might be. The prudential judgement that was contextualised in an obligatory context could make the effort to produce a beneficent action if such an action constituted an interpretation which fitted the conception of harm embodied in this obligatory context. However, the prudence which was generated under an obligatory context could, as a result of an exchange of ideas and a change of perspective, prove wanting. In such a case, prudence may involve a critical reflection upon an existing obligatory medium. Thus, a new communal conception of harm, and with it a new obligatory medium, could replace the old, wanting one.

This analysis reveals the structure of the ongoing activity which produces consensus formation backed by the sympathetic and the moral sanctions, and, in turn, gives rise to the motive of probity. This structure is as follows:

1. Discussion

This stage involves both influence of understanding over understanding, and of will over will through the medium of the understanding, which have been analysed above. As a result of exhausting communicative possibilities, people would arrive at new conceptions of what might or might not be in their interest. This communication would initially be facilitated and enlightened by virtue of its being conducted in some more general and obligatory context but could go on to transcend this context. This context could be created and justified by positive centralised coercion which might take the form of legislation and a code of

[75] *Deontology*, p. 179.

laws, or by any other behaviour established under existing moral and sympathetic obligations. Such obligatory context, as has been argued, would have to precede any exchange of ideas. However, it could also be modified by it. The obligatory context would enable a meaningful exchange of ideas, that is the influence of pure understanding over understanding, which would also be facilitated by the satisfaction of conditions for free communication. Therefore, for such a process to occur there is a negative requirement, namely the absence of obstacles to the exchange of ideas.[76]

[76] Free communication was crucial to the operation of Bentham's categorical, or constitutional, sphere. In order to be able to ascend to such a sphere of reflection the POT had to be independent. By stressing the importance of the *independence* of the POT, Bentham wanted to establish a system which generated disagreements among the people and between the people and the government. Any obstacles to communication would hamper inter-subjective communication. The virtue of Bentham's system lay in its asymmetrical nature. The moment there was symmetry in the system, that is the moment there was no antagonism between the public and the government, all motion in the constitution would stop. Stagnation in public attitudes was a social phenomenon which Bentham associated with the use of arguments, whose justification was based on ideas such as "legitimacy", "customary rules" and "men of principle". The acceptance of such ideas would infer intellectual weakness and indolence on the part of the public, which could allow a government to pursue its sinister interest, and to go on pursuing it without fear of censure.

Bentham was alive to the difficulties which the POT might face in functioning effectively and independently. He recognised that it might have to function in the face of divided interests, existing from the social division between the opulent few and the subject many (*First Principles*, pp. 69–70). Physical distance would also hamper proper communication. However, Bentham also pointed to "factitious" obstacles to communication. These factitious obstacles originated in government. *Independent* public opinion was only made possible by freedom of communication, which is to say, by the absence of factitious obstacles to communication. Such factitious obstacles could lead the people to support a bad government by not questioning existing obligations (*First Principles*, pp. 72, 154–5, *SAM*, pp. 26–7, 43, 67–72, 116–7). In short, a bad government would throw obstacles in the way of the POT.

The obstacles to communication were diverse. They included secret government, where procedures and dealings were not accessible to the public gaze (*SAM*, pp. 41–2).

A further obstacle to communication was *corruption*. Corrupt people conspired to advance their sinister interest. A corrupted member of the public would be uncritical, while a corrupted official would be unresponsive to public criticism (*First Principles*, pp. 17–25, 252–61, 187, 196). In short, corruption would have a disastrous effect on empathy, bad conscience, and sympathy.

A third obstacle to communication was *delusion*. Delusion was, in effect, "false consciousness", an erroneous conception or opinion. The government might engage in deceptive activities which would produce fallacies in the public's mind (*First Principles*, pp. 261–8). Delusion could be manifested in many ways. One of those manifestations was *prejudice*, especially a form of it which Bentham called *interest-begotten prejudice*. Such a prejudice meant that people would convince themselves that their own interest must also be the universal interest. They would fail to conceive any other interest *but their own as* the universal interest. This type of prejudice would lead to the preservation of bad governments. It would be debilitating in that, being under the influence of a false "conviction" with regard to the public interest, the people would, in effect, passively accept any government which promoted their immediate interest (*Deontology*, pp. 173–4, *First Principles*, pp. 151, 176–82). An example of a manifestation of corruption and delusion was *factitious dignity*. Individuals could become corrupted as a result of expecting to receive honour providing they played some role in an enterprise. Yet the public could also be deluded in fallaciously judging the person honoured by his title and not according to his deeds (*First Principles*, pp. 299–305, 315–6, 322–3, 311).

A fourth obstacle was *intimidation*. By generating fear, a government could prevent people from seeing their true interest (*First Principles*, p. 250).

This influence of understanding over understanding could generate communal obligation which would modify the justification for previous ones and, as a result, would modify preceding prudential judgements. In short, the obligatory context enabled the operation of influence, whereby the individual would both be subject to all sorts of obligations, and also informed about the existence of other interests through the arguments of other persons. The general obligatory context, involving the influence of will over will via the medium of the understanding was both the condition for, and could be modified as a result of, this discussional stage. At this stage of "discussion", self-regarding prudence and extra-regarding benevolence could join together in probity. The operation of "influence", or the "interaction" of sanctions and motives, represented the "public" or communal stage of consensus formation.

2. *Effect on Interest*

This was the individual stage (or individual context) of consensus formation. Here, the individual calculated how his own well-being would be affected by those ideas crystallised in the first stage. The individual formed some kind of a decisive opinion, as a result of calculations based on the communication of new information, as well as on some existing or modified conceptions in his own mind of the obligatory opinions of the community.

3. *Will to Act*

This stage involved a volition on the part of each individual which was based on the desire to bring about consequences calculated on the basis of prudence. This stage involved the formulation of a will by individuals, correspondent to their judgement, to undertake what could well turn out to be a collective action of the POT. Such a collective action could have a benevolent effect, namely one which promoted the well-being of fellow men. The collectivity of the action, and hence the greater probability of the benevolent effect, would derive from the motive of probity, involving a proposition backed by the moral sanction.

To summarise this section, consensus formation is facilitated by communication between people, and by reference to existing standards in a group, such as laws and communal obligations, be they sympathetic or moral. The memory and imagination of each individual is further enhanced by the free exchange of views. My argument is that, in the light of the continuous role which the people played in Bentham's legal and political theory, this interpretation makes the best sense of Bentham's statements in *Fragment*, with which this enquiry was begun.[77] The sympathetic and the moral sanctions operate to reinforce one another, and so create the possibility for communal integration under the auspices of the principle of utility. The interdependent operation of the external

[77] See pp. 216–17 above and 265–73 below.

agency and the individual, in both the sympathetic and the moral sanctions, is at the heart of what has been described above as the "panoptic principle". I have argued for an admittedly formal, but distinctly utilitarian, way of understanding "culture", and, as will be argued in the next section, of the process of cultural enlightenment. People would be able to "meet" each others' minds in the context of some obligatory culture which would unite them, but one which would be sensitive to, and even modified by, their individual contributions to communication. These individuals could, within the context of this "culture", reflect upon it, with a good chance that they would be understood by others. While participating in such an activity in a free manner, people would be able both to memorise and to imagine different conceptions or propositions to which painful or pleasurable consequences were attached.

The discussion of consensus formation in the public sphere so far has taken place at the level of universal theory, and has not referred to historical manifestations of it in different social groups. It is to this historical theme, which is important for an account of the broadest meaning of constitutional limits, that I will now turn.

IV

Deontology was that branch of morality which people arrived at through intersubjective communication. As such it related to consensus formation, and in turn to the operation of motives and sanctions. This section argues that by the operation of the sympathetic and moral sanctions, a social group could transform itself into what Bentham called a "community of sympathy".[78]

In a community of sympathy, at some level, there would be a common conception of harm and accordingly an obligatory medium concerning what was allowed and forbidden. No one would be able to disengage himself from communicative activity.[79] The task of deontology was to account for consensus formation between people. In other words:

> "In every instance to **bring out of their obscurity**, out of the neglect in which they have hitherto in so large a proportion been buried, **the points of coincidence** to the extent of which extra-regarding interest is connected and has by the hands of nature been identified with self-regarding interest: and this in such sort and with such effect that by the alliance thus formed, by this conjunct kind of interest, the force of self-regarding interest in those shapes in which it is purely self-regarding is commonly

[78] *First Principles*, p. 71. Bentham grounded the idea of a community of sympathy in the more basic idea of a "community of interest". However, the former will be focused upon because a community of interest, being broader than a community of sympathy, could encompass a community of law as well. A community of interest, whether achieved artificially or naturally, would be the utilitarian's end in terms of universal theory. A community of sympathy would be a particular historical manifestation of such a universal theory.

[79] Ibid., p. 72.

already in use, and by apt means may be rendered more and more in use, to be outweighed and overpowered."[80]

Communication between the public and governmental institutions was the crux of Bentham's constitutional theory. His constitutional theory was fundamentally communal in nature. It was rooted in sympathy, which was based on an empathic effort and the pain of bad conscience (or guilt). Through the capacity of each individual to imagine the pain of his fellow men, as well as his being influenced by communal obligations, he could begin to merge his pure self-regarding prudence with extra-regarding benevolence. This merging of self-regarding prudence and benevolence in the individual psyche would enhance the possibility of people arriving at a consensus. Sympathy was the most important factor in keeping a community together. Sympathetic affection, or the "desire for amity", would enable people to reconcile their opinions. As Bentham has been interpreted, the operation of the moral and the sympathetic sanctions would allow for some degree of "harmony", a harmony which would set the parameters for further individual, and in turn, communal reflection. In a vibrant community, many individuals could elevate the understanding of "harm" to the level in which they would come to believe that by harming other people's interests they would ultimately harm their own.[81] In a well-developed community of sympathy, *pure* self-regard would merge into extra-regard in many respects. In turn, within the parameters of the extra-regarding, individual imagination and the exchange of ideas could lead to the modification of the communal consensus. This process of formation and self-reflection of communities would be the story of cultural evolution, and would constitute a civilising process: "In proportion as the field of a man's particular connection enlarges itself, it approaches to a coincidence with that of the public at large."[82] The argument here is that self-regard embodied the notion of sympathy, and, in a well-developed community, it would be hard to distinguish the purely self-regarding from the sympathetic or moral-orientated self-regarding interest.

Although Bentham did not in fact take his analysis in *Deontology* further than a general description of social evolution, it is important to emphasise that the evolutionary process would, being utilitarian, involve a progression, as well as regression of sympathy. Social evolution could undergo reactionary stages in which patterns of sympathy would attempt to reassert themselves, and some other stages in which the political community could find no reconciliation and would break up. The whole idea of "community of sympathy", which embodied a communal conception of harm, would be first and foremost utilitarian and therefore, transient *not* according to a universal historical pattern. *Any* historical pattern in which some sympathy was crystallising would itself be transient in nature, and would be subject to criticism as a result of free exchange of ideas.

[80] *Deontology*, p. 193; see also ibid., pp. 196–7.
[81] Ibid., p. 195.
[82] Ibid.

This would entail a constant transformation of a conception of harm, obligatory mediums and perspectives of prudential considerations.

Focusing on the more immediate historical process through which sympathy would be crystallised, the notion of a "community of sympathy" has an implication for Bentham's theory as a whole. The social possibility of a self-reflective community, or a community of sympathetic utilitarians, depended on a given group's historical evolution. To speak about a society of sympathetic utilitarians, *without* reference to the actual state of communication and interpretation in the group concerned, would not make sense for Bentham. As has been argued above, there would have to be interdependence between individuals so that they would make the effort to consider the interest of their fellow men. This social stage would be difficult to attain, and hence law would be necessary to enable a people to move towards the formation of a "community of sympathy". Centralised, coercive, institutional authority, minimally justified in terms of security, would establish the initial collectivity by means of legislation and legal sanctions. However, the distributive role of centralised government, whether it was the approbation of certain practices to the exclusion of others, or whether it was the enforcement of some sphere of neutrality between certain practices, might gradually be supplanted by communal obligations, and eventually the need for state action might be reduced to a minimum. Legal intervention by the state, therefore, could end up to be, if one takes an evolutionary view of Bentham's enterprise, only secondary in importance. Viewed from the historical point of view of a given group, law would be merely an instrument which enabled a community of sympathy to develop. For Bentham, a historical goal could be a community in which the self- and the extra-regarding could be united—a perfect *society* of sympathetic utilitarians.[83] Law, the coercive power of government, legal punishment—all these would *make possible* the process of public enlightenment. Law would artificially bring together the self- and the extra-regarding motives. The law would be, according to Bentham, the subject-matter of *political deontology*.[84] The moral and the sympathetic sanctions, whose function was interdependent, would continue to operate in areas not already mirrored by the physical and the political sanction.[85] However, the balance between legislation and private ethics would change as the group evolved.

From a universal vantage point, Bentham assumed that there need not be *real* conflict between people, although at most stages of history such conflict would seem real enough. He described the way in which people would be enlightened as to their true interest:

> "**To bring to view** these comparatively latent ties—this, in so far as concerns the competition between *purely* self-regarding and social or say extra-regarding interest; this,

[83] See the quote at the head of the chapter from *First Principles*, p. 321.
[84] *Deontology*, p. 198.
[85] Ibid.

in so far as concerns the competition between probity and the self-regarding branch of prudence—this is what belongs to the field of deontology."[86]

Once the moral sanction was operating in a community, that community could take collective action according to what it thought to be in its best interest. Such collective action would imply that each individual (or at least the most influential individuals), was able to think in terms of the identification of the self-regarding and the extra-regarding. This capacity on the part of individuals would amount to an enlightenment of the community. This enlightenment, as has been argued, would result from influence which involved elements of both understanding and will. People would be able to detect an unjustified conception of harm and a pattern of obligations which results, whether established by the centralised authority, or among themselves. The sympathy which was crystallised into the moral sanction, or "public opinion", constituted the only proper basis on which the community might form a consensus with regard to the social justification of coercion.[87]

As far as the universal theoretical dimension of Bentham's enterprise was concerned, no goal or end was presumed. However, as far as the *historical* dimension of his enterprise, which involved an evolution of communities, was concerned, there would be a gap between the state of society as it WAS interpreted and as it OUGHT to be interpreted. Any historical OUGHT, being within the interpretative parameters of some ideological form, had the potential of evolving into a "community of sympathy" which embodied either self-government or, more likely, enforcement through legislation and judicial interpretation of communal sympathetic obligations. The universal utilitarian theory could account for such a historical evolution, and would emphasise its transient nature. History was only a "fragment of enlightenment" which itself would always be transient. From the universal point of view, any historical realisation would eventually fall short of full equilibrium between the self and the extra-regard. There were many institutional designs which could fall into a description of a historical evolution, despite the fact that in his institutional design Bentham did not go beyond the establishment of a representative democracy.

As far as the universal theoretical dimension of Bentham's enterprise was concerned, the force of the sanction of sympathy, and hence the force of the moral sanction and public opinion, would depend on the state of society. In no social group would the force of the sympathetic sanction be totally eliminated. Further, in no social group would it be possible completely to eliminate the exchange of ideas, that is the influence of the understanding over the understanding. Otherwise, it would be very difficult to explain how society could become enlightened, and move from the stage of brutal existence into a community of law and order, and then into a "community of sympathy":

[86] *Deontology*, p. 195.
[87] Ibid., p. 197.

> "In no state of society, which with the view of giving direction to human conduct [by] a work such as this I have in contemplation, can that social affection be wholly without place or wholly without the power of exercising in the direction here in question its influence on human conduct. In some states of society it is indeed in the whole extremely weak, and in every state the strength of it is susceptible of great variation as between individual and individual: in both which particulars it agrees in a considerable degree with the popular or moral sanction."[88]

To recapitulate, in terms of Bentham's universal *theory*, both empathy (the capacity of perceiving or imagining the pain suffered by another person), and sympathy (the interpretation of an empathic understanding), were of utmost importance for consensus formation. They would facilitate the formation of a consensus to some degree in *any* society. Empathy and sympathy would restrain an individual from doing something which appeared to the individual in question as likely to cause harm to another.[89] This required that each person was able to employ some "idea" of a likely pain, that is potential harm, in his own calculations, whether this pain would be suffered by another individual directly, or by the collectivity (in Bentham's language causing "private" or "public" mischief respectively). As an individual gained more experience he would become more adept at foreseeing certain sorts of pain which outweighed immediately tempting pleasures. A person could then acquire the ability to reflect generally upon the danger of being seduced by the immediately pleasurable.[90] In other words, when the moral and the sympathetic sanctions were well-rooted, a person would be able to reflect that hurting a fellow man would be to hurt himself in the long run.

Bentham produced a fascinating statement of social anthropology, envisaging an evolution from a society containing individuals with the propensity to act in a selfish manner, which would typically be subject to a mischievous and authoritarian form of rule, into a community of sympathy, in which authority was responsive to, indeed emanated from, the community, and operated only in those domains in which a social justification for such operations existed. The passage which contains this statement is remarkable, and illuminates many historical/anthropological aspects of Bentham's lifelong enterprise.[91] It reflects Bentham's lifelong insistence on portraying constitutional limits as socially dynamic in nature.

The first point to note about this passage is that Bentham saw legislation and private ethics as interdependent. Society might evolve from an aggregate of indi-

[88] *Deontology*, p. 201. Because one could not totally suppress the influence of understanding over understanding, one could not, even in a pure monarchy, stop the independent formation of sympathetic and moral obligations, which could, in turn, lead to the exercise of divestitive powers in some form. Thus, it is defensible to claim that sovereignty can be conceived as a split concept even where no split is apparent, for instance, in a pure monarchy: see chapter 2, pp. 57–8 above.

[89] Ibid., p. 201.

[90] Ibid., pp. 155–6.

[91] The passage is at *Deontology*, pp. 201–5. It is rather long and therefore is not quoted in full; see also ibid., pp. 73, 228.

viduals which justified coercion solely for reasons of security and co-ordination, into a state under a code of law, the limits to the justification of which incorporated, interpreted and enforced communal patterns of sympathy, and thereafter into a "community of sympathy" with minimal centralised coercion. Legislation and private ethics were parts of the same utilitarian enterprise. On the one hand, constitutional interpretation and reflection could signify the realm in which communal reflection already limited legislative powers. On the other hand, and more broadly, constitutional reflection could reflect the medium which would determine the balance of the respective operations of a "community of law" and a "community of sympathy". This broader level of constitutional reflection could reflect the level to which the community enforced its own imperatives without centralised institutions. It would mark a shift of the "political", namely from centralised institutions, into the community. So ultimately, constitutional law signified a balance, arrived at through historical evolution, which would in turn be mirrored in the demarcation between legislation and private ethics. The relationship between the realms of private and political deontology, or law, and the extent to which each left a mark on a given society, would depend on the historical stage in *a* (as opposed to *the)* civilising process which the society had reached.

It is important to notice in this passage the relation between the individual and society. Individuals felt sympathy through their imagining some moral sanction already in operation. This is why Bentham wrote in this passage about the "tutelary force" of sympathy—a term that he usually reserved for the moral sanction.[92] The degree of sympathy in each individual mind would depend on the strength of the moral sanction already existing as a collective norm in society. It goes without saying that, as has been argued in the previous section, an exchange of views between individuals could transform the mutual "sympathies" so as to create another social norm which would be backed by another moral sanction. The relationship between the interdependent moral and sympathetic sanctions would change as society changed in a course of civilisation. An uncivilised society would contain mainly self-regarding, beast-like people, who would have little empathy, and so would lack any understanding of the effects of their actions on other people, or of the longer term implications for themselves. It would be a society with hardly any sympathy. There would be little guilt and little compassion. Such a state of society might provide a utilitarian justification for Hobbesian political theory. As society grew, and the economy developed, and labour became more divided, people would become more dependent on the labour of other people, reciprocal relations of dependence would begin to form,[93] and people would begin to feel "bad conscience" about antisocial acts. A feeling of sympathy would begin to tie individuals together, so

[92] *Deontology*, p. 201.

[93] Bentham wrote in the passage: "[influence] extends itself successively, or at the same time, to other such individuals respectively connected with the individual in question by the ties of profession, class, town, province, political state".

that communication between them would give rise first to sympathetic sanctions, and then to a collective moral sanction aimed against the co-ordinating agency in the community (the government). The fields of human action, and the persons whose actions were the object of the sympathetic and moral sanctions, would become more diverse, and the sanctions themselves would extend to more people. They would embrace various groups of society, from the family to the worldwide community. The idea that sympathy was the "backbone" of society could gain greater and greater credence, at the expense of political deontology, which assumed a lack of sympathetic capacities in people. As free, inter-subjective communication became a dominant feature of society, the public sphere would gain cohesion, and sympathy would become its main characteristic. Bentham argued that each individual would gain the capacity to feel sympathy or "bad conscience" by observing other people. Through generalisations based on, and the observation of, the exchange of arguments, people would learn to conceive, that is memorise and imagine, other people's sentiments, and to feel a sense of obligation to take them into account.

People would be able to make signals, to communicate their sentiments, to their fellow citizens. In Bentham's language, they would learn how to develop "external expressions of their sentiments". With inter-subjective activity, the conditions for collective action would come into being. The force of the collectivity, backed by the threat of the moral sanction, could be applied against each member of the *group*, and against officials. What one can see here, in short, is a summing up by Bentham of the main thesis of his utilitarian enterprise, according to which the applications of universal theory are sensitive to the historical development of a society.[94] This passage arguably has application beyond Bentham's own historical experience, since the basic scheme of motives that he provided for here could remain operative in a society far more differentiated than a liberal, representative democratic one, as well as being compatible with an account of society derived from a more complicated ontology than the one with which Bentham operated.[95]

This idea of the historical development of the public sphere, involving the shifting borderline between political and private deontology, was arguably what Bentham had in mind, albeit in an undeveloped way, when he wrote the largely polemical *Fragment*. One can see in the account of political society

[94] In "Bentham on the Public Character of Law", *Utilitas* 1 (1989) 41–61 at 60–1, Postema argues that under Bentham's system the role of law was to put affairs beyond public debate after the law's appearance. Such a role, Postema argues, obscures another role law has, not discussed by Bentham, namely the *structuring* of public debate which continues after the law's appearance. Bentham's main aim was to achieve co-ordination, Postema insists, and not to use law as a means of facilitating continuous public debate once co-ordination was achieved. This argument portrays Bentham as a philosopher who advocated a socially static theory of law. Postema captures neither the manner in which an emphasis on law, though important, would be only a part, albeit a necessary one, of the historical development of a social group, nor that it was in the area of constitutional theory that the borderline between attaining co-ordination, as well as enforcing existing social co-operation, through law, and through communal and sympathetic obligations (private ethics), would be determined.

[95] This point will be discussed in Part 2.

offered there the embryo of the idea of the evolution of political society, developing from a society based on law and a centralised institutional scheme, into a community with only minimal spheres of legal obligation and coercion, having as its basis communal obligation originating within the community. This potential shift in the manifestation, or "locus", of obligation—from legislation to private ethics—would be determined, as has been argued in Chapter 4, by utilitarian calculations. This shift would imply that the unification of duty and interest in individual minds could be, to a large extent, embodied in culture. In such a social state there would be no need for law artificially to unify duty and interest. A community of law and political sanction would be transformed into a community of sympathy. The idea of "enlightenment", as transient as it would be, in this context meant that sources of pains and pleasures, propositions backed by sanctions, manipulated motives, and interest formation, all changed their social manifestations as a result of communal, and hence individual, evolution. This passage, together with the argument advanced in Chapter 4 above, regarding political society and free government,[96] provides the basis for the broadest possible account of the social operation of the principle of utility, and the socially dynamic, historically sensitive, though ever-transient, idea of the social justification of authority. Thus, this account in *Deontology* portrays the broadest meaning, socially speaking, of constitutional limits in the context of historical evolution.

The second issue which is highlighted by this remarkable passage is that of false consciousness.[97] Bentham explicitly referred to a point in the history of a given community, the "community" itself being a product of sympathy, or inter-subjective communication, at which people could come to see that the judgements which they had previously made, and the principles that they had previously adopted, had, in the light of experience, turned out to be erroneous. The greater extent to which free communication was conducted in the community, the more instructive would be the community's calculation of consequences, and in turn the consensus, even a consensus to break up, it would reach.[98] Bentham would insist that the inter-subjective process of self-evaluation takes place continuously. But, and this is crucial, he would deny that any particular substantive solutions to social problems were wholly enlightened solutions, incapable of amelioration.

A third issue which arises from reading this passage relates to minorities. A community of sympathy would be one in which, as has been argued, self-interest would be transparent to the degree that individuals would understand that by harming a fellow individual they would harm themselves as well.[99] This

[96] See chapter 4, pp. 119–22 above.

[97] See in this context chapter 4, p. 110 above, where it has been argued that Bentham had written in *Fragment* about the possibility of people not being able to conceive of states of affairs in their true light.

[98] See *IPML*, chapter 4, for these parameters (intensity, propinquity, etc.).

[99] In *First Principles*, p. 39, Bentham claimed that between groups there would be clashes of opinion, but that such a clash would not mean a clash of interest.

would imply that there could exist on the part of the individual some sensitivity to other conceptions of the good, that is some capacity to endorse pluralism; and further, that this pluralism could well be the subject of a consensus. Again, it must be emphasised that although Bentham can be understood as seeing a liberal pluralist society as the historical goal of communal development, it remains the case that no particular pattern of communal development, pluralist or otherwise, was assumed by his universal theory.[100]

In a community of sympathy, minority problems would be overcome by the social embodiment of a "sympathetic pattern", and hence a communal obligation, endorsing respect for the minority in question and its conception of the good. Such a sympathetic pattern embodied in a moral obligation would supply a prescriptive context for a great deal of prudential consideration by individuals in that community with regard to minorities. Constitutional limits on centralised coercion would point towards some neutrality or toleration with regard to different conceptions of the good. These constitutional limits would mirror an already cultivated sympathy in this regard amongst the people who composed the community.[101] Whether the "universal interest" of a community could contain the minority's interest or not would depend upon the quality of communication between individuals in this community, and, in turn, the stage of historical development of that community. In a society where sympathy predominated, the quality of the universal interest would be such that it would embody different interest groups.[102]

[100] It is important to avoid associating the idea of a "community of sympathy" with stagnation in public debate. A community of sympathy implied that some consensus existed, which would enable a free exchange of ideas to operate and to modify its central tenets. Stagnation would imply a passive and uncritical public.

[101] In *Bentham, Byron and Greece*, pp. 84–9, Rosen acknowledges that in *Deontology* Bentham made progress towards solving the problem of minorities.

[102] It is a pity that J.S. Mill did not read Bentham's *Deontology*, but only J. Bowring's edition of "Deontology". The result was that Bentham's remarks on deontology, as contained in these notes, suffered heavy criticism by Mill, on the ground of Bentham's alleged lack of attention to the importance of "sympathy": "Bentham", *The Collected Works Of J.S. Mill*, vol. 10, pp. 95–9; see also M. Green, "Sympathy and Self-Interest: The Crisis in Mill's Mental History", *Utilitas* 1 (1989) 259–77, at 265–71. The evolution of communities envisaged in *Deontology* resembled in many ways Mill's account of democracy and social evolution. Mill believed that the root of any social change would lie in the community. In his "Considerations on Representative Government", Mill argued that there had to be a communal readiness to accept representative institutions. Mill also saw sympathy as an enlightening force, a force which could liberate a community from stagnant, indolent and dogmatic thought. One of the dangers of representative governments, he claimed, would be that of legislation uninformed by sympathy. In sympathy he saw an assurance that no single interest would dominate society: see *The Collected Works*, vol. 19, pp. 435–6, 445–7. Mill also saw in the communication and mutual influence between majorities and minorities (although the majority would be the ultimate force), the prime value of democracy. He would, like Bentham, see the "universal interest" in the context of such communication: see "De Tocqueville on Democracy in America [I]", *The Collected Works*, vol. 18, pp. 71–3.

The argument advanced in this chapter also resembles what Mill said in "The Spirit of the Age", about the two states in which society could exist. In a *natural* state of society, people were governed, and censored their government, within generally accepted parameters, known to all, regarding social organisation and the aptitude of the rulers. A representative democracy would be in such a state (an "optimisation of state institutions"). This state of society would be regarded as stationary,

Bentham's model of democracy and the application of the majority principle in a representative government has been discussed both by James[103] and Schwartz[104]. James makes the assumption that Bentham did not change his theory of law and sovereignty in his later writings.[105] This is a correct assumption on James's part, although based on the mistaken assertion that Bentham's legal theory required an unlimited despotism. Therefore, according to James, representative government would still be legally unlimited. James claims that Bentham implied that a legally unlimited government was needed in order to establish some unification of duty and interest among small interest groups, which could not form a genuine public interest, and hence could not achieve unification by themselves. Consensus formation would be local, and so minority groups would be able to form consensuses which would operate to prevent the formation and recognition of the universal interest. Each group would form a sinister interest,[106] and hence there would be no possibility of, or incentive for, arriving at a majority universal interest. James assumes that, for Bentham, people were egoists who would ignore on every occasion the interest of others, and that the same would be true of groups, except where there was no contradiction between self-regarding and extra-regarding interest.[107] James is clearly mistaken in his account of Bentham's theory of motivation, in that he fails completely to discuss sympathy between individuals, let alone between groups. Further, the fact that minorities could compromise and reach a consensus implied that this consensus could *become* the universal interest. There was nothing impossible or undesirable in such a social process. Indeed, minorities could also arrive at a consensus with the majority group. *All* types of consensus would exemplify the unification of self- and extra-regard.

Schwartz also totally divorces self-regard from sympathy, and comes to the conclusion that under Bentham's account there would be nothing to stop the ruler from changing society as he wished.[108] Schwartz does not take account of the role of the POT in facilitating consensus between the majority and

or as progressing only slowly towards questioning the basic principles upon which society was built. When society reached a certain stage of self-reflection as a result of freedom of communication, a questioning of the basic order could occur. All existing patterns of opinion would be in chaos, which might in turn lead to a new understanding and construction of society and its institutional organisation. At this stage, society would be in a *transitional* state: *The Collected Works*, vol. 22, pp. 252–3. Mill's argument here can be seen as a statement of critical theory.

Further, Bentham's idea of a "community of sympathy" resembled in many ways Mill's idea of the "stationary state", in which enlightened individuals would enjoy fundamental rights and substantial equality: see "Principles of Political Economy", *The Collected Works*, vol. 3, pp. 752–7; and also in this context, J. Riley, "J.S. Mill's Liberal Utilitarian Assessment of Capitalism Versus Socialism", *Utilitas* 8 (1996) 39–71, at 46–55.

103 M. James, "Public Interest and Majority Rule in Bentham's Democratic Theory" *Political Theory* 9 (1981) 49–64.

104 P. Schwartz, "Jeremy Bentham's Democratic Despotism" in R. D. Collison Black (ed.), *Ideas in Economics* (Basingstoke, 1986), pp. 74–103.

105 James, "Public Interest and Majority Rule", p. 51.

106 Ibid., p. 54.

107 Ibid., p. 53.

108 Schwartz, "Jeremy Bentham's Democratic Despotism", p. 81.

minorities as a society developed under a democratic government. His view of Bentham's psychology is binary. He portrays people's interests under Bentham's theory as either coinciding or incompatible.[109] He does not discuss the possibility of social interaction, that is influence and dialogue. Schwartz's analysis does not therefore capture the complexity of Bentham's insight regarding the manner in which social arrangements had the capacity to enhance interaction among members of the public, and between the public and central institutions. His claim, that in Bentham's democracy there was nothing to stop the increase of government power under the majority,[110] is an oversimplification and therefore mistaken.

The claim regarding the social complexity of the formation of the universal interest with which the inquiry of this chapter began may now be better appreciated. The universal interest was a socially dynamic concept, the means of expression, though not the nature of which, would change, depending on whether the community was one of law, one of sympathy, or some hybrid form. The universal interest was embodied in a conception of harm which materialised as a result of a reciprocal process of mutual influence, or a struggle between many self-informed interests. Hence, the universal interest would be constantly changing. Under all circumstances, its formation involved more than just adding up static preferences. The moral and intellectual aptitude of individuals, and hence of the community, would change over time through communication.[111] Constitutional theory was a conception of the organisation of a group, based on some global utilitarian consensus regarding social relationships within it. As such, the utilitarian justification of a given constitutional theory would always mirror communal reflections regarding the balance between private ethics and legislation.[112]

V

It has been maintained that the relationship of understanding over understanding could also operate through the medium of the will. However, in the constitutional sphere, the moral sanction as exercised by the population would be predominant, so the superiority would belong to the people rather than to the government. Of course, influence of pure understanding would flow in both directions. If the government remained stubborn, the antagonism between it and the people could lead to a situation where the people exercised their will over the holders of supreme operative power.[113] The degree to which the people

109 Ibid., p. 90.

110 Ibid., p. 81.

111 See in this context, *First Principles*, p. 70.

112 Bentham declined to give an exact account of what such a balance should be: *IPML*, p. 281. See in this context, H.L.A. Hart, "Bentham's Principle of Utility and Theory of Penal Law", in *An Introduction to the Principle of Morals and Legislation* (CW), J.H. Burns and H.L.A. Hart (eds) (Oxford, 1996), pp. lxxix–cxii, at xciii–xcvi.

113 See *First Principles*, pp. 67–8, 30; see also Bowring, ix. 41.

interacted in this way with government would be the degree to which constitutional freedom existed. The more possibilities there were for free inter-subjective communication among the people, and between the people and the government, the better informed and effective would be the will of the people to which the moral sanction was attached. Further, under such conditions it would be reasonable to expect the holders of the operative power to perceive the popular will as imposing on them an obligation—a constitutional obligation:

> "Constitutional liberty depends upon and is proportioned to the dependence of the possessors of efficient public power upon the will of the body of the people, in virtue of the originative power they possess."[114]

Constitutional limits reflected a socially dynamic conception of harm in a social group. As such, constitutional limits (and of course, sovereignty) represented a moral judgement. This social dynamism would be enabled only under the condition of free communication within the public sphere. "Constitutional freedom", ultimately, would be freedom of communication—of influence arising from an exchange of opinions.[115] Constitutional limits were not related merely to some entrenched social beliefs which were "accepted" as true, but reflected a socially dynamic process of enlightenment in which conception of harms, patterns of sympathy could be formed and revised.

As has been argued in Chapter 2, Bentham's concept of law embodied a moral judgement. His legal and political theory had the reshaping and realisation of social *possibilities* at its heart. From *Fragment* to *Deontology*, he was committed to this democratic aim. *The key value was participation.* The participatory community could reflect critically on the degree of coercion existing, and hence on the extent to which such a community conceived of itself as a *political* one. Thus, the democratic process—the social process of the transformation of the community—would accelerate sharply after a representative government had been put in place.

[114] *On the Efficient Cause and Measure of Constitutional Liberty*, UC clxx. 168; see also *Political Tactics*, p. 73.

[115] See the discussion of the meaning of a free government in *Fragment*, chapter 4, section IV, above. This again resembles Mill's "On Liberty", in which flexibility in the borderline between the spheres of collective intervention and individual inviolability, the giving force to minorities' opinions (usually the most innovative and enlightening ones), the avoidance of the tyranny of the majority and of stagnation in public opinion (*inter alia* as a result of the acceptance of "custom"), in short the maintenance of a vibrant social dynamism, were the chief characteristics of constitutional liberty, and hence of free government: "On Liberty", *The Collected Works*, vol. 13, pp. 219–31, 242–3, 262–73; see also pp. 230–1, note 102 above.

PART 2

Utility, Indeterminacy and Harm

7

The Dynamic Connection between Ethics and Politics

> When a man attempts to combat the principle of utility, it is with reasons drawn, without his being aware of it, from the very principle itself. His arguments, if they prove anything, prove not that the principle is *wrong*, but that, according to the applications he supposes to be made of it, it is *misapplied*. Is it possible for a man to move the earth? Yes; but he must first find out another earth to stand upon.
>
> *IPML*, pp. 14–5.

This chapter has two main parts: first, it summarises the main arguments of the reconstruction of Bentham's legal and political enterprise. Secondly, some further thoughts about utilitarianism take Bentham's work, as interpreted here, into contemporary debates about the ethical foundations of political theory.

I

The first part of this book has put forward a constructive interpretation of Bentham's legal and political thought. At the most general level, the level of universal theory, Bentham's legal and political thought has been reconstructed to show a conceptual connection between, on the one hand, his account of constitutional limits, and on the other hand, his account of the realisation of communicative possibilities in the public sphere. Throughout Bentham's career, he saw the people as the body which was responsible for "determining and effectuating constitutional limits". This formula captures his meaning more accurately than the much criticised idea of the "habit of obedience", or "the disposition to obey". Bentham's concern at the level of universal theory was with what was *possible* rather than with what was *desirable*. The unfolding of communicative *possibilities* with regard to, on the one hand, the justification for centralised coercion (security through rules), and, on the other hand, with regard to the limitation of such coercion (security from rule), lay at the centre of Bentham's political philosophy. Instead of justifying morality upon a priori substantive metaphysical ideals, his main goal was to liberate the public sphere and to unfold communicative possibilities within it. Arguably, his criticisms of the common law, his own theory of legislation and law, as well as his constitutional theory, all shared the rationale of contributing to the realisation of the aim, admittedly broad, of liberating the public sphere. His ambition was to account for the limits of the social justification of authority and law, always bearing in mind the manner in which human psychology could be the basis of radically different prudential judgements, as the process of unfolding communicative possibilities in the public sphere continued.

Bentham was conscious, from a very early stage of his career, of the enormous potential which public opinion had for freeing people from well-established, and falsely-justified, coercive patterns. Bentham had always seen the people as the prime source of virtue. Public discussion could develop from an activity which barely existed, or existed only for a small number of individuals, into a full-scale exchange of ideas between every member of the community. Such a development would be mirrored in the realm of constitutional limits. Both the transparent nature of the exchange of views, and, in turn, the possibility of arriving at critical constitutional reflections in the "public sphere", were crucial to Bentham's utilitarian enterprise. Constitutional limits reflected the extent to which individual judgements were transparent to exchanges of views as well as to the development of communal obligations as a result of such exchanges. Utilitarian political theory conceived instances in which a shift in the locus of obligation could occur from centralised institutions into the community, so that self-government would predominate.

From a substantive point of view, constitutional limits represented communal self-reflection on the central moral principles around which a community revolved. In this context, constitutional limits could be seen as general, critical reflections in the public sphere resulting from communication within it. These reflections concerned the justification of a given pattern, which was charted between unity in conceptions of good and differentiation or neutrality between such conceptions. In other words, for Bentham, constitutional limits in the context of a utilitarian theory realised the communicative possibility of forming and revising a consensual notion of harm. Such a notion of harm could evolve to bring about neutrality between differing conceptions of the good.

Bentham assumed that as communication between people became more transparent, they would be enlightened with regard to the extent of the real conflict between them. This enlightenment would mean that, gradually, some *limits* to the exercise of coercion could be realised. In a utilitarian system, general prescriptive propositions with regard to the limits to the exercise of coercion would be socially entrenched. As such, these limits would reflect the culture of the community. So entrenched, these propositions would serve as a moral threshold in communication among people, and between the people and the government. They would form an obligatory context in which prudential utilitarian calculations would be carried out, either by officials or by every individual. These prescriptive propositions could be entrenched in the imposition of self-limitations by the legislature in a code of law, and could be further interpreted by courts.[1]

Law, or the exercise of political deontology, was a coercive instrument for the co-ordination of, and co-operation towards the crystallisation of, moral beliefs. Law was effectuated by creating certain offences, which were arrived at by the legislature utilising some conceptions of harm (or in Bentham's language, mischief). These conceptions of harm might reflect a communal conception of harm to a greater or lesser extent. Some purely instrumental conception of harm, one which led to the investment of authority in legal institutions, would have to exist in every political community—even in a pure monarchy. Such an instrumental conception identified harm as insecurity, which would result from the absence of the co-ordination of moral beliefs. However, even this purely instrumental, co-ordinative role of centralised coercion would facilitate communication in the public sphere with regard to the limits of justified, institutionally-based coercion. This communication, which could result in the crystallisation of increasingly sophisticated, communally-based obligations, would be reflected in a two-way influential activity between the government and the people.

Thus, in a political community, to a greater or lesser extent, an ongoing tension might evolve between crystallised communal conceptions of harm, as embodied in co-ordinated communal principles, and the government's conception of harm upon which coercion was based. Indeed, this tension could also exist between a representative government which re-presented, coerced and enforced the majority's view *as* a "public" conception of harm, and the conception of harm which existed among people in the community. This tension would lead to self-reflection on the part of the public sphere upon the extent of the powers of such a representative government. This popular collective reflection would establish certain communal principles as an obligatory context which would operate to limit governmental powers. These principles would form constitutional limits in that they would serve as an entrenchment of a given communal conception of harm. This conception would condition *and* circumscribe *any* justification of, and limitations upon, institutional activity which was based on immediate expediency. Communal obligations would form the basis for constitutional offences, in that their transgression might be perceived by members of the community as harmful. Hence, a communal "learning process" would signify a shift of the obligatory media from central institutions to the community.

Communal obligations would operate as reflections *vis à vis* any form of unified expression of coercion, whether institutionally–or communally–based. These reflections would be conducted in a "constitutional" sphere in which the reasons for justifying certain measures of coercion *qua* obligations would be the

[1] It is well beyond the scope of this book to construct a theory of adjudication. However, justification of judicial decisions which resolved constitutional disputes would have to relate at the most general level to a communal conception of harm based on these prescriptive propositions. See J. Habermas, *Between Facts and Norms* (Cambridge, 1996), pp. 222–5.

subject-matter. This constitutional sphere was contrasted in Chapter 4 with an immediate sphere of reasoning. In the immediate sphere, uncritically justifying a particular exercise of coercion would be the subject-matter. The interaction and critical reflection in the constitutional sphere, the sphere of "constitutional permissibility", may be seen as an alternative to what Hart called the rule of recognition. The elements of censuring coercive measures, and seeing them "as" valid authoritative utterances, were conceptually linked in the idea of "constitutional permissibility". "Validity" was a notion which embodied critical interpretation.

Constitutional limits would be ultimately established as moral and sympathetic obligations. However, communally-based coercion did not point towards the stagnation of public debate. Full publicity of governmental business, and the maintenance of a free exchange of ideas, which could operate to expose certain patterns of unjustified domination (for example claims for social unity which went too far at the expense of social differentiation), might be effectuated by institutions, or by the community itself. However, the account offered here does, under the auspices of the principle of utility, allow for the possibility that collective communal attitudes could regress as well as progress, for instance, leading to a strengthening of centralised institutional coercive mechanisms. Thus, over time, constitutional limits or general communal principles would change as a community evolved. These changes would occur as a result of an ongoing process of the exchange of ideas, and the embodiment of this exchange in general communal obligations. To summarise, communal obligations signified constitutional limits arrived at as a result of communication in the public sphere. Such communication helped to expose the limits to the necessary domination of institutionally-based coercion. As such, the development of constitutional limits would reflect the transparency, both to the prudential reasoning of officials and to that of each member of the public, of the communicative activity between people, or within the public sphere.

In the light of this broad understanding of constitutional limits, many particular areas of Bentham's thought, often regarded as problematic or incoherent, have been subjected to a new interpretation. Sovereignty has been interpreted as a "split", or two-dimensional concept. Any exercise of political authority had to imply the judgement of another body with regard to the moral justification of that authority. This "judging" body was an entrusting body, whose "suspended" conditional command to a prospective authority was the essence of the trust which would constitute any "political" society. The conditions of this trust would change as the community changed. This was the jurisprudential framework in which a "judging" public sphere was shown to be conceptually connected to the determination and effectuation of constitutional limits. The two interdependent dimensions which formed the concept of sovereignty were mirrored in a conceptual account of constitutional "law", under the command theory of "a law".

Sovereignty was not only of a "split", but also of a relative and plural nature. In abstract terms, sovereignty could be described as a relationship of superiority and subordination existing within a validating, "permitting" context, itself featuring relationships of superiority and subordination. The "split" nature of sovereignty implied a dynamic social activity which operated at a given level of the hierarchy of relationships of superiority and subordination. In contradistinction to this hierarchical relativity, sovereignty could exist as a plurality of hierarchies, horizontally manifested across each hierarchical stage. Both vertical relativity and horizontal plurality of sovereignty could help to resolve the tensions which arose in the attempt to explain the relations between the multiplicity of "legal" operations on the one hand, and the operation of sovereignty as a trust between a *unified* social judgement of a people and a coercive body, on the other. The connection was again established here between constitutional limits and the public sphere. Constitutional limits and law would mirror the extent to which the diversification of the public sphere could be contained by any unified representation of a group, this unified representation being required for utilitarian reasons of certainty, and hence, security.

Constitutional limits determined the extent to which the united hierarchy of a "community" should prevail over, or contain, the plurality of hierarchies which cut across it. This paradigm remained applicable whether state law or international law was under consideration. Constitutional law, as a mirror of a communal change, would reflect the ways in which the various domains of relationship of superiority and subordination could influence and modify one another. This mutual influence could determine two aspects of constitutional limits. First, the unity/plurality relationships at each level of hierarchy could be determined. The extent to which individuals or individual communities would manage their own affairs within a larger whole would be determined. Secondly, the determination of unity/plurality could lead to another determination and effectuation of the exact social manifestation of sovereignty (i.e. the "split") within any hierarchical level between an entrusting judging body and a central coercive authority. Thus the idea of "validity" had to embrace not only the nature of the concept of sovereignty, but also its relative social manifestation.

The basis of a flexible account of social evolution is arguably found in *A Fragment on Government*, in which the universal features of political society, and the way in which these features related to constitutional limits, were discussed. Yet again, the relationship between constitutional limits and the public sphere was shown to be a central theme of this early work. In *Fragment,* Bentham advocated a position which has been termed "utilitarian-based anarchism". This philosophical anarchism, which implied the existence of a residual moral autonomy, was based on Bentham's epistemology. This epistemology criticised any theory which asserted the existence of (as opposed to an argument for the existence of) imprescriptible moral obligations. Bentham's utilitarianism and his epistemology were both compatible with the existence of political societies, founded on the expediency of political authority. However, it has been argued that "political society", which consisted in popular, participatory, collective reflection as to whether to obey the institution of law, was capable of existing in various forms, reflecting different cultures and times. Bentham's philosophical anarchism, under the auspices of the principle of utility, implied that there could be many possibilities for the realisation and development of schemes of obligation within a social group. These possibilities could become actual social manifestations in the course of a group's history. However, only if people possessed this "philosophical anarchic attitude" (the ability to question centralised coercion in the categorical/constitutional sphere) would they be able to seize these opportunities, and to reflect upon the way their society was organised. This attitude could override any existing ideological justification of political authority. As such, this attitude was the most important liberating force in civilised societies. Bentham wanted to cultivate such an attitude in the population. No argument about the justification of the exercise of authority, and the utilitarian gains consequent upon it, could wholly exclude the moral autonomy of the population, that is their capacity to think at the categorical, constitutional level about obligations *qua* valid obligations. Thus, Bentham's theory could accommodate the anarchistic attitude, and even a community based on an anarchistic ideology, without compromising security, without abandoning the epistemic necessity of his sanction theory of duties, and without assuming any inherently bad or virtuous characterisation of human nature. As far as the social operation of the principle of utility was concerned, any indirect operation of the principle at the immediate level was subjected to, and confined by, a constitutional context, in which the operation of the principle was direct. Under the categorical, constitutional operation of the principle, the people, in Bentham's enterprise, had a direct participatory role in determining and effectuating constitutional limits.

A participatory role for the people existed also in Bentham's mature constitutional writings. In these writings, Bentham conceived of constitutional limits, that is the *extent* of the exercise of power by the government, in terms of the *quality* of its exercise. Generally, a good government could be maintained only if it were subjected to the continuous judgement of the people. More particularly, a bad government would not yield to public judgement with regard to the limits of acceptable coercion. In seeing constitutional limits as a continuous judgement of the people, Bentham formed his "enabling rationale" for good government. The government was not a priori limited, but was *a posteriori* limited by the check of a vibrant popular judgement, which related to the pattern which mediates between various abstract prescriptive propositions. A good government would be responsive in such a way as to tie its own hands in regard to the extent of the coercion it *could* exercise. If it failed so to do, the people would be able to resist it. Bentham in fact used the language of *Fragment* in his mature constitutional writing, in linking constitutional limits to a public judgement which would, if necessary, lead to disobedience. In his mature constitutional thought, Bentham recognised that to facilitate resistance in the case of a transgression of constitutional limits was to make a prime contribution to the attainment of free government. His democratic theory was the logical conclusion of the participatory role which he provided for the people as early as *Fragment*, in relation to the conditions for the existence and persistence of a free government. In his democratic theory, Bentham gave effect to his life-long enterprise by proposing a system in which the activity central to the concept of sovereignty, the interaction between the public sphere and the government, would be in a state of greatest intensity. However, the implication of this continuous role of the public sphere in Bentham's enterprise was that representative democracy did not exhaust the democratic potential of the public sphere in determining and effectuating constitutional limits.

Bentham's conception of the public sphere has been analysed both in its general, abstract formulation, and in terms of his theory of human motivation. The Public Opinion Tribunal has been interpreted as an "observer" which each person creatively imagines for himself as a result of the process of communication. Bentham wanted to establish a government which would be constantly improved under the panoptic principle. A situation where there was a high level of participation, and in particular, where constitutional limits were established, maintained and improved by such participation, has been referred to as "panoptic democracy". The cultivation of the panoptic principle was the basis upon which Bentham's idea of the "enabling rationale" for good government could be plausibly defended.

In discussing the concept of "influence", it was argued that Bentham believed that a free exchange of ideas in the public sphere would lead to enlightenment. Influence, which included both understanding and a volitional element, could focus public debate on constitutional issues in exposing unnecessary or iniquitous obligatory patterns within a community. The role of the sympathetic and the moral sanctions, and the relationship between them, accounted for the motivational basis for these activities of "influence" within the public sphere, activities which were at the heart of consensus formation.

In the first part of this book, a unifying rationale for Bentham's legal and political enterprise has been constructed. In justifying this construction, issue was taken with scholars who hitherto have not attempted to explain his texts in the light of some unifying theme. Hart, Kelly, Rosen, Hume and James have all provided important illuminations of certain aspects of Bentham's theory. Their arguments make sense in the context of the problems they were addressing, but they all erred in not relating their enquiries to the fundamental question in Bentham's thought, namely how can coercion within a social order be limited under the auspices of the principle of utility? All of them developed interesting interpretations of certain aspects of Bentham's enterprise. However, all of them, in their different ways, had a profoundly limited view of Bentham's endeavours.

Postema's work stands as an exception to the accounts which have failed to make sense of Bentham's theory as a whole. Postema looks at many published and unpublished texts, and presents a unified interpretation of some aspects of Bentham's enterprise. This book accepts and builds upon many of his conclusions. In particular, it shares the view that Bentham retained the same theory of law throughout his career, a theory which embraced an interaction between the people and the government which determined the limits of sovereignty. It accepts also that Bentham ultimately provided for a direct operation of the principle of utility.

However, this reconstruction arguably both refines and goes further than Postema's account in two respects. First, it seeks to show that the direct participation of the people in determining and effectuating constitutional limits remained a concern for Bentham in his mature constitutional writings, and in his writings on private ethics. Postema does not consider these mature texts in depth. In fact, Postema pays insufficient attention to Bentham's constitutional theory and his theory of private ethics. Secondly, the book goes further than Postema in developing a constructive interpretation of Bentham's legal and political enterprise. Postema rightly introduces an interactive element into the very understanding of Bentham's theory of sovereignty. This he does, however, without considering the implication such an introduction may have to the plausibility of reading Bentham as a fully-fledged legal positivist. The argument in this book presents Bentham's account not as resembling modern theories of law, such as Hart's, but as a highly abstract theory of law, linked to his understanding of the dynamism of social interpretation and change. Bentham's scientific approach to motivation, combined with highly abstract ideas such as the POT, reveal him in a totally different light from the positivistic one in which Hart, or indeed Postema, saw him. In short, Postema does provide a broad rationale for Bentham's legal theory, but this is not sufficient to account for the many lacunae in Bentham's theory. As a result, his interpretation does not appreciate the scope of Bentham's enterprise.

Postema's underestimation of the scope of Bentham's theory has particular implications. First, he provides only a limited insight into Bentham's understanding of the public character of law. Secondly, his interpretation of Bentham's theory of sovereignty is misguided. His idea of "interactional custom" is incoherent, and fails to capture Bentham's understanding of sovereignty as a "split", two-dimensional concept, which embodies the critical judgement of an entrusting body. Thirdly, as far as the operation of the principle of utility is concerned, Postema does not explain the significance of the constitutional sphere and its relation to the direct operation of the principle. This omission leads Kelly to suggest that Postema's account ultimately fails to adhere consistently to Bentham's sanction theory of duties, and to Bentham's assignment of prime importance to security in his scheme. Arguably, therefore, despite its many insights, Postema's account does not succeed in accounting for constitutional limits in Bentham's theory, and fails to exhaust the potential of that theory. The consequence of this general failure is Postema's denial that Bentham provided for fundamental rights which could and in fact did, limit governments (despite his explanation of Bentham's idea of limited sovereignty). Further, Postema argues that Bentham was hostile to the very notion of fundamental rights, and to their accommodation in his legal and political enterprise.[2]

[2] See chapter 5, pp.157–8.

In general, the arguments about Bentham's relevance depend on the assertion that his ultimate notion of democracy valued participation, not merely as a tool for ensuring the responsibility of officials, but also as a means of liberating the public sphere from dogma, *including* any myths about the goodness of an existing system according to which society was understood and, in turn, organised. Indeed, freedom of communication in the public sphere, the maintenance of the random nature of the exchange of opinions within it, was the ultimate basis for his defence of democracy. The reconstruction of Bentham's enterprise identifies a latent realm of freedom, one which would simply mean an absence of centralised obstacles for communication, from the exchange of views about future possibilities, and from consensus formation within the public sphere. To this freedom, Bentham was, to some degree, committed in all his legal and political writings.

The first part of the book has attempted to effect a change of *emphasis* in the reading of some of Bentham's writings. It shows Bentham as a thinker whose universal enterprise did not aim at establishing once-and-for-all solutions. It has emphasised that aspect of his thought which continuously sought to unlock the emancipatory potential, through which any form of social organisation could be criticised and changed in fundamental respects. His POT offered day-to-day criticism within a democratic system. However, it could also serve a much wider emancipatory social role, related to how the community saw itself. Perhaps ironically, Bentham, in producing his model of democratic government, did not exhaust the potential of his own theory. His theory was formal in that it could accommodate many forms of social organisation, some of which he was unable to envisage in his own time.

II

Many features discussed in the first part of this book constitute different perspectives of the same social dynamism that characterises Bentham's constitutionalism. These features include the "split", "relative" and "plural" understanding of sovereignty; the flexible social contract which Bentham referred to in *Comment* and developed in *Fragment*; the utilitarian-based anarchism; and the ever-changing relationships between community of law and community of sympathy. The taste which is left after completing the constructive interpretation of Bentham is one of constant flux, characterising the utilitarian foundations of his constitutionalism. Constitutional limits seem a contingent phenomenon and a free government is supposed somehow to respond to such a contingency. I imagine the reader to be left with a question of what substantive principles might form the justificatory basis for, and the limitations on, centralised coercion in a free society. What is the perspective from which to interpret social conflicts? From the reconstruction, it emerges that Bentham's utilitarian constitutionalism assigns importance—moral importance—*both* to the possibility of arriving at some consensus based on a moral perspective, *and* to the transient nature of such a perspective and, in turn, a consensus. A theme that constantly re-emerges in the book is that pain and pleasure that people feel operate in communication in the public sphere so as to form a conception of harm which shapes social norms, which in turn justify and limit coercion. The conception of harm operates to maximise pleasure in one distributive manner or another. However, in time, it is this very communication and exchange of sentiments which is derived from motives, desires and sanctions, that operates to discredit a previously constructed conception of harm, proving the necessity for it to be seen as contingent and transient in nature. It is *pain*, real pain under an existing conception of harm which generates the social dynamism to outgrow it. In that sense, a more general maximisation of pleasure is conditioned by the experience of that kind of pain.

This ambiguity which characterises the utilitarian calculus, namely between construction and dissolution of conceptions of harm through communication between people who feel pain and pleasure, gives rise to some unease. Real pains and pleasures as influencing communication create a feeling of instability that is arguably bound to re-emerge under any form of constructive political reasoning. Arguably, it is the unease, represented both by the need to construct foundational arguments in politics and the inherent instability of such a construction, which translates into the very intuition by virtue of which utilitarianism has been criticised for lacking inherent *commitment* to moral principles, fundamental rights and justice. Could the fact that pain and pleasure can explain both a temporal commitment to justice and the transient nature of such commitment be of ethical significance? What emerges is a picture of an ever-transient social tension, an unresolved asymmetry and indeterminacy, between a given state of the conceptualisation (including the interpretation) of issues underlying social conflicts, and the justification of centralised coercion. The purpose of this chapter is to examine generally this socially dynamic oscillation between the need for determinacy and the inevitability of the re-emergence of indeterminacy. I would like at least to begin to unravel how the dynamic utilitarian understanding of constitutionalism may relate to a field of enquiry broader than constitutionalism, namely critical ethical foundations for political theory.

What are the implications of such a socially dynamic understanding of constitutional limits? Let me reiterate the problem. Constitutionalism under the auspices of utility seems both to defend the necessity (i.e. good utilitarian reasons) of maintaining a constitutional arrangement and, at the same time, to predict that such a constitutional arrangement will somehow fall short in the face of social and political conflicts. A utilitarian conception of constitutionalism connotes two levels of reflection, namely one which constructs, interprets and makes coherent, and another, arguably more general, whose interpretation disproves, forces radical renegotiation and even political secession.

There are three underlying core ideas, or implications, to be drawn from the dynamic import of constitutionalism as understood in the first part of this book.

The first is linguistic and concerns the way in which utilitarian terms such as pain, pleasure, desire and happiness, should be understood. For the utilitarian, the basic human condition is that of feeling and interpreting pain and pleasure. Moral sentiments are created, developed and revised as a result of communication between people who feel and interpret pain and pleasure. Any calculus and generalisation that might be made out of it is based on this communicative process. Any social situation in which a given state is conceived as conducive to happiness (or more elementary and less interpretatively, to pleasure) can become painful to a person, and in turn to a group of people, who may try to influence and change a given social state of affairs. The capacity for feeling pain and pleasure shows something essential in the human condition, something which can function within, but also beyond, any ideological framework. With pertinence to the human condition, pains, pleasures, motives and desires which mould, and are being moulded by other motives and desires, precede ideology. Thus understood, motives and desires also constitute the force which allows people through communication to transcend ideologies which to a large, but not exclusive, extent pre-empt their existing motives and desires.

It seems, therefore, that it is always the destiny of politics to fail, in the understanding, let alone the accommodating, of the social complexity which is entailed by the capacity of human beings to feel pain and pleasure. An acknowledgement of the double role of pain and pleasure, the double role that stirs social and political struggles, opens the possibility of asking how utilitarian terms can explain what opens a person's mind to new communicative possibilities which lead to a radical transformation of the justificatory basis of political community, and possibly to the secession and formation of a new one. A linguistic turn of this kind would clearly be an intellectual move "beyond" Bentham. Yet, it is the reconstruction of Bentham's thought which points out the need to make it.

The inconclusivness argued for in this book which was so central to Bentham's legal and political thought, hints at a tension, not articulated by Bentham, which exists in the very characterisation of utilitarianism's commitment to enlightenment, and *a fortiori*, to the period referred to as "The Enlightenment". I do not want my argument to be understood as constituting yet another tack of post-modern, or what is sometimes referred to as post-metaphysical, thought. Arguably, the utilitarian would refuse to admit the plausibility of a historical move from modernity to post-modernity. Both the need to construct justifications for ethical and political decisions in a rational and coherent way, and the inconclusivness such a construction generates, constitute a *part and parcel* of the dilemma that exists in human beings because of the pain and pleasure that they are capable of experiencing. It is not as if one moves from determinacy and objectivity into indeterminacy and subjectivity, giving up the real human need to construct a coherent justificatory basis for ethics and politics. It is not as if, by abandoning the coherence associated with modernity, one can simply emphasise only the indeterminate part of the picture. Arguably, for real people, both the need to cohere about what the rationale for ethical and political togetherness ought to be, and the suffering—the pain—which emanates as a result of sustaining a stable and coherent ethical and political framework, constitute a real and generally insoluble dilemma. It is the potential of the reconstruction of Bentham's constitutionalism to unravel the insight that utilitarianism can provide to account for the reason real people can and will experience this kind of human dilemma. One can know this dilemma, sympathise with it, but cannot undo it by emphasising either determinacy or indeterminacy to be the only right perspective. Nor does utilitarianism resort to advocating the promotion of some kind of vague "middle". The dilemma arises precisely because people need to construct and for some time act on, some coherence. There is no point in ducking either side of that dilemma.

So, the second implication of the understanding of constitutional limits in this book mirrors the dynamism which ought to characterise an authentic description of the relationship between ethics and politics. The conception of enlightenment that utility adopts and the intuitive appeal of such a conception, has to engage with the ethical indeterminacy and even incompatibility of human political societies, which are culturally differentiated and historically contingent. In very general terms, my argument in this chapter is that the inconclusiveness and indeterminacy in ethical reflections have themselves a residual, intuitive impact. It is a result of such a residual intuition that indeterminacy does carry ethical and with it, constitutional, weight. The pursuit of happiness, and the remoulding of political communities has to account for the *pain* which is involved in not accounting for this residual intuition. Utility can relate to an intuition which is sensitive to different forms of ethical experiences. Some pain will be averted by the creation of a given framework of moral reasoning and decision. However, some pain will result from a rigid and dogmatic identification with this very framework. Utility recognises the ethical weight of the various particular, actual experiences of real human beings within different associations, but also the possibility of communicating many other possibilities. In other words, the truth of residual and inconclusive, but nevertheless operative, ethical intuition, is a space which is constantly at conflict not only with the outcome, but also with the very existence of the constructivist method of political argument. This is the case despite the fact that such a constructive argument is the basis for generating future motives, desires and expectations. Ethics can develop critically within an overarching ethical perspective. In the course of time, however, ethics outgrows ethics-in-politics, and pain and pleasures characterise the human condition which strives for such an outgrowing. If ethics outgrows politics it also has the potential of shaping political perspectives, or more accurately, it shapes the ethical perspective from which politics acts and reasons. A comprehensive self-description of the task of utilitarian theory embraces an ethical aporetic experience which is fuelled by real social conflicts, translating them into political struggles. Utilitarianism, understood properly, takes an experiential route to such ethical inconclusivness (though by no means the *only* route to it). This broad point implies that a socially dynamic utilitarian understanding of constitutionalism argued for in the first part of this book implies a dynamic understanding of the relationship between a critical ethical reflection, both by individuals and communities and a political construction of an umbrella which coheres about, and justifies, coercion for a given period of time.

The third implication of the socially dynamic understanding of constitutional limits concerns *harm*. Looking for the constructive side of utility, the main theme of this book is that utility always functions to generate some conception of harm from the perspective of which existing social relations are critically interpreted and justified in politics. A conception of harm reflects *both* a given prioritization of values *and* the enforcement of this particular priority through interpretation and action. During the period in which a conception of harm predominates, there is a perspective which preconditions interpretation. A given conception of harm forms that space within which human beings debate, communicate and generate social norms which are mirrored in the rationale of their political systems. During the reign of a dominant conception of harm, its force, and the distribution of rights and obligation that it generates *seems* to "trump" utilitarian calculation. A conception of harm generates a moral threshold which makes apparently neutral utilitarian calculation self-contradictory (a theory which, because being apparently neutral, must give equal weight and hence open-mindedness to non-neutral moral and political theories) and at any rate, dangerously insufficient for being committed to a just result.[3] Having said that, there exists a tension, perhaps even a *telling* contradiction, in utility as far as harm is concerned. The dynamic understanding of constitutionalism advocated in this book means that utility, communication and exchange of sentiments of pains and pleasures, keeps reopening a schism between the harm which is averted by a political system and the harm of suppressing the authenticity of people's and groups' voices by the coercive political system under which they live.

The purpose of this chapter is to develop these three points, namely the different aspect in which pain and pleasure operate, the dynamic relationship between ethics and politics and the dual understanding of harm. It may be that the dynamic nature of the connection between constitutionalism, ethics and politics, harm, and pain and pleasure of real people, forms the basis for the timeless intuition all utilitarians share but never fully articulate—an intuition to which the elements constructed in Bentham's work open a small window. As has just been mentioned, the field of enquiry which concerns ethics, politics and utilitarianism is very broad and potentially complex, so we cannot hope to achieve more than the opening up of its potential on this occasion. Nevertheless, it is remarkable that so many leading scholars have been swayed by the technical nature of utilitarianism's felicific calculus and condemned it as crude, reductionist, and above all, as insensitive to differences between persons.[4] I hope this

[3] See R. Dworkin, "Rights as Trumps", in J. Waldron (ed.), *Theories of Rights* (Oxford, 1984), pp. 153–67.

[4] See, e.g., Rawls, *A Theory of Justice*, pp. 22–7, and M. Walzer, *Interpretation and Social Criticism* (Cambridge, Mass., 1987), pp. 7–8.

chapter will show that the exact opposite might be the case. I hope to show that utility might be plausibly defended as a theory that provides the deepest basis for social criticism which is based on the diversity between persons and groups. Being open both to different existing ethical experiences, and to the dynamic formation of alternative types of ethical experiences, utility is the enemy of ethical and moral dogma. For utility, the complexity and dynamism of social forms mirror the complexity of the way in which the entities of pain and pleasure are critically involved in self-realisation.

A more plausible criticism of my account of utility would be on the lines advanced by Rawls, namely that the public use of utility is too complex to function as a simple standard with which public reason can work.[5] To reiterate, it is nothing short of remarkable that utilitarianism is strikingly absent from theories about the interdependence between enlightenment and counter-enlightenment; theories about the connection of the self and community and theories of self-realisation.[6] The "enlightenment" utilitarianism advocates, it will be argued, has more in common with communitarians like Walzer, agonistic liberals and moral pluralists like Berlin, advocates of communicative rationality and inter-subjectivity like Habermas, and critical theorists of society like Roberto Unger who describes his programme as "super-liberalism",[7] than with any contemporary, egalitarian, liberal account.

The argument in this chapter contains four parts. The first discusses the dynamism that characterises the relationship between personal, critical, ethical reflection and the rationale for politics. The second and third explore two perspectives, each embodying a tension, from which the relationship between ethics and politics can be viewed. One perspective is the negative liberty/positive freedom perspective. The other perspective is the intuition/identity/identification perspective. The fourth discusses how these tensions relate to the liberal/communitarian debate.

The relationship between ethics and politics

The connection between ethics and politics has been discussed, as a foundational puzzle for liberal equality, by Dworkin in his Tanner Lecture.[8] Dworkin develops what he refers to as a "strategy for continuity" between ethics and politics. I shall discuss his argument in more detail below, but for now I would like to restate the general puzzle as developed by him. Dworkin's main line of argument is that morality shapes personal, critical, ethical reflections which in turn shape one's conception of justice. There is a connection between the extent to

[5] J. Rawls, *Political Liberalism* (New York, 1993), pp. 13, 162, 260–1.

[6] A distinct exception is T.L.S. Sprigge, *The Rational Foundations of Ethics* (London, 1988), esp. chapters 7, 8.

[7] R. Unger, *The Critical Legal Studies Movement* (Cambridger, Mass., 1986), pp. 40–2.

[8] R. Dworkin, "Foundations of Liberal Equality", in G. Peterson (ed.), *The Tanner Lectures on Human Values* (Salt Lake City, 1990), pp. 1–119.

which the community is just, and the degree of well-being of each member of that community. In order to achieve some critical gain in well-being, namely gain that one *ought* to achieve, one needs both to participate in, and to evaluate continuously the rationale for the structure and reasoning of political institutions. In so participating, one would realise, refine and reflect upon, conceptions of justice from a viewpoint of personal ethics. Dworkin thus establishes a *functional* connection between ethics, justice and politics. If my political rationale and my participation in political life give effect to a given conception of justice in my ethical life, my well-being is thereby enhanced in a way in which it ought morally to be enhanced. In short, the just man in a just polity is an ethically satisfied man, in the sense that whatever he is or has in leading his life is truly critically his.[9] This means that his role in life, his possessions are what they should be.

Dworkin's concern to connect ethics to politics is a serious one, one that lies at the foundation of political philosophy. However, the onus that it puts upon the shoulders of political theorists is huge. So huge is the burden of showing a connection between ethics and politics, that one constantly runs the risk of overseeing the complexity it entails. This is because what is involved in answering the question "what is the justification for this and that?" must relate to the question of "what is involved in an evaluative ethical question?" or "how is an evaluative judgement possible?" If the first question does not take the latter two seriously on board, it runs the risk that its outcome will be divorced from what is going on in a social group. Theories which connect what an evaluative agent does in relation to his justification of a political scheme must involve some *functional* elements in them. Whatever causes a person to see that action A is wrong because of reason R1, rather than R, may later lead to the replacement of R1 with R2. To put it more generally, in order to make a foundational claim, one has to engage with the problem of how critical, practical reason functions. This is fundamental to "doing" things with this or that substantive theoretical claim.

On a general and preliminary level, bearing in mind the complexity of social interaction, intuitive doubts arise when the functional connection between ethics and politics is channelled in an all-too-dominant direction. The process of materialisation, moral materialisation, of certain principles of justice which connect ethics to politics need not follow one formula. As I will argue below, most contemporary, liberal, political philosophers, with the possible exception of Joseph Raz, are vulnerable to the charge of channelling and aligning ethical diversity according to one model. Principles of justice under modern liberalism, it is argued by these theorists, constitute first principles which are held to have critical but also long-standing and stable intuitive appeal to every participant in a political system which upholds and enforces them. In their different ways, contemporary liberals claim to have succeeded in connecting ethics to politics. Under a liberal polity, people can come to unify their critical, ethical reflection

[9] R. Dworkin, "Liberal Community", in S. Avineri and A. de-Shalit (eds), *Communitarianism and Individualism* (Oxford, 1992), pp. 205–23, at 220–3.

upon their well-being with moral intuition along the lines of liberal principles of justice.

My argument takes on board the burden of connecting ethics to politics. However, I shall claim, if the connection between ethics and politics is to be maintained, the cultural and historical dynamism that characterises ethical self-reflection applies to any ethical rationale of politics. Foundational claims for political theory are socially dynamic and change in the endlessly inventive human process of self-realisation and experience. In other words, any critical story that some ideology may tell us about the connection between ethics and politics is transient. Existing incommensurability and incompatibility in critical ethical reflection, as well as the human construction of new possibilites for ethical reflection, must be mirrored in politics which must also function and evolve on that level. The tension between unity and difference will continue indefinitely under a single rationale for politics. An attempt to sustain a given rationale for politics for too long may well lead to the undesirable schism legal sociologists refer to as the distinction between law in books and law in action. More specifically, an attempt to find a single formula which unites ethics and politics may lead to cynicism towards politics. Any dogmatic identification between ethics and politics would lead to a rift between politics and social reality. The connection between ethics and politics must be sought in the nature of the dynamic process of renewal. My argument from a utilitarian perspective claims that people can live flourishing lives under many formulas which unite their ethical and political lives. The critical, moral common denominator which would characterise different societies would be something much more minimal than the form of one ideology or another.

Any materialisation of a conception of harm within different reflective ethical worlds runs the risk of being blind to different instrumental and symbolic relationships that it does not have the language to engage with, or comprehend. Any social contract, either instrumental or symbolic, runs this risk. The risk exists *vis à vis* other social groups but also *vis à vis* the conflicts that arise within the social group in which a given conception of harm predominates. The social contract can hold only if the contract is to change constantly.[10] It is the inability to listen to a different voice which comes from people's evaluations of their deepest authentic selves which provides the perfect scenario for politics to become reactionary. A critical theory of practical reason, I shall claim, will always operate to destabilise the point where politics becomes either too distant from the social world and people's ethical evaluations, or too strongly embedded within a certain perspective, so that it attempts to intrude into the real social life of the people under its jurisdiction. There is a fine line to chart here between how subjectivity realises itself within certain objective social and political forms, yet may be capable of overcoming the perspective imposed by those forms. The self and the scheme within which this self sees its interest in relation

[10] See Bentham's remark in *Comment*, above chapter 4, p. 106. note 19.

to others can have many forms in terms of the harm that the collectivity accepts and tries to avert.

The reason why the connection between ethics and politics is a difficult problem to resolve under one set of principles, is that the cultural variety existing in the world is pervasive. The fact that these cultures are diverse is significant in relation to how members of those societies, with an ethical reflective attitude, will approach the understanding of goods, including ranking and distributions of those goods expected to be delivered by politics.[11] This is not to say that they cannot improve upon a given social state of affairs, but that the improvement will be the result of some ordering of goods and values that their culture entails. So can the rationale of politics be made so general and less committed once it faces social and hence ethical diversity, or should politics reflect diversity through a continuous fundamental reconstruction of its main principles, or even by breaking up? What is the price to pay for *containing* the diversity of ethical reflection among people belonging to diverse commonalties? Is there a point at which the answer to the question "what should I have?" would be too remote for it to penetrate people's consciousness? How general can one's authentic ethical being really be?

I find it appropriate to approach a detailed discussion of the dynamism which characterises the relationship between ethics and politics from two well-canvassed perspectives, namely that of negative liberty/positive freedom, and that of intuition/identity/identification. As utilitarianism starts from pain and pleasure my choice of liberty, intuition, identity and identification may seem odd. However, I shall argue that the discussion of these terms is not in lieu of utilitarianism. The discussion of constitutionalism on these terms presumes utilitarianism, although in significantly different ways. That is how I would read the main motto of the introductory quote for this chapter and Wittgenstein's quote at the beginning of the book: we *are and always have been*, ethically and thus politically, beings who feel and interpret pain and pleasure. This capacity of feeling pains and pleasures is our *nature*—we *are* through and in them— and thus they "govern us in all we do, in all we say, in all we think".[12] They are ontological, rather than epistemological qualities. I shall later argue that only the human experience of pain and pleasure can account for the human experience of an aporetic tension that the discussion of liberty, intuition, identity and identification come up with. Indeed, I shall claim that utility does provide a basis for a normative description of the relationship between ethics and politics that a discussion in those terms cannot plausibly provide, and that in so far as attempts have been made by political theorists to provide such a normative description on those terms, their accounts are wanting.

[11] See M. Walzer, *Spheres of Justice: A Defence of Pluralism and Equality* (Oxford, 1983), pp. 3–20 and chapter 13. See also D. Miller, "Complex Equality", in D. Miller and M. Walzer (eds), *Pluralism, Justice and Equality* (Oxford, 1995), pp. 197–225, at 197–204.

[12] *IPML*, p. 1.

Negative liberty/positive freedom

Bentham understood liberty as an absence of coercion. I have argued above in Chapter 5 that his replacement of liberty with ideas of security by a rule and security from a rule can recast the debate about liberty as one about security as far as constitutional limits are concerned.[13] Just to reiterate, an ultimate conception of harm can relate to how extensive the sphere of non-intervention is (security from rule), or to what distributive pattern people are subject to in using a given sphere of action (security by rule). As I have argued in Chapter 5, the quality of the sphere of liberty was determined by a socially dynamic process. The freedom effectuated by this social process, never fully articulated by Bentham, reveals the way in which the debate about liberty can help to unravel a latent realm of freedom that utilitarian theory facilitates. Bentham was always committed to this freedom by being first and foremost utilitarian, but somewhat disappointingly, he never paused to articulate and refine it. In this respect, the discussion which follows refines and extends Bentham's general approach to the relationship between freedom and political theory.

The following discussion of liberty is based on Berlin's famous exposition which distinguishes between negative and positive liberty.[14] Negative liberty is a *sphere* without restraint, constraint or interference by others, summed up in the question "how much am I governed?" The lesser the constraint, the more extensive the sphere of liberty. This sphere of non-intervention has been referred to as a sphere of individual inviolability. Taking an absence of constraint as a characteristic of negative liberty, as such, it is about provision for choice. *Within the sphere* of liberty no one dictates to a person what to be, what to have, or what community to belong to. It follows that, in political terms, arguments about negative liberty relate to the *ambit* of the individual sphere, or conversely to the extent of justified coercion. The debate of negative liberty is a debate about constitutional *limits*.

As an abstract idea, negative liberty as absence of constraint means just a sphere of choice. *Some kind* of constraint gives meaning to this choice. As will be argued shortly, in the abstract, this choice is exercised within a sphere of liberty which critically assesses any system within which choice is more immediately constrained. As such, the generality of level at which negative liberty may be understood need not relate to the plausibility of social and political realisation of any rationale for the constraint upon choice. Discussing the importance of negative liberty need not be coupled with a discussion of a defensible, unified

[13] See pp. 120–1 above. See in this connection, F. Rosen, "Thinking About Liberty", an inaugural lecture, University College London, 1990.

[14] I. Berlin, "Two Concepts of Liberty", in *Four Essays on Liberty* (London, 1969), pp. 118–72, especially pp. 127–34, and ibid., *Introduction*, pp. xxxviii–xl and xliii–l. See also C.J. Galipeau, *Isaiah Berlin's Liberalism* (Oxford, 1994), chapter 4, and J. Gray, *Isaiah Berlin* (London, 1995), pp. 23–37.

political system within which this type of choice can be realised. Anything may be the *object* of choice, for instance, ways of life, choices between states, cultures or communities. The discussion of negative liberty, taken to its limits, as it arguably has been by Berlin, relates to plurality of forms of life and therefore moral pluralism subject to a very minimal common moral constraint.

Arguably, however, some gap may exist between the position of the moral philosopher who strives to articulate, and to defend, the enhancement of negative liberty as a moral goal, and the political philosopher who tries to develop a rationale for a constitution by which political authority should be required and limited. It does not follow from the fact that a more general pattern of choice between forms of life can be articulated, philosophically speaking, that this pattern can be conceivably effectuated through politics. In short, political theory does not capture the *philosophical* implication of negative liberty. Having said that, it can be argued that the whole point of questions involving negative liberty is that they are socially meaningful. These questions can be socially meaningful only in the context of socially realisable politics, namely when there *is* some political, and hence coercive, constraint, however sophisticated, to which people may connect in their evaluations, and to which people may have practical reasons to connect. It is important, therefore, that people can justify and limit political action in a coherent way in order to reach politically some realisation of the value of negative liberty. By "coherent", I mean a system of reasoning which has at its roots some form which amalgamates and ranks some values, and in which the justifications to the outcome of conflicts fit this form. In this respect, if one wants to "do" things with theory, it may be conceived as more meaningful to talk about "political systems" or in short "systems" of negative liberty rather than about negative liberty in the abstract.

Positive freedom, by contrast, is an abstract question of self-determination. Although Berlin admits that positive freedom does not start from a great logical distance from negative liberty, it is nevertheless a logically distinct question about liberty.[15] Self-determination involves questions which relate to the *capacity* of human beings. The reason that it cannot be reduced to negative liberty is that although some "absence of constraint" is also involved here, this absence is considered with regard to the positive capacity for self-realisation, rather than just implying a sphere in which the individual is left alone. In other words, it represents a capacity to reflect upon the adequacy of a given choice or upon a given perspective from which a range of choices is given. The constraint under which it can be said "apart from that, do what you want" reflects a different understanding of liberty from the one involved in the reflection "this existence is adequate for me".

Understood as a capacity, positive liberty can be manifested in many ways. I would like to focus on three. First, it can be understood as an abstract question: who governs me? This question is a critical question, as it points towards the

[15] Berlin, *Four Essays on Liberty*, p. xliii.

capacity to evaluate any political system *qua* a political system in the name of self-government. Thus, the question is: "to what extent can a realisation within a political system further my *self?*" and in turn, "what is the extent to which a political system *x* ought to govern me?" As will be argued shortly, the potential of this question, and the moral burden it generates, is enormous, as it encompasses not only a self which participates within the parameters that a political system allows, but also a self which in the process of unfolding itself, questions the desire to participate in that political system in the first place. In short, this question of positive freedom implies that the self can transcend any belonging to a given political system as a part of its own realisation.

The second broad question of positive freedom concerns self-realisation, and as such it involves the capacity of the self to ask the question: "is what I am/do/have authentic?" "Is it really me?" This question has been discussed by Taylor, and concerns the internal limitations to self-realisation such as irrational fear or delusion. These limitations constitute internal fetters on a person's realising himself, whatever his choices actually are.[16] Provision of choice is hardly sufficient for the requirement of authenticity. The dimension of authenticity relates to the capacity of a person neither merely to choose, nor to reflect upon his choices. Authenticity means that a person should be able to reflect upon his choice authentically and hence, adequately. A person who cannot adequately reflect upon his choices, because he is deluded or suffers irrational fear, is not really a free person. As Taylor puts it, if he chose under false consciousness, his choice would only deepen his unfreedom.[17]

An attempt could be made to argue that the problem of authenticity is one which is important for liberty, but not for politics. It may be claimed that politics provides facilitating conditions for self-realisation, but cannot pretend to deal with internal fetters, the latter being too individually orientated and therefore too complex for an all-too-general political understanding to deal with. However, despite acknowledging the doubts about the relevance of politics to the issue of internal fetters, it will be argued that the existential rift of authenticity, namely "no doubt that I am but is this *really* me?", is very important to politics, as it may cause a person to question the very perspective which is normally accepted without question as the basis for the rationale of a political system. The dimension of authenticity for self-realisation can generate a quest for a new form of life, and with it a social conflict. In this way, authenticity can be relevant for the critical question of the relationship between politics and freedom.

The third issue encapsulated in positive freedom also relates to self-realisation and concerns what Rawls has referred to as "worth of liberty".[18] It concerns the external possibilities of a person to realise his chosen life plans and goals. The concern for self-realisation of chosen plans and goals leads to ques-

[16] C. Taylor, "What's Wrong with Negative Liberty', in A. Ryan (ed.), *The Idea of Freedom* (Oxford, 1979), pp. 175–93.

[17] Ibid., p. 179.

[18] Rawls, *A Theory of Justice*, p. 204.

tions about how people use opportunities or resources in relation to other people, and hence connects the issue of self-realisation to distribution and to some conception of equality. I say *some* conception of equality because conceptions of equality vary.

Self-realisation in this context involves, for example, a distribution of resources and rights so as to enable every person to self-realise. Further, this question relates to the very possibility that a person might *realise* his reflection upon his choice. If a person is not given, say, an opportunity or a resource to realise his potentially revised, self-reflected goal, he would be frustrated, unrealised and hence unfree.[19]

Questions of both negative liberty and positive freedom involve aspects of free will and with it individuality. If one has too limited a choice, or, if one has adequate choice but for all sorts of reasons is unable to reflect adequately upon the chosen options, or unable to realise one's reflection upon them, one is frustrated in that one is denied in advance the possibility of realising one's own interpretation of one's life. Being so frustrated means that one would remain—morally speaking—"potential". Obviously, this is not to say that all people self-reflect all the time. Also it does not suggest that anybody should do so. Finitude of reflection is a characteristic of most human beings.

For a socially meaningful, and *critical,* discussion, questions of positive freedom and negative liberty are meshed within a political system. Both questions of negative and positive liberty require coercion, but also specify the limits to coercion. In designing a rationale for a political system, one must be coherent about what coercion *should* prevent, and by what means coercion should be limited. Now, political actions and limits upon political actions are there to prevent harm. Some shared conception of harm is needed in order to make arguments about the limitation and justification of coercion. Under any political system, one needs a shared conception of harm which people use to refine their critical reasoning about acceptable coercion. If politics is to provide justification and reasoning, its ability to relate the resolutions of conflicts to some general conception of harm must be presumed. It is to such a general conception of harm which the justification in the resolution of more concrete moral disputes would be referred and adapted. In terms of coherence, this conception of harm would make more sense of some political arguments than others. A shared conception of harm, which gives context and meaning to arguments about avoidance of more particular instances of that harm, is the point where law and political theory connect to general questions in moral theory, and around which the realisation of moral goals within a political system can be discussed. This conception of harm must form some boundary to the exercise of coercion. Beyond the specification of harm, no coercion is justified. I call the idea of a sphere of political action, which is limited by a conception of harm, a system of negative

[19] Arguments about equality can also relate to questions of self-determination: see R. Dworkin, *Freedom's Law: The Moral Reading of the American Constitution* (Oxford, 1996), pp. 21–31.

liberty. I refer to negative liberty here because the dominant question is still "how much am I governed?" A conception of harm *limits* coercion. No coercion is permitted if harm is not averted by it. While the introduction of harm fuses the quantity and quality of coercion, it ultimately constitutes a quantitative imperative. Conceptions of harm within a system of negative liberty turn the question of "how much am I governed?" into a *purposive* question which may, to various degrees, include questions concerning positive freedom.

A conception of harm, in short, transforms negative liberty into a *system* of negative liberty. This distinction, for example, is the root distinction between neutrality and liberal neutrality. The former does not include an articulated conception of harm, the latter does. Conceptions of harm are the foundation of political theory, and with it the foundation of constitutions and constitutionalism. So questions of positive freedom can, and have been asked, within the context of a negative liberty debate. A mixture of the two questions does indeed characterise the thesis of modern egalitarian liberals: to what extent coercion (a negative liberty question) should be taken so as to further possibilities of self-determination (a positive freedom question). The modern egalitarian liberals' answer, given by liberals like Rawls and Dworkin, is that of liberal equality. Egalitarian distribution of resources, morally consistent interpretation and enforcement of fundamental rights and freedoms, equality of opportunity, are all, on the one hand, the *only* ultimate sphere in which political coercion is required, in which political coercion should be permitted. In this sense they all constitute questions about the sphere of negative liberty. On the other hand, they are also questions about creating possibilities of self-determination and the duties of government to facilitate and enforce these possibilities. This common theme, generally expressed, of all liberal egalitarians is that basic liberties and egalitarian distribution of resources, expressed in political and economic rights, are to be the basis for resolutions of political disputes. The premise of positive freedom, namely that of self-determination, is realised only if a person is treated as *morally* equal to another and to achieve that purpose, some conception of harm and therefore a scheme of politics is to be reasoned about and designed accordingly. Self-determination and absence of constraint (including the coercive enforcement of this absence of constraint) are interwoven in liberal equality.

Positive freedom is an abstract question which people may, and in many senses will, ask in self-realising in *any* system of negative liberty. Indeed, Berlin cautioned that a potentially anarchical or totalitarian political community can be justified upon some abstract idea of self-determination and freedom.[20] He cautions against overrating positive freedom, and warns against the potentially disastrous consequences, in terms of collective oppression, in the name of freedom, as in the case of Rousseau's social contract, or in terms of the other

[20] Berlin, *Four Essays on Liberty*, Introduction, pp. xlv–xlvii, and "Two Concepts of Liberty", pp. 132–3.

extreme anarchy, namely an a priori rejection of all types of centralised coercive constraints.

However, putting those extreme cases aside, no perspective of harm and therefore of a system of negative liberty (which, as I have argued, incorporates positive and negative dimensions) exhausts the capacity entailed in positive freedom. The potential of positive freedom can relate to self-determination and self-realisation under *different* systems of negative liberty. It can also relate to the possibility of emancipation of the self that exists within a given system of negative liberty from the conception of harm it imposes on it. Thus, questions of positive freedom are wider than any realisation of positive freedom within a system of negative liberty.

The point is that human possibilities of self-realisation-within-a-given-conception-of-harm are limited. Certain possibilities of positive freedom, generated by individual and cultural authenticity, may be suppressed. The call of authenticity may mean that individuals conceive of possibilities which cannot be allowed for under a system of negative liberty. These possibilities face a real threat of being subjected to the perspective imposed by *any* particular system of negative liberty which is founded upon a self-justifying system of harm. Thus, questions about positive freedom can transcend any dominant, materialised perspective of harm. This transcendence can, but need not, have the disastrous results that Berlin warns us against. The transcendence of self-realisation involves many shades of grey, not only black and white. Positive freedom may warrant self-determination and realisation in a way which is not transparent to the reasoning and language in which certain goods are ordered, prioritised and realised in a certain structure of values, which itself gives rise to an abstract perspective materialised in a given conception of harm, and therefore in a system of negative liberty. Any system of negative liberty with a real social "bite", even a system which is based on liberal–equality, will be a system that *limits* growth in certain ways. The point of discontinuity in historical evolution, the point which makes this historical evolution fascinating and unpredictable, arises because "harm" can be understood as something which is articulated within a particular ordering of a large number of values.[21] Human moral experience, and with it the moral contexts for human self-realisation, is itself marked by a plurality of possibilities. Questions of positive freedom are sensitive to the existence of such plurality, and require speculation about the possibility that this plurality may overcome any critical channelling of experience towards adaptation to a fixed moral perspective with its resultant conception of harm. Positive freedom can transcend and disrupt any pattern that the very existence of a moral, and with it a political, dialogue presumes. At one level, realising one's own free will

[21] See in this context I. Berlin, "Herder and the Enlightenment" in *Vico and Herder: Two Studies in the History of Ideas* (London, 1976), pp. 145–216, and "Historical Inevitability", in *Four Essays on Liberty*, pp. 41–117.

means being open to a world one does not yet know and cannot yet fully feel to be right.[22]

The imposition of a perspective upon which a political system of negative liberty depends must, by its very nature, take sides in order to settle human conflicts, and limit possibilities of self-determination according to some conception of harm. It may be silent about a specific realisation of human life within a group, but it cannot be silent about how to deal with a conflict when it arises. Now, what happens if differentiation in a social group leads to social conflicts which embody fundamental moral conflicts? Reasoning, and with it justified coercion, within a system of negative liberty will either pretend to show that these conflicts are not as deep as they seem, that is to contain them, or will attempt to resolve the conflicts under one conception of harm. By its very nature therefore, any system of negative liberty will be ineffective or reactionary towards the dynamics that social reality produces.

The critical question from a positive liberty perspective connects to the issue of capacity to realise choice, and hence to the most abstract question of the nature of restraint of human possibilities *as a question of choice*. The problem of free will unites the most abstract question of positive liberty as a capacity for self-determination and the idea of negative liberty as a philosophical question of choice under a constraint. From the point of view of freedom, the extent to which politics can remain responsive to social change is the most fundamental issue. Political theorists who advocate systems of negative liberty do not hear a lot of what the debate about positive and negative liberty has to say. For most modern, egalitarian, political theorists, positive liberty does not signify difference and incompatible ways of being, but is mere noise. The moral intuition about difference that they possess is a justifiable one and this prompts their willingness to accommodate radically different human possibilities. However, in attempting to realise that intuition within a political system of negative liberty they interpret it all too narrowly. Thus, to their willingness to accommodate difference under a conception of harm, they call "neutrality between different conceptions of the good". This formula, which signifies different ways of life or different life-plans, different ways of interest formation and pursuit, is deemed

[22] This "feeling" relates to the residual moral intuition about some possible, yet unrecognisable, injustice, which is discussed in the next section. Under an all-encompassing view of justice many unjust acts would be conceived as "misfortune". Further still, even if one was receptive towards a novel form of injustice one could still be passively unjust: see J. Shklar, *The Faces of Injustice* (New Haven, 1990), pp. 8–9, 36–8, 48–50, 54–9. The lack of an optimal point of closing the gap between, on the one hand, the level of *ideally* accepting principles of justice and, on the other hand, an intuitive *personal* reflection on the degree of a departure from the ideal, is discussed by S. Cavell in his comments on Rawls's *A Theory of Justice*, in *Conditions Handsome and Unhandsome: The Constitution of Emersonian Perfectionism* (Chicago, 1990). See in this context, D. Owen , "Cultural Diversity and The Conversation of Justice: Reading Cavell on Political Voice and The Expression of Consent", *Political Theory* 27 (1999) 579–96. Cavell's argument is that Rawls assumes all too simply an intuitive continuum from the first level (the "Original Position"), to the second, materially/culturally-oriented, level. Rawls's account is thus intuitively static, while in fact the relation between these levels, and hence the whole idea of individual actual consent to be an equally-spoken-for member of a just polity, is dynamic, revisable and transformative.

sufficient to satisfy the human potential for difference and self-realisation. By using the formula of "neutral between different conceptions of the good" egalitarian liberals create the illusion of the appropriate distancing of politics from real-life realisations. However, in parallel, they silence the implications of the "just so long as" that their conception of harm entails to that variety of individual lives and common pursuits.

Any system of negative liberty which transforms a general intuition, and with it insights in moral philosophy, into a political programme does not hear the diversity of authenticated selves which are embodied in diversity of values, ordering of values, symbolic relationships of subordination and superiority, or, in short, the give and take of which individual and communal life can consist. This diversity exists, and arguably will constantly re-emerge, within a political community and *between* political communities. The implication of this last point is that positive freedom as an abstract question of self-determination, a human capacity for transcending any system of negative liberty, is in fact connected to the philosophical understanding of negative liberty. The positive and negative dimensions of liberty function together on a philosophical level, as well as on a political level. These two levels represent different levels of well-being. On the philosophical level, positive freedom connotes the all-important human capacity of self-realisation which may arise within different moral perspectives, as well as the human capacity to reject moral perspectives. A grasp of this capacity connects an understanding of negative liberty to moral intuition. But *this* intuition must mean that humans can transcend any *political system* of negative liberty.

It would be helpful to express this idea in terms of harm. The understanding of positive freedom, as being an abstract question of self-determination, means that negative liberty, as an absence of constraint upon human possibilities, is itself harmed by any political realisation of it as a system of negative liberty. Positive freedom is about the human potential to discover, see, and imagine other people as being "within" other ethical experiences. Positive freedom relates to the human capacity to realise fully but also to transcend any political conception of harm, however sophisticatedly expressed. Having once transcended a socially oriented conception of harm, a person may both see and empathise with other incompatible ethical experiences, and realise himself in a newly constructed ethical experience. As from this moment, the nature of a socially orientated constraint upon possibilities within a political community becomes itself the subject of criticism and is itself recognised as harmful. Positive freedom and negative liberty are different only to the extent that a full realisation of the former leads to the full philosophical implications conveyed by the latter. Positive freedom is too narrowly understood within a *system* of negative liberty, but is fully accounted for in relation to a proper philosophical understanding of negative liberty.

This in turn connects to the functioning of the idea of harm within what constitutes an aporia of moral reasoning. The aporia exists between a politically realised, as well as more concretely interpreted, conception of harm, and the harm that exists by accepting that very conception. Putting aside arguments about some very minimal, and surely controversial, universal harm, any system of negative liberty fails fully to realise negative liberty. Absence of constraint, qualified within a social and political constraint, is felt as intuitively wrong as against a more abstract thinking about "absence of constraint". The aporia manifests itself in the inability to articulate and hence, more concretely to interpret, the philosophical *constraint* upon choice. The aporia manifests itself in the fact that questions about harm can be asked on two different, unbridgeable levels. One level says: I harm/do not harm him because I do *x*. The other level says: I harm him because harm-as-*x* distorts what he may become. No system of negative liberty, and hence of constitutional limits, can realise that second level of negative liberty. It does not follow that this more abstract thinking does not involve a constraint at all, but only that the constraint is not politically articulable and realisable.[23]

Terms such as "liberty", "equality", "neutrality", "individuality", "autonomy" and "democracy", can all be framed into a general moral premise without dressing them with full cultural and historical meaning. Once this general, admittedly diluted, meaning, is materialised by a system of negative liberty, the aporia becomes operative between the general understanding and the materialised "conceptions" of those terms. Only according to the latter, however, some operable constraint can be articulated. Of course, one can only think in terms of experiencing the aporia not in terms of resolving it. However, in experiencing the aporia, one would have to change the aspect from which the general understanding of terms is materialised into conceptions and indeed into a conception of harm. The result of such a change is difficult to predict. It may lead to a different conception of harm which replaces the old one—a newly renegotiated settlement. Alternatively, experiencing the aporia may awaken the conscious reflective acknowledgement of the impossibility to accommodate difference under the conception of harm which underlines the system of negative liberty.

Experiencing the aporia, and the possibility of action upon such an experience, is perhaps the greatest challenge facing political theory. It is a huge challenge because it would mean that "interpretation" can no longer have the constructivist pretence of achieving some kind of coherence, or integrity. The aporia means that the attainment of coherence implies that at the point where some new argumentative complexity is resolved under some coherent reasoning, another complexity is not being accounted for, perhaps not even heard and

[23] Which is arguably why libertarianism, as a philosophical doctrine, is not politically realisable. Nozick's individual libertarianism already employs a political conception of harm, namely the non-violation of the philosophical understanding of the side-constraint upon people's inalienable rights. Once politically realised, the harm encapsulated in the "side" constraint would arguably be destroyed by a "patterned" distribution of recources and rights under a conception of harm. *Some* utility would be inevitable: see *Anarchy, State and Utopia*, pp. 28–35, 155–7. Cf. Raz, *The Morality of Freedom*, pp. 145–8.

recognised. A voice that attempts to bring to the fore such a complexity would be at the risk of an active suppression, or worse, a suppression from "innocent" deafness created by a prison of perspective. The avoidance of such a suppression would be the case where political argument would claim, needless to say implausibly, coherence which is based on "fitness" to the general, not-yet fully contextualised understanding of terms. Such a claim would merely be an equivalent to the statement that indeterminacy exists. The implication of the aporia is that any representational device aimed at distancing the rationale for the foundations of politics from conceptions of good (e.g. a "veil of ignorance")—a device that elevates discussion about harm to a second-order and partially disengaged level—must be morally wanting. The act of distancing politics from the so-called "politics of common good" would still fall short at the very point when the aporia can be felt to bite morally. A theory which embodies distancing rhetorical devices would in fact be in a bind, and would use these devices to disguise both this bind and the double-language this bind necessitates. For example, in order to purify itself, the theory would speculate about a state of "as-if" ignorance, a state which the theory paradoxically counts on heavily as *non-existent*. In such a theory, the materialised and contextualised use of such terms as "intuitively-right 'conceptions' ", could be in operation only up to a point where their basic appeal and justification *would have to* rely on some unexplained fitness to their general acontextualised sense. At this point, the materialised conceptions would be called again for help. The necessity for such double-language of using the terms would mean that the relationship between philosophy and politics is, and will always be, a big non sequitur: concrete "conceptions" of terms do not follow from the general understanding of those terms. However, this non sequitur does not prevent the general understanding of terms from being invoked whenever the materialised conceptions are in need of re-assessment and re-interpretation. Thus, the dynamism between ethics and politics, dynamism which allows experiencing the aporia, is the most authentic philosophical expression of constitutional limits.

In sum, the notion of negative liberty recognises a dichotomy between the abstract understanding of it, which implies variety of human possibilities and its political realisation under a conception of harm, which curtails those possibilities. Evaluations under the co-ordinates of a conception of harm stand in an aporetic relation to evaluations made about the more abstract conception of harm which relates to human possibilities. Questions of positive freedom do not only function within a conception of harm, but constitute a capacity to destabilise the politically or socially realisable conception of harm. Ultimately, and hence beyond any transient political realisation, self-determination pertains to different human possibilities.

I shall argue below that some political theorists attempt to divorce philosophical questions arising out of social-in-relation-to-self realisation from the actual social conflicts which may be implicated by confronting these questions. This could only be an attempt, however, for had they taken seriously the separation between fundamental insights in moral philosophy and the realisation of this insight *all across the board*, they would face the very aporia of reason which is hidden in any transformation of moral philosophy into a self-justifying political programme. In short, political theorists, by "doing" things with theory through realisation of a political programme, reduce critical morality into a one that functions under a socially recognised conception of harm. This is so because they presume a broad consensus about a conception of harm which would predetermine any moral conviction aimed at resolving a given and more concrete social conflict. The tension between the *philosophically* desirable and the *politically* realisable is prone to the danger of dogmatism and reactionism by reason of not facing the aporia of practical reason. Berlin's background sensitivity to that aporia, I believe, is the ground for an authentic but unresolvable tension, metaphorised by Gray as agonistic,[24] in his liberalism, which is very different from modern liberal egalitarianism.

Positive freedom and the potential it signifies for the moral intuition of negative liberty is, in truth, the most extensive understanding of freedom possible with its bad and good sides. Freedom means that the moment we construct a political system we improve certain aspects of human existence with one hand, silencing others with the other. Positive freedom and negative liberty listen to the wonder of the human condition and self-realisation. As such, though positive freedom may be misused to supress that wonder, it can be more sophisticatedly suppressed by any *system* of negative liberty.

Differences between groups can be based on different conceptions of harm. Further, people will always form and dissolve collectivities. Formations and dissolutions of conceptions of harm result from some endless dynamism of self-realisation and have to be confronted. If such dynamism is confronted it should make political theory *critical* rather than a containing, or a reactionary, controlling device. Any system of negative liberty, a range of choice realised from, and limited by, the perspective of a conception of harm will, sooner or later, fail.[25] The quest for positive freedom means that conflicts which our selves create, when seeking for sociability will tend to demolish any dominance of moral perspective. Any system of negative liberty will be temporary. Reflections made in the process of self-determination and in turn, the change of systems of negative liberty within the wider sphere of negative liberty, are not reflections which merely re-affirm what one already deeply knows, but which create new possibilities. Despite positive freedom being prone to the charge of being a recipe for anarchism, totalitarianism and relativism, the price for sanctifying and avoiding those dangers is an equally damaging reduction of human potential.

The above discussion points to the dynamic connection between ethics and politics. The aporia characterises such dynamism. The capacity of leading a life

[24] J. Gray, *Isaiah Berlin*.

[25] See my reference to J. Shklar, *The Faces of Injustice*, p. 260, note 22 above.

in realising an ethical *experience* can outgrow any system of negative liberty. Still, the question is to what extent such a debate about liberty needs to presume something else in order to explain the experience involved in driving persons and groups to transcend a system of negative liberty. Self-realisation must, arguably, relate to the capacity of striving towards pleasure (and indeed happiness). However, it must also relate to the pain which may drive people to reconsider their common ethical considerations and to reshape any system of negative liberty which suppresses those considerations. Authentic politics must be able to experience, and to respond to, the ongoing and dynamic social-in-relation-to-self differentiation rather than to the challenge of containment. Neither such an experience nor the response to it is easy to envisage or articulate. This is so because it entails that politics must find the ability, as well as the will, to outgrow the perspective—the conception of harm—from which it operates. Sometimes such a response can be found in a sophisticated generalisation of a second-order conception of harm. But by the very supposition of the aporia any conception of harm, however generalised, may well come to a dead end. It is not my concern here to articulate how political response to ethical dynamism might be done institutionally, but only to point out the necessity for such a response. It does not involve the setting up of a so-called "post-modern" constitutional theory and constitution. Perhaps all one can do is to wait. I merely stress the need for politics to respond to that dynamic space embodied in the recognition of the most general, philosophical possibility of human choice and self-determination.

Intuition, identity and identification[26]

Various methodological attempts have been made to connect ethics to politics on the basis of moral intuition. It is vital to discuss intuition here because the nature of attaining some equilibrium in moral reflection is essential to an account which connects personal ethical reflection to politics. One has to reflect upon the "rightness" or "wrongness" of one's actions or possessions. There must be some intuition to provide the light in which one can reflect upon whatever one does or has. A closer look at intuition, identity and identification forms another route for discussing the dynamic way in which politics can relate to ethical reflections. However, a discussion of intuition, identity and identification approaches the aporia mentioned in the last section from an angle which is arguably closer to real human motivations. Intuition, identity and identification, being qualities the understanding of which clarify *how* real people think and reflect, constitute suitable terms with which to explain how utilitarian notions, pain and pleasure that real people feel, their real motives and desires,

[26] I thank Ariella Atzmon for introducing me to the tension between identity and identification.

come to explain the dynamic relationship between ethics and politics. Further, a discussion of intuition, identity and identification shows that although the aporia can be *understood* in terms of liberty, something else is needed in order to explain why the aporia *matters* for real people. The need to discuss intuition here arises because, together with the identity and identification, it shows utilitarian notions to be vital both to the adoption, and to the transcendence, of ethical perspectives.

Some kind of intuition lies at the heart of all moral theories. In the absence of intuition of rightness or wrongness there would be no need for a change from any social state of affairs to another. Intuitionism, as an ethical doctrine, argues that ethical statements can have real ethical significance only if that significance is *independent* of our feeling of pleasure. My purpose is not to defend that ethical doctrine. However, I share Moore's point that one cannot reduce an "ought" statement into what people "are", for that would be to commit the naturalistic fallacy. This fallacy consists of an attempt to define a simple entity by equating its meaning with one of its manifestations. The definition of yellowness cannot be equated with the appearance of the colour yellow. Similarly, in ethics, there has to be something simple and indefinable which constitutes the ethical goodness of an ethical term, something which cannot be equated with a way that experience manifests itself. The "addition", that makes certain things "right" or "wrong" in themselves, must have an intuitive appeal *independent* from any feeling of pleasure that one might have.[27]

However, even if one concedes the indispensable place of intuition about ethical goodness, the methodology with which one approaches moral intuition is crucial. The kind of questions that a discussion of intuition might wrestle with are, for example, what makes intuition possible? Further, what makes *critical* intuition possible? What makes one person's critical intuition better than another's? In other words, what is the point of reference by which to evaluate so as to obtain critical intuitions? What is the kind of "progress" or "improvement" that one goes through in examining intuitions critically? Is it a universal type of progress or is it a process of self-fulfilment and realisation which connects to what a person is? If it is a universal process, how can the universality be characterised? To what extent does what is "me" precede any channel of progression and critical reflection upon my intuitions?

What is included in finding ethical foundations on the basis of intuition? To reiterate, the task of connecting ethics to politics must account for critical ethical reflections such that, once adopted, people can, through their politics, live a better life, critically speaking. So we are in search of two levels of explanation.

[27] Cf. B. Williams, *Ethics and the Limits of Philosophy* (London, 1985), pp. 125–8, especially p. 127:

> "Once you get beyond the matter of practical reasoning and its 'all-in' conclusions, the deepest questions that have been discussed under the title of the naturalistic fallacy or the *is–ought* distinction could not possibly be solved, or even revealed, by an analysis of language."

The first level is what is the orientation in which one's intuitions are situated? What constitutes the moral "isness" of ourselves?[28] In Chapter 6, it was argued that under the auspices of the principle of utility, an individual's calculations will be embedded in general moral obligations that operate upon his motivations and can be referred to as a community or culture. This means that the limits of the first level (which constitutes the ambit of what a moral judgement which pertains to our consciousness—our most inner "first" principles) are a result of the crystallisation of general, community oriented, moral ideals. Arguably, ethical meanings have developed and will be developed in the future on those lines.[29]

Notice two features of this first level. First, it allows for criticism and self-reflection. Some generally accepted co-ordinates, some general pointers—themselves materialised, general conceptions of some values—situate our reflections and practical reasoning. These conceptions will delimit the horizon of our arguments. Further, the concrete meaning of the conceptions can be refined through interpretation over time. Yet, some key points, some basic instrumental and symbolic ordering of certain abstract goods and values, as Taylor called them hyper-goods,[30] as well as some general conception of harm which they entail, will precondition the progress and even reflection on the concretised meaning of this conception of harm.

In this context, Rawls's principles of justice in *A Theory of Justice*, as based on primary goods and a thin theory of the good, are already based on a materialised conception of the general terms which signify those primary goods. So materialised, Rawls's principles of justice presume a conception of harm. The purpose of Rawls's methodology was to elucidate the conception of harm that we all deeply recognise as intuitively true, regardless of refinement of that conception through interpretation. This elucidation would be the basis for all our reflections. For the utilitarian, this conception of harm would channel our

[28] This is a question which C. Taylor confronted; see *Sources of the Self: The Making of Modern Identity* (Cambridge, 1989), pp. 3–52.

[29] This question could be rephrased in asking "what is the basis for our innermost *ethical* confidence?": See B. Williams, *Ethics and the Limits of Philosophy*, pp. 170–3. Williams proposes to ground objectivity in ethical life not on arguments from a single overarching morality, but on an ethically confident ongoing communication which gives rise to critical use and, if needed, a replacement of what he calls "thick", or "action-guiding", concepts. "Thick" concepts, such as "brutality" or "gratitude", differ from "thin" concepts, associated with abstract morality (such as, presumably, "equality" and "individuality") which are not action-guiding: ibid. chapter 8. In this ongoing activity, ethical *knowledge*, as being the import of the fact and ways of using thick concepts, can be re-evaluated and if needed, be set aside. The problem of grounding objectivity in ethics on a general moral theory is replaced with the problem of grounding the *ethical content* of the confidence which is required for reflection. The open-endedness changes its rhetoric and locus. The point which I try to pursue here is that the aporia implies that the unfulfilled ethical intuition, which characterises a dynamic connection between ethics and politics, involves conflicts with the very process of "thickening" any meaning of concepts to the point when these concepts *could* be acted, as well as coherently reasoned, upon (including concepts like "equality" and "individuality"). My question is where could one go in order to master the "ethical confidence" needed to challenge a conception of harm which culturally colonises one's intuition?

[30] Taylor, *Sources of The Self*, pp. 62–8.

feeling of "lack" or "guilt" by which we examine our calculation of pain and pleasure. This "channelling", being intuitively acceptable, would supply the necessary "flesh" to the "bones", namely to the general meaning of general terms such as "liberty" and "equality". The language of *A Theory of Justice* is a double-language which relies on pre-exisiting intuition to justify what is apparently a universal truth about rational human beings.[31] The conception of harm presumed by Rawls, which specifies a universal rationale for politics, will be to some extent metaphysical, but of course it will arise from "our" shared metaphysics.[32] Some basic priority and ordering of goods, and therefore of harm, functions through language and symbols in our mind and limits our deepest sentiments and interests-formation and arguments in reflecting upon those interests. Our intuitions about the "rightness" of discriminating one pleasure from another, or as Bentham sometimes refers to it, one "lot" of pleasure from another, the way we articulate what others feel, our intuitive sympathy towards them, will form our consciousness on the basis of that "metaphysics". Community, whether ethnic or political, and the harm it embodies, constitutes more than a certain role, or a certain way of life. Such a community signifies a certain abstract form which constitutes the co-ordinates for our own moral being.

The distinction between the "right" and the "good" is possible precisely because what is metaphorised as "right" is based on the acceptance of some bundle of goods which constitutes our most inner conception of harm. This acceptance can be manifested in many ways. The most general manifestation of it is the acceptance of goods and ordering of values which then form the hidden assumptions that colonise and dominate reflection in a moral discourse. Such an assumption can relate to the value of individuality as manifested through the value of choice. This assumption directs towards a particular connection between liberty and equality. Such assumptions, and the justificatory connection they establish between abstract terms, are then elaborated in the discourse's

[31] See my reference to Cavell, pp. 260, note 22 above and p. 278 note 46 below.

[32] The idea of "some" metaphysics short of a totally disembodied self is presented by A. Gutmann: "By requiring us to abstract from our particular but not our shared interests, the original position with its 'veil of ignorance' and 'thin theory of the good' avoids reliance on both existing preferences and a priori considerations in reasoning about justice" and " The characterisation of liberalism [by Rawls] as nonmetaphyiscal can be misleading, however. To be justified as the *political* ideals most consistent with the 'public culture of a democratic society', Rawlsian principles therefore have to express some (though not all) of our deepest self-understanding. Rawls must admit this much metaphysics—that we are not radically situated selves.": "Communitarian Critics of Liberalism", in S. Avineri and A. de-Shalit (eds), *Communitarianism and Individualism* (Oxford, 1992), pp. 120–36, at 124–7. I shall argue below that it is precisely this "partial", culturally contingent, metaphysics which triggered the aporia of moral reasoning in Rawls's own mind. This trigger and its intuitive implication were the reasons which pushed Rawls to modify his account of justice in *A Theory of Justice*, without abandoning Kantian constructivism.

Note also Bentham's remark: "The business of metaphysics is neither more nor less than this, to examine what ideas we have belonging to the terms we use, and whether they are clear or not. . . . Every science . . . has its metaphysics: for every science has its leading terms, terms that are in constant use in every discourse that is held upon the subject of it. . . ." UC lxix., 124.

more elaborate "conceptual analysis" and pretended open-minded "interpretation". In fact, however, the discourse becomes a socially-ridden metaphysics which is dressed in universal properties. By erecting a discourse which colonises the intuition, the extent to which potential social complexity is reduced by the inner logic of the relationship between terms is determined. Further, the potential non sequitur of the deliberations, namely the extent to which a truth-value of the use of a term leads to the truth-value of use of another, will be determined by this socially-ridden metaphysics. For example, the claim "it does not follow from the fact that cultural membership is important that liberal–equality is wanting" will be made possible by the defenders of the conceptual account of modern liberalism.

The second feature of this first level of intuition is that it connotes fundamental differences between moral intuitions. Acknowledging the predominance of this level suggests that there is no global morality. Moralities in this sense are worlds of meaning, orders of values and conceptions of harm. Rawls's project, to extract people's deepest *common* interest, does not accept the existence of different *moral* worlds in which people can realise themselves in different ways. An acknowledgement of difference shows how people's self-interest and calculations and their interaction with fundamental conceptions of harm is indeterminate *between those conceptions*. The acknowledgement of such indeterminacy, which utility adopts, is about the different ways in which human beings realised moral experience of balancing pains and pleasure in relation to some social collective consciousness. The individual arguments which participate, by way of intuition-based evaluation, are to be seen as situated within this socially-ridden consciousness. Humanity has created different gives and takes, which can self-reflect, but nevertheless still do so within the basic co-ordinated people constructs, as a result of them feeling pain and pleasure in themselves and others.

So much for moral intuition on this level, and I hope it is clear that the naturalistic fallacy is not committed here as the "ought" is immanent in the social "is". People's dissatisfaction with the goodness of their immediate calculation would lead them to calculate differently on the basis of reflecting upon the basic common, social good. Pleasure and dissatisfaction with immediate pleasure create the sense of "ought" through ascending to a more general level of argument. Intuition at this level is embodied in a conception of harm, which is first and foremost communal. Justification, and any equilibrium in one's ethical intuitions, and reflections based on this justification, has to admit a certain level which it accepts without justification. Intuition at this level, namely the circular "fit"—orientated critical reflection upon, and reaffirmation through, some abstract conception of harm, means that our moral reasoning consists of something we already know. At this level intuitions are *not* really critical. The desire they generate, the most abstract motives, are already, in a basic sense, enframed. Our critical progression is merely conventional. From a utilitarian perspective, pain and pleasure experienced by people would be situated in existing norms which characterise existing social reflection.

Now, the question of intuition may well enter at another level of reflection with which pain and pleasure interact. A reinterpretation of that second level of intuition must reflect the aporia of practical reason, this time from what a person, and in turn, a community can feel. Though possible, such re-interpretation is difficult to undertake and would most certainly be generally regarded, at least initially, as irresponsible and unreasonable and hence, immoral. The reason for such disapproval would be that if the foundation for an intuition is challenged, abandoned and reconstructed, the new reconstruction has to be according to a standard which this first level of intuition cannot supply. If there is an intuitive "beyond", what does it consist of, what does it relate to? In the context of discussing ethics and politics, the question now relates to the point in which ethical, critical intuitions outgrow given social co-ordinates to which political arguments relate. The basic question now is about how intuition can be disinterested and intuitive at the same time, and how pain and pleasure that real people feel and communicate upon can explain both the nature and the cause of such an intuition. Surely, the first level of intuition creates a gap between intuition and disinterestedness because the moral co-ordinates make one "interested" at some level. The "is" and the "ought" are now considered at another level. Can intuition relate to something on this level or is there literally "nothing" to relate to? If some interpretative closure, or comprehensiveness, exists in the sense of the first level of intuition, with the acknowledgement that any bridge between them would distort their deep difference, can one move out of moral worlds or, alternatively, gradually create a new form of human moral realisation? Surely, this must be very difficult for two reasons: first, because this second-level intuition implies that presumably one is in a position of "seeing" the possibilities open to one, acknowledging that there *is* something different. But on the basis of what should one "see" that difference? Secondly, what moral intuition would determine whether to stay aloof from this difference, gradually being open to become part of such a different moral world, or even form a new, different moral commonality? Is this second-level intuition conscious? Mere recognition of other moral perspectives can enlighten one's perspectives but not really solve the intuition issue. What could intuition consist of at this second level?

A theory of practical reason should encompass both levels of intuition. This is the only way a moral theory can be critical and universal. How should one view the conflict between ethics and politics in this context? Is it not true that, from a universal perspective, any conflict between ethics and politics on the first level of intuition would imply a limited view of what the connection between ethics and politics *should* be about?[33]

[33] Arguably, in the second level of intuition we try to find the basis of reasoning from within some kind of "void". In *Anarchical Fallacies* Bentham had this to say about natural, imprescriptible rights: "look to the letter, you find nonsense—look beyond the letter, you find nothing" Bowring, ii. 497. If there is "nothing" beyond some kind of prescription how could utility actually reason from it? Being constructive here, I think that Bentham would point to the potential and actual damage that can be done by the impossibility of dogmatic substantive content of an intuition to reflect upon itself. I believe this was the root of his objection to imprescriptible natural rights. Utility rejects the view

The question of intuition on this second, critical and disinterested level distinguishes between two ways of realising one's identity. The first is what may be called *identity-in-identification* or in short, *identification.* This sort of identity means that one interprets one's moral self within a communal web that conceptualises a certain abstract conception of harm. It is clear that people are different although they may all fit to a communal conception of harm. The "filter" through which you make order of the world will ultimately be communal. People maintain their difference within this communal conception of harm. Individual moral identities, in this sense, would be like the different shapes in a kaleidoscope that are nevertheless determined by the shape and angle of the mirrors. This connection to a communal conception of harm is called fraternity.[34]

However, orienting and self-interpreting one's identity-in-identification does not exhaust one's identity. There may be a point when one's own complexities will push one to move between communities, to accept different language and different symbolism. Alternatively, one can gradually form a different identification when following one's identity. This would be very difficult because one would have to lose and renounce oneself in order to find one's tru*er* self. It is more than changing what one does or what one "is" by way of one role play or another. Individual identity, as opposed to identity-in-identification, is the striving for an inner pleasure that itself can cause a certain pain in one's life-in-identification. Following one's identity survives any identity-in-identification.

One's discontent with identification will be reflected in some "openness" in communication with other people. It will open one's imagination in order to find others to build a language which could form a new commonality or to renegotiate radically the old one. One would gradually stop seeing the possibilities for one's own self in terms of the common parameters. One would no longer limit one's differentiation only through what is permitted under the common conception of harm.

Different identifications can account for different cultures in the world in which we find ourselves. The rich, different cultures in which subjects map themselves is something to admire and to be astonished by. It is a reduction even to describe this difference and evaluate it in binary terms of "ours is good" and "theirs is repressive". In this respect, there are many forms in which continuity between ethics and

that there is an *inherently* true ordering of values embodied in universal first principles. Any distribution of rights must be culturally prescriptible and as such, defeasible. As was argued in chapter 5, rights are certain moral thresholds which can be realised on different levels. The intuitive appeal of certain interpretations of rights that are represented as "justified" are interpreted and "exist", indeed critically, on the first level of intuition. Such an interpretation would be justified within a structure of "fit", to the prescribed ideals which stem from the cultural conception of harm. So why cannot there "be" a fully materialised, however abstract, rights stemming from the second level of intuition? Because it will be to invoke the language of rights only in relation to a general understanding of terms (see above, pp. 262–3) and the inconclusive conception of harm that stems from it.

[34] Both ideas of "reflective equilibrium" and the quality of "fitness" in interpretation presume a common conception of harm. The inherent limitation of these ideas comes to the fore when different conceptions of harm clash. Which "community" does one try to fit one's judgement to? See J. Habermas, *Between Facts and Norms*, pp. 221–9.

politics can exist and critically persist. Nevertheless, we can speculate from the existence of difference in conceptions of harm. We can say that the differences between people will prevent one conception of harm from becoming universal, and subjecting humanity to a single instrumental and symbolic conception of harm. Identity can lead to the change of dogma and to further differentiation, in terms of creating new commonalties and new conceptions of harm.

However, existing differences between different conceptions of harm are accounted for, the feeling that there is no one best conception of harm, does not solve the problem of intuition. There comes a point, which I shall argue utility recognises, where an intuition exists but there are no more first principles to relate to, because every first principle will be communally "situated". Affirming communitarian views, the metaphysics which we are concerned with here does mean that the self is at this point, to use Sandel's term, disembodied or unencumbered.[35] It is not constituted by its end. So what would be the basis for intuitions? One could simply defer, as a mark of respect, to a different world of meaning one knows exists but cannot fully understand. But can one take sides? Can one abandon one's "situation" and move to another? Can one form a new commonality?

At this stage, when intuitive commitment compels in a disinterested way, any "moral talk" becomes problematic. One is left with one's own very basic, minimal but deep sense of lack. Being "naked" in this sense connects to the most authentic intuitions that one has. At this point communitarianism is insufficient. One can see oneself, after going through these big changes in one's life, and say "whatever I did was the real authentic me". There is a gap between what a person actually is and a person at each stage of his life knowing about what he is. If pain and pleasure mean something here it is something other than pain and pleasure which are communally situated. If pain and pleasure create a certain openness to communication and new type of inter-subjectivity, it will be based, and start from, what one has always been but never realised. Intuitions have no basis to relate to except what one's deepest self-interest and pleasure were and will be—the interest, perhaps never to be fulfilled, of self-realisation. The way pains and pleasures operate here will be according to what a person authentically is. As a result, one can, because of a view one has of what one *really* is ("really is" connotes "ought to be"), suffer pain because of one's unrealised existence. This pain can lead to the fundamental renunciation of one's realisation within a commonality and can either lead one to move to another or create another one for oneself. This perhaps is the basic philosophical issue of autonomy. It is autonomy in the pursuit of identity, not autonomy within the paradigms of a given community or culture.[36]

[35] M. Sandel, *Liberalism and the Limits of Justice* 2nd edition (Cambridge, 1998), pp. 168–72. See also his "The Procedural Republic and the Unencumbered Self", in S. Avineri and A. de-Shalit (eds), *Communitarianism and Individualism*, pp. 12–28, at 18–20.

[36] It should not be understood that I imply some form of libertarianism here. Libertarians would try to implement a philosophical primacy of liberty into politics and thus try to "enact" the aporia

The significance of all this is that it is in one's own true self generally that one can feel pleasure and pain *within and between* different social worlds which are based on different orderings of values and conceptions of harm. It is our self-realisation that operates to demolish any intuitive dogmatism of the first level of intuition. Arguably, our seeking moral commonality is a reflection of our own desire for self-realisation. Our desire is the start of ideology, of our practical reasons, of our truly authentic conception of harm. If ethics is to be connected to politics, to borrow Dworkin's way of expression, critical self-realisation must shape critical ethical reflections. Self-realisation and differentiation mean that one's well-being, one's striving for self-realisation, can be pursued in different, ethically incompatible ways. Self-realisation and hence human psychology, as connected to the satisfaction of one's pleasures, is the key to moral psychology, which is in turn the key to understanding the dynamics of the relationship between a self and a collectivity through a conception of harm.

Self and community

Communitarians are convincing as far as the first level of intuition is concerned. They are right in so far as they claim that any conception of harm, however partially uncommitted the fashion in which it is articulated, rests in fact upon some shared ends as far as human possibilities are concerned. Perfectionism has many manifestations. The neutrality which is achieved under an egalitarian-oriented conception of harm, namely *liberal* neutrality, is, in truth, one manifestation of perfectionism with regard to that conception. It will rule out ways of life which do not conform to that conception of harm, and will try to contain difference as long as different groups refrain from challenging it. The point is not about whether the right is prior to the good or vice versa, but that the whole distinction between the right and the good is incoherent. The term "right" is a metaphor for the dominant conception of good. The whole distinction between teleological and deontological theories relates to a conventional understanding of two different kinds of accounts of the achievement of disinterestedness, namely the Kantian versus the experiential.[37] These accounts may not really be as different as they seem. They have very little to do with a distinction between right and good. Rawls exploits our predetermined cultural assumptions and belonging, to differentiate an intuitive sentiment which can be metaphorised under the name "right", but it is important to see that he does that. Communitarians rightly deny that there is a realisable political principle by

into politics, shrinking its meaning and moral force. Utility and libertarianism would coincide when the aporia bites, namely when any common constraint in the form of a conception of harm became reactionary.

[37] See A. Halpin, *Rights and Law: Analysis and Theory*, (Oxford, 1997) pp. 216–26. See also R.M. Hare, "Could Kant have been a Utilitarian", *Utilitas* 5 (1993) 1–16 and T.L.S. Sprigge, *The Rational Foundations of Ethics*, chapter 10.

which people are bound together and which does not prioritise some good at the expense of other goods. There is no distinction between a thick and thin "good": good is thick all the way through.

Attempts by liberals, such as Dworkin, to distinguish a metaphysical community which forms a collective consciousness that imposes some conception of good upon members of the community, and a formal community wherein people feel fraternal towards one another through institutions which enforce a certain conception of harm, is arguably untenable. [38] Both are substantive communities espousing different and particular manifestations of perfectionism.

The honesty of communitarianism lies in the connection it establishes between identity-in-identification, which is communal, and the "metaphysical" identity and self. As I have argued in Chapter 1, there is *nothing* in-between which can be *realised* politically. It is the gap between philosophy and politics that communitarians have acknowledged. There is no interim stage between communitarian politics and metaphysics. One can generalise communal moral thresholds according to which some communal form of life will be assessed, but if this moral threshold is to be realised politically, it has to be communitarian. Critical theory is not something that can be *realised* politically even on an interpretative basis. Critical ethical experience and re-interpretation which correspond to the second level of intuition analysed above, are *possible* but their realisation and interpretation in politics will always eventually fall short, causing injustice in falling short, precisely because such realisation is communally-imposed unity and coherence about a conception of harm.

I do not want to be interpreted as arguing that because there is indeterminacy in ethical reflections we can only be ironical about coherent politics. In other words, I would not like my argument to be read as pulling the carpet from under any constructive interpretation in political theory. Arguing that would be to militate against the utilitarian understanding of constitutional limits, as argued for in the first part of the book. To emphasise ethical indeterminacy as the only side of constitutionalism would be inauthentic, as far as experiences of real communicating human beings are concerned, and will duck the very tension that utilitarian conception of constitutional limits reveals to be so pervasive and inescapable. From the point of view of pain and pleasure, there are good utilitarian reasons, such as security, stability, or more generally, the feeling of being in control, over the ambit of justification used in politics to construct a coherent political system. This is the force that pushes politics to be a rational container of social conflicts. However, while politics is communitarian, ethics need not be. There are good utilitarian reasons, based on the pain and pleasure people feel, for reaching the social state that ethics outgrows ethics-in-politics and so pushes political argument to be effective only to the extent that it renegotiates its conception of harm or splits up. I do not think this latter type of critical utilitarian reason implies that politics is more than communitarian. Whether a renegotia-

[38] Dworkin, "Liberal Community", pp. 212–6.

tion or splitting up is involved, communitarianism is the "already"—the point where politics closes its eyes only to open them in it again. A free government is *always* a residual potential within, but which lies further. All it implies is that one could imagine an ethical experience that public deliberation, but not a politically interpretation-for-decision, can accommodate.

If one understands communitarianism as a common conception of harm, then much of the distinction between liberalism and communitarianism falls away. The social fact of human potential, of diverse and incompatible self-realisation within an ethical community and between ethical communities, is of paramount importance. Such a diversity means that the horizons to which a person's own conception of self-respect might reach and be felt ought not be fully colonised by any imposition by politics of a conception of harm. The *kind* of frustration that humans might suffer is very varied and complex and leads to dynamism which cannot be contained within this or that articulation of a conception of harm. However, once moral intuition is conceived from an anthropological perspective, namely the empathic ability to feel others' pleasures and pains, one can begin to reconsider the methodology by which the whole relationship between ethics and politics leads to generalisations. Bearing this ethically significant diversity of self-realisation-within-a-conception-harm in mind, self-respect at its deepest level means that one can realise that an adherence to possibilities under one conception of harm is itself wrong. Such wrongness cannot be addressed by any ideology, including egalitarian liberals' interpretation of liberal ideology. I shall criticise in the next chapter recent contemporary accounts, some of which claim to have established an overarching "middle" between on the one hand, the act of "distancing" in order to allow for the diversity of human possibilities, and on the other hand, the act of "taking sides" according to some conception of harm. There is no qualitative distinction between so-called perfectionism and the so-called comprehensive moral doctrine. There are only different conceptions of harm built on the dominance of different goods.

Ethics and politics—a short summary

It has been argued that the dynamism which characterises the connection between ethics and politics is reflected by a residuary, unfulfilled state both on the axis of positive freedom/negative liberty and the one of intuition, identity and identification. Both discussions give rise to an aporia which characterises the relationship between ethics and politics. However, it is the axis of intuition, identity and identification which connects to utilitarian notions of pains, pleasures, motives and desires which gets us somewhat closer to an explanation of *experiencing* that aporia both by individuals and by groups. Identity and hence some kind of intuition, remains unfulfilled and this residuary unfulfilled state will operate to seek difference in communication. Identity will always build up differentiated individual and collective forms of life. This means that the connection between ethics and politics cannot be unconditionally comprehensive and perfectionist. The critical standard must allow for plurality of comprehensive conceptions of harm and allow for critical change to existing different communities on the basis of a newly-formed conception of harm. Communitarian politics explains the first part, namely the existence of incompatible moral differences between communities. Communitarianism does not elaborate on the critical standard by which communities will always change. There must be the potential to destabilise and question any comprehensive politics, but not by means of one comprehensive moral ideal which will capture a true, universal ethical reflection. Ethical pluralism, which situates individuals' consciousness under legitimate politics (communitarianism) and ethical dynamism, which breaks up politics through individuals communicating with one another and emancipating their identity (inter-subjectivity) is another process that should be allowed to happen. Communitarians connect ethics to politics but, despite their ability to accommodate social criticisms, their vision is still socially static. Communitarians cannot resolve social conflicts, and by suppressing an emancipating communication between individuals, communitarianism ends up becoming reactionary. People who communicate in the public sphere will create some life for themselves which the political culture may obstruct if it becomes dogmatic. Alternatively, they may become cynical towards politics and just ignore it, that is to find other routes to address their differences. As far as a utilitarian, socially dynamic account of constitutionalism is concerned, pains and pleasures interpreted within existing socially generated conceptions of harm will always regenerate the very process which generates and re-opens the gap between ethics and politics. The pain and pleasure which function under the dominance of a given conception of harm would make interpretation in politics progressive and teleological. The pain and therefore, the striving for pleasure which destabilises such a progression involve some mutation, some suspension of rationality, if politics is to catch-up with ethical change. From this destabilising aporetic perspective, stability is a utopia, an illusion.

Any critical ethical theory is arguably metaphysical, but the question is what type of metaphysics one adopts. Is it a metaphysics that arrives at difference either through ideas, or through the striving towards the pleasure of authentic self-realisation in relation to others? We cannot hope to decide the question on this occasion. Perhaps the two types of metaphysics are not so different. The important point is, however, that if this *kind* of response does not come *from* politics it will come *despite* it, sooner or later. Political rationales which are inauthentic will ultimately fail because people will not be able to be free under them. The truly *foundational* account must recognise the dynamic connection between ethics and politics, and must constitute an account of critical theory, namely a theory which emancipates the people who use it from dogmatic, coercive, and hence, unfree world-views.[39] Indeterminacy in personal ethics must emancipate politics and lead

[39] For a useful summary of the characteristics of Critical Theory, see R. Geuss, *The Idea of Critical Theory, Habermas and the Frankfurt School* (Cambridge, 1981), chapter 3.

to indeterminacy in politics of which this ethics constitutes the foundation.[40] Utility and in turn, utilitarian conception of constitutionalism, can explain the need for substantive ethical foundations and in *this sense* it *is* foundational. However, utility is uncommitted to the foundations of this or that ethical substantive view. Utility is always hard-nosed about the same thing, namely that pain and pleasure that real communicating people feel is the only evaluative basis both for ethics and, *as a result*, politics. This evaluative principle must display some openness towards disinterestedness that comes from a person's deep, unconstituted, intuitive identity.

A brief point should be made here. The dynamism which characterises the relationship between ethics and politics means that there is always the possibility of renegotiating the basic terms of the political settlement, instead of the breaking up towards the formation of a new one.[41] However, the justification for the re-negotiated settlement would have to be based either on a more refined conception of harm, based on a *better* understanding of the real conflict, or under a more general conception of harm, based on recognition of incompatibility and hence the critical acknowledgement of the desirability for containment. But, as Bentham recognised in *Fragment*, it is not inconceivable for transparent communication to expose incompatibility on a level which does not warrant the continuity of "togetherness" and therefore one which yields secession. Working through the aporia comes a long way towards, and may even achieve, understanding, through a suspension of the operation of a one-sided, embedded, materialised "court of reasons" upon the intuitions. Recognition of the different forms of life that humanity can produce may well have to involve the letting go of that craving towards the attempt of constructing a new settlement, a new collective umbrella of inauthentic, yet strangely tranquillising, concepts. We cannot expect just to "resolve" matters within a newly shaped container, nor can we pretend that a proper, deliberative procedure can somehow overcome the aporia that any materialised substantive perspective leads us into. At most, such a procedure can bring us to the verge of experiencing such an aporia.[42] Even if we do not resolve matters by way of a new containment, we are likely to fall short of expressing the aspirations of all people. This is clear enough. The possibility of politics to experience the aporia and respond to ethical change is possible on the one hand, but is a no-win situation on the other. The choice does not include an end-construction. Constitutions may continue to pretend to contain successfully contradictions under some opaque, unified conception of harm, a conception which pays lip-service to difference through the rhetoric of "overlapping" and "multiculturalism". Such will arguably be the distributive result of the logic of "continuous" renegotiation. Alternatively, constitutions may resort to the "poly-logic" of *modus vivendi*, or indeed secession,

[40] See D. Luban, "The Self: Metaphysical not Political", *Legal Theory* 1 (1995) 401–37, at 428–32 and 435–7.

[41] See my discussion of Tully's argument, pp. 303–6 below.

[42] See J. Waldron, *Law and Disagreement* (Oxford, 1999).

as a result of the recognition of indigenisation and difference. As I argued, there is much room for distinguishing between a successful resolution of the aporia which is impossible, and experiencing the aporia. The latter means that political settlement always falls short by our own conception of collectivity. The evolutionary, and somewhat tragic, nature of politics[43] is tantamount to the choice between containing more and more contradictions, or separating and creating other contradictions. Furthermore, an attempt to perpetuate the ever-unsatisfactory political construct will be manifested in the fact that even when people try to go through the aporia, ridding themselves of ideological dogma as hard as they can, there will always be influential people who would resolve political conflicts, suppressing the implications of genuine social conflicts in the process.[44] The aporia's moral lesson is the *knowledge*, indeed the ethically confident knowledge, that it is impossible to construct an ideal for the amelioration of the balance between freedom and authority. Rousseau's dictum looms large: "Man is born free; and everywhere he is in chains", he said in *The Social Contract*. Rousseau's social contract, whereby one is free only by giving all one has to the collective general will, can be read as the symbolic expression of the need to confront the aporia. The necessity for Rousseau's contract is arrived at in recognition of the inevitable moral deficiency of any form of politics. Arguably, Rousseau's intellectual move was a desperate manoeuvre to produce a *philosophical* contract in which every subjectivity would find political expression in a collective general will which constituted the "sum of differences". Being "forced to be free" serves here as an ironic mirror for the pretended, yet enslaving, resolution of conflicts through politics to contain successfully human difference.[45] The combination of an intuitive appeal and practical oddities in Rousseau's contract stems from this contract being an expression of the very impossibility by virtue of which all systems of negative liberty are oppressive.[46]

[43] I thank D. Owen for the use of this term.

[44] I thank A. Halpin for raising this point.

[45] J.J. Rousseau, "The Social Contract", in *The Social Contract and Discourses* (London, 1973), pp. 203–4. Cf. R. Rorty, *Contingency, Irony and Solidarity* (Cambridge, 1989), chapters 3 and 4 in which liberal ethics are achieved through irony. Only through constant irony can public arguments be trustworthy. The trustworthiness is achieved by privatising the "public" in a way which challenges the misguided totalising, metaphysically dogmatic, perspective under which an ideologically-ridden conception of the "public" operates.

[46] See S. Cavell, *The Claim of Reason: Wittgenstein, Skepticism, Morality and Tragedy* (Oxford, 1979), pp. 25–8.

8

Contemporary Attempts to Bridge the Gap between Ethics and Politics

In this chapter I shall briefly survey four recent liberal accounts in respect of the gap that exists between ethics and politics. In general, modern liberals, in their different ways, are torn between their desire to connect ethics to politics on a stable, long-term basis, and their need to distance themselves from conventional morality and ethics, so that politics can respond and enforce something meaningful, morally independent of the fact of its belonging to this or that society, in this or that stage of its historical development. All liberal accounts are driven by a philosophical intuition about liberty and difference between people and ways of life, much like Berlin's account, but they also take the further step, adopting various methodologies, of trying to design a polity which will give effect to this philosophical intuition. Arguably, as far as this extra step is concerned, they all fail. Their methodologies are different, but the root of the failure is the same, namely the corruption of a background moral intuition through its institutionalisation in politics. The moral foundation which this politics ends up promoting is the very one that the background moral intuition rejects.

Arguably, the common problem that modern liberals face is that they all attempt to contain philosophical insight about difference, incommensurability and incompatibility between forms of life within a single, *coherent* political system. They attempt to reconcile an irreconcilable aporia, the very aporia of unlocking reason through unreason, and the result is an inauthentic political theory that not only fails to implement itself fully within a single social group, but also fails to do so between social groups. All these accounts, in different ways, fail to account for the dynamism that characterises the relationship between ethics and politics. Their failure lessens the force of the aporia which, somewhat ironically, is not only highlighted by a utilitarian theory through the realisation of pain and pleasure in intuition, identity and identification, but also by a general discussion of liberty.

Rawls's Political Liberalism

> "Combined with an index of primary goods the principles of justice detach reasons of justice not only from the ebb and flow of fluctuating wants and desires but even from sentiments and commitments."
>
> Rawls, *Political Liberalism*, p. 190.

Rawls's attempts to address the gap that exists between ethics and politics is an attempt to differentiate a *political* conception of justice. This political conception of justice differentiates a realm of communication, deliberation and reflection which functions alongside, but overlaps with, comprehensive philosophical doctrines (including comprehensive ethical doctrines). As a part of the basic structure of a democratic society, the political conception of justice acknowledges that public reason can yield an overlapping consensus between different, yet reasonable, comprehensive views in a scheme of fair co-operation between free and equal people. In order to justify this political conception of justice, Rawls invokes the same methodology as in *A Theory of Justice*. The Original Position is used this time as a device of representation under which rational and reasonable people can construct principles of justice, knowing only the factual possibility of a society which is characterised by a fact of pluralism of reasonable, comprehensive doctrines.[1]

Rawls thus creates a different order of reasons—a political one, in which people conceive a conception of harm in the light of which, in the name of free society, comprehensive doctrines should be interpreted and if necessary, limited, by coercion. In order to achieve and maintain stability in a pluralistic society, a political conception of justice is not completely distinct from the comprehensive doctrines that it tries to control.[2] People who adopt incommensurable comprehensive doctrines ought to be able to reason in a way which accepts a conception of harm which subjects their comprehensive doctrines to the requirement of "reasonableness" which, if the case requires, would be enforced by coercive means. People would be able to relate to this political conception "from the inside". This conception of harm, in the name of reasonableness and reciprocity, marks the boundary of an overlapping consensus. Overlapping consensus means much more than mere *modus vivendi* which relates to a doctrine of mutual advantage. The political-based rationality can be constructed so as to limit rationality under any comprehensive doctrine.

Rawls's account contributes, directly and indirectly, to the divorce of ethics from politics in three respects. The first, indirect respect, is not peculiar to Rawls but is characteristic of all Kantians, and related to the distinction that exists within the "personal". Rawls's account of the moral psychology, which explains the formation of moral ideas in the mind, is deliberately unrelated to empirical human psychology. Moral reasoning is constructed and interpreted on a personal level as an order of reasons which should be understood as distinct from human psychology.[3] Secondly, Rawls distinguishes between ethical reflection based on comprehensive doctrines and ethical reflection based on a political

[1] For a critical discussion of Rawls's methodology, see B. Barry, *Theories of Justice* (Berkeley, 1989), pp. 257–82 and chapter 9.

[2] *Political Liberalism,* p. 134.

[3] Ibid., pp. 81–8.

order of reasons.[4] He explicitly divorces political and ethical reasoning as related to the exercise of full autonomy by citizens of a well-ordered society:

> "[full autonomy] is realised in public life by affirming the political principles of justice and enjoying the protections of the basic rights and liberties . . . This full autonomy of political life must be distinguished from the ethical values of autonomy and individuality, which may apply to the whole of life, both social and individual. . ."[5]

Thirdly, Rawls claims a distinct capacity for moral reasoning which flows from a concept of the "reasonable". This idea of the "reasonable", as distinct from the "rational", constitutes an independent, fundamental type of moral sensibility which rational people as such may or may not share.[6] The "reasonable" signifies some practical reciprocity between people, and even between their comprehensive doctrines, in order to attain stability. This moral sensibility can operate to "round" one's own moral convictions *qua* moral conventions. Reasonableness constitutes a higher type of moral sensibility which attaches itself to people's comprehensive doctrines. Reasonableness as reciprocity of self-imposed limitation upon comprehensive doctrines, themselves reasonable, stems from a desire to build "a social world in which [people], as free and equal, can cooperate with others on terms all can accept".[7]

[4] See ibid., pp. 137–8:

> ". . .questions about constitutional essentials and matters of basic justice are so far as possible to be settled by appeal to political values alone. . . . it is vital to the idea of political liberalism that we may with perfect consistency hold that it would be unreasonable to use political power to enforce our own comprehensive view, which we must, of course, affirm as reasonable or true."

On p. 139, Rawls attempts to locate the possibility of reconciling comprehensive and political reasoning by appealing to values such as

> "the basic framework of social life—the very groundwork of our existence . . . values of equal political and civil liberty; fair equality of opportunity; the values of economic reciprocity; the social basis of mutual respect between citizens. Other great political values—the values of public reason—are expressed in the guidelines for public inquiry and in the steps taken to make such inquiry free and public, as well as informed and reasonable."

See also ibid., pp. 150, 153, 155. Finally, Rawls attempts to discharge the burden of reconciling a free-standing political reasoning, for which he no doubt gives a conceptual account, with people's own comprehensive doctrines—p. 140.

[5] Ibid., pp. 77–8.

[6] Ibid., pp. 48–54, esp. p. 51.

[7] Ibid., p. 50. When Rawls discusses the overlapping consensus his foundation for the substance of the overlap relates to his idea of the "reasonable". Unreasonableness constitutes the conception of harm by which, according to the free-standing political conception of justice, comprehensive doctrines are to be limited. The idea of reasonableness connects *all* Rawls's ideas: it is the fact of *reasonable* pluralism which gives rise to an independent conception of political justice based on overlapping consensus between *reasonable*, comprehensive doctrines, each limited by what is judged to be *reasonable* by public reason. Public reason operates according to what is required by the basic structure of a democratic society which includes people who are equal and free. Our unity-in-reasoning depends on the understanding of the "reasonable" according to which a conception of harm is deduced. Can one be reasonable beyond what one believes to be comprehensively good? An obscure passage sums up the length to which Rawls wishes to take his doctrine of reasonableness: "To apply the principles of toleration to philosophy itself is to leave to citizens themselves to settle the questions of religion, philosophy, and morals in accordance with views they freely affirm." *Political Liberalism*, p. 154.

This is a very crude statement of Rawls's seminal argument. The relevance to my point is that the success or failure of this conception of political justice depends upon two questions. First, would it be *possible* to reason consistently according to the conception of harm advocated by political justice in order to achieve stability? Secondly, even if it was possible to reason according to this conception of harm, would the result of such reasoning be reflected upon as true by a participant in the system who holds this or that comprehensive doctrine? Would it be *critically* acceptable to people not merely to live under a comprehensive doctrine, but under an overlapping consensus between comprehensive doctrines? A political conception of justice, in the way Rawls develops it, divorces the moral requirement of reasonableness from moral authenticity. Rawls's politically-orientated reasonableness foists on people an extra layer of reasonableness which they may well not seek. Why should the political imperative force people together? There are many ways in which people can co-operate to achieve mutual benefits without compromising their comprehensive doctrines.

As a piece of constructivism, a political conception of justice may be criticised. First, it may not persist long enough to penetrate and inform people's evaluations on a stable basis. This is because it requires people to be schizophrenic. They need to engage, on the one hand, in comprehensive ethical reasoning, and on the other in political reasoning about the "reasonable". Personal reflection may go as follows: "I am required not to be really me because this is unreasonable, so I allow the political process to enable me to be me only up to the point when it decides that my conduct is reasonable in relation to other comprehensive doctrines." It is questionable whether people can transcend their deepest, critical, ethical convictions in the way Rawls expects them to. Why should they intuit in a Rawlsian fashion? To broaden a conception of harm beyond people's deepest ethical convictions requires those people to put "togetherness", in the name of an abstract free and stable society, before their deepest critical convictions and it is not clear why they should, or indeed can, do that. There seems to be little reason for people to be together politically if their *comprehensive* ethical reflections differ to the degree Rawls suggests they do. In short, either one accepts some plurality under a comprehensive conception of harm, according to which people can limit their judgements, or there is not sufficient reason for people to live together. This seems to present a moral dilemma, which Rawls tries to resolve by means of some further layer of reasoning which itself seems to be impossible to reach.

Secondly, even if sometimes people do seem to engage in Rawls's kind of reasoning, it may be impossible to sustain a stable political society on that basis. If political liberalism itself does amount to a comprehensive doctrine, the conception of harm it invokes may be so diluted that the theory does not provide a sustainable basis for effective coercion. Rawls specifically says that his liberalism is connected to, and embedded in, a political conception of justice which means that the state will not do "anything intended to favour any particular comprehensive view".[8]

The idea of "reasonableness" is, arguably, too insubstantial to bite. It creates a vacuum that may degenerate into arbitrariness, inconsistency and instability. By creating a very open-textured, uncommitted, over-abstract system of negative liberty, political reasoning may infuriate some, confuse others, and in short, may create instability to the extent that a system of de facto local justice will re-emerge to replace the ineffective and abstract political system. Rawls thus tries too hard to do the impossible, namely to contain philosophical pluralism under a single political system. His system dilutes morality too much and therefore does not establish a stable and coherent link with legal and political reasoning.

A constitution framed according to Rawls's rationale in *Political Liberalism* is a recipe for cynicism towards politics; for the attitude that social reality goes on regardless of the rule of law. "Law in books" and "law in action" would be as far apart as they can be. With this abstract idea of reasonableness governing political decisions, it is more likely, therefore, that a Rawlsian Republic would collapse back and re-integrate into what would be consistent comprehensive doctrines, into various polities, with conceptions of harm that people can reason, abstract, concretise and above all, intuit about. A political conception of justice, as distinct from comprehensive philosophical doctrines, either threatens peaceful, stable coexistence, or, alternatively, it makes this loose coexistence needless.

All these problems stem from Rawls's adherence to the methodology of the veil of ignorance and the Original Position, this time as an attempt to overcome its initial shortcomings in *A Theory of Justice*. One criticism of his methodology in *A Theory of Justice*, made by Sandel, is that Rawls in fact presumes a comprehensive communal good which makes sense in real people's ethical reflection. In this case, the original position is a needless distancing device of representation, "distancing" because it presumes more information than it cares to say. If this is the case, then the procedure he advocates is not pure at all because people come to find what they already know. The alternative has metaphysical implications about disembodied selves that Rawls wants to avoid, since the ethical reflection of a radically disembodied self, once it materialises, will not necessarily follow a liberal direction.[9] The upshot of Sandel's criticism is that Rawls is either a self-denying communitarian or a disembodied Kantian, both being possibilities he tries to avoid. Either the procedure is not really pure or it is too pure.[10]

So there have been problems for the operation of reflective equilibrium in *A Theory of Justice*. These problems indicate some unsatisfied moral intuition

[8] *Political Liberalism*, p. 196.

[9] M. Sandel, *Liberalism and the Limits of Justice*, chapter 3, esp. pp. 122–32.

[10] For Sandel's criticisms of *Political Liberalism*, see ibid., 2nd edition., pp. 195–218. For a similar argument in relation to *A Theory of Justice*, drafted before the publication of *Political Liberalism*, see R.P. George, *Making Men Moral: Civil Liberties and Public Morality* (Oxford, 1993), pp. 130–9.

which has to be accounted for. Rawls arguably recognised these problems, in part, as a result of communitarian challenges. He felt the need to refine *A Theory of Justice* because he had the insight based on the residual moral intuition about incommensurability and difference. The outcome of *A Theory of Justice* was not distanced enough from the different, actual, moral experiences that people can have. As far as making *this* intuition the basis of politic's concern, it is doubtful whether one can go beyond a mere *modus vivendi*. In adhering to the same methodology in *Political Liberalism*, Rawls simply imported problems of difference and of the incommensurability of moral perspectives into the Original Position, allowing his imaginary people to see such difference as a possibility. He then coupled this importation with a corresponding dilution of the moral basis for the agreement as to the harm to be avoided. There seems, therefore, to be no limit to the transcendence in the name of ideas which can be attached to the people in the original position. So, in *Political Liberalism*, by acknowledging too strong an adherence to a comprehensive theory in *A Theory of Justice*, Rawls transcends the comprehensive doctrine it provides at the expense of creating an ontological schizophrenia, coupled with dilution of harm, which really cannot bite convincingly on social reality.[11]

Rawls fails to appreciate the ethical *significance* of the aporia of practical reason and in turn fails to nail politics to its implications. On the one hand, he does not sufficiently allow for the fact that actual people, with actual motives, in communication, people who feel pain and pleasure, create and construct comprehensive doctrines and conceptions of harm in order to justify coercion under a system of negative liberty. On the other hand, and here he fails to acknowledge the aporia, he pretends that once a conception of harm which justifies a system of negative liberty causes pain, the problem can, *and ought to*, be contained within another kind of "political" reasoning. Instead of being honest and loyal to people's real sentiments, honesty and loyalty which must arguably lead him to some dead-end once conceptions of harm come to be in conflict, Rawls produces a complicated construct which degrades the aporia and its wrestling with authenticity into a concept of an "overlapping consensus". Not only does Rawls fail to account for the pains and pleasures which create the harm to be averted by politics, but he also underplays the authentic pain felt by people (and groups) holding a different comprehensive doctrine and a different conception of harm,

[11] Rawls writes:

> "Thus, when the political conception is supported by an overlapping consensus of reasonable comprehensive doctrines, the paradox of public reason disappears. The union of the duty of civility with the great values of the political yields the ideal of citizens governing themselves in ways that each thinks the others might reasonably be expected to accept;":

Political Liberalism, p. 218. See also ibid., p. 246:

> "A reasonable and effective political conception may bend comprehensive doctrines toward itself, shaping them if need be from unreasonable to reasonable. But even granting this tendency, political liberalism itself cannot argue that each of those comprehensive doctrines should find the conclusions of public reason nearly always within its leeway. To argue that transcends public reason."

whose voice might not be even heard by the time the overlapping consensus is interpreted. The last sentence would not bemuse him. It would not strike him as a telling contradiction (as far as pains and pleasures felt by people are concerned) but as a layered constructive continuum.

The danger of Kantian constructivism is apparent. Under it, ideas can be generalised regardless of the people who are supposed to make real use of them. It is possible to make sense of the idea of a conceptually consistent account which goes beyond comprehensive doctrines. Indeed, *Political Liberalism* does that admirably. Terms like "reasonable comprehensive", "overlapping consensus", "public reason" create a more generalised conceptual umbrella which can make sense as such, but one doubts whether people can actually *be* what the theory requires them to be. Any ascent in abstraction must coincide with what people *are*, in the sense of what might constitute a realistic horizon of critical reflection for them. Rawls's account in *Political Liberalism* demands people try not to be really, deeply themselves. At this point they would renounce the political union altogether. *Political Liberalism*, as opposed to *A Theory of Justice*, is a recipe for incoherence in the rationale for political and legal reasoning.

In sum, Rawls was morally right to acknowledge the need to go beyond a comprehensive doctrine. However, he erred in adhering to the same methodology which forced unity upon difference on such a diluted basis. If people in the Original Position are not moral persons in the full sense of the term, namely people who are at least able to reflect *vis à vis* some different comprehensive conception of harm, they will adjourn the meeting, knowing the nature of the barrier that must tear them apart politically. When devising a complete a priori order of reasons, Kant saw difference, not togetherness. Only from an independent order of reasons can one appreciate the pluralism and incommensurability of comprehensive doctrines. Rawls follows Kant and captures the insight but distorts its implications for politics. *Political liberalism* is an impressive conceptual construct which it is possible to understand but not to realise. At best, ontologically speaking (i.e. in relation to what people *are*), it is superfluous. Political constructivism is invented by Rawls to create a needless and hence unsustainable extra layer of reflection. Rawls's reasonableness ducks the issue of strong moral evaluation by people through politics and the aporetic relations it bears to the moral evaluation which outgrows politics. His theory collapses into the circularity of defining reasonableness as the basis of averting the very harm this reasonableness tries to transcend. His claim that the justice is political, not metaphysical, involves both concealment and distortion. He conceals what is a truly metaphysical insight and he distorts the implication of this insight in declaring something to be "political" which is in fact distinct from it.

Dworkin's Foundations of Liberal Equality

In his Tanner Lecture, Dworkin tries to find "ethical foundations" for liberalism.[12] His argument is complex and subtle and so one cannot hope to do full justice to it here. However, I shall try to follow in general terms his methodology of connecting ethics to politics. In his lecture, Dworkin explains what ethical reasons people might have to be liberals. In what sense does liberalism enhance one's well-being? His argument is an attempt to show how considerations of justice and morality may penetrate people's critical motivations and reflections upon their well-being.

Dworkin's methodology, unlike Rawls's, involves a search for critical reasons which real people might have for adopting liberalism and embodying it in their ethical judgements.[13] Self-reflection upon one's well-being takes sides, morally speaking. Dworkin resorts to the Platonist idea that the moral implications of what we do or have affect our well-being. Interpretations of conceptions of social justice shape personal ethical considerations and therefore shape well-being. The reason I wish to be a just person is that if I get what I get by unjust reasons, I will never be fully satisfied with what I am or have, because I will not be able to accept critically that I *should* have what I have or be what I am. As long as I have what I have or am what I am as a result of social injustice, whatever I have or am cannot be *critically* mine.

What are the *critical* foundations upon which people reflect upon their well-being, namely upon what they *ought* to be or have? These questions relate to what Dworkin calls critical well-being as opposed to volitional well-being. It is critical because a constant critical challenge makes people reflect upon the justification of what they are and what they have by virtue of the immediate fulfilment of their volition. Life poses an ethical challenge for the fulfilment of critical interests which Dworkin calls a "challenge model".

This ethical challenge assumes a justificatory continuum between critical personal ethical judgement and the moral basis for politics. It connects ethics to politics. Put generally, in a socially just scheme of institutions and political

[12] Dworkin, "Foundations of Liberal Equality" (hereafter *FLE*), p. 3.

[13] See ibid., pp. 12–22 esp. pp. 15–16. Dworkin wants to find foundational, ethical, categorical force to liberalism as opposed to basing it on a hypothetical contract. Categorical force here means some moral truth that serves as a critical point for reflection upon any actual consent to it by contracting people. Rawls's problem would be:

> "If a particular political conception of justice would be agreed upon by artificial people in the right circumstances, he believes, real people each have a moral reason to accept decisions in accordance with that conception of justice now, even though they have not collectively agreed to do so. Can we identify moral reason[s] that have that categorical force, and locate these moral reasons in a plausible personal perspective?" p. 26.

The idea of categorical force is not divorced from intuitionism. The problem of categorical force persists not only if conceptions of harm are not collectively shared but also, perhaps even more sharply, when they *are* actually shared.

reasoning, people's lives are critically better. The moral rationale for a scheme of institutions and reasoning is what formally binds people together as a community. This idea of community is to be distinguished from the idea of community as a metaphysical entity which consists of some common good people should look after. Through the moral rationale underlying the activity of political institutions, such as parliament and courts, people's ethical and political life are bound together.[14] The extent to which people are parts of a social group which develops a socially just basis for both its political institutions and their reasoning, will mark also the extent of the success or failure of their critical ethical lives. Community and politics respond to the same challenge that people respond to in their ethical life, namely the challenge of social justice. To reiterate, only in a just polity can people say that whatever they have, however partially, is critically speaking *theirs*.[15]

This model differs from Rawls in its methodology. Rawls wants to establish a reasoned and intuitive equilibrium between a hypothetical procedure and people's actual intuitions about justice, but it is not clear why actual and different people would connect to Rawlsian justice as the outcome of a hypothetical contract. This problem becomes more acute, as has been argued, in *Political Liberalism*. By contrast, Dworkin tries to relate the rift between ethics and politics to the rift that exists *within* people's ethical reflections. However, he does very little to improve the solution to the *foundational* problem. Rawls's foundational problem centres on the different possible conceptions of harm that the critical evaluation may be amenable to. The connection between ethics and politics in fact implies a critical connection which characterises the problem of people's ethical reflection in *both* Rawls and Dworkin.[16]

The problem is that if one wishes to say something about the foundation of liberal equality one must consider ethical theory generally and see whether the operation of such a theory would justify liberal equality as opposed to some other result. To connect ethics to politics is a noble aim, but it is arguable that

[14] Dworkin, "Liberal Community", pp. 208–16. See also *FLE*, pp. 86–93.

[15] Ibid., p. 222.

[16] There is a revealing ambiguity relating to the role of motivation in Dworkin's account of which he is aware and which he discusses in a footnote at p. 5 of the lecture. The overcoming of this ambiguity, which Dworkin transforms into two allegedly *different* questions, is nevertheless crucial for the success of his argument. Dworkin distinguishes between the motivation people already have and the motivations they *should* have. However justified this distinction might be, Dworkin wants to connect people's motivations in a critical sense to broader schemes of ideas and *not* to psychology. Criticisms and the defence of liberalism should not relate to the fact that it is socially unworkable because it fails to penetrate people's psyche. Criticisms have to be levelled not at the likelihood of realisation but at something "that the most perceptive ethical theory, supported by the soundest opinions in other departments of philosophy, would reject". Dworkin hopes "to construct an attractive picture of the goals and ambitions we believe people *should* have, and then show that liberal politics *in some way* flows from or coheres with that picture". However, Dworkin cannot avoid discussing the connection between moral and actual psychology in the same manner as Rawls does it because he wishes real people to change their critical reflections. He is involved more than Rawls in constructing the case for the manner in which moral psychology is related to the question of *what it is to have a motivation*. His theory builds on people changing their motivation, and the connection between empirical psychology and moral psychology is therefore vital to ethical liberals.

Dworkin's approach succeeds no better than Rawls's. Dworkin uses the harm prevented by liberal equality as the best ethical argument people can have. However, people can *reflect critically* upon their well-being according to different conceptions of harm. Existing and future fundamental social conflicts will show that.

There is no foundational ethical argument in Dworkin at all. A foundational argument of the kind required must ask questions like: what constitutes an ethical value, ethical knowledge, ethical intuitions? The argument that I present, one from pain and pleasure, is foundational in that it relates to an explanation of ethical possibility, not to the fundamental presumption of the rightness of this or that ethical view. The latter would be to put the cart before the horse. An argument from such foundation, such as the real experience of pain and pleasure, makes any allegedly substantive "foundational" justification dependent on substantive presumptions and hence contingent and unconvincing. Foundations can, of course, relate to justifications rather than to explanations, as in Kant's moral theory, but, as I have argued above,[17] it will be difficult to sustain an authentic connection between the abstract *substantive* foundation and a preferred particular view for a given conception of harm which underlines political morality. In Dworkin's argument, the foundations are in fact presumed. The ethical significance of the aporia is not even felt by him, as opposed to the Rawls of *Political Liberalism* who does feel it. All that one learns is that critical ethical reflection works best for liberal egalitarians because they are liberal egalitarians. It is one thing to argue that ethical reflection can yield liberal egalitarian results but it is a very different thing to claim that, by doing that, one provides an ethical *foundation* for liberalism. If a person belongs to a culture which understands harm differently, or, to use Rawls's example, adopts a different comprehensive doctrine, Dworkin's argument will not find an ally. Dworkin's argument faces the same foundational problem that *A Theory of Justice* faces. Rawls's hypothetical contract articulates all the presumptions Dworkin wants us to embody in our interpretation of our critical well-being within a challenge model of ethical value. In other words, Rawls assumes that his readers *are* all liberal in his hypothetical methodology, while Dworkin assumes that we are liberal in the channel chosen to satisfy the ethical challenge. The problem in Dworkin and Rawls is that both try to justify critically what they assume, and thus the reflective equilibrium in the latter and the meeting of the challenge for the former will be circular and hence superfluous. If Dworkin's audience is a liberal audience, his mission is needless. If they do not subscribe to the liberal conception of harm, his mission will be unsuccessful and potentially reactionary. The critical connection between ethics and politics can take many forms. The connection between ethics and politics must be much more socially dynamic than Dworkin suggests. If ethics is to be connected to politics, the challenge is to make politics responsive to the different directions in which ethical judgement might proceed.

[17] See pp. 262–3 above.

Rawls is aware of the real problem involved in connecting ethics to politics, but adheres to a methodology which cannot possibly allude to it. Dworkin's comprehensive liberalism does not take the challenge which his own foundational account creates seriously enough. This is the light in which Habermas's criticism of Dworkin should be read:

> "In Dworkin's own project, however, we can discern the dilemma in which every ethic claiming universal validity inevitably gets caught today under conditions of post-metaphysical thinking. Namely, as long as such an ethic makes substantive statements, its premises remain confined to the context in which particular historical or ever personal interpretations of the self and the world arose. As soon as it is sufficiently formal, however, its substance at best consists in elucidating the procedure of ethical discourses aimed at reaching self-understanding."[18]

At one point, Dworkin distinguishes between limitations and parameters in ethical thinking. Parameters are qualities which challenge us ethically. Limitations define for us how to live well. The quality of limitations depends on the existence of parameters, and parameters can stir up a challenge only in the context of limitations. Therefore, ethical life must contain both parameters and limitations. Our existing ethical limitations are interpreted in the light of parameters. But the way Dworkin channels the challenge model of ethical values makes liberalism an untranscendable limitation because the challenge stops at the point of a given (liberal) conception of harm. The challenge model is no better as a device of representation than the original position. The rationale for politics must serve as the *only parameter* in the life of a person that accepts Dworkin's view.[19]

Finally, Dworkin seems undecided as to whether the critical challenge posed by ethical value is transcendent or historically indexed. He seems to be arguing that *to some extent* transcendence has to be involved as far as one critically transcends one's cultures. In other words, it must run into conflict with the cultural horizon that makes people the moral persons that they are.[20] At another place, however, Dworkin resolves this question by arguing that an understanding of the challenge as transcendent would entail that it calls for the fulfilment of a certain value in the best way.[21] This would be superficial, says Dworkin, because ultimate values do change in history. So, being argumentative, the challenge model is indexed to history. However, if it is so indexed surely it encompasses a change in the comprehensive conception of harm as well. Otherwise, the model *is* transcendent in the sense that Dworkin wishes to avoid.[22]

[18] J. Habermas, *Between Facts and Norms,* p. 64.
[19] *FLE*, pp. 66–71.
[20] Ibid., p. 48.
[21] Ibid., pp. 62–6.
[22] See Rawls, *Political Liberalism,* p. 211, note 42 in which it is revealing that Rawls does not see any problem in the challenge model of ethical value, being a formal model which is historically indexed, serving as a comprehensive cultural background and supporting role for political liberalism. Yet, it would seem absurd for Dworkin to accept this position in his attempt to find a

In other words, to see the challenge model as indexed is fatal to Dworkin's liberal equality as well, because there is no way to channel the historical evolution of the interpretation of the challenge towards any particular conception of harm, precisely because it is not possible to subject it to the dominance of any ulterior values. If one admits that the challenge model is indexed, one has to abandon the "progress towards . . ." approach as well for there is nothing to give the grist to the mill of the challenge. The challenge model is, in truth, a philosophical model, and it is at the point when one wants to *do* things with the theory that its foundational claims become unconvincing. So Dworkin must choose either to admit that the challenge model holds a transcendent conception of harm, or that the challenge is indexed so that the judgemental conception of harm is itself subject to challenge. Dworkin has his cake and eats it. This can hardly count as a foundational argument. Being transcendent means that the challenge never stops.

Dworkin does not take the moral intuition of difference seriously. Foundations must be based on something else other than the conception of harm which they support. If the foundation Dworkin seeks to discuss is the connection between ethics and politics, then any interpretation of this relationship must be connected to the foundation of ethics. This means that a discussion is needed of how ethical judgement is possible and how it evolves and is transformed. A genuine foundational argument (whether utilitarian or not) would be more receptive to the different ways evolution of critical ethical experience may go. An argument from foundation will not necessarily lead to liberalism, and need not sustain liberalism.

Kymlicka's Cultural Membership

The attempt to accommodate cultural membership within the rationale of egalitarian liberalism was undertaken by W. Kymlicka in two works—*Liberalism, Community and Culture* and *Multicultural Citizenship*. Essentially, Kymlicka argues that liberal values can form the rationale for politics in a multicultural society. His liberalism constructs a defensible liberal case for cultural membership within polyethnic societies.

The factual existence of multi-ethnic society, Kymlicka argues, calls for a more complex account than normally allowed for in liberal discussions. Cultural membership has not been taken seriously by egalitarian liberals when considering the problem of treating *individual* people as morally equal. Kymlicka argues that the morally equal treatment of individuals by liberals,

comprehensive ethical foundation for liberal equality. Dworkin has never used his idea to elaborate upon the constraint which would limit comprehensive ethical doctrines. This is the very schizophrenia that he tries to avoid. The insight that one can get from the compatibility of Dworkin's indexed account of the challenge model with Rawls's account is precisely that the challenge model cannot serve as a comprehensive foundation for liberal equality, for the challenge continues.

which includes egalitarian distribution of resources and rights under a liberal state politics, has been too simplistic in polyethnic societies. The existence of various cultures within a political community calls for the integration of a cultural dimension into the understanding of individual autonomy which underpins the rationale of liberal politics. Liberals must acknowledge that cultural membership gives meaning to individual choices.

Cultural shared language and history provides an arena within which individuality can be exercised on various levels. First, individual choices have meaning and acknowledgement only within existing, culturally shared meanings and aspirations. Secondly, individuals can reflect upon, and modify through their choices, existing cultural characteristics without discrediting the general cultural structure itself. Thirdly, individuals can abandon some or all elements of their culture if they do not consider them to be worthwhile.

Cultural membership is a variant which must be taken into account because it functions as the meaningful context within which individuals can form, rationally pursue and revise, their conception of the good. Provision for cultural membership is in fact an enhancement of individuality and an enhancement of individual choice and reflection upon the adequacy of that choice, activities which are associated with the liberal understanding of self-respect.[23]

Understood as a context of choice, a liberal recognition of cultural membership as a primary good, together with liberty, equality and self respect, refutes communitarian worries about the atomistic nature of liberal political theory. Liberalism allows individuals to revise their lives should they come to acknowledge that they were wrong about their life plans. The ability to lead a satisfying life for oneself is entirely compatible with, indeed it requires, social recognition as embodied in a culture. Individuality as a value is not to be identified with atomism. The dependence of individual reflection on communal values, as a matter of the way the self reflects upon its life, is entirely compatible with the *moral* individualist premise that individuals can be wrong about their life pursuits, and hence should be allowed to reflect for themselves upon their current life, whatever the communal values to which they subscribe.

Liberalism does not require the self to be beyond its ends and therefore unencumbered, disembodied or atomistic. It does acknowledge that the constitution of, and self-reflection on, personal identity gain meaning within a cultural context. It does also acknowledge the individually-various empirical limits to reflection, namely that to various degrees persons may well not spend all their existence reflecting upon their lives. However, it emphasises that politics should not dictate either the parameters or the ambit of self-reflection upon one's life. It is morally wrong that people should limit their self-reflection under a given formula, when this formula imposes a certain overwhelming good which surpasses all or some other goods. The possibility of an individual living a full life, which is reflectively acceptable for him as sufficient, is

[23] W. Kymlicka, *Liberalism, Community and Culture* (Oxford, 1989), pp. 64–5.

valuable regardless of the extent to which different individuals choose to exercise that self-reflection.

However, the understanding of cultural membership as an essential, contextual variant for the exercise of individual autonomy can be abused and the case for it overstated, so it is important to acknowledge what Kymlicka does not say. First, he does not say that the recognition of cultural membership implies moral rights on the part of cultures. Cultures cannot be the subject of moral claims. The survival or fall of cultures is a matter of reflection for the individuals who constitute those cultures. Secondly, the recognition of cultural membership in the context of choice does not lead to communitarian politics. Where Kymlicka differs from communitarians is in his claim that it is not the business of the state to provide protection for a given culture by the reason that this culture's goods are to be considered paramount. The preservation of culture is not the same as the preservation of the conditions in which cultural membership could be experienced and be reflected upon by individuals. It is for the sake of individuals that all cultures should be allowed to compete in the cultural marketplace on equal terms, not for the sake of cultures. Communitarians use politics to promote cultural goods and as such would put cultures beyond the rationale of preservation of cultural membership in the context of individual choice. Communitarian politics, according to Kymlicka, is paradoxical because it sacrifices the end that it tries to proclaim as ultimately important, namely cultural membership, for the sake of politics of the common good or shared cultural ends. Communitarian politics, by its very nature, ends up being repressive of the value of cultural membership and as such it has the paradoxical effect of curtailing the variety of relationships within a society by allowing dominant shared ends to curtail everything that is different from them.[24]

Unlike some liberals who see culture as a kind of form of life which gives some "off the shelf" experiences for the cosmopolitans to enjoy,[25] Kymlicka seems to take cultures seriously by acknowledging that belonging is not only something which an individual may choose but a context, the parameters of which constitute a way of life which gives meaning to some choices of individuals. This understanding of the importance of cultural membership to individuality has implications for the foundation of liberal politics in polyethnic nations. Cultural membership demands the active protection of disadvantaged groups within a dominant culture, protection that might be needed because of unpopularity within the dominant culture or because of the disadvantages a given culture faces due to participatory problems which can be linguistic or otherwise related to their culture. Essentially, Kymlicka calls for the protection, in the name of individuality, of certain minority cultures by what he calls measures of external protection.[26]

[24] *Liberalism, Community and Culture*, pp. 168–70.

[25] J. Waldron, "Minority Cultures and the Cosmopolitan Alternative", in W. Kymlicka (ed.), *The Rights of Minority Cultures* (Oxford, 1995), pp. 93–119.

[26] W. Kymlicka, *Multicultural Citizenship: A Liberal Theory of Minority Rights* (Oxford, 1995), pp. 35–44.

Distribution of resources and rights should address cultural disadvantage in competing on equal terms, in the same way it protects individual qualities that put individuals at a disadvantage in realising and revising their life plans in ways which, as Rawls put it, are "arbitrary from the moral point of view". To reiterate, cultures do not have a moral status in the same way as individuals, but it is important that cultures be treated as equals to the degree that they may equally express their importance in the cultural market place. If a culture does not survive after it has been given an equal chance of articulating its main tenets to the market, including the possibility of participating in the polity on equal terms, then the state should not intervene to protect it. Hence, liberalism should be occupied with culture and should not wash its hands of dealing with cultural membership and rights of minority cultures within polyethnic society. The protection of minority cultures or the provision of group-differentiated rights would prevent harm to the liberal value of individual autonomy. The state's *liberal* neutrality is effectuated though the sensitivity of an egalitarian distribution to cultural context by means of minority rights.

Kymlicka's account establishes a subtle line between the recognition of cultural difference and uniqueness, and liberal principles. His account does not overstate the case for culture but does recognise the importance of cultural difference to individuals. Kymlicka's intuition, like Rawls's in *Political Liberalism*, is the intuition of difference and *to some extent* moral incompatibility. Different cultures mean fundamental differences between the people who constitute them. It is not the business of the state to promote one cultural form or another. Its business is just to help certain disadvantaged minority groups to compete in the cultural market place.

However, Kymlicka's account is a refinement of something that we all already know and feel intuitively to be right about being liberal. When one reads his account one feels that something, which will be the prime tool of the anthropologist's approach to morality, is missing, namely a recognition of, and humility before, different types of moral experiences. Such an approach recognises the incompatibility of different foundational conceptions of harm. Not only is the anthropologist's hermeneutic approach sensitive to this incompatibility, but it can enable the translation of this sensitivity into a moral intuition about the diverse ways open to individual self-realisation. Such an approach, in short, will open up the possibility for a moral intuition, the object of which would be the very importance of respect to different forms of moral experiences. This anthropologist's intuition would be bigger than any identification with any of those experiences. It would be open to many possibilities of "rightness" brought about by different moral experiences, different forms of life. Arguably, such type of intuition and the empathy it entails, is missing from Kymlicka's liberal account of cultural membership. It does not take the complexity implied by cultural membership to the full. The idea of "cultural membership as a context of choice" must imply also moral incommensurability and incompatibility.

Kymlicka acknowledges the limited scope of his argument, and states that his aim in these two books is to provide a defensible liberal case for the polyethnic societies which exist on the globe. He tries to add a cultural dimension to the general liberal conviction that people from different cultures ought to reflect for themselves upon their participation in a given culture. It is difficult to combine the idea of respect for cultural membership with the idea of the containment of the implications of such membership under a single comprehensive conception of harm. By containing cultures within a liberal conception of harm, one subjects them to a single cultural perspective on harm, and in turn limits the ways in which individuality can be realised within a culture and the ways in which it may reflect upon a culture. Cultures have inherent *moral* importance as a form of life which contains moral experiences. The value of individuality, namely the capability to realise certain types of moral experience, stems from a bigger moral insight than any temporal, historical or cultural realisation of individuals—itself stemming from insights which presume a given conception of harm. If Kymlicka admits that value of cultural membership in the context of choice is more important than the maintenance of a culture as it is manifested at any particular time,[27] why cannot he acknowledge that the realisation of individuality in a culture is more important than realisation-of-individuality-within-a-culture-in-compatibility-with-a-conception-of-harm? This is not just a statement of realpolitik but a moral argument. By arguing that cultures are important as they serve as a context of *individual choice*, Kymlicka arguably puts too heavy a burden on the shoulders of liberal theory.

The containment of cultural membership under a liberal egalitarian conception of harm has two undesirable implications for individuality. First, because the conception of harm is entrenched, it will limit the ambit of any cultural difference that may exist or arise. This may prevent a person from belonging to a chosen culture, if that culture offends the hegemonic conception of harm. This point relates to the limits of toleration of illiberal practices which is discussed below. For liberals, morally speaking, individual choice and reflection upon the adequacy of choice can be sufficiently fulfilled *within* roles or fundamental shared ends which may limit to some extent individual choice, *only as a result of, and subject to*, individual reflection. Some cultures may not see it that way and appreciate, say, choice within unquestionably shared ends, or a certain segregation which creates give and take between segregated groups. Kymlicka's liberal interpretation of cultural membership has already and implicitly determined the cultural co-ordinates, and therefore permissible ways, within which competition between cultures in a market place is to be allowed.[28]

The second point relates to individual autonomy. Should a person desire to transcend his present culture and establish a commonality which is incompati-

27 *Liberalism, Community and Culture*, p. 169.

28 See in this context, C. Kukathas, "Are There any Cultural Rights?", in W. Kymlicka (ed.), *The Rights of Minority Cultures*, pp. 228–56, and "Cultural Rights Again: A Rejoinder to Kymlicka", *Political Theory* 20 (1992) 674–80.

ble with any of the cultures contained within the liberal co-ordinates, he will be unable to do so. Individuality and with it, cultures and cultural membership in the context of individual choice, are bigger than the liberal interpretation of it. If individuality breaks the cultural, including the cultural moral pattern, it may well do so in all sorts of ways, some of which may not be allowed under a liberal conception of harm. From the point of view of individual autonomy, excepting perhaps for some very minimal common features of all cultures, there is an unbridgeable gap between the philosophical respect for individuality and the way it is realised under a given, cultural and political, conception of harm.

So, bearing in mind these two points, namely the individual flourishing within existing cultures, cultures which may be incompatible with one another, and the exercise of autonomy which potentially goes beyond any existing range permitted under a conception of harm, there should be some respect for cultures which goes beyond what Kymlicka allows. Certain cultures are not open to us because we do not have the language to understand them, including a moral language. The term "discrimination" may not do justice to all cultures whose symbolic relationships of subordination and superiority are not open to us or, to be more precise, open to us only on our own terms. This is precisely an instance of what may stimulate the residual moral intuition of existing difference, and the prediction that new differences will be formed. In that respect, a liberal perspective of harm according to which cultural membership is being understood and appreciated already dominates our perspective. A philosophy which conceptualises freedom in such a dominant way runs the risk of suppressing human possibilities. When one reads Kymlicka's argument, one feels a certain reduction, a certain neglect of moral intuition. It is this residual moral intuition, the one between different and incommensurable conceptions of harm, this freedom which may well not be felt by me or you which has prompted Rawls, at least on a philosophical level, to attempt (albeit unsuccessfully) a refinement of *A Theory of Justice* in *Political Liberalism*. Perhaps it was this intuition that prompted Kymlicka to introduce culture as an element of the liberal equation in the first place. However, Kymlicka does not take the intuition to its conclusion, since he does not allow culture to question the liberal perspective *as a culture*.

To summarise, the diversity of cultural membership may imply the recognition of some, alternative conceptions of harm according to which people build a flourishing life for themselves. This means that some degree of respect should be accorded to existing differences, subject perhaps to what writers referred to as a minimum content of universal moral law.[29] Further, the argument predicts that difference will be recreated under any system which imposes a single conception of harm. Any system of negative liberty, even one that recognises cultural membership under a given conception of harm, will be transient. The point

[29] See H.L.A. Hart, *The Concept of Law* (Oxford, 1961), pp. 189–95, M. Walzer, *Interpretation and Social Criticism* (Cambridge Mass., 1987), pp. 23–7. Berlin also argued for the existence of universal objective values as well as for their minimal realisation in a minimal code of law: see J. Gray, *Isaiah Berlin*, pp. 64–5.

is that there is something to be learnt from the fact that people have created different cultures, to the extent also that these cultures maintained certain conceptions of harm which excluded some forms of individual reflection upon them. Liberal egalitarians, for all their efforts to contain difference, must also disallow some forms of reflection.

This argument connotes that, barring extreme cases of inhumanity, cultures do deserve respect and deference. This is so because respect for different kinds of moral experience is respect for what humanity can produce and will produce. Any morally justifiable attempt to contain politically cultural indeterminacy, and the human possibilities it implies, would result in the artificial anchoring of a conception of harm which must in turn curtail certain possibilities for individuality. From a Kantian perspective, treating others as ends in themselves, *as potential members of different cultures*, is an interpretation of the moral Categorical Imperative which competes with the egalitarian interpretation of this imperative as cultural membership in the context of individual choice. Both interpretations regard cultural membership and individuality as primary goods. The first, however, is the thinnest possible because it is philosophical and does not depend on any materialisation in social and political reality. Arguably, cultural membership cannot be conceptualised beyond such a thin threshold in a morally satisfying way. Both the immorality of any thicker conceptualisation, with regard to a given social group, and the existence of the de facto different conceptualisations in different social groups, are the manifestations of the aporia. Liberalism in effect imposes a normalising conception of harm upon cultures, an exercise which is immoral in itself because it subjects all cultures to its own moral scheme.

The second point about Kymlicka's account follows from the first. The idea of tolerating and protecting illiberal cultures in a liberal polity is problematic. Kymlicka recognises this problem.[30] His preferred polity would ensure that the promotion of cultural difference under liberal principles involved "*freedom within* the minority group, and *equality between* the minority and majority groups".[31] Cultural complexity is to be scrutinised, and evaluated according to liberal ideology. To the extent that cultures infringe individual freedom and autonomy they should not be protected within a liberal polity: "I have defended the right of national minorities to maintain themselves as culturally distinct societies, but only if, and in so far as, they are themselves governed by liberal principles."[32] Kymlicka recognises toleration within a certain conception of harm which requires promotion of cultural variation under it. This is to be distinguished from toleration between incompatible conceptions of harm, some of them illiberal, a kind of *modus vivendi*-liberalism—"reciprocal non-interference".

[30] *Multicultural Citizenship*, ch. 8.

[31] Ibid., p. 152.

[32] Ibid., p. 153.

Regarding the liberalising of cultures, Kymlicka accepts that coercive liberalising intervention is unjustified both between states and within a multicultural state. Instead, he advocates mutual discussion and persuasion as well as what he regards as "non coercive" liberalising interference. Peaceful liberalising means could also include various incentives for liberal reform such as making membership conditional upon liberalisation (e.g. the European Union). However, he admits that the line between incentive and coercion is not a sharp one.[33] However, for the reason explained above, what he suggests does amount to coercion, coercion which is manifested by being insensitive to the richness that constitutes the morality of other cultures. In this I am in agreement with Walzer's claim that an over-rigid and allegedly universal political rationale is undemocratic.[34] The moral intuition about difference should be respected between political communities, but it cannot be so within them. To attempt such respect within them is to go the Rawlsian way. This means that, even if one succeeds in persuading other cultures, the result will be transient.

In summary, cultural membership cannot be convincingly conceptualised.[35] If one takes cultural membership seriously, one should see the limits it imposes both between and within polities which construct a conception of harm. No construction of a conception of harm will ever do justice to it. Thus, no conceptualisation of its general and thin meaning would do. It would face the very aporia that other terms such as "liberty", "equality" and "individuality" face. Cultural membership, if it is to enhance individuality, demands a dynamic connection between ethics and politics. In using a critical methodology to account for the moral intuition of difference, one has both to acknowledge some deference towards existing cultural difference, and to make politics responsive to newly emerging human possibilities. Human possibilities must return to political debates in a critical way. Cultural membership and the dynamic relationship between ethics and politics lie at the heart of the aporia, the aporia between any actualised and institutionalised system of negative liberty and negative liberty as a philosophical notion about human choice and possibilities.

Raz's Liberal Perfectionism

This brings me to the fourth attempt, arguably the most successful, to connect ethics to politics, and individuals to their community. Raz's *Morality of Freedom* is an impressive attempt to reconcile individual autonomy with state action. The upshot of his liberalism is that the state has a moral duty to enhance individual autonomy.[36]

[33] *Multicultural Citizenship*, pp. 168–70.

[34] M. Walzer, "Philosophy and Democracy", *Political Theory* (1981) 379–99, at 386–9, 393–5.

[35] See my discussion of Tully, pp. 303–6 below.

[36] My account is based on J. Raz, *The Morality of Freedom* (Oxford, 1986), chapters 5–6, 12–15. See also his "Autonomy, Toleration, and the Harm Principle", in R. Gavison (ed.), *Issues in Contemporary Legal Philosophy: The Influence of H.L.A. Hart* (Oxford, 1987), pp. 313–33, and

Raz's conception of harm upon which politics should be based centres on the notion of autonomy. One is harmed if one does not enjoy autonomy. Therefore, the state has a moral duty to nourish and enhance individual autonomy. Autonomy for Raz is a means for attaining well-being, which in turn means being able to choose between a variety of life projects and relationships. Once a person regards certain projects and relationships as wrong, there must be other life options to choose from. It is because well-being relates so closely to individual self-realisation that autonomy is an important means for its attainment. However, Raz maintains that some ulterior judgements have to be exercised about the quality of the options available. Autonomy for Raz consists of a range of *valuable* options. Hence, some discriminating exercise must be made in order to eliminate invaluable options. Choice, and reflection upon choice, between valuable and invaluable options does not amount to autonomy. It is the duty of the state to promote valuable options and to discourage invaluable ones.

Now, some life options may be incommensurable and incompatible with one another. The incommensurability essentially means that there is not always a common quality by which to measure the value of options. Incompatibility means that the choice of some options entails the exclusion of others. However, the fact that some options are incommensurable and incompatible does not mean that all options can be regarded as valuable. In this, Raz echoes Berlin's insight that different life options represent different ways of combining and ordering values, and that therefore there are different ways in which well-being can be attained.

Raz's liberalism is based on the duty of the state to distribute resources so as to promote a variety of valuable options, even if these options are incommensurable or incompatible with one another. The state has a duty to be the guardian of a variety of valuable options, and as such a guardian of individual autonomy. Because this range of choice must consist of valuable options, Raz trusts the state to discriminate between valuable and non-valuable options. Raz interprets Mill's harm principle to mean that the state has a positive duty to enhance individual autonomy, and not merely to enforce a certain pattern of distribution if this pattern is not followed by individuals or governments.[37] The state has a duty to promote autonomy and, as such, not only is it to be trusted to decide which options are valuable but also, once it decides that an option is valuable, it has a duty, in the name of maintaining autonomy, to resource that option and not to let it disappear in the cultural market place. Raz therefore does not believe in a liberal neutrality which, apart from ensuring certain just distributions, does not advocate a positive action by the state. He does not trust the cultural market place, in the same way egalitarian liberals do, to maintain the range

"Multiculturalism: A Liberal Perspective" in J. Raz (ed.), *Ethics in the Public Domain: Essays in the Morality of Law and Politics* (Oxford, 1994), pp. 170–91. See also J. Waldron, "Autonomy and Perfectionism in Raz's *Morality of Freedom*", *Southern California Law Review* 62 (1989) 1098–152 and Raz's response at pp. 1223–35.

[37] *The Morality of Freedom*, pp. 412–20.

of valuable options. Further, he does not believe in liberal neutrality because this neutrality itself entails one pattern of distribution which may exclude many valuable options. In short, if survival of options is left to the cultural market place or is aligned to one dominant principle of distribution, many life options will be degraded and so individual autonomy will be harmed.

These are the general features of Raz's political theory. The most apparent feature is that the state is trusted to make an assessment of the value of life options. Raz does not go to a great length to specify what "valuable" means. Indeed, he admits that the state may make mistakes. However, it does not follow from the possibility of mistakes that the state should not take any action in assessing the value of options.

The initial judgement of value by the state filters options. Once acknowledged by the state as valuable, options would be encouraged *even if they are incompatible and incommensurable* with each other. The tension of the argument lies in the fact that the rationale for the state's initial judgement entails some vantage point that all options must satisfy, and this may not sit comfortably with the idea of incompatibility of options. The attempt to make sense of this tension suggests that options must be, to some extent, compatible according to the standard by which the state exercises its judgement. This is a vague point in Raz's thesis. His thesis about incommensurability is a philosophical insight that is shared by liberals like Berlin and Rawls. It is also based on the intuition about difference that prompts many modern liberals, like Rawls and Kymlicka, to modify liberal accounts in a non-comprehensive and comprehensive manner respectively. We saw that Rawls tried to accommodate this insight within his methodology in *Political Liberalism*. We saw also that Kymlicka accommodated difference as an *object* of egalitarian distribution, and thus within the formula of egalitarian liberalism and state neutrality, through the notion of "cultural membership".

So Raz's account is to an extent compatible with their accounts. We now see that Raz wants to enhance autonomy which can only be done by encouraging incompatible and incommensurable, or, in short, fundamentally different options, to flourish under one polity. So, Raz also tries to realise the philosophical insight of difference and incompatible perspectives in politics. The significant absence, however, is that Raz, while acknowledging the heavy burden of autonomy, namely the burden of difference, is silent about the specific ways in which his theory may be implemented. He does not take sides as to what constitutes value.

There is a moral and philosophical commitment to autonomy and difference in his account, as well as an acknowledgement that the state has a duty to enhance that autonomy, but he does not say anything about any specific formulation in which the all-important initial filter, that of value, is to operate. I think that his silence on this matter has moral significance. It is significant because one cannot reduce a Razian state to the egalitarian liberal state. There are many ways in which the philosophical insight can be implemented and autonomy promoted. It is worth emphasising, however, that once the initial filter of value is passed, there is a duty on the state to maintain plurality though the distribution of rights and resources. In this sense, in recognising the necessity of state action but being silent about what this action might entail, Raz has produced perhaps the most honest account of liberalism to date. It is also important to note that the term "neutrality" is not completely redundant in Raz's theory, because the state distributes resources to allow different options to exist once it establishes their valuable nature. As such, it does not let any option become dominant and so it is, to that extent, neutral. Arguably, his neutrality is more far-reaching than the type of neutrality that egalitarian liberals advocate, more akin, though not identical to, the philosophical neutrality aimed at by Rawls in *Political Liberalism*.

Let me examine some possible implementations of the Razian account. His account may be interpreted as saying that, in order to enhance autonomy, the state has to cater for life options that are morally incompatible, in that they subscribe to different conceptions of harm. This interpretation unites the most abstract application of the principle of autonomy directly with politics and the state, and would mean that a state should support morally incompatible doctrines. This would, in effect, mean moral neutrality, because the state would make sure that no conception of harm becomes dominant. The question then arises as to what the judgement of "value" is based on? If "valuable" in this context means another layer of reasoning, then it may resemble Rawls's *Political Liberalism,* with one significant difference; as long as the state allows a conception of harm to predominate, it must support its predominance in the name of autonomy. But this difference carries little weight. Thus interpreted, the Razian state would be prone to the same criticisms to which Rawls's account was. Applying a very abstract idea of autonomy to the positive duty of the state would mean that the state's initial judgement of what options are "valuable" would be diluted. The plurality that the state has a duty to promote would be incoherent. It would not be clear on what basis incompatible ways of life should be allowed to exist. The claim "but this option is also valuable" would be pervasive. The state would enforce moral pluralism. A less diluted conception of harm may relate to the extent to which a given option respects autonomy, namely the extent to which a given option does something, either physical or mental, to people which prevents them from living their lives or changing their options.[38] However, it is unclear why people would want to stay in the political community if so many of their common moral beliefs are not respected by their state. The basis for justifying state distribution of resources may be so thin as to degenerate into instability. It will make the political judgement of "value" too easy to satisfy, so as to relieve the state of responsibility for its moral commitments. Ethics and politics would be dangerously divorced. If this is what Raz means, he faces all the problems in Rawls's account and, in addition, faces the

[38] Raz, *The Morality of Freedom*, pp. 424–9.

potential problem of infuriating people by distributing resources to sustain conceptions of harm that they strongly oppose. In truth, people will be forced to be free. If there is a plurality of conceptions of harm, there is no reason to force people to associate together except for some form of *modus vivendi*. The implementation of such a Razian system would probably result in radical decentralisation towards more comprehensive reasoning.

More realistically, "value" may be interpreted in terms of a more concrete moral justification in which it will adhere to some comprehensive conception of harm. Raz does not say which conception of harm he prefers and one can assume that he acknowledges, quite rightly, that there may be various comprehensive conceptions of harm, according to which a state can protect a variety of options which are conformable to it. The state's decision about "value" might relate, for example, to a liberal egalitarian conception of harm. If it does, then the state would recognise the benefit to autonomy of options which are considered valuable in this respect. Here, different ways of life would have to be promoted by the state as long as they are recognised as valuable, in the sense of being just according to liberal egalitarianism. However, the difference in Raz, as has been seen, is that the state would have to support quite different options and not just allow them to compete in the cultural market place. In this respect, his theory resembles that of Kymlicka. The difference between them is subtle but significant. Kymlicka would refine an egalitarian distribution by allowing different cultures to compete on equal terms in the market place, *and to this extent* would require some distributive intervention. However, he does not approve of state intervention beyond that point. Kymlicka's model of accommodating difference would leave it to the market place to determine the survival of difference.[39] The Razian state would have to go further. It would "encourage" the survival of different options. Kymlicka would not see it as a state role to preserve options but only wants to make sure that different life options compete on equal terms. Raz trusts the state to support vulnerable options. The difference stems, perhaps, from different assumptions about the market place. Kymlicka's, perhaps naïve, assumption is that it can be trusted to maintain and to recreate different options as different cultures. Raz is justly more suspicious of it and requires state action to enhance and nourish difference.

However, and this is important, it is the similarity rather than the difference that is of significance. Under both theories, the state, whether in deciding to assist a minority culture in the case of Kymlicka, or in going even further than that in Raz, would determine the merits of its intervention according to a conception of harm. The variety which is assisted, or positively promoted, would already be a screened variety under both models. The difference may turn out to be functionally important depending on the capability of the market place. If

[39] W. Kymlicka, "Liberal Individualism and Liberal Neutrality", in S. Avineri and A. de-Shalit (eds), *Communitarianism and Individualism* (Oxford, 1992), pp. 165–85, at 177–84.

people can maintain variety by themselves then, to that extent, the duty of the state to resource plurality must become minimal.

But this is the point where both Raz's silence, as well as his acknowledgement that the state can make mistakes, are significant. This silence almost amounts to the recognition that no perfect polity can exist. It almost amounts to an acknowledgement that autonomy either can be promoted under different conceptions of harm, or, conversely, that the state will fail to support or even actively discourage options which are potentially valuable. This silence by Raz creates a theoretical vacuum that still leaves very much alive the aporia that will always exist between philosophy and political constructivism. Exhibiting unparalleled honesty, Raz's liberalism is situated between liberalism as a philosophical insight and liberalism as political realisation.

The Razian state's decision upon the "valuable" determines a conception of harm under which different ways of life are to be promoted. That decision may be, but need not be, egalitarian. The conception of harm may give a prominence to a certain good, say a given religion. The state of Israel is the prime example of that situation. Autonomy is allowed only to the extent that permissible options are compatible with a conception of harm which embodies an ultimate good. In this case, Razian politics would become more like a communitarian polity in which autonomy is enjoyed.

So the gist of Raz's honesty is first the admission that once politics is involved, *precisely because the realisation of autonomy is at stake,* a screening judgement by the state upon value and therefore perfectionism, is needed. This perfectionism would consist of a comprehensive conception of harm. Second comes his silence about what the "valuable" consists in. Raz takes sides in his analysis only up to the point beyond which "valuable" might thicken into some ethical *knowledge*. Thus, the dynamic connection between ethics and politics, which depends on some ethical dynamism, is adhered to very jealously by Raz. Moral communities can evolve, *in different ways*, so as to come to recognise both their commonalties and the difference between life options of people that make them up.

Raz's theory excels in explaining difference. Also, it does not pretend to contain all differences. Although harm to autonomy may be valuably discussed in philosophical terms, the political realisation of that philosophical discussion would necessitate the limiting of toleration according to a comprehensive conception of harm. This point reveals a critical omission from Raz's theory. A criticism of this interpretation of Raz might be that autonomy is generated within a given conception of harm, which, to reiterate, may not be liberal egalitarian. However, there is no clue in Raz's theory about how the state should react to life options which are not "valuable", according to the dominant conception of harm. This concern is expressed by critical social theorists such as Habermas. At what point would the Razian state become prone to dogmatism and reactionary in the face of human difference? The gap between the philosophical insight concerning autonomy and difference, and its political realisation, reinvents itself under any given polity. It always will. Despite the capacity of Raz's account to explain existing difference, and significantly, difference which is *unbridgeable in terms of political unity*, it falls short of connecting ethics and politics in a socially dynamic way. Raz's idea of politics is critical only to the extent of enhancing plurality under a given conception of harm; it does not explain, as it should, the dynamic and critical aspects of the connection between ethics and politics; a dynamic aspect according to which ethics can shape politics. For one needs a critical principle according to which existing conceptions of harm could be modified, and perfectionist intuitions transformed, in response to social change. From this perspective, the relevant arena is not political but the practical reason underlying moral philosophy. It is not good enough, therefore, to trust the state to enforce a conception of harm, whether that state is liberal egalitarian or not.

Consideration of maintaining difference within a conception of harm cannot be trusted to the market place for the reason that the "market place" will itself be operating in terms of a comprehensive conception of harm. It is for the public, and public communication alone, to emancipate politics from the dogma that a given conception of harm imposes upon it. The Razian state, however democratic, does not explain how democracy may imply the secession of adherents of the different conceptions of harm that develop in the public sphere. Raz faces the aporia but does not *use* it to account for the different moral experiences that might evolve within the public sphere, perhaps the most important constitutional change that a community shuts its eyes from seeing. To some extent, this will amount to bursting through an open door as far as Raz is concerned because, arguably, he did not see it as part of his task to account for such a change.

Tully's Politics of Cultural Recognition

A new diversity-accommodating approach to cultural membership which allegedly goes beyond a liberal *and indeed a communitarian*, umbrella is argued for by J. Tully in his book *Strange Multiplicity*.[40] It is not possible on this occasion even to begin to do justice to this groundbreaking work which is full of rich examples of social struggles. Neverthless, a summary and a general reflection are pertinent. Tully's argument for a new political and constitutional language which embraces cultural recognition adopts *by analogy*[41] Wittgenstein's method of rejecting background rules which facilitate monological shared understanding. Tully takes on board Wittgenstein's method of arriving at a general understanding of the nature of the "game" in a language game, this nature being based on a critical exposition of "family resemblances" and

[40] J. Tully, *Strange Multiplicity: Constitutionalism in an Age of Diversity* (Cambridge, 1995). See also D. Owen, "Political Philosophy in a Post-Imperial Voice: James Tully and the Politics of Cultural Recognition", *Economy and Society* 28 (1999) 520–49.

[41] *Strange Multiplicity*, p. 112.

"connextions", similarities and overlaps between apparently different world-views.[42] In importing this method to the discussion of cultural diversity, Tully contests an essential, closed, shared conception of "culture" and instead sees culture as standing in permanent ambivalence to its own self-description. Cultures are therefore aspectival, overlapping, interactive and internally negotiated, rather than containing an essential core, general, "true" self-description.[43]

Tully's argument is that the language of modern constitutionalism is imperialist in that it assumes a central, monological perspective, accepted in the form of unexamined conventions, both procedural and substantive. Such a monological view of constitutionalism is imprisoned within various tensions between liberal–communitarian–nationalist co-ordinates. Further, it is imprisoned in seven unexamined conventions, such as an abstract conception of popular sovereignty exercised by rational and equal people, uniformity as opposed to irregularity of "ancient" constitutions, and the recognition of custom within the theory of progress.[44] The result of such imprisonment is the tendency to view and hear cultures either as "in" or "out" of a dominant perspective. Such imprisonment blinds and prevents *listening to*, as opposed to *hearing*, difference. In the case of cultures being "out", the dominant perspective cannot even recognise justice or injustice according to the indigenous perspective of the culture in question.

Thus, Tully's broad argument is that the modern view of conceiving cultures as closed phenomena based on shared understanding is the root of having a modern, monological, constitutional language which captures indige only in terms of apparent containment. "Apparent" because such a containment is in fact conditional upon the assimilation into a dominant perspective or a point of view. Tully aspires to and calls for the initiation of a new intercultural language mirrored in constitutional debates and dialogue. Constitutions would *be* fully open and dialogical and would entrench, as a constitutional principle, the continuous renegotiation of cultural boundaries. Such a continuous renegotiation of relationship between centralisation and decentralisation would be the result of the ongoing dialogue and self-redescription of cultures in the light of discussions with other cultures.

Tully wants the rationale for unity encapsulated in popular sovereignty to be based on equality of being belonging to different cultures and speaking in different voices. In this respect, all people are "in the same boat".[45] Tully does, however, (as I shall argue, *apparently)* depart from the monological language of containment and adopts instead some amorphous notion of an ever-renegotiated unity which accommodates a flexible, ongoing intercultural influence and dialogue. My general point questions whether the analogy Tully draws from

[42] *Strange Multiplicity*, pp. 103–113.
[43] Ibid., pp. 7–17.
[44] Ibid., pp. 62–70.
[45] This is illustrated in the statue which inspires the whole work— *The Spirit of Haida Gwaii* by Bill Reid.

Wittgenstein holds to account for different cultural conceptions of harm. Consequently, my question is whether an intercultural dialogue can, as a presumption, serve as a rationale of politics, namely as I understood it, a system of reasoning which aims at averting harm according to a cultural, or even ideological conception of harm. I think the response to both points should be "no". It is a subtle yet important difference that constitutes my point of departure. This point relates to what we can in all honesty expect from intercultural dialogue and as a result, from politics. The lesson of the aporia is that there is a limit, at least on an ideological level, in which people of different cultures can be taken to be analogous to a "family", and hence to be contained within a dialogical forum set to expose "family ressemblances". We can understand difference but such understanding does not necessarily connote togetherness under a single constitution.[46]

Arguably, a closure will exist between various cultural conceptions of harm. This will be the case despite the culture being to some degree aspectival in nature. The opposition of cultures being *either* aspectival or essential can be doubted. As the argument is about a conceptual possibility there is much to be debated here. Cultures are probably both. If this binary opposition is doubted (it seems that Tully would acknowledge the wrongness of binary oppositions), then it is not clear how plausible it is to argue that a constitutional framework *can* be based *solely* on dialogue. Certainly, the plausibility of such a framework does not follow from the capacity, and indeed the desirability, to renegotiate the boundaries of cultural self-description. I share a great deal of Tully's philosophical view about the importance of accounting for cultural recognition and difference. I also share his dynamic understanding of the conception of the social contract and popular sovereignty.[47] Indeed, such an understanding constitutes the central core of this book. However, I depart from seeing cultures as *exclusively* aspectival and thus I argue that cultural difference may, but cannot always, renegotiate the political settlement.[48] Nowhere in the book does Tully mention the need for unity around a conception of harm. His account does not resort to the concepts of reasonableness of Rawls's *Political Liberalism*, but in effect is not really different from it. There is something, I feel, which is not right, something which pretends that renegotiation and togetherness is always possible but which in fact ducks the issue of incompatibility of conceptions of harm. The good (utilitarian) reasons, for people's sense of *some* security and interpretative predictability will always establish some unity, which of course would fall short. Constitutionally speaking, difference exists *within* a unified conception of harm and this is what makes politics tragic and the relationship between ethics and politics aporetic. A unity which falls short as a result of incompatibility of

[46] See, I.M. Young, "Communication and the Other: Beyond Deliberative Democracy", in S. Benhabib (ed.), *Democracy and Difference: Contesting the Boundaries of the Political* (Princeton, 1996), pp. 120–35.

[47] *Strange Multiplicity*, pp, 194–5.

[48] See pp. 277–8 above.

conceptions of harm is arguably a truer conception of constitutionalism than a pretence that the unity exists as some kind of a general symbolic unity of human beings which are united in the never-ending dialogue about the nature of their differences.

Tully underplays, and would probably deny the existence of, the aporia because he underplays the importance for people to establish unified secure and predictable constitutional reasoning and with it justification for coercion. There are reasons, utilitarian reasons, for constructing a monological constitution and this monologism creates the aporia. Under Tully's constitutional arrangement, because of the fluid and aspectival nature of conceptions of harm, no one would ever feel that ethical reasoning which justifies given arguments about the need to enforce a right or a conception of justice head into a brick wall. If there is no unity, no closure, there is no wall and there is no aporia. The aporia as I have described it would probably be caricatured by Tully as a phenomenon of the dogmatism of modernity, and a result of the close, essentialist and dogmatic view of politics. The case for Tully to answer is whether there are reasons for coherent constitutions to be created and function. If there are such reasons one cannot just wipe them out. They are here with a view to stay. Admitting that they are here to stay is the very fact that enables us to capture their ethical aporetic implications.

My departure from Tully recognises the tragic nature of monologic political and constitutional reasoning. However, it is behind subtlety that evil can hide and therefore be the most wicked. Tully in fact enacts indeterminacy into politics in the most direct way of all. It is understandable that Dworkin, Kymlicka, the earlier Rawls (although to some extent also the later Rawls) are hooked on their own perspectives. At the very least, their theories manifest the very reasons why we have constitutions. By reducing the reasoned need for stable constitutional reflection, Tully leaves people with no constitutional claims about harm at all. The ambivalence in the self-description of harm makes this harm potentially assimilable and defensible. Re-enacting the secret, the wonder, at the expense of unified politics errs for reasons of inauthenticity in the same way the unified perspective does. To reiterate, our ability to understand difference does not lead to the possibility of the enactment of this ability into politics or, "[to] exchange and juxtapose [cultural] myths, narratives and further descriptions of their interrelated histories together".[49] The need to enforce a conception of harm in the name of some security, by some coercive authority cannot be *replaced*. Never. It is the temporal incapacity of popular sovereignty to engage with the aporia which, we know, must produce an oppressive, moralising, monological, politics. This, I feel, is the *most* we can admit. To go beyond that conflates saying the right things in the wrong place and as a by-product, not being honest to the tragedy of the human condition.

[49] *Strange Multiplicity*, p. 206. See also pp. 183–4:

"Constitutions are not fixed and unchangeable agreements reached at some foundational moment, but chains of continual intercultural negotiations and agreements in accord with, and violation of the conventions of mutual recognition, continuity and consent."

Utility, indeterminacy and harm

The reconstruction of Bentham's project undertaken in the first part of this book has argued that, as a result of communication between people, they can form a utilitarian consensus which is based on a conception of harm that enter every person's calculations, and as such form part of that person's moral identification. The pains and pleasures that one feels depend on some forms of communal sanctions which will be manifested in guilt, shame, care and other feelings arising in one's sympathetic imagination. In other words, moral feeling, to start with, is always within our consciousness, which is itself embedded in some socially preconceived conception of harm. As such, morality will always depend on our ability to imagine the impact of our actions on others. To the extent that we identify in our pains and pleasures with the pain of others, we conceptualise and prioritise values and build a communal conception of harm which is cyclically re-interpreted and refined. So the initial cycle of communication between individuals' articulations of their sentiments can produce a moral world which then articulates itself in people's future consciousness. We evaluate within the communal matrix of harm that has been created through people's communication and exchange of sentiments. Our consciousness contains morality to that extent but not exhaustively. This conception of harm seeks to mark the limit of our moral intuition. It is from desire and psychology that harm, values, moral intuitions, and indeed ideologies are in many instances moulded, refined and reflected upon. On this view, moral psychology is derived from real psychology. Our horizon in this respect is largely, but not exhaustively, dominated by a conception of harm the aversion of which we metaphorise as "rightness" and "wrongness". This point will shape the map of moral thresholds that we metaphorise as "rights". This morality as an expression of unity can contain difference in different ways, and in different degrees. What is clear is that at any moment in time people can intuit and relate to some communal conception of harm as the basis according to which they criticise their conventions and evaluations. The way in which this conception of harm is a product of communication marks, to some extent, our empathic capabilities. This harm constitutes in itself a layer of moral obligations which penetrates, and to some degree preconditions, individuals' intuitions as against their evaluations. Utility explains how moral ideals can grow out of people's motives and communications but recognises the plurality of ways in which morality can realise itself and form part of people's critical ethical evaluations. Prescriptive propositions, which are the result of a collectively formed conception of harm, will mirror the extent to which people's capacity to incorporate ideas about how other people might be affected by their own evaluations. Up to this point, utility sides with the view that the moral self can exist only within a social matrix. To such an extent, utility and communitarianism go hand in hand.

However, throughout the book, the question of the "right" conception of harm was not part of the field of enquiry. This "absence" characterises the themes that have been discussed in each and every chapter. The reason for this is that what is "right", because preconditioned by communication and exchange of sentiments, namely by the exchange of pains and pleasures, can transcend any potential constructed conception of harm. Throughout the book utilitarianism has been argued for as entailing a specially dynamic conception of constitutionalism. This conception has developed in Part 2 into a possible general suggestion that pain and pleasure are the foundations by which the dynamic connection between ethics and politics can be appreciated and alluded to. A reconstruction of Bentham on the basis of a close reading of his writings showed them to contain this insight about such dynamism between ethics and politics. However, Bentham did not generally reflect upon, let alone refine, the insights and potential encapsulated in his utilitarian project. Nevertheless, he did contribute a novel and a far-reaching insight, namely, that pain and pleasure are the only qualities, admittedly psychological qualities, which are the efficient causes of desire, and hence of will formation, and ultimately of ethics, morality and politics. This, admittedly reductionist, claim opened the way for utilitarianism to account for the different ethical experiences humanity can produce. It opened the way for the utilitarian to appreciate, through the experience of real communicating people who feel pain and pleasure, the aporetic relationship that characterises the relationship between ethics and politics. Utility provided the reasons for people, through communication with one another, to generate values and to produce a conception of harm which they expect politics to avert. This conception of harm gives rise to a system of negative liberty which could represent a coherent and hence "rational" interpretative constitutional framework. The conception of harm also constituted the point of reference which "situates" people's intuitions. Yet a drive for authenticity could produce pain in individuals and so in groups whose view could not be accommodated within the bounds of rationality that a conception of harm entailed.

Conceived as a critical theory, utility is ethically sensitive to suffering, suffering which is not alluded to under the single perspective of monological political reasoning. It is this suffering which enables persons, and in turn, groups, not to succumb to, or worse, assimilate into, a single perspective of harm. Utility is well-placed to generate social conflicts with the result of achieving greater congruity between the political and the authentic singularity of persons-in-groups. It is *pain* which could generate the conceptual shortcomings, both instrumental and symbolic, which hamper the attainment of greater happiness.[50]

In opposition to Kantianism, psychology for Bentham was the *only* resource available to generate ethics and morality. What people *are* is the basis of morality, strictly speaking. The quote opening this chapter ought to be understood as

[50] See in this context N. Lacey, "Bentham as Proto-Feminist? or An Ahistorical Fantasy on 'Anarchical Fallacies' ", *Current Legal Problems* 31 (1998) 441–66 at 453–63.

supporting a special kind of metaphysical foundation for ethics, but is incompatible with others (although Bentham might have meant to use it to refute metaphysics). The direction that the book points to, and it can only be a direction on this occasion, is that the thrust of utilitarian metaphysics might reside in people's infinite quest with what they are. Elaborating on that must be resisted, but it may be useful to end up with some remarks that seek to capture the argument pursued in this book in general and the second part in particular.

"Is this *really* me?" is a critical question that can be asked on a number of levels, which may represent different levels at which ethics can be connected to politics. Politics can accommodate a certain space (system of negative liberty) which would allow people to reflect and be closer to what they are. The seminal achievement of liberal egalitarian theories is that they hammered home the need to engage with constitutional provisions which would allow people to be authentic. However, the field of enquiry that starts from pain and pleasure experienced by real people makes a quasi-anthropological claim that whatever ethical world people identify with, however critical this identification may be, may not exhaust what they actually are *and that this lack may have moral and ethical implications which go beyond ethics-in-politics*. From a utilitarian perspective, ethical *knowledge*, and a resulting political argument which presumed this ethical knowledge, may become the obstacle rather than a liberator. The type of experience that politics must undergo is far from being clear at the point of concluding this book and requires a great deal more thought. Utility's commitment to authenticity and to the pain and pleasure that actual people feel can indicate that historically, culturally and even ideologically-ridden pains and pleasures constitute the process by which ethics', and as a result politics' being is explained. Utility, as understood in this book, can simply now be seen as having the potential of claiming not only that "this is a better morality (or ethical theory) than another" but also that as long as people inauthentically calculate (or put less scientifically, evaluate), the calculation (or evaluation) would be wanting. If language and communication are based on a conceptual structure that is inauthentic, utility ultimately operates to challenge it and expose this inauthenticity.[51]

It is difficult to decide whether utility, if it is to be critical theory, has to be metaphysical. I have proclaimed, both in the introduction and above in this chapter, that it does. Arguably, one central feature of metaphysics is that it constructs *because* it disproves. Its truth-value endure despite the agnosticisms and contradictions that its interpretative materialisations entail. Any critical principle of ethics, and its dynamic connection to politics, implies that as far as its social realisation is concerned, it recognises barriers in social reality which

[51] In Heideggerian terminology, pains and pleasures may be seen as the qualities in Dasein through which it understands, interprets or uses the "isness" of the rightness of law in its everyday understanding of the world: see P. Minkkinen, *Thinking Without Desire: A First Philosophy of Law* (Oxford, 1999), pp. 66–70.

frustrate attempts to bring fundamental conflicts "together", according to ever-more general methods of representation and conceptual coherence.

But types of metaphysics differ. The metaphysician can assume a position of disinterestedness by representing an independent order of reasons, generalised from a first-category ahistorical principle. As has been argued above in relation to Rawls's liberalism, the interpretation of such a metaphysics can fall into the trap of constructing a coherent but implausible conceptual account as far as actual evaluation by real people might operate. The alternative approach, the inter-subjective, as adopted by utility, centres on the unfolding of authentic sentiments through communication. It is through communication that such metaphysics attains disinterestedness. According to the principle of utility, pains and pleasures are the entities which cause different prescriptive propositions to be formed in communication. The inter-subjective exchange and entrenchment of certain sentiments can explain the human tendency to construct an order of reasons to which one can relate and within which one can identify. However, the drive for authentic self-realisation and the pleasure it entails operates to create communicative possibilities. Thus understood, pain and pleasure, in whatever form, open up possibilities for new will-formation from a disinterested perspective. In this sense, only through inter-subjective communication can people reshape the ethical and political worlds. The kind of metaphysics that utility might give effect to, and the transient way in which it sees reason, continuously resists unconditional identification with dogma. Utility resists essentialising conceptions. To borrow a liberal egalitarian phrase, pain and pleasure are the only masters which cause us to form, refine through interpretation, and revise values and conceptions of harm. Utility claims that morality grows from what we are, but admits that what we are "identified" with may cause us not to be transparent to what we really are. Utilitarianism will operate to the full as a critical principle only in conditions of free communication, and as such it shares many aspects of Habermas's ideas.

Being also a critical theory means that the very process of formation of desire and will for pleasure creates, refines and transforms conceptions of harm. People's imagination, expanded as a result of communication, can open them up to new possibilities in which their action affects others. People's evaluations are influenced by communal conceptions of harm, but something in them has the potential, and indeed the desire, to listen to difference, to open to different orderings of value. Despite people's identification, they can understand what is said to them in the deepest sense of the term, if something in them creates the openness to it.

It is through feeling pain, the pain of being inauthentic, that one is pushed to be open to others and to imagine oneself through others, in a way one desires to imagine oneself. Reason is unfolded through unreason *because* greater pleasure *for a person* unfolds through pain. This is the utilitarian route to disinterestedness. Utility is metaphysical precisely *because* we are maximisers of pleasures for *ourselves,* and so endeavour to break from ourselves as "identified" people.

This is why difference progresses towards unity, which then regresses again towards difference. The capacity for empathy and the sympathetic conception of harm entail the building and breaking of ideologies and conceptions of harm that are attached to them. Political constitutions follow this process, which makes any history temporal. Pains and pleasures are ultimate sovereign masters, as Bentham put it, precisely because individuals and communities which are realised according to them can *never* be fully identified with any type of good. The principle of utility cannot and need not be proved, as Bentham put it, because any proof will be subverted by the operation of the principle itself. Pains and pleasures do not constitute a substantive idea to be proved, because they are ontological qualities which both constitute and transcend the person who proves.

Bibliography

Bentham's works

Bentham Papers, University College London Library:
Preparatory Principles, UC lxix.
On the Efficient Cause and Measure of Constitutional Liberty, UC cxxvi., cxxvii., clxx.
Necessity of an Omnipotent Legislature, UC cxlvi.
On the Influence of the Administrative Power over the Legislative, UC cxxvi.
The Collected Works of Jeremy Bentham, General Editors, J.H.Burns, J.R. Dinwiddy, F. Rosen and P. Schofield (London and Oxford, 1968—in progress):
—*An Introduction to the Principles of Morals and Legislation*, J.H. Burns and H.L.A. Hart (eds) (London, 1970 (new edition, 1996)).
—*Of Laws in General*, H.L.A. Hart (ed.) (London, 1970).
—*A Comment on the Commentaries and A Fragment on Government*, J.H. Burns and H.L.A. Hart (eds) (London, 1977).
—*The Correspondence of Jeremy Bentham,* 10 volumes, I. Christie, T.L. Sprigge, A.T. Milne, J.R. Dinwiddy and S.R. Conway (eds) (London and Oxford, 1968–94).
—*Deontology, together with A Table of the Springs of Action and Article on Utilitarianism*, A. Goldworth (ed.) (Oxford, 1983).
—*Chresthomathia*, M.J. Smith and W.H. Burston (eds) (Oxford, 1983).
—*Constitutional Code*, vol. 1, F. Rosen and J.H. Burns (ed.) (Oxford, 1983).
—*First Principles preparatory to Constitutional Code*, P. Schofield (ed.) (Oxford, 1989).
—*Securities against Misrule and other Constitutional Writings for Tripoli and Greece*, P. Schofield (ed.) (Oxford, 1990).
—*Official Aptitude Maximized; Expense Minimized*, P. Schofield (ed.) (Oxford, 1993).
—*Colonies, Commerce, and Constitutional Law: Rid Yourselves of Ultramaria and other writings on Spain and Spanish America*, P. Schofield (ed.) (Oxford, 1995).
—*Political Tactics,* M. James, C. Blamires and C. Pease-Watkin (eds) (Oxford, 1999).
—*The works of Jeremy Bentham*, J. Bowring (ed.), 11 volumes (Edinburgh, 1843):
vol. i: *On the Influence of Time and Place in Matters of Legislation.*
vol. ii: *Principles of Judicial Procedure.*
Essay on Political Tactics
Principles of International Law.
On the Liberty of the Press, and Public Discussion.
Anarchical Fallacies.
vol. iii: *Pannomial Fragments.*
A General View of a Complete Code Of Laws.
Nomography.
Equity Dispatch Court Proposal and Bill.
Parliamentary Reform.
Radicalism not dangerous.
vol. iv: *Draught of a Code for the Organization of the Judicial Establishment in France.*

vol. v: *Scotch Reform.*
vols vi & vii: *Rationale of Judicial Evidence (including Introductory View).*
vol. ix: *Constitutional Code.*

—*Theory of Legislation*, C.K. Ogden (ed.) (Kegan Paul & Co, London, 1931).

—*Bentham's Theory of Fictions,* C.K. Ogden (ed.) (Kegan Paul & Co, London, 1932).

—*The Book of Fallacies*, from unfinished papers, by a friend, P. Bingham (ed.) (London, 1824).

—*Supplement to Papers Relative to Codification and Public Instruction* (London, 1817).

Secondary books and articles

ALTMAN A., *Critical Legal Studies: A Liberal Critique* (Princeton University Press, Princeton, 1990).

ARISTOTLE, *The Politics* (Penguin Classics, London, 1962).

—*Nicomachean Ethics* (Oxford University Press, Oxford, 1925).

ATKINSON C.M., *Jeremy Bentham—his life and work* (Methuen & Co., London, 1905).

AUSTIN J., *The Province of Jurisprudence Determined, and the Uses of the Study of Jurisprudence* (Weidenfeld and Nicolson, London, 1954).

AYER A.J., "The Principle of Utility", in G.W. Keeton and G. Schwarzenberger (eds), *Jeremy Bentham and the Law* (Stevens & Sons, London, 1948), pp. 245–59.

BAHMULLER C.F., *The National Charity Company: Jeremy Bentham's Silent Revolution* (University of California Press, Berkeley, 1981).

BAKUNIN M., *God and the State*, G. Aldred (ed.) (Bakunin Press, London 1920).

BARRY B., *Theories of Justice* (University of California Press, Berkeley, 1989).

BAUMGARDT D., *Bentham and the Ethics of Today* (Princeton University Press, Princeton, 1952).

BERLIN I., *Four Essays on Liberty* (Oxford University Press, London, 1969).

—*Vico and Herder: Two Studies in the History of Ideas* (The Hogarth Press, London, 1976).

BLACKSTONE W., *Commentaries on the Laws of England*, R.I. Burn (ed.) (London, 1783).

BOZOVIC M., "Introduction", *The Panopticon Writings*, M. Bozovic (ed.) (Verso, London, 1995), pp. 1–27.

BRAND A., *The Force of Reason: an Introduction to Habermas's Theory of Communicative Action* (Allen and Unwin, Sydney, 1990).

BURNS J.H., "Bentham and the French Revolution", *Transactions of the Royal Historical Society* 16 (1966) 95–114.

—*The Fabric of Felicity: The Legislature and the Human Condition* (H.K. Lewis & Co, London, 1968).

—"Bentham on Sovereignty: An Exploration", *Northern Ireland Legal Quarterly* 24 (1973) 399–416.

—"Bentham's Critique of Political Fallacies", in B. Parekh (ed.), *Jeremy Bentham—Ten Critical Essays* (Cass, London, 1974), pp. 154–67.

—"Dreams and Destinations: Jeremy Bentham in 1828", *Bentham Newsletter* 1 (1978) 22–30.

—"Jeremy Bentham: from Radical Enlightenment to Philosophic Radicalism", *Bentham Newsletter* 8 (1984) 4–14.

—"Utilitarianism and Reform: Social Theory and Social Change 1750–1800", *Utilitas* 1 (1989) 211–25.
—"Bentham and Blackstone—A Lifetime's Dialectic", *Utilitas* 1 (1989) 22–40.
—"Nature and Natural Authority in Bentham", *Utilitas* 5 (1993) 209–19.
CALHOUN C., *Habermas and the Public Sphere* (MIT Press, Cambridge, Mass., 1992).
CAVELL S., *The Claim of Reason: Wittgenstein, Skepticism, Morality and Tragedy* (Oxford University Press, Oxford, 1979).
—*Conditions Handsome and Unhandsome: The Constitution of Emersonian Perfectionism* (University of Chicago Press, Chicago, 1990).
CONWAY S.R., "Bentham on Peace and War", *Utilitas* 1 (1989) 82–101.
COTTERRELL R., *The Politics of Jurisprudence: a Critical Introduction to Legal Philosophy* (Butterworth, London, 1989).
—*The Sociology of Law* (Butterworth, London, 1992).
CRAIG P.P., *Public Law and Democracy in the UK and the United States of America* (Clarendon Press, Oxford, 1990).
CRIMMINS J.E., *Secular Utilitarianism: Social Science and the Critique of Religion in the Thought of Jeremy Bentham* (Clarendon Press, Oxford, 1990).
CRISP R., "Sidgwick and Self-interest", *Utilitas* 2 (1990) 267–80.
CROOK D.P., "The United States in Bentham's Thought", *The Australian Journal of Politics and History* 10 (1964) 196–204.
CROSS R., "Blackstone v. Bentham", *The Law Quarterly Review* 92 (1976) 516–27.
DEVLIN P., *The Enforcement of Morals* (Oxford University Press, Oxford, 1965).
DICEY A.V., *An Introduction To The Study of The Law of The Constitution* (Macmillan, London, 1959).
DINWIDDY J.R., "Bentham's Transition to Political Radicalism 1809–10", *Journal of the History of Ideas* 36 (1975) 683–700.
—"Bentham on Private Ethics and the Principle of Utility", *Revue Internationale de Philosophie* 36 (1982) 271–309.
—*Bentham* (Oxford University Press, Oxford, 1989).
—"Adjudication under Bentham's Pannomion", *Utilitas* 1 (1989) 283–9.
DUBE A., *The Theme of Acquisitiveness in Bentham's Political Thought* (Garland, London, 1991).
—"Hayek on Bentham", *Utilitas* 2 (1990) 71–87.
DWORKIN R., *Taking Rights Seriously* (Duckworth, London, 1977).
—"What is Equality? Part 2: Equality of Resources", *Philosophy and Public Affairs* 10 (1981) 283–345.
—"Law as Interpretation", *Texas Law Review* 60 (1982) 527–50.
—"Rights as Trumps", in J. Waldron (ed.), *Theories of Rights* (Oxford University Press, Oxford, 1984).
—*A Matter of Principle* (Clarendon Press, Oxford, 1985).
—*Law's Empire* (Fontana, London, 1986).
—"Foundations of Liberal Equality", *The Tanner Lectures on Human Values* 1988, G. Peterson (ed.) (University of Utah Press, Salt Lake City, 1990), pp. 1–119.
—"Liberal Community", in S. Avineri and A. de-Shalit (eds), *Communitarianism and Individualism* (Oxford University Press, Oxford, 1992), pp. 205–23.
—*Freedom's Law: The Moral Reading of The American Constitution* (Clarendon Press, Oxford, 1996).

EHRLICH E., *Fundamental Principles of the Sociology of Law* (Harvard University Press, Cambridge, Mass., 1936).
ENTREVES A.P. De, *Natural Law: An Introduction to Legal Philosophy* (Hutchinson, London, 1951).
EVERETT C.W. (ed.), *The Limits of Jurisprudence Defined* (Columbia University Press, New York, 1945).
FINNIS J., *Natural Law and Natural Rights* (Clarendon Press, Oxford, 1980).
FISH S., *Doing What Comes Naturally: Change, Rhetoric, and the Practice of Theory in Literary and Legal Studies* (Clarendon Press, Oxford, 1989).
FOUCAULT M., *Discipline and Punish: The Birth of The Prison* (Penguin, London, 1977).
FLATHMAN R.E., *Political Obligation* (Atheneum Press, New York, 1972).
FREEDEN M., *Rights* (Open University Press, Buckingham, 1991).
—*Ideologies and Political Theory* (Clarendon Press, Oxford, 1996).
FULLER L., *The Morality of Law* (Yale University Press, New Haven, 1969).
—"Positivism and Fidelity to Law: a reply to Professor Hart", *Harvard Law Review* 71 (1958) 630–72.
GADAMER H-G., *Truth and Method* (Sheed & Ward, London, 1975).
GALIPEAU C.J., *Isaiah Berlin's Liberalism* (Clarendon Press, Oxford, 1994).
GANS C., "The Normativity of Law and its Co-ordinative Function", *Israel Law Review* 16 (1981) 333–49.
—*Philosophical Anarchism and Political Disobedience* (Cambridge University Press, Cambridge, 1992).
GEORGE R.P., *Making Men Moral: Civil Liberties and Public Morality* (Clarendon Press, Oxford, 1993).
GEUSS R., *The Idea of Critical Theory, Habermas and the Frankfurt School* (Cambridge University Press, Cambridge, 1981).
GEWIRTH A., "Can Utilitarianism Justify any Moral Rights?", in J.R. Pennock and J.W. Chapman (eds), *Ethics, Economics and The Law NOMOS* XXIV (New York University Press, New York, 1982), pp. 158–93.
GODWIN W., *Enquiry Concerning Political Justice* (Penguin, Harmondsworth, 1976).
GLOVER J., *Causing Death and Saving Lives* (Penguin, Harmondsworth, 1977).
GRAY J., *Liberalism* (Open University Press, Milton Keynes, 1986).
—*Isaiah Berlin* (HarperCollins Publishers, London, 1995).
GREEN M., "Sympathy and Self Interest: The Crisis in Mill's Mental History", *Utilitas* 1 (1989) 259–77.
GREENAWALT K., "Utilitarian Justification for Observance of Legal Rights", in J.R. Pennock and J.W. Chapman (eds), *Ethics, Economics and The Law NOMOS* XXIV (New York University Press, New York, 1982), pp. 139–47.
—*Conflicts of Law and Morality* (Clarendon Press, Oxford, 1989).
GRIFFIN J., *Value Judgement: Improving our Ethical Belief* (Clarendon Press, Oxford, 1996).
GUEST S., *Ronald Dworkin* (Edinburgh University Press, Edinburgh, 1992).
GURVITCH G., *Sociology of Law* (Routledge & Kegan Paul, London, 1947).
GUTMANN A., "Communitarian Critics of Liberalism", in S. Avineri and A. de-Shalit (eds), *Communitarianism and Individualism* (Oxford University Press, Oxford, 1992), pp. 120–36.
HABERMAS J., *The Philosophical Discourse of Modernity* (Polity Press, Cambridge, 1987).

—*Legitimation Crisis* (Polity Press, Cambridge, 1988).
—*The Structural Transformation of the Public Sphere: an Inquiry into a Category of Bourgeois Society* (Polity Press, Cambridge, 1989).
—*Between Facts and Norms* (Polity Press, Cambridge, 1996).
—"Reconciliation Through the Public Use of Reason: Remarks on John Rawls's Political Liberalism", *Journal of Philosophy* 92 (1995) 109–31.
HACKER P.M.S., "Sanction Theories of Duties", in A.W.B. Simpson (ed.), *Oxford Essays in Jurisprudence* (Oxford University Press, London, 1973), pp. 131–70.
—"Hart's Philosophy of Law", in J. Raz and P.M.S. Hacker (eds.), *Law, Morality and Society—Essays in Honour of H.L.A. Hart* (Clarendon Press, Oxford, 1977), pp. 1–25.
HALÉVY E., *The Growth of Philosophic Radicalism* (Faber and Faber, London, 1928).
HALPIN A., *Rights and Law: Analysis and Theory* (Hart Publishing, Oxford, 1997).
—"Concepts, Terms, And Fields of Enquiry", *Legal Theory* 4 (1998) 187–205.
HAMILTON A., MADISON J. and JAY J., *The Federalist* or *The New Constitution*, M. Beloff (ed.) (Basil Blackwell, Oxford, 1948).
HAMMOND M. (and J. Howarth, R. Keat), *Understanding Phenomenology* (Blackwell, Oxford, 1991).
HARDIN R., *Collective Action* (John Hopkins University Press, Baltimore ,1982).
HARE R.M., *Freedom and Reason* (Clarendon Press, Oxford, 1963).
—"Political Obligation", in T. Holderich (ed.), *Social Ends and Political Means* (Routledge, London, 1976), pp. 1–12.
—"Utility and Rights: Comment on David Lyons's Essay", in J.R. Pennock and J.W. Chapman (eds), *Ethics, Economics and The Law NOMOS* XXIV (New York University Press, New York, 1982), pp. 148–73.
—"Could Kant have been a Utilitarian", *Utilitas* 5 (1993) 1–16.
HARRISON R., *Bentham* (Routledge and Kegan Paul, London, 1983).
—*Democracy* (Routledge, London, 1993).
HART H.L.A., "Are There any Natural Rights?", *Philosophical Review* 64 (1955) 175–91.
—"Positivism and the Separation of Law and Morals", *Harvard Law Review* 71 (1958) 593–629.
—*The Concept of Law* (Clarendon Press, Oxford, 1961, and 2nd edition, 1994, Postscript).
—*Law, Liberty and Morality* (Oxford University Press, Oxford, 1962).
—"Bentham", Lecture on a Mastermind, *Proceedings of The British Academy* 48 (1962) 297–320.
—"Bentham on Sovereignty", in B. Parekh (ed.), *Jeremy Bentham—Ten Critical Essays* (Cass, London, 1974), pp. 145–53.
—"Law in the Perspective of Philosophy 1776–1976", *New York University Law Review* 51 (1976) 538–51.
—"Between Utility and Rights", in A. Ryan (ed.), *The Idea of Freedom* (Oxford University Press, Oxford, 1979), pp. 77–98.
—*Essays on Bentham: Studies on Jurisprudence and Political Theory* (Clarendon Press, Oxford, 1982).
—*Essays in Jurisprudence and Philosophy* (Clarendon Press, Oxford, 1983).
—"Bentham's Principle of Utility and Theory of Penal Law", in *An Introduction to the Principle of Morals and Legislation* (CW), J.H. Burns and H.L.A. Hart (eds), Clarendon Press, Oxford, 1996), pp. lxxix–cxii.

HENKIN L., R.C. PUGH, O. SCHACHTER and H. SMIT (eds), *International Law—Cases and Materials* 2nd edition (West Publishing Co., Minnesota, 1987).
HIMMELFARB G., *Victorian Minds* (Weidenfeld and Nicolson, London, 1968).
HINSLEY F.H., *Power and the Pursuit of Peace* (Cambridge University Press, Cambridge, 1967).
HOBBES T., *Leviathan* (Penguin, London, 1975).
HOLUB R.C, *Jurgen Habermas—Critic in the Public Sphere* (Routledge, London, 1991).
HORTON J., *Political Obligation* (Macmillan, London, 1992).
—"Moral Conflict and Political Commitment", *Utilitas* 5 (1993) 109–20.
HUME D., *A Treatise of Human Nature*, P.H. Nidditch (ed.) (Clarendon Press, Oxford, 1978).
—*Essays Moral, Political and Literary*, E. Miller (ed.) (Liberty Classics, Liberty Fund, Indianapolis, 1987).
HUME L.J., "The Political Functions of Bentham's Theory of Fictions", *Bentham Newsletter* 3 (1980) 18–27.
—*Bentham and Bureaucracy* (Cambridge University Press, Cambridge, 1981).
JAMES M., "Bentham on the Individuation of Laws", *Northern Ireland Legal Quarterly* 24 (1973) 357–82.
—"Public Interest and Majority Rule in Bentham's Democratic Theory", *Political Theory* 9 (1981) 49–64.
JENNINGS I., *The Law of the Constitution* (University of London Press, London, 1933).
JOWELL J., "The Rule of Law Today", in D. Oliver and J. Jowell (eds), *The Changing Constitution* (Clarendon Press, Oxford, 1994), pp. 57–78.
KANT I., *Foundations of the Metaphysics of Morals* (Macmillan, London, 1990).
—"What Is Enlightenment?", in *The Foundation of the Metaphysics of Morals* (Macmillan, London, 1990).
KELLY P.J., "Utilitarian Strategies in Bentham and J.S. Mill", *Utilitas* 2 (1990) 245–66.
—*Utilitarianism and Distributive Justice: Jeremy Bentham and the Civil Law* (Clarendon Press, Oxford, 1990).
—"More on Bentham on Utility and Rights", *Utilitas* 10 (1998) 165–7.
KELSEN H., *General Theory of Law and State* (Harvard University Press, Cambridge, Mass., 1949).
—*Pure Theory of Law* (University of California Press, Berkeley, 1970).
KING M., "The 'Truth' About Autopoesis", *Journal of Law and Society* 20 (1993) 218–36.
KROPOTKIN P., *Mutual Aid: A Factor of Evaluation* (Heinemann, London, 1910).
KUKATHAS C., "Are There any Cultural Rights", in W. Kymlicka (ed.), *The Rights of Minority Cultures* (Oxford, Oxford University Press, 1995), pp. 228–256.
—"Cultural Rights Again: A Rejoinder to Kymlicka", *Political Theory* 20 (1992) 674–80.
—and P. PETTIT, *Rawls: A Theory of Justice and Its Critics* (Polity Press, Cambridge, 1990).
KYMLICKA W., "Liberalism and Communitarianism", *Canadian Journal of Philosophy* 18 (1988) 181–204.
—*Liberalism, Community and Culture* (Clarendon Press, Oxford, 1989).
—*Contemporary Political Philosophy: an Introduction* (Clarendon Press, Oxford, 1990).
—"Liberal Individualism and Liberal Neutrality", in S. Avineri and A. de-Shalit (eds), *Communitarianism and Individualism* (Oxford University Press, Oxford, 1992), pp. 165–85.

—*Multicultural Citizenship: A Liberal Theory of Minority Rights* (Clarendon Press, Oxford, 1995).

LACEY N., "Bentham as Proto-Feminist? or, An Ahistorical Fantasy on 'Anarchical Fallacies'" *Current Legal Problems*, 31 (1998) 441–66.

LETWIN S.R., *The Pursuit of Certainty: David Hume, Jeremy Bentham, John Stewart Mill* (Cambridge University Press, Cambridge, 1965 (reprint 1993)).

LIEBERMAN D., *The Province of Legislation Determined: Legal Theory in Eighteenth-century Britain* (Cambridge University Press, Cambridge, 1989).

LLEWELLYN K.N., "The Normative, The Legal and The Law Jobs: the Problem of Juristic Method", *Yale Law Journal* 49 (1940) 1355–400.

—and HOEBEL E.A., *The Cheyenne Way* (University of Oklahoma Press, Oklahoma, 1941).

LOBBAN M., *The Common Law and English Jurisprudence 1760–1850* (Clarendon Press, Oxford, 1991).

LOCKE J., *Two Treatises on Government* (Everyman, J.D. Dent & Sons Ltd, London, 1990).

LOLME J.L. de, *The Constitution of England* (Hodge and Campbell, New York, 1792).

LONG D., *Bentham on Liberty: Jeremy Bentham's Idea of Liberty in Relation to his Utilitarianism* (University of Toronto Press, Toronto, 1977).

LUBAN D., "The Self: Metaphysical not Political', *Legal Theory* 1 (1995) 401–37.

LYONS D., *Forms and Limits of Utilitarianism* (Clarendon Press, Oxford, 1965).

—*In the Interest of the Governed: A Study in Bentham's Philosophy of Utility and Law* (Clarendon Press, Oxford, 1973).

—"Utility and Rights", in J.R. Pennock and J.W. Chapman (eds), *Ethics, Economics, and The Law NOMOS* XXIV (New York University Press, New York, 1982), pp. 107–38.

LYSAGHT L.J., "Bentham on the Aspects of A Law", *Northern Ireland Legal Quarterly* 24 (1973) 383–98.

MacCARTHY T., *The Critical Theory of Jurgen Habermas* (Polity Press, Cambridge, 1984).

MacCORMICK N., *Legal Reasoning and Legal Theory* (Clarendon Press, Oxford, 1978 (2nd edition, 1994)).

—*H.L.A. Hart* (Edward Arnold, London, 1981).

—"Beyond the Sovereign State", *Modern Law Review* 56 (1993) 1–18.

—"The Dialectic of Might and Right: Legal Positivism and Constitutional Change", *Current Legal Problems* 31 (1998) 37–63.

MACK M. P., *Jeremy Bentham: An Odyssey of Ideas, 1748–1793* (Heinmann, London, 1962).

MACKIE J.L., *Ethics: Inventing Right and Wrong* (Penguin, Harmondsworth, 1977).

MACPHERSON C.B., *The Life and Times of Liberal Democracy* (Oxford University Press, Oxford, 1977).

MACPHERSON T., *Political Obligation* (Routledge, London, 1967).

MacREYNOLDS P., "The Motivational Psychology of Jeremy Bentham", *Journal of the History of Behavioural Science* 4 (1968) 230–44, 349–64.

—"Jeremy Bentham and the Nature of Psychological Concepts", *The Journal of General Philosophy* 82 (1970) 113–27.

MARMOR A., *Interpretation and Legal Theory* (Clarendon Press, Oxford, 1992).

MARSHALL P., "Human Nature and Anarchism", in D. Goodway (ed.), *For Anarchism and History, Theory and Practice* (Routledge, London, 1989), pp. 127–49.

MILL J.S, *The Collected Works*, J.M. Robson (ed.) (University of Toronto Press, Toronto), 33 volumes, 1963–91.

MILLER D., *Philosophy and Ideology in Hume's Political Thought* (Clarendon Press, Oxford, 1984).

—*Anarchism* (Dent, London,1984).

—"Complex Equality" in D. Miller and M. Walzer (eds), *Pluralism, Justice and Equality* (Oxford University Press, Oxford, 1995).

MINKKINEN P., *Thinking Without Desire: A First Philosophy of Law* (Hart Publishing, Oxford, 1999).

MOFFAT R.C.L., "Two English Views of Constitutionalism: a Bicentennial Retrospective", *Oklahoma City University Law Review* 12 (1987) 849–62.

MOLES R.N., *Definition and Rule in Legal Theory: a Reassessment of H.L.A. Hart and the Positivist Tradition* (Basil Blackwell, Oxford, 1987).

MONTESQUIEU Baron De, *The Spirit Of The Laws* (Hafner Press, New York, 1949).

MULHALL S. and SWIFT A., *Liberals and Communitarians* (Blackwell, Oxford, 1992).

MURPHY W.T., "The Habermas Effect: Critical Theory and Academic Law", *Current Legal Problems* 42 (1989) 135–65.

NAGEL T., "Moral Conflict and Political Legitimacy", in J. Raz (ed.), *Authority* (Blackwell, Oxford, 1990), pp. 300–23.

NATTRASS M.S., "Devlin, Hart, and the Proper Limits of Legal Coercion", *Utilitas* 5 (1991) 91–107.

NELKEN D., "Law in Action or Living Law? Back to the Beginning in Sociology of Law", *Legal Studies* 4 (1984) 157–74.

NORRIS C., "Law, Deconstruction and the Resistance to Theory", in C. Norris, *Deconstruction and the Interest of Theory* (Pinter Publishing, London, 1988).

NOZICK R., *Anarchy, State and Utopia* (Blackwell, Oxford, 1974).

OWEN D., "Political Philosophy in a Post-Imperial Voice: James Tully and the Politics of Cultural Recognition", *Economy and Society* 28 (1999) 520–49.

—"Cultural Diversity and The Conversation of Justice: Reading Cavell on Political Voice and the Expression of Consent", *Political Theory* 27 (1999) 579–96.

PAREKH B., *Bentham's Political Thought* (Croom Helm, London, 1973).

PARFIT D., *Reasons and Persons* (Oxford University Press, Oxford, 1984).

PATEMAN C., *Participation and Democratic Theory* (Cambridge University Press, London, 1970).

PATON H.J., *The Moral Law: Kant's Groundwork of the Metaphysics of Morals* (Hutchinson, London, 1948).

PEARDON T.P., "Bentham's Ideal Republic", in B. Parekh (ed.), *Jeremy Bentham—Ten Critical Essays* (Cass, London, 1974), pp. 120–44.

PETRAZYCKI L., *Law and Morality* (Harvard University Press, Cambridge, Mass., 1955).

PITKIN H., "Obligations and Consent", in P. Laslett, W.G. Runciman and Q. Skinner (eds), *Philosophy, Politics, and Society* (Basil Blackwell, Oxford, 1972), pp. 45–85.

PLAMENATZ J., *Man and Society* (Longman, New York, 1992).

PLATO, "Crito", in *Plato—The Trial and Death of Socrates* (Aldine Press, London, 1963).

—*The Republic* (Oxford University Press, Oxford, 1941).

POSTEMA G.J., "Coordination and Convention at the Foundation of Law", *Journal of Legal Studies* 11 (1982) 165–203.
—*Bentham and The Common Law Tradition* (Clarendon Press, Oxford, 1986).
—"The Normativity of Law", in R. Gavison (ed.), *Issues in Contemporary Legal Philosophy: The Influence of H.L.A. Hart* (Clarendon Press Oxford, 1987), pp. 81–104 (commentary by N. MacCormick and D. Lyons, pp. 105–26).
—"Facts, Fictions and the Law", in W.L.T. Twining (ed.), *Facts in Law*, Ninth Annual Conference of the Association for Legal and Social Philosophy, Wiesbaden, Steiner, Durham, pp. 37–64.
—"Bentham on the Public Character of Law", *Utilitas* 1 (1989) 41–61.
—"In Defence of 'French Nonsense': Fundamental Rights in Constitutional Jurisprudence", in N. MacCormick and Z. Bankowski (eds), *Enlightenment, Rights and Revolution* (Aberdeen University Press, Aberdeen, 1989), pp. 107–33.
POWERS M., "Repugnant Desires and the Two-Tier Conception of Utility", *Utilitas* 6 (1994) 171–6.
RAWLS J., "Two Concepts of Rules", *Philosophical Review* 64 (1955) 3–32.
—"Legal Obligation and the Duty of Fair Play", in S. Hook (ed.), *Law and Philosophy* (New York University, Institute of Philosophy, New York, 1964), pp. 3–18.
—*A Theory of Justice* (Harvard University Press, Cambridge, Mass., 1971).
—'Kantian Constructivism in Moral Theory", *Journal of Philosophy* 77 (1980) 515–72.
—'Distributive Justice', in A. Ryan (ed.), *Justice* (Oxford University Press, Oxford, 1993).
—*Political Liberalism* (Columbia University Press, New York, 1993).
—"Reply to Habermas", *Journal of Philosophy* 92 (1995), 132–80.
RAZ J., "Legal Principles and the Limits of Law", *Yale Law Review* 81 (1972) 823–54.
—"On the Functions of Law", in A.W.B. Simpson (ed.), *Oxford Essays in Jurisprudence* (Oxford University Press, London, 1973), pp. 278–304.
—"Authority, Law and Morality", *Monist* 68 (1975) 295–324.
—*The Authority of Law* (Clarendon Press, Oxford, 1979).
—*The Concept of a Legal System* (Clarendon Press, Oxford, 1980).
—"The Problem about the Nature of Law", *University of Western Ontario Law Review* 21 (1983) 203–18.
—*The Morality of Freedom* (Clarendon Press, Oxford, 1986).
—"Autonomy, Toleration, and the Harm Principle", in R. Gavison (ed.), *Issues in Contemporary Legal Philosophy: The Influence of H.L.A. Hart* (Clarendon Press, Oxford, 1987), pp. 313–33 (commentary by C.L. Ten, pp. 334–41).
—"Facing Up: A Reply", *Southern California Law Review* 62 (1989) 1153–235.
—*Practical Reasons and Norms* (Princeton University Press, Princeton, 1990).
—"Introduction", and "Authority and Justification", in J. Raz (ed.), *Authority* (Blackwell, Oxford, 1990), pp. 1–20, 115–41.
—"H.L.A. Hart 1907–1992" *Utilitas* 5 (1993) 145–56.
—"The Obligation to Obey—Revisions and Traditions", in J. Raz (ed.), *Ethics in The Public Domain* (Clarendon Press, Oxford, 1994), pp. 341–54.
—"The Politics of the Rule of Law", in J. Raz (ed.), *Ethics in the Public Domain* (Clarendon Press, Oxford, 1994), pp. 370–8.
—"Multiculturalism: A Liberal Perspective", in J. Raz (ed.), *Ethics in the Public Domain: Essays in the Morality of Law and Politics* (Clarendon Press, Oxford, 1994), pp. 170–91.

RILEY J., "J.S. Mill's Liberal Utilitarian Assessment of Capitalism Versus Socialism", *Utilitas* 8 (1996) 39–71.

RITTER A., *Anarchism, a Theoretical Analysis* (Cambridge University Press, Cambridge, 1980).

ROBERTS W., "Behavioural Factors in Bentham's Conception of Political Change", *Political Studies* 10 (1961) 163–79.

—"Bentham's Conception of Political Change: A Liberal Approach", *Political Studies* 9 (1961) 254–66.

RORTY R., *Contingency, Irony, and Solidarity* (Cambridge University Press, Cambridge, 1989).

ROSEN F., "Jeremy Bentham—Recent Interpretations", *Political Studies* 30 (1982) 575–81.

—*Jeremy Bentham and Representative Democracy: A Study of The Constitutional Code* (Clarendon Press, Oxford, 1983).

—"Bentham and Mill on Liberty and Justice", in G. Feaver and F. Rosen (eds), *Lives, Liberties and the Public Good* (Macmillan, London, 1987), pp. 121–38.

—"Thinking About Liberty", an inaugural lecture, University College London, 1990.

—"Jeremy Bentham", in D. Miller, J. Coleman, W. Connolly and A. Ryan (eds), *The Blackwell Encyclopedia of Political Thought* (Blackwell, Oxford, 1991).

—*Bentham, Byron, and Greece: Constitutionalism, Nationalism, and Early Liberal Political Thought* (Clarendon Press, Oxford, 1992).

—"Introduction", in *An Introduction to the Principles of Morals and Legislation* (CW), J.H. Burns and H.L.A. Hart (eds), new edition (Clarendon Press, Oxford, 1996), pp. xxxi–lxix.

—"Individual Sacrifice and the Greatest Happiness: Between Utility and Rights", *Utilitas* 10 (1998) 129–43.

ROSENBLUM N., "Bentham's Social Psychology for Legislatures", *Political Theory* 1 (1973) 171–85.

—*Bentham's Theory of the Modern State* (Harvard University Press, Cambridge, Mass., 1978).

—*Another Liberalism: Romanticism and the Reconstruction of Liberal Thought* (Harvard University Press, Cambridge, Mass., 1987).

ROUSSEAU J. J., *The Social Contract and Discourses* (Everyman, J.D. Dent & Sons, London, 1973).

SANDEL M., *Liberalism and the Limits of Justice*, 2nd edition (Cambridge University Press, Cambridge, 1998).

—"The Procedural Republic and the Unencumbered Self" in S. Avineri and A. de-Shalit (eds), *Communitarianism and Individualism* (Oxford University Press, Oxford, 1990).

SANDLER T., *Collective Action, Theory and Application* (Harvester Wheatshelf, London, 1992).

SARTORIUS R., *Individual Conduct and Social Norms: a Utilitarian Account of Social Union and The Rule of Law* (Echino, Dickinson Publishing Co, California, 1975).

—"Positivism and the Foundation of Legal Authority", in R. Gavison (ed.), *Issues in Contemporary Legal Philosophy: The Influence of H.L.A. Hart* (Clarendon Press, Oxford, 1987), pp. 43–61 (commentary by J. Finnis and H. Ben-menachem, pp. 62–80).

SAVIGNY F.K. von, *Of the Vocation of Our Age for Legislation and Jurisprudence* (Arno Press, New York, 1975).

SCHOFIELD P., "Bentham on Public Opinion and the Press", in D. Kingsford-Smith and D. Oliver (eds), *Economical with the Truth, the Law and the Media in Modern Society* (ESC Publishing, Oxford, 1990), pp. 95–108.

—"The Constitutional Code of Jeremy Bentham", *King's College Law Journal* 2 (1991–2) 40–62.

—"Bentham on the Identification of Interests", *Utilitas* 8 (1996) 223–34.

—"Utilitarian Politics and Legal Positivism: the Rejection of Contractarianism in Early Utilitarian Thought", in S. Guest (ed.), *Positivism Today* (Dartmouth Press, Aldershot, 1996), pp. 99–118.

SCHWARTZ P., "Jeremy Bentham's Democratic Despotism", in R.D. Collison Black (ed.), *Ideas in Economics* (Macmillan, Basingstoke, 1986), pp. 74–103.

—"The Procedural Republic and the Unencumbered Self", in S. Avineri and A. de Shalit (eds), *Communitarianism and Individualism* (Oxford University Press, Oxford, 1992).

SEMPLE J., "Foucault and Bentham: A Defence of Panopticism", *Utilitas* 4 (1992) 105–20.

—*Bentham's Prison, A Study of the Panopticon Penitentiary* (Clarendon Press, Oxford, 1993).

SHKLAR J., *The Faces of Injustice* (Yale University Press, New Haven, 1990).

SIMMONDS N., *Central Issues in Jurisprudence* (Sweet and Maxwell, London, 1986).

SIMMONS A.J., *Moral Principles and Political Obligations* (Princeton University Press, Princeton, 1979).

—"Voluntarism and Political Association", *Virginia Law Review* 67 (1981) 19–37.

SINGER P., *Democracy and Disobedience* (Clarendon Press, Oxford, 1973).

SKINNER Q., "Meaning and Understanding in the History of Ideas", in Q. Skinner and J. Tully (eds), *Meaning and Context: Quentin Skinner and his Critics* (Polity Press, Cambridge, 1988), pp. 29–67.

—*Liberty Before Liberalism* (Cambridge University Press, Cambridge, 1998).

SMART J.J., "Extreme and Restricted Utilitarianism", *Philosophical Quarterly* 6 (1956) 344–54.

—(and WILLIAMS B.), *Utilitarianism For and Against* (Cambridge University Press, Cambridge, 1973).

SMITH M.B.E., "Is there a *Prima Facie* Obligation to Obey the Law?", *Yale Law Journal* 82 (1973) 950–76.

SOPER P., *A Theory of Law* (Harvard University Press, Cambridge, Mass., 1984).

—"The Obligation to Obey the Law", in R. Gavison (ed.), *Issues in Contemporary Legal Philosophy: The Influence of H.L.A. Hart* (Clarendon Press, Oxford, 1987), pp. 127–55 (commentary K. Greenawalt and C. Gans, pp. 156–90).

SPRIGGE T.L.S., *The Rational Foundations of Ethics* (Routledge & Kegan Paul, London, 1988).

—"The Relation Between Jeremy Bentham's Psychological, and his Ethical, Hedonism", *Utilitas* 11 (1999) 296–319.

STANKIEWICZ W. J., "Introduction', in W.J. Stankiewicz (ed.), *In Defence of Sovereignty* (Oxford University Press, 1969).

STEARNS J.B., "Bentham on Public and Private Ethics", *Canadian Journal of Philosophy* 5 (1975) 583–94.

STEINER G., *Errata: An Examined Life* (Weidenfeld and Nicolson, London, 1997).

STEINTRAGER J., *Bentham* (Allen and Unwin, London, 1977).

STEPHEN L., *The English Utilitarians* (London School of Economics, London, 1950).

TARLTON C.D., "The Overlooked Strategy of Bentham's Fragment of Government", *Political Studies* 20 (1972) 397–406.

TAYLOR C., "What's Wrong with Negative Liberty", in A. Ryan (ed.), *The Idea of Freedom* (Oxford University Press, Oxford, 1979), pp. 175–93.

—*Sources of the Self: The Making of Modern Identity* (Cambridge University Press, Cambridge, 1989).

—"Atomism", in S. Avineri and A. de-Shalit (eds), *Communitarianism and Individualism* (Oxford University Press, Oxford, 1992), pp. 29–50.

—*The Ethics of Authenticity* (Harvard University Press, Cambridge Mass, 1995).

TEN C.L., "Moral Rights and Parties in Wicked Legal Systems", *Utilitas* 1 (1989) 135–43.

TEUBNER G., "How the Law Thinks: Toward a Constructivist Epistemology of Law", *Law and Society Review* 23 (1989) 727–52.

—*Law as an Autopoetic System* (Blackwell, Oxford, 1993).

THOREAU H.D., "On The Duty of Civil Disobedience", in *Walden or, Life in the Woods and On the Duty of Civil Disobedience* (Harper and Row, New York, 1965), pp. 251–71.

TOCQUEVILLE A. de, *Democracy in America* (The Modern Library College Edition, New York, 1945).

TULLY J., *Strange Multiplicity: Constitutionalism in an Age of Diversity* (Cambridge University Press, Cambridge, 1995).

TWINING W.L., *Karl Llewellyn and the Realist Movement* (Weidenfeld and Nicolson, London, 1973).

—"The Contemporary Significance of Bentham's Anarchical Fallacies", *Archiv fur Recht und Sozialphilosophie* 61 (1975) 325–56.

—"Why Bentham?", *Bentham Newsletter* 8 (1984) 34–49.

—*Theories Of Evidence—Bentham and Wigmore* (Weidenfeld and Nicolson, London, 1985).

—"Reading Bentham", Maccabean Lecture in Jurisprudence, in *Proceedings of The British Academy* 75 (1989) 97–141.

—"Alternative to what? Theories of Litigation, Procedure and Dispute Settlement in Anglo-American Jurisprudence: Some Neglected Classics", *Modern Law Review* 56 (1993) 380–92.

—"General and Particular Jurisprudence—Three Chapters in a Story", in S. Guest (ed.), *Positivism Today* (Dartmouth Press, Aldershot, 1996), pp. 119–46.

UNGER R.M., *The Critical Legal Studies Movement* (Harvard University Press, Cambridge Mass., 1986).

VILE M.C., *Constitutionalism and the Separation of Powers* (Clarendon Press, Oxford, 1967).

WALDRON J., *Nonsense Upon Stilts: Bentham, Burke and Marx on the Rights Of Man* (Methuen and Co, London, 1987).

—"Autonomy and Perfectionism in Raz's *Morality of Freedom*", *Southern California Law Review*, 62 (1989) 1098–152.

—"Minority Cultures and the Cosmopolitan Alternative", in W. Kymlicka (ed.), *The Rights of Minority Cultures* (Oxford University Press, Oxford, 1995), pp. 93–119.

—*Law and Disagreement* (Clarendon Press, Oxford, 1999).

WALZER M., *Essays on Disobedience, War and Citizenship* (Harvard University Press, Cambridge, Mass., 1970).

—"Philosophy and Democracy", *Political Theory* (1981) 379–99.
—*Spheres of Justice: a Defence of Pluralism and Equality 19* (Basil Blackwell, Oxford, 1983).
—*Interpretation and Social Criticism* (Harvard University Press, Cambridge Mass., 1987).
—*Thick and Thin: Moral Argument at Home and Abroad* (University of Notre Dame Press, London, 1994).
WILLIAMS B., *Ethics and the Limits of Philosophy* (Fontana Press, London, 1985).
WILLIAMS G. L. (ed.), *John Stuart Mill on Politics and Society* (Fontana, London, 1976).
WITTGENSTEIN L., *Philosophical Investigations* (Basil Blackwell, Oxford, 1953).
—*On Certainty* (Basil Blackwell, Oxford, 1969).
WOLFF J., *Robert Nozick: Property, Justice and the Minimal State* (Polity Press, Cambridge, 1991).
—"Hume, Bentham and the Social Contract", *Utilitas* 5 (1993) 87–90.
WOLFF R.P., *In Defence of Anarchism* (Harper and Row, New York, 1976).
YOUNG I.M., "Communication and the Other: Beyond Deliberative Democracy", in S. Benhabib (ed.), *Democracy and Difference: Contesting the Boundaries of the Political* (Princeton University Press, Princeton, 1996).
ZWIEBACH B., *Civility and Disobedience* (Cambridge University Press, Cambridge, 1975).

Index

67

95, 97

utilitarian bases [illegible] 101, 241

155

163-4

187

229

279

310

SUMs

66

93

159

185

223

237 sq

263

275